Architecting Cloud Native Applications

Design high-performing and cost-effective applications
for the cloud

Kamal Arora
Erik Farr
John Gilbert
Piyum Zonooz

BIRMINGHAM - MUMBAI

Architecting Cloud Native Applications

First published: April 2019

Production reference: 1110419

Published by Packt Publishing Ltd.
Livery Place
35 Livery Street
Birmingham
B3 2PB, UK.

ISBN 978-1-83864-331-7

www.packtpub.com

mapt.io

Mapt is an online digital library that gives you full access to over 5,000 books and videos, as well as industry leading tools to help you plan your personal development and advance your career. For more information, please visit our website.

Why subscribe?

- Spend less time learning and more time coding with practical eBooks and Videos from over 4,000 industry professionals

- Improve your learning with Skill Plans built especially for you

- Get a free eBook or video every month

- Mapt is fully searchable

- Copy and paste, print, and bookmark content

Packt.com

Did you know that Packt offers eBook versions of every book published, with PDF and ePub files available? You can upgrade to the eBook version at www.packt.com and as a print book customer, you are entitled to a discount on the eBook copy. Get in touch with us at customercare@packtpub.com for more details.

At www.packt.com, you can also read a collection of free technical articles, sign up for a range of free newsletters, and receive exclusive discounts and offers on Packt books and eBooks.

Contributors

About the authors

Kamal Arora is an inventor, author, and technology leader with more than 15 years of IT experience. He currently works at Amazon Web Services and leads a diverse team of highly experienced solutions architects who enable global consulting partners and enterprise customers on their journey to cloud. Kamal has also led the creation of biggest global technical partnerships, set his team's vision and execution model, and incubated multiple new strategic initiatives.

Erik Farr is a technology leader with over 18 years in the IT industry. He has been on the leading edge of cloud technology and enterprise architecture, working with some of the largest companies and system integrators in the world. In his current role at Amazon Web Services, he leads a team of experienced solution architects to help global system integrator partners design enterprise scale cloud native architectures.

John Gilbert is a CTO with over 25 years of experience of architecting and delivering distributed, event-driven systems. His cloud journey started more than five years ago and has spanned all the levels of cloud maturity—through lift and shift, software-defined infrastructure, microservices, and continuous deployment. He finds delivering cloud native solutions to be by far the most fun and satisfying, as they force us to rewire how we reason about systems and enable us to accomplish far more with mu

Piyum Zonooz is a global partner solution architect at Amazon Web Services, where he works with companies across all industries to help drive cloud adoption and re-architect products to cloud native. He has led projects in TCO analysis, infrastructure design, DevOps adoption, and complete business transformation. Prior to AWS, Piyum was a lead architect as part of the Accenture Cloud Practice where he led large-scale cloud adoption projects.

Packt is searching for authors like you

If you're interested in becoming an author for Packt, please visit `authors.packtpub.com` and apply today. We have worked with thousands of developers and tech professionals, just like you, to help them share their insight with the global tech community. You can make a general application, apply for a specific hot topic that we are recruiting an author for, or submit your own idea.

Table of Contents

Preface

Cloud computing has proven to be the most revolutionary IT development since virtualization. Cloud native architectures give you the benefit of more flexibility over legacy systems.

This Learning Path teaches you everything you need to know for designing industry-grade cloud applications and efficiently migrating your business to the cloud. It begins by exploring the basic patterns that turn your database inside out to achieve massive scalability. You'll learn how to develop cloud native architectures using microservices and serverless computing as your design principles. Then, you'll explore ways to continuously deliver production code by implementing continuous observability in production. In the concluding chapters, you'll learn about various public cloud architectures ranging from AWS and Azure to the Google Cloud Platform, and understand the future trends and expectations of cloud providers.

By the end of this Learning Path, you'll have learned the techniques to adopt cloud native architectures that meet your business requirements.

This Learning Path includes content from the following Packt products:

- Cloud Native Development Patterns and Best Practices by John Gilbert
- Cloud Native Architectures by Erik Farr et al.

Who this book is for

This Learning Path is designed for developers who want to progress into building cloud native systems and are keen to learn the patterns involved. Software architects, who are keen on designing scalable and highly available cloud native applications, will also find this Learning Path very useful. To easily grasp these concepts, you will need basic knowledge of programming and cloud computing.

What this book covers

Chapter 1, *Understanding Cloud Native Concepts*, covers the promise of cloud-native: to enable companies to continuously deliver innovation with confidence. It reveals the core concepts and answers the fundamental question: what is cloud-native?

Chapter 2, *The Anatomy of Cloud Native Systems*, begins our deep dive into the architectural aspects of cloud-native systems. It covers the important role that asynchronous, message-driven communication plays in creating proper bulkheads to build a reactive, cloud-native system that is responsive, resilient, and elastic. You will learn how cloud-native turns the database inside out and ultimately turns the cloud into the database.

Chapter 3, *Foundation Patterns*, covers the patterns that provide the foundation for creating bounded isolated components. We eliminate all synchronous inter-component communication and build our foundation on asynchronous inter-component communication, replication, and eventual consistency.

Chapter 4, *Boundary Patterns*, covers the patterns that operate at the boundaries of cloud-native systems. The boundaries are where the system interacts with everything that is external to the system, including humans and other systems.

Chapter 5, *Control Patterns*, covers the patterns that provide the flow of control for collaboration between the boundary components. It is with these collaborations that we ultimately realize the intended functionality of a system.

Chapter 6, *Deployment*, describes how we shift deployments all the way to the left and decouple deployment from release to help enable teams to continuously deploy changes to production and continuously deliver innovation to customers with confidence.

Chapter 7, *Testing*, describes how we shift testing all the way to the left, weave it into the CI/CD pipeline, and leverage isolated and transitive testing techniques to help enable teams to continuously deploy changes to production and deliver innovation to customers with confidence.

Chapter 8, *Monitoring*, describes how we shift some aspects of testing all the way to the right into production to assert the success of continuous deployments and instill team confidence by increasing observability, leveraging synthetic transaction monitoring, and placing our focus on the mean time to recovery.

Chapter 9, *Security*, describes how we leverage the shared responsibility model of cloud-native security and adopt the practice of security-by-design to implement secure systems.

`Chapter 10`, *Cloud Native Application Design*, dives deep into the development of cloud native architectures, using microservices and serverless computing as a design principle.

`Chapter 11`, *How to Choose Technology Stacks*, explores the common technology that is used to create cloud native architectures, from open source to licensed software. It will explore marketplaces that can be used to consume resources in the cloud. Finally, it will discuss the procurement process and licensing models that are common in the cloud.

`Chapter 12`, *Scalable and Available*, talks about available tools/features and strategies to employ when designing cloud native systems for scale and HA. The chapter will explore how these tools/features work, how they enable cloud native applications and how to deploy them.

`Chapter 13`, *Optimizing Cost*, covers the pricing model for Cloud environments. We will then discuss how to approach costing exercises as well as the differences between the old and cloud models.

`Chapter 14`, *Amazon Web Services*, focuses on providing a perspective on Amazon Web Services' cloud native application development capabilities, strengths, ecosystem maturity, and overall approach.

`Chapter 15`, *Microsoft Azure*, focuses on providing a perspective on Microsoft Azure's cloud native application development capabilities, strengths, ecosystem maturity, and overall approach.

`Chapter 16`, *Google Cloud Platform*, focuses on providing a perspective on Google Cloud Platform's cloud native application development capabilities, strengths, ecosystem maturity, and overall approach.

`Chapter 17`, *What's Next? Cloud Native Application Architecture Trends*, looks at future trends and what to expect from various cloud providers in this space.

To get the most out of this book

Cloud experience is not a prerequisite for this book, but experienced readers will find the content readily applicable. The examples used in this book require an AWS account. You can sign up for a free trial account via the AWS website (`https://aws.amazon.com/free`). The examples are written in NodeJS (`https://nodejs.org`) and leverage the Serverless Framework (`https://serverless.com/framework`). The `README` file in the code bundle contains installation instructions. The examples leverage the powerful HighlandJS (`http://highlandjs.org`) streaming library.

Download the example code files

You can download the example code files for this book from your account at `www.packt.com`. If you purchased this book elsewhere, you can visit `www.packt.com/support` and register to have the files emailed directly to you.

You can download the code files by following these steps:

1. Log in or register at `www.packt.com`.
2. Select the **SUPPORT** tab.
3. Click on **Code Downloads & Errata**.
4. Enter the name of the book in the **Search** box and follow the onscreen instructions.

Once the file is downloaded, please make sure that you unzip or extract the folder using the latest version of:

- WinRAR/7-Zip for Windows
- Zipeg/iZip/UnRarX for Mac
- 7-Zip/PeaZip for Linux

The code bundle for the book is also hosted on GitHub at `https://github.com/PacktPublishing/-Architecting-Cloud-Native-Applications`. In case there's an update to the code, it will be updated on the existing GitHub repository.

We also have other code bundles from our rich catalog of books and videos available at `https://github.com/PacktPublishing/`. Check them out!

Conventions used

There are a number of text conventions used throughout this book.

`CodeInText`: Indicates code words in text, database table names, folder names, filenames, file extensions, pathnames, dummy URLs, user input, and Twitter handles. Here is an example: "Notice that the `ItemChangeEvent` format includes both the old and new image of the data."

A block of code is set as follows:

```
const raiseTestError = () => {
    if (Math.floor((Math.random() * 5) + 1) === 3) {
        throw new Error('Test Error'); // unhandled
    }
}
```

Bold: Indicates a new term, an important word, or words that you see onscreen.

There is a concise diagramming convention used throughout this book. Cloud-native components have many moving parts, which can clutter diagrams with a lot of arrows connecting the various parts. The following sample diagram demonstrates how we minimize the number of arrows by placing related parts adjacent to each other so that they appear to touch. The nearest arrow implies the flow of execution or data. In the sample diagram, the arrow on the left indicates that the flow moves through the API gateway to a function and into the database, while the arrow on the right indicates the flow of data out of the database stream to a function and into the event stream. These diagrams are creating using Cloudcraft (`https://cloudcraft.co`).

 Warnings or important notes appear like this.

 Tips and tricks appear like this.

Get in touch

Feedback from our readers is always welcome.

General feedback: If you have questions about any aspect of this book, mention the book title in the subject of your message and email us at customercare@packtpub.com.

Errata: Although we have taken every care to ensure the accuracy of our content, mistakes do happen. If you have found a mistake in this book, we would be grateful if you would report this to us. Please visit www.packt.com/submit-errata, selecting your book, clicking on the Errata Submission Form link, and entering the details.

Piracy: If you come across any illegal copies of our works in any form on the Internet, we would be grateful if you would provide us with the location address or website name. Please contact us at copyright@packt.com with a link to the material.

If you are interested in becoming an author: If there is a topic that you have expertise in and you are interested in either writing or contributing to a book, please visit authors.packtpub.com.

Reviews

Please leave a review. Once you have read and used this book, why not leave a review on the site that you purchased it from? Potential readers can then see and use your unbiased opinion to make purchase decisions, we at Packt can understand what you think about our products, and our authors can see your feedback on their book. Thank you!

For more information about Packt, please visit packt.com.

Understanding Cloud Native Concepts

1

Our industry is in the midst of the single most significant transformation of its history. We are reaching the tipping point, where every company starts migrating its workloads into the cloud. With this migration comes the realization that systems must be re-architected to fully unlock the potential of the cloud.

In this book, we will journey into the world of cloud-native to discover the patterns and best practices that embody this new architecture. In this chapter, we will define the core concepts and answer the fundamental question: *What is cloud-native?* You will learn that cloud-native:

- Is more than optimizing for the cloud
- Enables companies to continuously deliver innovation with confidence
- Empowers everyday teams to build massive scale systems
- Is an entirely different way of thinking and reasoning about software architecture

Establishing the context

We could dive right into a definition. But if you ask a handful of software engineers to define cloud-native, you will most likely get more than a handful of definitions. Is there no unified definition? Is it not mature enough for a concrete definition? Or maybe everyone has their own perspective; their own context. When we talk about a particular topic without consensus on the context then it is unlikely we will reach consensus on the topic. So first we need to define the context for our definition of cloud-native. It should come as no surprise that in a patterns book, we will start by defining the context.

What is the right context for our definition of cloud-native? Well, of course, the right context is your context. You live in the real world, with real-world problems that you are working to solve. If cloud-native is going to be of any use to you then it needs to help you solve your real-world problems. How shall we define your context? We will start by defining what your context is not.

Your context is not Netflix's context. Certainly, we all aim to operate at that scale and volume, but you need an architecture that will grow with you and not weigh you down now. Netflix did things the way they did because they had to. They were an early cloud adopter and they had to help invent that wheel. And they had the capital and the business case to do so. Unfortunately, I have seen some systems attempt to mimic their architecture, only to virtually collapse under the sheer weight of all the infrastructure components. I still cringe every time I think about their cloud invoices. You don't have to do all the heavy lifting yourself to be cloud-native.

Your context is not the context of the platform vendors. What's past is prologue. Many of us remember all too well the colossal catastrophe that is the **Enterprise Service Bus** (**ESB**). I published an article in the *Java Developer's Journal* back in 2005 (`http://java.sys-con.com/node/84658`) in which I was squarely in the *ESB is an architecture, not a product* camp and in the *ESB is event-driven, not request-driven* camp. But alas, virtually every vendor slapped an ESB label on its product, and today *ESB* is a four-letter word. Those of you who lived through this know the big ball of mud I am talking about. For the rest, suffice it to say that we want to learn from our mistakes. Cloud-native is an opportunity to right that ship and go to eleven.

Your context is your business and your customers and what is right for both. You have a lot of great experience, but you know there is a sea change with great potential for your company and you want to know more. In essence, your context is in the majority. You don't have unlimited capital, nor an army of engineers, yet you do have market pressure to deliver innovation yesterday, not tomorrow, much less next month or beyond. You need to cut through the hype. You need to do more with less and do it fast and safe and be ready to scale.

I will venture to say that my context is your context and your context is my context. This is because, in my day job, I work for you; I work alongside you; I do what you do. As a consultant, I work with my customers to help them adopt cloud-native architecture. Over the course of my cloud journey, I have been through all the stages of cloud maturity, I have wrestled with the unique characteristics of the cloud, and I have learned from all the classic mistakes, such as lift and shift. My journey and my context have led me to the cloud-native definition that I share with you here.

In order to round out our context, we need to answer two preliminary questions: *Why are we talking about cloud-native in the first place?* and *Why is cloud-native important?*

We are talking about cloud-native because running your applications in the cloud is different from running them in traditional data centers. It is a different dynamic, and we will cover this extensively in this chapter and throughout this book. But for now, know that a system that was architected and optimized to run in a traditional data center cannot take advantage of all the benefits of the cloud, such as elasticity. Thus we need a modern architecture to reap the benefits of the cloud. But just saying that cloud-native systems are architected and optimized to take advantage of the cloud is not enough, because it is not a definition that we can work with.

Fortunately, everyone seems to be in relative agreement on why cloud-native is important. The promise of cloud-native is speed, safety, and scalability. Cloud-native helps companies rapidly deliver innovation to market. Start-ups rely on cloud-native to propel their value proposition into markets and market leaders will need to keep pace. But this high rate of change has the potential to destabilize systems. It most certainly would destabilize legacy architectures. Cloud-native concepts, patterns, and best practices allow companies to continuously deliver with confidence with zero downtime. Cloud-native also enables companies to experiment with product alternatives and adapt to feedback. Cloud-native systems are architected for elastic scalability from the outset to meet the performance expectations of today's consumers. Cloud-native enables even the smallest companies to do large things.

We will use these three promises—speed, safety, and scale, to guide and evaluate our definition of cloud-native within your context.

Rewiring your software engineering brain

First and foremost, cloud-native is an entirely different way of thinking and reasoning about software architecture. We literally need to rewire our software engineering brains, not just our systems, to take full advantage of the benefits of the cloud. This, in and of itself, is not easy. So many things that we have done for so long a certain way no longer apply. Other things that we abandoned forever ago are applicable again.

This in many ways relates to the cultural changes that we will discuss later. But what I am talking about here is at the individual level. You have to convince yourself that the paradigm shift of cloud-native is right for you. Many times you will say to yourself "we can't do that", "that's not right", "that won't work", "that's not how we have always done things", followed sooner or later by "wait a minute, maybe we can do that", "what, really, wow", "how can we do more of this". If you ever get the chance, ask my colleague Nate Oster about the "H*LY SH*T!!" moment on a project at a brand name customer.

I finally convinced myself in the summer of 2015, after several years of fighting the cloud and trying to fit it into my long-held notions of software architecture and methodology. I can honestly say that since then I have had more fun building systems and more peace of mind about those systems then ever before. So be open to looking at problems and solutions from a different angle. I'll bet you will find it refreshing as well, once you finally convince yourself.

Defining cloud-native

If you skipped right to this point and you didn't read the preceding sections, then I suggest that you go ahead and take the time to read them now. You are going to have to read them anyway to really understand the context of the definition that follows. If what follows surprises you in any way then keep in mind that cloud-native is a different way of thinking and reasoning about software systems. I will support this definition in the pages that follow, but you will have to convince yourself.

Cloud-native embodies the following concepts:

- Powered by disposable infrastructure
- Composed of bounded, isolated components
- Scales globally
- Embraces disposable architecture
- Leverages value-added cloud services
- Welcomes polyglot cloud
- Empowers self-sufficient, full-stack teams
- Drives cultural change

Of course you are asking, "*Where are the containers?*" and "*What about microservices?*". They are in there, but those are implementation details. We will get to those implementation details in the next chapter and beyond. But implementation details have a tendency to evolve and change over time. For example, my gut tells me that in a year or so we won't be talking much about container schedulers anymore, because they will have become virtually transparent.

This definition of cloud-native should still stand regardless of the implementation details. It should stand until it has driven cultural and organizational change in our industry to the point where we no longer need the definition because, it too, has become virtually transparent.

Let's discuss each of these concepts with regard to how they each help deliver on the promises of cloud-native: speed, safety, and scale.

Powered by disposable infrastructure

I think I will remember forever a very specific lunch back in 2013 at the local burrito shop, because it is the exact point at which my cloud-native journey began. My colleague, Tim Nee, was making the case that we were not doing cloud correctly. We were treating it like a data center and not taking advantage of its dynamic nature. We were making the classic mistake called **lift and shift**. We didn't call it that because I don't think that term was in the mainstream yet. We certainly did not use the phrase *disposable infrastructure*, because it was not in our vernacular yet. But that is absolutely what the conversation was about. And that conversation has forever changed how we think and reason about software systems.

We had handcrafted AMIs and beautiful snowflake EC2 instances that were named, as I recall, after *Star Trek* characters or something along those lines. These instances ran 24/7 at probably around 10% utilization, which is very typical. We could create new instances somewhat on demand because we had those handcrafted AMIs. But God forbid we terminate one of those instances because there were still lots of manual steps involved in hooking a new instance up to all the other resources, such as load balancers, elastic block storage, the database, and more. Oh, and what would happen to all the data stored on the now terminated instance?

This brings us to two key points. First, disposing of cloud resources is hard, because it takes a great deal of forethought. When we hear about the cloud we hear about how easy it is to create resources, but we don't hear about how easy it is to dispose of resources. We don't hear about it because it is not easy to dispose of resources. Traditional data center applications are designed to run on snowflake machines that are rarely, if ever, retired. They take up permanent residency on those machines and make massive assumptions about what is configured on those machines and what they can store on those machines. If a machine goes away then you basically have to start over from scratch. Sure, bits and pieces are automated, but since disposability is not a first-class requirement, many steps are left to operations staff to perform manually. When we lift and shift these applications into the cloud, all those assumptions and practices (aka baggage) come along with them.

Second, the machine images and the containers that we hear about are just the tips of the iceberg. There are so many more pieces of infrastructure, such as load balancers, databases, DNS, CDN, block storage, blob storage, certificates, virtual private cloud, routing tables, NAT instances, jump hosts, internet gateways, and so on. All of these resources must be created, managed, monitored, understood as dependencies, and, to varying degrees, disposable. Do not assume that you will only need to automate the AMIs and containers.

The bottom line is: if we can create a resource on demand, we should be able to destroy it on demand as well, and then rinse and repeat. This was a new way of thinking. This notion of disposable infrastructure is the fundamental concept that powers cloud-native. Without disposable infrastructure, the promises of speed, safety, and scale cannot even taxi to the runway, much less take flight, so to speak. To capitalize on disposable infrastructure, everything must be automated, every last drop. We will discuss cloud-native automation in Chapter 6, *Deployment*. But how do disposable infrastructure and automation help deliver on the promise of speed, safety, and scale?

There is no doubt that our first step on our cloud-native journey increased Dante's velocity. Prior to this step, we regularly delivered new functionality to production every 3 weeks. And every 3 weeks it was quite an event. It was not unusual for the largely manual deployment of the whole monolithic system to take upwards of 3 days before everyone was confident that we could switch traffic from the blue environment to the green environment. And it was typically an all-hands event, with pretty much every member of every team getting sucked in to assist with some issue along the way. This was completely unsustainable. We had to automate.

Once we automated the entire deployment process and once the teams settled into a rhythm with the new approach, we could literally complete an entire deployment in under 3 hours with just a few team members performing any unautomated smoke tests before we switched traffic over to the new stack. Having embraced disposable infrastructure and automation, we could deliver new functionality on any given day. We could deliver patches even faster. Now I admit that automating a monolith is a daunting endeavor. It is an all or nothing effort because it is an all or nothing monolith. Fortunately, the divide and conquer nature of cloud-native systems completely changes the dynamic of automation, as we will discuss in `Chapter 6`, *Deployment*.

But the benefits of disposable infrastructure encompass more than just speed. We were able to increase our velocity, not just because we had automated everything, but also because automating everything increased the quality of the system. We call it *infrastructure as code* for a reason. We develop the automation code using the exact same agile methodologies that we use to develop the rest of the system. Every automation code change is driven by a story, all the code is versioned in the same repository, and the code is continuously tested as part of the CI/CD pipeline, as test environments are created and destroyed with every test run.

The infrastructure becomes immutable because there is no longer a need to make manual changes. As a result, we can be confident that the infrastructure conforms to the requirements spelled out in the stories. This, in turn, leads to more secure systems, because we can assert that the infrastructure is in compliance with regulations, such as PCI and HIPAA. Thus, increased quality makes us more confident that we can safely deploy changes while controlling risk to the system as a whole.

Disposable infrastructure facilitates team scale and efficiency. Team members no longer spend a significant amount of time on deployments and fighting deployment-related fires. As a result, teams are more likely to stay on schedule, which increases team morale, which in turn increases the likelihood that teams can increase their velocity and deliver more value. Yet, disposable infrastructure alone does not provide for scalability in terms of system elasticity. It lays the groundwork for scalability and elasticity, but to fully achieve this a system must be architected as a composition of bounded and isolated components. Our soon-to-be legacy system was still a monolith, at this stage in our cloud maturity journey. It had been optimized a bit, here and there, out of necessity, but it was still a monolith and we were only going to get vertical scaleout of it until we broke it apart by strangling the monolith.

Composed of bounded, isolated components

Here are two scenarios I bet we all can relate to. You arrive at work in the morning only to find a firestorm. An important customer encountered a critical bug and it has to be fixed forthwith. The system as a whole is fine, but this specific scenario is a showstopper for this one client. So your team puts everything else on hold, knuckles down, and gets to work on resolving the issue. It turns out to be a one-line code change and a dozen or more lines of test code. By the end of the day, you are confident that you have properly resolved the problem and report to management that you are ready to do a patch release.

However, management understands that this means redeploying the whole monolith, which requires involvement from every team and inevitably something completely unrelated will break as a result of the deployment. So the decision is made to wait a week or so and batch up multiple *critical* bugs until the logistics of the deployment can be worked out. Meanwhile, your team has fallen one more day behind schedule.

That scenario is bad enough, but I'm sure we have all experienced worse. For example, a bug that leads to a runaway memory leak, which cripples the monolith for every customer. The system is unusable until a patch is deployed. You have to work faster than you want to and hope you don't miss something important. Management is forced to organize an emergency deployment. The system is stabilized and everyone hopes there weren't any unintended side effects.

The first scenario shows how a monolithic system itself can become the bottleneck to its own advancement, while the second scenario shows how the system can be its own Achilles heel. In cloud-native systems, we avoid problems such as these by decomposing the system into bounded isolated components. Bounded components are focused. They follow the single responsibility principle. As a result, these components are easier for teams to reason about. In the first scenario, the team and everyone else could be confident that the fix to the problem did not cause a side effect to another unrelated piece of code in the deployment unit because there is no unrelated code in the deployment unit. This confidence, in turn, eliminates the system as its own bottleneck. Teams can quickly and continuously deploy patches and innovations. This enables teams to perform experiments with small changes because they know they can quickly roll forward with another patch. This ability to experiment and gain insights further enables teams to rapidly deliver innovation.

So long as humans build systems, there will be human error. Automation and disposable infrastructure help minimize the potential for these errors and they allow us to rapidly recover from such errors, but they cannot eliminate these errors. Thus, cloud-native systems must be resilient to human error. To be resilient, we need to isolate the components from each other to avoid the second scenario, where a problem in one piece affects the whole. Isolation allows errors to be contained within a single component and not ripple across components. Other components can operate unabated while the broken component is quickly repaired.

Isolation further instills confidence to innovate, because the blast radius of any unforeseen error is controlled. Bounded and isolated components achieve resilience through data replication. This, in turn, facilitates responsiveness, because components do not need to rely on synchronous inter-component communication. Instead, requests are serviced from local materialized views. Replication also facilitates scale, as load is spread across many independent data sources. In Chapter 2, *The Anatomy of a Cloud Native Systems*, we will dive into these topics of bounded contexts, isolation and bulkheads, reactive architecture, and turning the database inside out.

Scales globally

There are good sides and bad sides to having been in our industry for a long time. On the good side, you have seen a lot, but on the bad side, you tend to think you have seen it all. As an example, I have been riding the UI pendulum for a long time, from mainframe to 4GL client-server, then back through fat-client N-tier architecture to thin-client N-tier architecture, then slowly back again with Ajax and then bloated JavaScript clients, such as GWT, with plenty of variations along the way.

So when a young buck colleague named Mike Donovan suggested that we really needed to look at the then new thing called **Angular**, my initial reaction was "oh no, not again". However, I strive to stay in touch with my inner Bruce Pujanauski. Bruce was a seasoned mainframe guru back when I was a young buck C++ programmer. We were working on a large project to port a mainframe-based ERP system to an N-tier architecture. Bruce pointed out that we were re-inventing all the same wheels that they had already perfected on the mainframe, but as far as he could tell we were on the right track. Bruce understood that the context of the industry was changing and a new generation of engineers was going to be playing a major role and he was ready to embrace the change. That moment made a lasting impression on me. So much so, that I don't think of the UI pendulum as swinging back and forth. Instead, I see it and software architecture in general as zigzagging through time, constantly adjusting to the current context.

So, I heeded Mike's recommendation and gave Angular my attention. I could see that Java UI veterans could easily feel at home with this new crop of JavaScript UI frameworks. However, I wasn't convinced of its value, until I realized that we could run this new presentation tier architecture without any servers. This was a true "what, really, wow" moment. I could deploy the UI code to AWS S3 and serve it up through the AWS CloudFront CDN. I wouldn't need an elastic load balancer (ELB) in front of a bare minimum of two EC2 instances running Apache, in turn in front of another (ELB) fronting a cluster of at least two EC2 instances running a Java App server, with all the necessary elbow grease, to run the presentation tier in just a single region. I would have to be completely nuts not to give this approach full measure.

Running the presentation tier on the edge of the cloud like this was a game changer. It enabled virtually limitless global scale, for that tier, at virtually no cost. What followed was a true "how can we do more of this" moment. How can we achieve this at the business layer and the data layer? How can we run more at the edge of the cloud? How can we easily, efficiently, and cost-effectively support multi-regional, active-active deployments? Our journey through this book will show us how. We will push the API Gateway to the edge, enforce security at the edge, cache responses at the edge, store users' personal data on devices, replicate data between components and across regions, and more. For now, suffice it to say that scalability, even global scalability, no longer keeps me awake at night.

Embraces disposable architecture

Not enough emphasis is placed on the *Big R* in conversations about cloud-native. Independent DURS ultimately comes up in every discussion on cloud-native concepts; to independently Deploy, Update, Replace, and Scale. The focus is inevitably placed on the first and the last, *Deploy* and *Scale*, respectively. Of course, *Update* is really just another word for *Deploy*, so it doesn't need much additional attention. But *Replace* is treated like a redheaded stepchild and only given a passing glance.

I think this is because the Big R is a crucial, higher-order concept in cloud-native, but many discussions on cloud-native are down in the technical weeds. There is no doubt, it is essential that we leverage *disposable infrastructure* to independently deploy and scale bounded isolated components. But this is just the beginning of the possibilities. In turn, *disposable architecture* builds on this foundation, takes the idea of disposability and replacement to the next level, and drives business value further. At this higher level, we are driving a wedge in monolithic thinking at the business level.

The monolith is etched on our brains and permeates our way of thinking. It leads us to architectural and business decisions that may be optimal in the context of the monolith, but not in the context of cloud-native. Monolithic thinking is an *all or nothing* mindset. When something has to be *all or nothing,* it frequently leads us to avoid risk, even when the payoff could be significant if we could only approach it in smaller steps. It just as frequently drives us to take extreme risk, when it is perceived that we have no choice because the end game is believed to be a necessity.

Disposable architecture (aka the **Big R**) is the antithesis of monolithic thinking. We have decomposed the cloud-native system into bounded isolated components and disposable infrastructure accelerates our ability to deploy and scale these components. One rule of thumb, regarding the appropriate size of a component, is that its initial development should be scoped to about 2 weeks. At this low level of investment per component, we are at liberty to experiment with alternatives to find an optimal solution. To put this in business terms, each experiment is the cost of information. With a monolith, we are more likely to live with a suboptimal solution. The usual argument is that the cost of replacement outweighs the ongoing cost of the suboptimal solution. But in reality, the budget was simply blown building the wrong solution.

In his book, *Domain Driven Design: Tackling Complexity in the Heart of Software* (`http://dddcommunity.org/book/evans_2003/`), Eric Evans discusses the idea of the breakthrough. Teams continuously and iteratively refactor towards deeper insight with the objective of reaching a model that properly reflects the domain. Such a model should be easier to relate to when communicating with domain experts and thus make it safer and easier to reason about fixes and enhancements. This refactoring typically proceeds at a linear pace, until there is a breakthrough. A breakthrough is when the team realizes that there is a deep design flaw in the model that must be corrected. But breakthroughs typically require a high degree of refactoring.

Breakthroughs are the objective of disposable architecture. No one likes to make important decisions based on incomplete and/or inaccurate information. With disposable architecture, we can make small incremental investments to garner the knowledge necessary to glean the optimal solution. These breakthroughs may require completely reworking a component, but that initial work was just the cost of acquiring the information and knowledge that led to the breakthrough. In essence, disposable architecture allows us to minimize waste. We safely and wisely expend our development resources on controlled experiments and in the end get more value for that investment. We will discuss the topic of lean experiments and the related topic of decoupling deployment from release in `Chapter 6`, *Deployment*. Yet, to embrace disposable architecture, we need more than just disposable infrastructure and lean methods; we need to leverage value-added cloud services.

Leverages value-added cloud services

This is perhaps one of the most intuitive, yet simultaneously the most alienated concepts of cloud-native. When we started to dismantle our monolith, I made a conscious decision to fully leverage the value-added services of our cloud provider. Our monolith just leveraged the cloud for its infrastructure-as-a-service. That was a big improvement, as we have already discussed. Disposable infrastructure allowed us to move fast, but we wanted to move faster. Even when there were open source alternatives available, we chose to use the cloud provided (that is, cloud-native) service.

What could be more cloud-native than using the native services of the cloud providers? It did not matter that there were already containers defined for the open source alternatives. As I have mentioned previously and will repeat many times, the containers are only the tip of the iceberg. I will repeat this many times throughout the book because it is good to repeat important points. A great deal of forethought, effort, and care are required for any and every service that you will be running on your own. It is the rest of the iceberg that keeps me up at night. How long does it take to really understand the ins and outs of these open source services before you can really run them in production with confidence? How many of these services can your team realistically build expertise in, all at the same time? How many "gotchas" will you run into at the least opportune time?

Many of these open source services are data focused, such as databases and messaging. For all my customers, and I'll assert for most companies, data is the value proposition. How much risk are you willing to assume with regard to the data that is your bread and butter? Are you certain that you will not lose any of that data? Do you have sufficient redundancy? Do you have a comprehensive backup and restore process? Do you have monitoring in place, so that you will know in advance and have ample time to grow your storage space? Have you hardened your operating system and locked down every last back door?

The bulk of the patterns in this book revolve around data. Cloud-native is about more than just scaling components. It is ultimately about scaling your data. Gone are the days of the monolithic database. Each component will have multiple dedicated databases of various types. This is an approach called polyglot persistence that we will discuss shortly. It will require your teams to own and operate many different types of persistence services. Is this where you want to place your time and effort? Or do you want to focus your efforts on your value proposition?

By leveraging the value-added services of our cloud provider, we cut months, if not more, off our ramp-up time and minimize our operational risk. Leveraging value-added cloud services gave us confidence that the services were operated properly. We could be certain that the services would scale and grow with us, as we needed them to. In some cases, the cloud services only have a single dial that you turn. We simply needed to hook up our third-party monitoring service to observe the metrics provided by these value-added services and focus on the alerts that were important to our components. We will discuss alerting and observability in `Chapter 8`, *Monitoring*.

This concept is also the most alienated, because of the fear of vendor lock-in. But vendor lock-in is monolithic thinking. In cloud-native systems, we make decisions on a component-by-component basis. We embrace disposable architecture and leverage value-added cloud services to increase our velocity, increase our knowledge, and minimize our risk. By leveraging the value-added services of our cloud provider, we gave ourselves time to learn more about all the new services and techniques. In many cases, we did not know if a specific type of service was going to meet our needs. Using the cloud-provided services was just the cost of acquiring the information and knowledge we needed to make informed long-term decisions. We were willing to outgrow a cloud-provided service, instead of growing into a service we ran ourselves. Maybe we would never outgrow the cloud-provided service. Maybe we would never grow into a service we ran ourselves.

It is important to have an exit strategy, in case you do outgrow a value-added cloud service. Fortunately, with bounded isolated components, we can exit one component at a time and not necessarily for all components. For example, a specific cloud provider service may be perfect for all but a small few of your components. In `Chapter 3`, *Foundation Patterns*, we will discuss the Event Sourcing and Data Lake patterns that are the foundation for any such exit strategy and conversion.

Welcomes polyglot cloud

The willingness to welcome polyglot cloud is a true measure of cloud-native maturity. Let's start with something more familiar: **polyglot programming**. Polyglot programming is the idea that on a component-by-component basis, we will choose to use the programming language that best suits the requirements of the specific component. An organization, team, or individual will typically have a favorite or go-to language but will use another language for a specific component when it is more appropriate.

As an example, JavaScript is now my go-to language. When I started my cloud journey, Java was my go-to language. I had been using Java since it was born in the mid-1990s and it was a great full-stack option in my pre-cloud days. But then native mobile apps and single page web apps changed everything. These new presentation tiers dictated the language that was used. Even when you could choose between languages, the wrong choice would leave you swimming against the current. Then function-as-a-service emerged and full-stack JavaScript became the most compelling baseline. But even though I have a favorite, there are still components in specific domains, such as analytics and artificial intelligence, that can benefit from another language, such as Python.

Moving on, **polyglot persistence** is a topic we will cover in depth in this book. This too is the idea that on a component-by-component basis, we will choose to use the storage mechanism that best suits the requirements of the specific component. One unique characteristic of polyglot persistence is that we will often use multiple storage mechanisms within a single component in an effort to get the absolute best performance and scalability for the specific workload. Optimal persistence is crucial for global scale, cloud-native systems. The advancements in the persistence layer are in many ways far more significant than any other cloud-native topic. We will be discussing cloud-native database concepts throughout this book.

Polyglot cloud is the next, logical, evolutionary step. In a mature cloud-native system, you will begin to choose the cloud provider that is best on a component-by-component basis. You will have a go-to cloud provider for the majority of your components. However, you will find that competition is driving cloud providers to innovate at an ever-faster pace, and many of these innovations will help give your system its own competitive advantage, but alas your go-to cloud provider's offering in a specific case may not be sufficient.

Does this mean that you will need to lift and shift your cloud-native system from one cloud provider to another? No, absolutely not. It will take less time and effort and incur less risk to perform a quick, potentially disposable, experiment with the additional provider. After that, there will be a compelling reason to try a feature offered by another provider, and another, and so on. Ultimately, it will not be possible to run your cloud-native system on just one provider. Thus, a mature cloud-native system will be characterized by polyglot cloud. It is inevitable, which is why I welcome it in our cloud-native definition.

Today, does your company use both Office 365 and AWS? The answer to this question, or one of its many permutations, is very often, yes. If so, then you are already polyglot cloud and you should find ways to integrate and leverage both. Has your company acquired another firm that uses another cloud provider? Is it possible that your company might acquire such a company? Can you think of any other potential scenarios that will inevitably lead your company to be polyglot cloud? I suspect most companies are already polyglot cloud without realizing it.

It is important to make a distinction between polyglot cloud and another common term, multi-cloud. Polyglot cloud and multi-cloud are different. They come from completely different mindsets. Multi-cloud is the idea that you can write your cloud-native system once and run it on multiple cloud providers, either concurrently for redundancy or in an effort to be provider-agnostic. We have seen this before in the Java application server market and it didn't pan out as promised. It did not pan out because the providers offered compelling value-added features that locked in your monolith. With cloud-native, we do not have a monolith. Thus, vendor lock-in is only on a component-by-component basis. There will always be compelling reasons to leverage vendor-specific offerings, as we have already discussed. A least common denominator approach does not provide for this flexibility. Thus we welcome polyglot cloud.

Furthermore, moving an entire system from one provider to another is a high-risk proposition. Big-bang migrations have always been and will always be problematic. Migrating a cloud-native system to another cloud provider is no different. This holds true even when a cloud abstraction platform is employed. This is because your system on top of the cloud abstraction platform is just the tip of the iceberg. All the real risk lies below the surface. A cloud abstraction layer adds significant project overhead to your system in its infancy when it is needed the least, requires more operational effort throughout the product life cycle, and does not mitigate the significant risks of migration should you ever actually need to do so.

Essentially, multi-cloud is characteristic of the monolithic, all or nothing thinking of the past. Polyglot cloud focuses instead on the promise of cloud-native. Welcoming polyglot cloud up front keeps your system lean, avoids unneeded layers and overhead, and frees your team to choose the right provider on a component-by-component basis.

Empowers self-sufficient, full-stack teams

Developers often ask me how they can learn to write infrastructure as code when they do not know enough about the infrastructure resources they are deploying. I typically respond with several probing questions, such as:

- When you were first hired straight out of school as a programmer, were you hired because you were an expert in that company's domain? No. The domain experts gave you the requirements and you wrote the software.
- Did you eventually become knowledgeable in that domain? Yes, absolutely.

- Have you ever been given just the documentation of an external system's API and then asked to go figure out how to integrate your system with that system? Sure. You read the documentation, you asked follow up questions, and you made it happen.

Then I just reiterate what they have already begun to realize. An infrastructure resource is just another functional domain that happens to be a technical domain. In the cloud, these resources are API-driven. Ultimately, we are just integrating our build pipelines with these APIs. It is just code. We work our agile development methodology, write the code, ask questions, and iterate. More and more we can do these deployments declaratively. In `Chapter 6`, *Deployment*, we will dive into more detail about how to do deployments and integrate these tasks into the development methodology.

Sooner than later, we all become domain experts of the cloud-native resources we leverage. We start simple. Then as our components mature, they put more demands on these resources and we learn to leverage them as we go. As we discussed previously, this is why value-added cloud services are so valuable. They give us a strong foundation when we know the least and grow with us as we gain expertise. This is one of the ways that being cloud-native empowers teams. The cloud works on a shared responsibility model. Everything below a certain line is the responsibility of the cloud provider. Everything above this line is the responsibility of your team. As you use more and more value-added cloud services, such as database-as-a-service and function-as-a-service, that line is drawn higher and higher. Your team becomes self-sufficient by leveraging the power of value-added cloud services, which allows you to focus on the value proposition of your components. Your team controls the full-stack because you can provision your required resources at will.

You may have heard of Conway's Law:

> *"organizations are constrained to produce application designs which are copies of their communication structures"*

Let's put this in the context of an example. Many companies are organized around the architectures of N-tiered monoliths and data centers. Teams are organized by skillset: user interface, backend services, database administrators, testers, operations, and so forth. Conway's Law essentially says that organizations like this will not successfully implement cloud-native systems.

Cloud-native systems are composed of bounded isolated components. These components own all their resources. As such, self-sufficient, full-stack teams must own the components and their resources. Otherwise, the communication and coordination overhead across horizontal teams will marginalize the benefits of bounded isolated components and ultimately tear them apart. Instead, companies need to re-organize to reflect the desired system architecture.

Self-sufficient, full-stack teams own one or more components for the entirety of each component's full life cycle. This is often referred to as the *you build it, you run it* mentality. The result is that teams tend to build in quality up front because they will be directly on the hook when the component is broken. The patterns in this book for creating bounded isolated components help teams control their own destiny by controlling the upstream and downstream dependencies of their components. In Chapter 6, *Deployment*, Chapter 7, *Testing*, and Chapter 8, *Monitoring*, we will discuss the techniques that teams can leverage to help ensure their confidence in their components. Self-sufficient, full-stack teams are at liberty to continuously deliver innovation at their own pace, they are on the hook to deliver safely, and companies can scale by adding more teams.

Drives cultural change

It was a big event when we completed our first fully automated deployment of our monolith using disposable infrastructure. There was a celebration. It was a big deal. Then we did another deployment in a couple of days and the naysayers nodded their heads. Then we did another deployment the next day and congratulatory emails went out. Before long we could do a deployment, even multiple deployments, on any given day, without even a whisper or a pat on the back. Deployments had become non-events. Successful, uneventful deployments had become an expectation. The culture had begun to change.

We still have celebrations. We have them when we complete a feature release. But a release is now just a marketing event; it is not a development event. They are milestones that we work towards. We have completely decoupled deployment from release. Components are deployed to production with the completion of every task. A release is made up of a large number of small task scoped deployments. The last task deployment of a release could very well have happened weeks before we flipped the feature on for general availability. In Chapter 6, *Deployment*, we will discuss the mechanics of decoupling deployment from release. In Chapter 7, *Testing* and Chapter 8, *Monitoring*, we will discuss the techniques that help ensure that deployments can safely happen at this pace. Many of these techniques were considered heresy until their value was demonstrated.

Ultimately, cultural change comes down to trust. Trust is earned. We must incrementally demonstrate that we can execute and deliver on the promise of cloud-native. The monolith has been the cultural norm forever, in software terms. It is a mindset; it is a way of thinking. Many software-related business practices and policies revolve around the expectations set by the realities of monolithic systems. This is why cloud-native must drive cultural change. When we show that the downstream practices truly can deliver, only then can the upstream practices and policies really begin to change and embrace lean thinking. With cloud-native driven lean thinking, the pace of innovation really accelerates through experimentation. The business can quickly and safely adjust course based on market feedback and scale by minimizing the effort required to perform the business experimentation. All the while knowing that the solutions can scale when the experiments prove fruitful.

Summary

In this chapter, we covered the fundamental concepts of cloud-native systems. Our definition of cloud-native is focused on your context. You need an architecture that will grow with you and not weigh you down now. Cloud-native is more than architecting and optimizing to take advantage of the cloud. It is an entirely different way of thinking and reasoning about software architecture and development practices. Cloud-native breaks free of monolithic thinking to empower self-sufficient teams that continuously deliver innovation with confidence. This confidence is derived from the knowledge that cloud-native systems are powered by disposable infrastructure, composed of bounded isolated components, and scale globally, so that they remain responsive in the face of failures. Cloud-native teams embrace disposable architecture, leverage value-added cloud services, and welcome polyglot cloud to provide the strong foundation that enables them to take control of the full-stack, focus on the value proposition, and drive cultural change from the bottom up by earning trust through successful execution.

The Anatomy of Cloud Native Systems

2

In the first chapter, we identified that the promise of cloud-native is the ability for everyday companies to rapidly and continuously deliver innovation, with the confidence that the system will remain stable as it evolves and that it will scale to meet users' demands. Today's users demand far more than in the past. They expect to access applications around the clock from all kinds of devices, with zero downtime and sub-second response times, regardless of their geographic location. If any of these expectations are not met then they will seek out alternatives. Meeting these demands can seem daunting, but cloud-native empowers every day teams to deliver on this challenge. However, it requires us to approach software architecture with an open mind to new ways of thinking.

In this chapter, we begin our deep dive into the architectural aspects of cloud-native systems. In our definition, cloud-native is powered by disposable infrastructure, composed of bounded isolated components, scales globally, and leverages value-added cloud services. We put these technical concepts in context and pave the way for understanding cloud-native patterns. We will cover the following topics:

- The cloud is the database
- Reactive architecture
- Turning the database inside out
- Bulkheads
- Event streaming
- Polyglot persistence
- Cloud-native databases
- Cloud-native patterns
- Decomposition strategies for bounded isolated components

The cloud is the database

In the first chapter, I told the story of my first *wow* moment when I realized that we could run our presentation layer entirely from the edge with no servers. From that point on, I wanted to achieve the same level of scalability for the rest of the layers as well. Let's start this chapter with a continuation of that story.

Like many of you, for a significant chunk of my career, I implemented systems that needed to be database agnostic. The relational database was the standard, but we had to support all the various flavors, such as Oracle, MySQL, in-memory databases for testing, and so forth. Object relational mapping tools, such as Hibernate, were a necessity. We built large relational models, crammed the database schema full of tables, and then tossed the DDL over the fence to the DBA team. Inevitability, the schema would be deployed to underpowered database instances that were shared by virtually every system in the enterprise. Performance suffered and we turned to optimizing the software to compensate for the realities of a shared database model. We added caching layers, maintained more state in the application sessions, de-normalized the data models to the nth degree, and more. These were just the facts of life in the world of monolithic enterprise systems.

Then came time to lift and shift these monoliths to the cloud, along with the shared database model. It did not take long to realize how complicated and expensive it was to run relational databases in the cloud across multiple availability zones. Running on a database-as-a-service, such as AWS RDS, was the obvious alternative, though this had its own limitations. A given database instance size could only support a maximum number of connections. Thus it was necessary to scale these instances vertically, plus add read replicates. It was still complex and expensive and thus there was still an incentive to run a shared database model. It was time to start looking for alternatives. I studied CAP theorem and sharding, evaluated the various NoSQL options, learned about the BASE and ACID 2.0 transaction models, and considered the different ways our system could support eventual consistency. NoSQL was deemed a nonstarter because it would require reworking the system. The NewSQL options promised a pluggable alternative to NoSQL, but these were just downright expensive.

When we moved to microservices, we started with a schema-per-service approach on top of the shared database-as-a-service model. It was a step in the right direction, but it still had several drawbacks: we needed a way to synchronize some data between the microservices, there was effectively no bulkhead between the services at the database level, and we still needed to scale the connections for the consumer-facing services. The new feature was a consumer-facing, mobile-first application. It had a click stream that pumped events through AWS Kinesis into a time series database running as-a-service. I knew this part of the new feature would scale, so we just had to repeat that pattern. We started using the event stream to synchronize the data between the microservices. This approach was very familiar because it was essentially the same event-driven pattern we had always used for **Enterprise Application Integration** (**EAI**) projects. How could we build on this to scale the consumer-facing services?

We had a set of back-office services with low user volumes for authoring content. Those could stay on the shared database for the time being. We would use the event stream to synchronize the necessary back-office data to high-octane Polyglot Persistence dedicated to the consumer-facing components. The consumer-facing databases included S3 plus AWS CloudFront for storing and serving the images and JSON documents and AWS CloudSearch to index the documents. We effectively created a bulkhead between the front-office and back-office components and allowed the two to scale completely independently. The documents were being served on a global scale, just like a single page app. We didn't realize it at the time, but we were implementing the Event Sourcing and **Command Query Responsibility Segregation** (**CQRS**) patterns, but with a cloud-native twist. We will discuss these patterns in `Chapter 3`, *Foundation Patterns*, and `Chapter 4`, *Boundary Patterns*, respectively.

Along the way on my cloud-native journey, I came across two documents that drew my attention, *The Reactive Manifesto* (`https://www.reactivemanifesto.org/`) and Martin Kleppman's excellent article, *Turning the Database Inside-out* (`https://www.confluent.io/blog/turning-the-database-inside-out-with-apache-samza/`). These documents formalized what we were already doing and led to another *wow* moment, the realization that the cloud is the database. This is where our discussion will go next.

Reactive Manifesto

The *Reactive Manifesto* embodies a concise description of the system properties we are striving for. There are just four, seemingly straightforward, properties. A system should be responsive, resilient, elastic, and message-driven. We all certainly want our systems to be responsive, and if you are building a cloud-based system then elasticity is definitely a goal. But the magic lies in how we achieve resilience, because the responsiveness and elasticity of a system are a function of how it achieves its resilience. It is important to recognize that the message-driven property is the means to achieve the other properties.

These properties will manifest themselves in our cloud-native systems. Our objective is to use asynchronous, message-driven, inter-component communication to build resilient components that are responsive and elastic. We want to accomplish this in the context of our cloud-native definition such that the architecture is approachable by everyday companies. We will leverage value-added cloud services to empower self-sufficient, full-stack teams to create bounded isolated components that scale globally. Event streaming will be the mechanism for inter-component communication. We will effectively turn the database inside out to achieve cost-effective resilience through data replication in the form of materialized views. These materialized views act as a cache to make components responsive and provide proper bulkheads between components. They also make the system more elastic as the database load is spread across many independent data stores.

Let's continue to dive deeper into how we turn the database inside out and ultimately turn the cloud into the database.

Turning the database inside out

As our industry progresses through its cloud-native metamorphosis, we are also experiencing a revolution in database thinking. The amount of advancement we have seen in database technology over the past decade is significant. It started with the NoSQL movement, but then expanded into the Polyglot Persistence arena. Database sharding techniques finally enabled databases to scale horizontally by spreading disk access across commodity hardware. Polyglot Persistence expanded on this technique by optimizing how data is stored on these disks for different read and write patterns. CAP Theorem taught us to embrace eventual consistency in our designs in favor of availability.

However, with this advancement comes a significant increase in operational complexity and the workforce needed to administer these databases. With this overhead comes the tendency to operate in a shared database model. As was previously mentioned, this means that there are no bulkheads between the various components sharing these monolithic database clusters. Without isolation, at best these components just compete for the cluster's scarce resources and impact each other's performance, at worst a catastrophic failure in the database cluster causes an outage across all the components.

Yet, in most cases, a company's value proposition is its data. A company's most valuable asset warrants more than a shared database model. This is where the real revolution is happening; a complete break from monolithic thinking at the persistence layer. We are turning the database completely inside out, replicating the data across many databases of different types to create the necessary isolation, outsourcing some of the responsibilities of these databases to the cloud provider, and leveraging the innovations of cloud-native databases, such as global replication. Let's dissect how we turn the database inside out.

We need to understand a bit about how databases work, to understand how we are turning them inside out. Martin provides a very thorough description in his article, which I will paraphrase here. At the heart of any database is the transaction log. The transaction log is an append-only structure that records all the events that change the state of the data. In other words, it records all the insert, update, and delete statements that are executed against the database. The database tables hold the current state representation of these events. The transaction log can be replayed to recreate the current state of the tables if need be. This is what happens during replication. The logs are replayed against another node to bring it up to date. The database also manages indexes. These indexes are just another copy of the data sorted in the desired sequence.

Traditional databases are notoriously slow and contention for connections is high. This drives the need for caching query results on the consuming side. A cache is yet another copy of the data, but this copy can be incomplete and stale. Performance can be very slow when we have complex queries over large sets of data. To solve this problem databases maintain materialized views. A materialized view is yet another copy of the data, which is the result of a query that is continuously kept up to date by the database. These are examples of derived data, that, other than the cache, are managed by a single database cluster. We ask our databases to do a great deal of work and then wonder why they are slow.

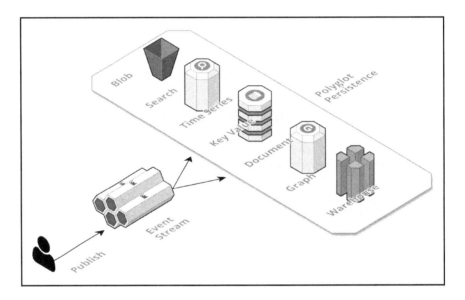

Our objective is to take all this processing and turn it inside out, so that we can spread this processing across the cloud, to achieve massive scale and sufficient isolation. Lets first revisit the Reactive properties. Our components should be responsive, resilient, elastic, and message-driven. Our *message-driven* inter-component communication mechanism is event streaming. As depicted in the preceding diagram, the event stream is the externalized transaction log. Components publish their events to the stream. Other components consume these events from the stream and create read replicas of the data in their own Polyglot Persistence stores by programmatically populating materialized views (that is, tables) that are optimized for their own usage. These local representations of the data help the system achieve Reactive properties.

First, they make a component *responsive* by providing an optimized cache that effectively eliminates the stale cache and cache miss problems, because it is continuously warmed. Second, they act as a bulkhead to make a component *resilient* to failures in upstream components, because the component will always retrieve the latest known state from its own storage. Finally, this makes the system extremely *elastic*, because the read replicas are spread across many databases in many components. The main patterns at work here are the Event Sourcing and CQRS patterns. We will discuss these in `Chapter 3`, *Foundation Patterns*, and `Chapter 4`, *Boundary Patterns*, respectively.

Bulkheads

I have already mentioned bulkheads several times in this chapter. Let's get more specific about the role of bulkheads in cloud-native systems. In the first chapter, we discussed how monolithic systems are their own bottleneck to advancement because they must be deployed as a whole, even for the smallest of changes. The natural reaction to this reality is to batch up changes and thus produce a bottleneck. This reaction is driven by a lack of confidence that the system will remain stable in the face of change. This lack of confidence is rooted in the fact that monoliths are prone to catastrophic failures because a failure in one component can infect the whole system. The problem is that monoliths have no natural system bulkheads. Ultimately, monolithic systems mature and evolve at a glacial pace, because the feedback loop is protracted by this bottleneck and lack of confidence.

The solution is to instill confidence by decomposing a system into bounded isolated components. We can reason about well-bounded components much more easily. Conversations about the functionality of bounded components are much more coherent. We can be far more certain that we understand the implications and side effects of any controlled change to a bounded component. Yet it is inevitable that there will be failures, both human and technical. We strive to minimize this potential with bounded components, but we design for failure and make preparations to recover quickly when failures do occur. Well-isolated components make the system as a whole resilient to these failures by containing the failures and limiting the blast radius to a single component, thus providing teams with breathing room to rapidly respond and recover from the failure.

The apt analogy for bounded isolated components is the bulkhead. As depicted in the preceding diagram, ships are divided into compartments that are separated by walls, known as **bulkheads**, to form watertight chambers. A breach in the hull will contain the flooding to the affected chambers to help prevent the ship from sinking. Unfortunately, it is not enough to just have bulkheads; they must be properly designed. The Titanic is the classic example of poorly designed bulkheads. Its bulkheads were not watertight, allowing water to flow from compartment to compartment over the top of the bulkheads and we all know how the story ends.

A primary focus of this book is dedicated to designing for failure by creating proper bulkheads for our cloud-native components. This is where much of the rethinking lies. We will be using event streaming and data replication as the implementation mechanisms for isolating components from each other and cover those patterns in depth throughout the book.

Event streaming

Event streaming is our message-driven, publish, and subscribe mechanism for asynchronous inter-component communication. Asynchronous, event-based messaging has long been known for its ability to create loosely coupled systems. Producers publish events without knowledge of the consumers and the consumers are only coupled to the event type definitions, not the producers of the events. The location of producers and consumers is transparent, which facilitates elasticity and resilience. Producers and consumers need only access the messaging system, there is no need for service discovery to determine the location of other components. The components operate in complete isolation. Messages can be produced even when the consumers are not available. When an unavailable consumer comes back online, it can scale up to process the backlog of messages. Producers can increase their responsiveness by delegating processing to other components so that they can focus their resources on their single responsibility.

There are a two, separate but related, aspects of event streaming that make it stand out from traditional messaging systems: scale and eventual consistency. Event streaming belongs to the *dumb pipes, smart endpoints* generation. Traditional messaging middleware of the monolithic generation can be considered smart pipes, too smart for their own good. These tools receive messages, perform routing and delivery, track acknowledgments, and often take on message transform and orchestration responsibilities. All this additional processing is a drain on their resources that limits their scalability. Their value-added features of transformation and orchestration increase coupling and decrease cohesion, which limits isolation and turns them into a single point of failure.

Event streams have a single responsibility, to receive and durably store events, lots of events, at massive scale. An event stream is an append-only, sharded database, that maintains an ordered log of events and scales horizontally to accommodate massive volumes. It is important to note that an event stream is a modern, sharded database. We will discuss the implications of modern, sharded databases shortly. It is the consumers of the stream (that is, stream processors) that have all the smarts, which first and foremost allows all the necessary processing to be spread across all the components. Stream processors read events from the stream and are responsible for checkpointing their current position in the stream. This is important for many reasons, but for now, it is just important that the streaming engine is relinquished of the need to track acknowledgments and all the overhead that this entails. Stream processors read events in batches to improve efficiency. Traditional messaging systems do this as well, but they typically do this under the covers and deliver the messages to consumers one at a time. This means that traditional consumers cannot capitalize on batch efficiencies as well. Stream processors leverage these batches in combination with functional reactive programming and asynchronous non-blocking IO to create robust, elegant, and highly concurrent processing logic. What's more, stream processors are replicated per shard to further increase concurrency. We will delve into more details with the event streaming pattern, in `Chapter 3`, *Foundation Patterns*.

The CAP theorem states that in the presence of a network partition, one has to choose between consistency and availability. In the context of modern consumer-facing applications, even a temporary increase in latency is considered to be equivalent to a network partition, because of the opportunity cost of lost customers. Therefore, it is widely preferred to choose availability over consistency and thus design systems around eventual consistency and session consistency. Embracing eventual consistency is a significant advancement for our industry. Event streaming and eventual consistency are interdependent. Eventual consistency is simply a reality of asynchronous messaging and event streaming is the mechanism for implementing eventual consistency.

Without both, we cannot increase responsiveness and scalability by allowing components to delegate processing to downstream components. More importantly, without both, we cannot build bounded isolated components that are resilient and elastic, because event streaming and eventual consistency are crucial to turning the database inside out and ultimately turning the cloud into the database.

There is a common misconception that eventual consistency equates to a lack of transactionality. Nothing could be further from the truth. Each hand-off in the flow of events through the system is implemented transactionally by the smart endpoints (that is, components) and their supporting architecture. The subsequent design of the aggregate flow produces the eventual consistency. When the system is operating normally, eventual consistency happens in near real-time but degrades gracefully when anomalies occur. We will discuss the architectural mechanisms, such as idempotency and the *Event Sourcing* pattern in Chapter 3, *Foundation Patterns*, and the *Saga* pattern in Chapter 5, *Control Patterns*. For now, keep in mind that the world we live in is eventually consistent. The classic example of event-driven, non-blocking, eventual consistency is the coffee shop. You stand in line at the coffee shop and wait for your turn to place and pay for your order. Then you wait for your cup of coffee to be prepared. If all goes to plan then your order is ready promptly. Otherwise, you inquire about your order when it is taking too long. If a mistake has been made then it is corrected and you are likely compensated with a discount for use on your next visit. In the end, you get your coffee and the coffee shop has a more effective, scalable operation. This is analogous to how event streaming and eventual consistency play their role in helping cloud-native systems achieve scale and resilience.

Polyglot Persistence

Traditional databases are unable to scale to meet the demands of global cloud applications because they were designed to scale vertically. Modern databases have been designed to leverage sharding, which allows them to scale horizontally by partitioning the data across multiple nodes. This improves responsiveness because it reduces contention for disk access; it provides resilience because the data is also stored redundantly across several machines; and allows the database to be elastic, as the demand grows, by adding partitions. Yet, sharding is not sufficient in and of itself. Many specialized databases have been built on top of sharding that are optimized for very specific workloads.

Gone are the days where one size fits all. The least common denominator of traditional general-purpose databases cannot effectively handle the large variety of modern workloads. To meet the performance requirements of cloud-scale workloads, many different kinds of databases have been created that are highly optimized for the read and write characteristics of specific usage scenarios. This specialization has led to the adoption of a Polyglot Persistence approach where the system is composed of many different types of databases. Each component in the system uses the right storage technology for the job and often multiple kinds of databases per component. Some of the different categories of databases include key-value stores, document stores, search engines, graph databases, time series databases, blob or object storage, mobile offline-first databases, columnar or column-oriented data warehouses, and append-only streams. Note the important fact that streams are databases. Many newer database products are multi-model, in that they support multiple database types and even support the dialects of other popular databases.

The following diagram depicts an example of the persistence layer of a hypothetical e-commerce system. The example consists of six bounded isolated components:

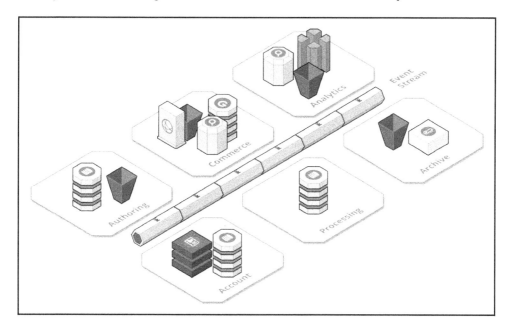

The **Authoring** component is responsible for managing the authoring of products. The product metadata is stored in a JSON document table and related multimedia is stored in a blob store. All data change events are published to the event stream for consumption by other components. The **Commerce** component is responsible for making products available to customers. The component consumes authoring events and refines the product metadata into its own materialized views. The data is indexed in a search engine and blob storage is used for multimedia and product details that are served from the edge via the CDN. The component also consumes customer clickstream events and populates a graph database for driving future product recommendations.

The **Account** component is responsible for managing a customer's profile, preferences, shopping cart, and order history. To facilitate session consistency the customer's profile, preferences, cart, and recent orders are stored in an offline-first, mobile database in local storage. This ensures that customers see a consistent view of their data even if the data is not yet eventually consistent with the rest of the system. In extreme cases, it allows customers to see their data in offline mode. The offline-first database is synchronized to the cloud and potentially other devices on a periodic basis and on discrete actions, such as checkout. Synchronization events are also published to the event stream. Order status events are consumed from the event stream and synchronized to local storage across devices. The customer's complete order history is stored in a document store. The **Processing** component is responsible for processing orders. The component consumes checkout events and stores the orders in a document table for further processing. The order table is essentially a materialized view of the order information joined with the customer's account information at the point in time of the order. The component produces events to reflect the status of orders. The order table is aggressively purged of completed orders, as the analytics and archive components are tracking all events for reporting and compliance.

The **Analytics** component consumes all events and stores them in their raw format in the data lake in perpetuity. The data is also stored in a search engine for a complete index of all the events and their contents and for robust time series analysis of the events. Events are also refined into materialized views and stored in a data warehouse. The **Archive** component consumes all events for compliance with regulations. The data is stored and versioned in blob storage and aged into cold storage.

As you can see, each of the database types excels at supporting different application usage scenarios. By selecting the right database types on a component-by-component basis we greatly simplify the work needed to implement these applications. Yet managing all these different database types can be a burden. We will address this problem in the following section.

Cloud native database

Managing a traditional database in the cloud is hard and risky. As we will discuss, it is necessary to replicate the data across availability zones to ensure the data is accessible and durable, and replicate it across regions to protect against regional outages. Managing a modern sharded database in the cloud is superhard and risky. We have all the complexity of managing the traditional database across availability zones and regions multiplied by the number of shards. Managing N modern, sharded databases in the cloud, to gain the advantages of Polyglot Persistence and bulkheads between components, is arguably an exercise in insanity, even for many unicorn companies. Imagine this oversimplified example: you have five components, each with two types of storage, each with four shards, deployed across two regions, with three availability zones each. So that is $5 * 2 * 4 * 2 * 3 = 240$ elastic block storage devices that must be provisioned, monitored, and managed. Obviously, this gets expensive pretty quickly, but that is not the real concern. With these numbers, and this is an oversimplified example, the probability that a storage device fails on any given day is very high. Of course, the point of this approach is to keep the database available during these failures, but the point here is that this is a maintenance nightmare. Does this mean we throw out the approach and go back to our shared monolithic database with no bulkheads and cross our fingers? No, because crossing your fingers won't help. That big outage will happen, it is only a matter of time, and it will happen at the most inopportune time, and the aftermath won't be pretty.

The alternative is to leverage value-added cloud services, as we discussed in the first chapter. We achieve more by managing less. However, any ole database-as-a-service offering is not what we are talking about. Those still tend towards a monolithic, shared database model. The best alternatives are the cloud-native databases. These databases are purchased, provisioned, and tuned one table at a time. This means that one table can be a document store, another table is a search index, and another table is blob storage, and so forth. They all operate across availability zones as a matter of course and more and more of these offerings have turnkey regional replication. Storage space for most offerings grows automatically, otherwise, storage space monitoring is provided. Read and write capacity will also auto scale. This is important at both extremes because it also means that they are a good alternative for small workloads as well. Many of these cloud-native databases are actually designed to support this inside-out database architecture and expose their transaction logs as an event stream, to facilitate the Event Sourcing and CQRS patterns. We will dive deeper into this in the *Cloud Native Databases Per Component* pattern section in Chapter 3, *Foundation Patterns*.

I think it should be starting to become clear that rewiring the way we think about systems, combined with leveraging value-added cloud services, can empower everyday companies to create reactive, cloud-native systems that are responsive, resilient, and globally elastic. It was a major *wow* moment for me when I realized that the *Cloud is the database* and how much that means we can accomplish with the fundamental cloud-native building blocks of event streaming and cloud-native databases.

Cloud native patterns

It is easy enough to say that we will architecture cloud-native systems based on Reactive principles and leverage event streaming to ultimately turn the cloud into the database, but it is another thing entirely to show how the pieces fit together. There is a relatively small collection of proven patterns that can be leveraged as templates to build cloud-native systems that solve a wide variety of valuable problems. Many of these patterns may already be familiar but have cloud-native twists.

Each pattern describes a solution to a specific problem in the context of cloud-native systems and addresses various forces, issues, and trade-offs. The patterns are interrelated and thus can be pieced together to build systems composed of bounded isolated components. There are many ways to document patterns. Martin Fowler has an excellent summary of various pattern forms in his posting on Writing Software Patterns (`https://www.martinfowler.com/articles/writingPatterns.html`).

Our cloud-native patterns are documented in the following form. Each will start with its name, a brief description of its intent, and a diagram that represents a sketch of the solution. These three pieces are critical to forming a pattern language that teams can use to facilitate architecture and design discussions and to train new team members. When additional details are needed we can refer to the body of each pattern.

Each pattern body includes sections discussing the context, problem, and forces; the solution, the resulting context, and one or more examples of the solution in action. The solution may include variations that can be applied in different scenarios. The resulting context section discusses the consequences, benefits, and drawbacks of applying the pattern, along with how it relates to the other cloud-native patterns. The patterns are grouped into three categories: Foundation, Boundary, and Control, to emphasize their relationships to each other and their place in cloud-native systems in general. The examples are real working solutions. However, they are purposefully simplified to focus in on the specific pattern.

Thus far we have established the overall context for our cloud-native patterns. The promise of cloud-native is to enable everyday companies to rapidly and continuously deliver innovation with confidence. To this end we want to empower self-sufficient, full-stack teams, leverage value-added cloud services, and embrace disposable architecture so that teams can focus on the value proposition of their bounded isolated components. We want to achieve global scale by recognizing that the cloud is the database, applying Reactive principles, and turning the database inside out to create proper bulkheads through the replication of data to materialized views built on event streaming, Polyglot Persistence, and cloud-native databases.

This context will be at the heart of all our cloud-native patterns. The following is a catalog of the patterns organized by category. Each category section includes a description of the category, the name, and intent of each pattern, and a summary diagram with a thumbnail image of each pattern sketch. Plus all the images are available for download as mentioned in the *Preface* of the book.

Foundation patterns

These patterns provide the foundation for reactive, asynchronous inter-component communication in cloud-native systems.

Cloud Native Databases Per Component: Leverage one or more fully managed cloud-native databases that are not shared across components and react to emitted events to trigger intra-component processing logic

Event Streaming: Leverage a fully managed streaming service to implement all inter-component communication asynchronously whereby upstream components delegate processing to downstream components by publishing domain events that are consumed downstream

Event Sourcing: Communicate and persist the change in state of domain entities as a series of atomically produced immutable domain events, using Event-First or Database-First techniques, to drive asynchronous inter-component communication and facilitate event processing logic

Data Lake: Collect, store, and index all events in their raw format in perpetuity with complete fidelity and high durability to support auditing, replay, and analytics

Stream Circuit Breaker: Control the flow of events in stream processors so that failures do not inappropriately disrupt throughput, by delegating the handling of unrecoverable errors through fault events

Trilateral API: Publish multiple interfaces for each component: a synchronous API for processing commands and queries, an asynchronous API for publishing events as the state of the component changes, and/or an asynchronous API for consuming the events emitted by other components

Boundary patterns

These patterns operate at the boundaries of cloud-native systems. The boundaries are where *the system* interacts with everything that is external to *the system*, including humans and other systems.

API Gateway: Leverage a fully managed API gateway to create a barrier at the boundaries of a cloud-native system by pushing cross-cutting concerns, such as security and caching, to the edge of the cloud where some load is absorbed before entering the interior of the system.

Command Query Responsibility Segregation (CQRS): Consume state change events from upstream components and maintain materialized views that support queries used within a component.

Offline-First Database: Persist user data in local storage and synchronize with the cloud when connected so that client-side changes are published as events and cloud-side changes are retrieved from materialized views

Backend For Frontend: Create dedicated and self-sufficient backend components to support the features of user focused, frontend applications

External Service Gateway: Integrate with external systems by encapsulating the inbound and outbound inter-system communication within a bounded isolated component to provide an anti-corruption layer that acts as a bridge to exchange events between the systems

Control patterns

These patterns provide the control flow for inter-component collaboration between the boundary components of cloud-native systems.

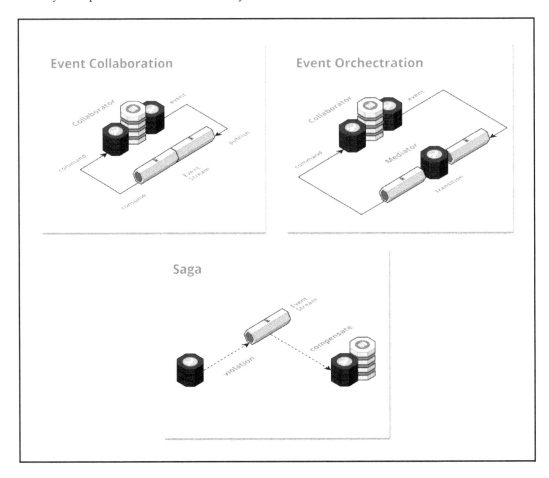

Event Collaboration: Publish domain events to trigger downstream commands and create a reactive chain of collaboration across multiple components

Event Orchestration: Leverage a mediator component to orchestrate collaboration between components without event type coupling

Saga: Trigger compensating transactions to undo changes in a multi-step flow when business rules are violated downstream

Bounded isolated components

We have defined the architectural vision for our cloud-native systems and enumerated the patterns used to build these systems. The next step is to decompose a system into bounded isolated components. However, *"What is the right size?"* is a fundamental question that everyone asks. Ultimately, every team has to answer this question for itself. You have to ask yourself how confident you are that you can continuously deploy and scale each component. If you cannot be certain of the implications of a given change to a component then the component is potentially too large. If you have to make compromises on the scalability and tuning of a specific component then it likely needs to be split apart. If the backlog of changes to a component starts to clog then this is an indication that it may need to be refactored into multiple components. The potential scenarios may be limitless. In this section, we discuss common strategies for decomposing cloud-native systems into bounded isolated components across both functional and technical dimensions. These are not independent strategies. You will use all these strategies in different combinations for different components. Embrace disposable architecture in an effort to reach the optimal decomposition by executing controlled lean experiments, as we will discuss in `Chapter 6,` *Deployment*.

Functional boundaries

Functional decomposition is by no means a new topic. For programmers, it is the fundamental topic of any programming 101 course. For software analysts, decomposing a system into domains and subdomains is part of the job description. At its core, none of this has changed. You know your functional domain. As a domain expert, you know how to best divvy up your system's functionality. What we are focused on here is how to use that knowledge and take it further to create bounded isolated components that you can deploy and scale with confidence. In essence, we are creating functional bulkheads around our components. We want to share a domain language across all teams to help ensure that everyone has a shared understanding of the innovations we are continuously deploying to these components. We want to apply relevant patterns to components to help ensure the cohesion of a specific component. We want to ensure that each component is focused on a specific responsibility.

Bounded context

One fallacy of monolithic thinking is the **master data model** (**MDM**). Virtually every decent-sized enterprise has made an attempt at crafting a master data model that describes all the data entities used by the enterprise and the relationships between those entities. It's a noble goal to create a shared definition of all the data within a company and across all its systems and processes. Yet these projects drag on and on, filled with meetings full of more people then can be fed with two pizzas. There is endless debate about the details of the model and ultimately any model that is created is utterly bloated with details that are irrelevant for most systems and scenarios. In the end, these models actually impede progress, because they lend themselves to the creation of monolithic systems that are neither bounded nor isolated. I was recently involved in a cloud migration project for a legacy system that was plagued by an unbounded data model. Several separate but somewhat related concepts were intertwined in the same relational data model. These concepts shared the same terms, but they had different meanings for different teams. Design discussions frequently went off track when the terms and meanings were mixed up. Ultimately, innovation in the legacy system came to a standstill, because no one was confident that they could make enhancements to the broken model. The model needed to be revamped into several bounded contexts.

No book on cloud-native would be complete without covering the concept of bounded contexts. Bounded contexts are a core concept in **Domain Driven Design** (**DDD**). Domain Driven Design embraces the fact that there is no single unified model. Large models are decomposed into multiple bounded contexts with well-defined interrelationships. Each bounded context is internally consistent, such that no terms have multiple meanings. When concepts do overlap between bounded contexts, these relationships can be depicted with a context map. Domain events are used to communicate between the different contexts. What emerges is a ubiquitous language that facilitates communication between developers and domain experts. This shared language helps elicit the confidence that teams need to continuously deliver innovation. Furthermore, these models map nicely to the notion of bounded, isolated, cloud-native components communicating via event streams. This consistency further instills confidence that the teams have a shared understanding of the functionality.

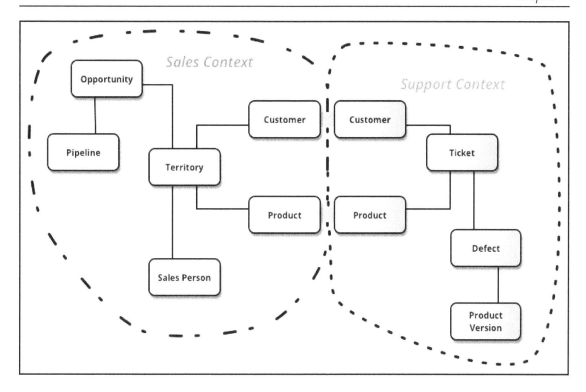

The preceding diagram is a classic bounded context example from Martin Fowler's blog on the topic (https://martinfowler.com/bliki/BoundedContext.html). It depicts two separate but related bounded contexts: the **Sales Context** and the **Support Context**. These contexts are interrelated in that they each have a concept of **Product** and **Customer**. Each context has its own definition of a **Customer** entity and a **Product** entity and each definition is unique to its context. The only thing that would need to be consistent across the contexts is the identifiers of the instances of these entities as depicted by the interrelationship. One very important thing to note is that there is no unified **Customer** context and no unified **Product** context. Each context is bounded and isolated and forms its own bulkhead, such that it can execute and even exist independently. Unfortunately, monolithic thinking would have us create those shared contexts and lead us to create inflexible and un-resilient systems.

Instead, we will integrate the contexts via the domain events. A customer instance may originate in the **Sales Context** and produce a `CustomerCreated` event that is consumed by the **Support Context**. A third context, the Catalog context could be the source of `ProductCreated` events that are consumed by both the **Sales Contexts** and **Support Contexts**, but neither would need to directly query products from the catalog. The Catalog context would only be responsible for the authoring phase of the data life cycle, as we will discuss shortly. Yet another context, such as a Customer Self-Service context, could also produce `CustomerCreated` events and potentially result in a bi-directional integration with the **Sales Context**. This brings into question the bounded context that is the official source of record. We will be discussing the idea that the data lake becomes the official source of record. We will cover these event driven patterns throughout the pattern chapters.

Component patterns

Another strategy for decomposing our components with proper boundaries is based on applying the component patterns. `Chapter 3`, *Foundation Patterns*, will cover the patterns that provide the mechanisms used by all components, whereas `Chapter 4`, *Boundary Patterns*, and `Chapter 5`, *Control Patterns* both contain patterns that pertain to specific flavors of components. The boundary patterns, such as **Backend For Frontend** and **External Service Gateway**, interact with external entities at the edge of the system, while the control patterns, such as **Event Orchestration**, deal with mediating, choreographing, and orchestrating the interactions between components.

Continuing our bounded context example, the Customer Self-Service and Catalog contexts focus on interacting with different user groups. As such, they would each follow the Backend For Frontend pattern. Let's say that **SalesForce** and **ZenDesk** fulfill the **Sales Contexts** and **Support Contexts**, respectively. This would indicate that each should have an External Service Gateway component that acts as an anti-corruption layer to adapt and integrate those systems. All inter-component communication and collaboration is achieved using events. When there are relatively few events and the business processes are straightforward, it is reasonable for the components to apply the Event Collaboration pattern and know about the event types of the other components specifically. However, as these processes become more complicated it is good to add in components in the middle that act as mediators, following the Event Orchestration pattern, to maintain loose coupling between the participating components.

Data life cycle

Another useful strategy for decomposing a system into components is based on the life cycle of the data in the system. This is similar in concept to dividing the system based on the value streams or business processes of the system, but stretches out over a longer period. For example, how long must data be retained before it can be deleted? Data may have to live long after a business process or value stream is complete. A case in a case management system is created, assigned, and ultimately completed, but the records of the case will need to be retained and managed for an extended period. A product in an e-commerce system is authored, published, offered, sold, and discontinued, but so long as a customer still owns the product there is still a reason to keep the product detail information available. Furthermore, as the data moves through its life cycle, it may be best to store the data in different formats and in different types of storage. Retention policies may vary between different stages of the life cycle, such as allowing high transaction volume stages to purge old data to free up resources and improve performance. Each stage in the data life cycle will typically be its own component, with different requirements and a different user base. The data will flow through these stages and components based on the life cycle events that are published as the data ages.

Single responsibility

The single responsibility principle says that a component should have one and only one responsibility; the entire responsibility should be encapsulated in that component; it should do that one thing and do it well; it should have high cohesion such that everything in the component belongs together; it should have only one reason to change. The trick is determining what that one responsibility should be. The bounded context, component patterns and data life cycle decomposition strategies help us whittle components down, but here I want to focus on *only one reason to change* part of the principle. Part of the goal of cloud-native systems is to enable teams to rapidly deliver innovation with confidence, in other words, to deliver change fast. At the other end of the spectrum, we have discussed how monolithic systems hinder innovation, because we have low confidence that any particular change won't have unintended consequences on the system. Cloud-native systems are always on, thus we need to perform zero downtime deployments. We need to have bounded isolated components, so that we avoid failures in the first place, but also so that we can recovery quickly when there is a problem with a component. We need to have cohesive components.

Your team will have to be its own judge about the cohesion of your components. What is your confidence level with a particular component? If your confidence level is low, then discuss why. One counter intuitive possibility is that your confidence may be low, because you have too many tests. So many tests that it is hard to reason about their correctness. This could be a sign that the component has too many responsibilities. Categorizing the tests and splitting apart the component may lead to a breakthrough in the team's understanding of the problem space. Alternatively, the code itself may have grown convoluted. The amount of code in a component is not necessarily a concern. If there is a large amount of code, but that code follows a very clear pattern that is repeated over and over again, such as a set of rules on a concept, and those rules are easy to reason about, then so be it. However, if the code is hard to review, no matter how much code it is, then that is an indication that the component may have taken on too much responsibility.

Technical isolation

When defining functional boundaries we have many degrees of freedom. There is a lot of good advice and a few hard and fast rules, but for the most part you rely on your domain expertise and practical experience. When it comes to technical isolation the realities of cloud computing are a bit more strict and make isolation equally elusive. Shared Nothing is certainly a guiding concept, but in practice there tend to be a lot of leaks. To provide the necessary bulkheads we need to consider regions and availability zones, cloud accounts and providers, deployment units and resource management, and data isolation.

Regions and availability zones

The cloud has been in the news recently with a first-class *disruption* that impacted a large swath of well-known sites. I tell my clients that they should expect these large disruptions about every one and half to two years, and this latest disruption was right on cue. Of course, naysayers used this as an opportunity to bash the cloud, but other cloud providers did not use it as an opportunity to one up each other, because they know that it's only a matter of time before the same will happen to their services as well. Yet all the while some companies were prepared and only experienced a minor blip in availability, while others experienced protracted outages.

As depicted in the following diagram, every cloud provider divides its offering into geographic regions, which in turn consist of two or more **availability zones** (**AZ**). Each availability zone is an independent data center with high-speed communication between all the availability zones in the region. AZs act as bulkheads within a region. For any resource clusters that you will be managing yourself, you will be deploying them across multiple availability zones for redundancy to help ensure your components stay available when there is an interruption in a specific AZ. Any value-added cloud services that you leverage, such as cloud-native databases and function-as-a-service, are already deployed across multiple AZs, which frees you from that responsibility.

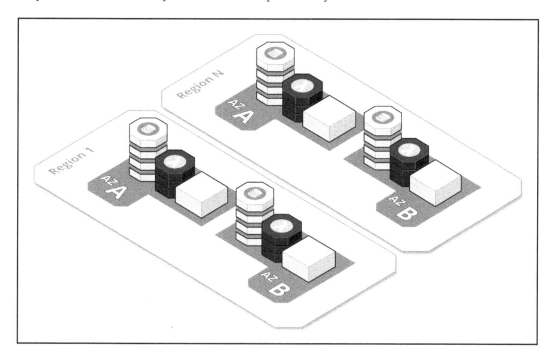

Regions act as a bulkhead within a cloud provider. The *disruption* mentioned earlier was limited to a specific region, because regions are designed to contain failures. The companies that only experienced a blip in availability had at least their critical workloads deployed in multiple regions. Their blip in availability lasted only as long as it took their regional routing rules to failover to the still available regions. In Chapter 6, *Deployment*, we will cover considerations for regional deployments.

Many, if not most, companies fail to take advantage of multi-regional deployments for a variety of reasons. Many just don't heed the warnings. This is often just a lack of experience, but it is usually because the value is not perceived to be worth the extra effort. I certainly concede this latter point if the objective is just to run an active-passive, multi-regional deployment. The cost of running duplicate resources just in standby mode is not attractive. Running an active-active, multi-regional deployment is much more palatable, because you can spread your load across the regions and give your regional users a lower latency experience. You may even have regulations that require you to store and access user data within regions in specific countries.

Of course running active-active is not without its challenges. It is fair to say that the value may still not be worth the effort, if you are running all your clusters yourself and particularly your own database clusters. However, this is not necessarily the case if you are leveraging value-added cloud services, such as cloud-native databases and function-as-a-service. These services have already made AZs transparent and freed you of the burden of scaling them across AZs. Thus, you can redirect that effort to multi-regional deployments. Plus, provisioning these services to multiple regions is becoming more and more turnkey. Expect cloud providers to be competing on this feature. The bottom line is that mature, cloud-native systems are multi-regional.

Components

With cloud-native, we are wholeheartedly going out of our way to create bounded isolated components, thus it is important that we don't lose sight of this when we actually deploy these components. We have already discussed strategies for decomposing the system into components at the functional level. However, the functional components do not necessarily translate one for one into deployment units. Deployment units are natural bulkheads. Each has its own resources, each will contain its own failures, and each is independently deployable and scalable. In `Chapter 3`, *Foundation Patterns*, we will discuss the *Trilateral API* pattern. This pattern brings the fact that components will be accessed through more than a synchronous interface, such as REST, front and center. They may also have inbound and outbound asynchronous interfaces based on streams. Some components will have all three and some will have just one or two in the various permutations. Each of these will typically be its own deployment unit and sometimes multiple deployment units.

We also have options to consider regarding containers versus functions. When choosing containers, we have to keep in mind that they are just the tip of the iceberg. Containers themselves are a bulkhead, but they also have to run in a cluster with other containers; a cluster must be managed by a scheduler, some sort of load balancer is required, and so on, and so on. All of these pieces have the potential for failure. I always recommend using the native scheduler of your cloud provider, such as ECS on AWS and GKE on GCP. The native solutions are simply better integrated with their cloud provider and thus are lower risk alternatives.

We also have to be wary of monolithic clusters. Anytime it takes extra elbow grease to provision and manage a set of resources, we will have a tendency to share and overburden those resources. This holds true for container clusters. I frequently see them become their own monolith, in that all containers get deployed to the same cluster, at which point a catastrophic failure to that one cluster would cripple the entire region. Instead, we need to treat the container cluster as a bulkhead as well and strategically allocate components and containers to focused clusters.

As an alternative to containers, we have function-as-a-service. Functions provide us with fine-grained bulkheads. Each function invocation is in essence its own bulkhead. Functions do not share resources, a failing function instance will be immediately replaced, and functions implicitly scale as volumes increase. Furthermore, while functions are the tip of their own iceberg, the cloud provider manages that iceberg. Deploying functions to multiple regions is also essentially a turnkey exercise.

We also need to prepare proper bulkheads within components, down in the code, where they interact with external resources. This is where we need to pool resources independently, have proper timeouts, retries, and circuit breakers, and implement backpressure. We will discuss these topics in the *Stream Circuit Breaker* pattern in Chapter 3, *Foundation Patterns*. One important concept for creating responsive, resilient, and elastic components that I have already mentioned and that we will cover thoroughly throughout the book, is asynchronous inter-component communications. We will strive to limit synchronous communication to only the boundaries of the system and intra-component communications with cloud-native resources. We will rely on event streaming for asynchronous, inter-component communications. Next we turn to isolating these resources themselves.

Data

The topics of single responsibility, independent DURS, bounded context, and isolation come up over and over again in the context of microservices. I cover these topics at length in this book as well. The topic of a database per service also comes up over and over again in the same context. It's the combination of these topics that is rarely covered, though that is beginning to change. Earlier in this chapter, we discussed the critical idea of *turning the database inside out* and in turn how the *cloud is the database*. Bounded isolated data, as a part of the whole of a component, is fundamental to building cloud-native systems that are responsive, resilient, and elastic. Unfortunately, there is a tendency to gravitate toward shared monolithic databases. This is in part because that is the way it has always been. The other reason for this tendency towards monolithic databases is that managing and operating a database in the cloud at a large scale is hard. Managing a sharded database is more difficult and managing Polyglot Persistence is even more difficult. We have already covered this briefly, but as a core tenet of this book it bears repeating.

The result of this shared monolithic database model is that we have no bulkheads for our data. More and more tables are added to the monolithic database, ever increasing the probability that these tables will be competing for the same, scarce resources. In the best case, the database requests only increase in latency as they compete for the available memory, I/O throughput, and CPU cycles. Or worse, lack of disk space causes the database to crash and results in an outage across the entire system. Ultimately, if we have no isolation at the persistence layer then we effectively have no isolation at the component layer. Instead, each component must have its own isolated databases. Taking this one step further, we discussed how mature cloud-native systems are multi-regional, because they need to be resilient to regional outages. This means that mature cloud-native data must also be multi-regional. Thus, the persistence layer is an example of where we need a different way of thinking and reasoning about software architecture.

Accounts

All too often, I see customers using only a single cloud account. Have you heard of a company named Code Spaces? More than likely the answer is no, because this is a bit of a rhetorical question. The company no longer exists. This company perished so that we can learn from its mistake. Their cloud account was compromised and ultimately everything in it was deleted, including their backups. They had backups, but they were stored in the same account. We will cover security topics in `Chapter 9`, *Security*, but the point here is that we can use cloud accounts as an isolation mechanism to create bulkheads to protect the system. My basic advice is that companies start with at least four accounts: a master account for only consolidated billing, a production account, a development account, and a recovery account for backups. Each account will have different access rights granted.

Each account has soft limits set on services that act as governors to impede runaway resource usage. This protects the cloud provider and your pocket book. So, as an example, the last thing you want to do is run a performance test in an account that houses your production workloads and inadvertently cause your users to be throttled, because the performance test pushed the account across these thresholds. Regulations, such as PCI, can have a big impact on your system and your company. It is typically advantageous to limit the scope of these regulations on your systems. These regulations are typically focused on the parts of a system that interact with certain types of data. As such, we can craft components around this data and then isolate those components in separate accounts and control access to these accounts independently. It may also be advantageous to isolate related components in separate accounts, just to ensure that a mishap in one account does not impact another. For example, separate accounts could be created to separate back-office components from front-office components. The front-office components used by your customers are of the utmost importance, therefore a dedicated account would be prudent.

Providers

For completeness, it is worthwhile to point out that there is a natural bulkhead between cloud providers. All cloud providers will have outages, but the likelihood that they will have simultaneous outages is low. In the context of polyglot cloud, where each component selects the most appropriate provider based on its needs, this simply means that when one provider has an outage then the components running on the other providers will not be affected. Maybe there is an argument to be made that your components should be well diversified across providers, but that is not the objective of polyglot cloud. On the other end of the spectrum, multi-cloud suggests running components redundantly across multiple providers to achieve high availability during an outage. I will wager that maybe 1% of companies have maybe 1% of their workloads which might benefit from all the extra elbow grease that is needed to achieve this type of topology. For the overwhelming majority of us, multi-regional deployments are quite sufficient. Regardless, in cloud-native systems these decisions are made on a component-by-component basis.

Summary

In this chapter, we learned that cloud-native systems are built on the principles of Reactive architecture. We use asynchronous, message-driven, inter-component communication to build resilient components that are responsive and elastic. Event streaming is the mechanism for inter-component communication. Components publish domain events to notify the system of their state changes. Other components consume these events to trigger their behavior and cache pertinent information in materialized views. These materialized views make components responsive by providing a dedicated cache that is continuously warmed. They act as bulkheads to make components resilient to failures in upstream components, because the latest known state is available in local storage. This effectively turns the cloud into the database by leveraging value-added cloud services, turning the database inside out, and spreading the processing across the elastic power of all the components in the system. This empowers everyday, self-sufficient, full-stack teams to build large systems composed of bounded isolated components that scale globally.

3
Foundation Patterns

In the previous chapter, we began our deep dive into the architectural aspects of cloud-native systems with a look at their anatomy. To create these globally scalable systems, we effectively turn the cloud into the database. Following Reactive principles, we leverage event streaming to turn the database inside out by replicating data across components to maximize responsiveness, resilience, and elasticity. Ultimately, we create proper functional and technical bulkheads, so that teams can continuously deliver innovation with confidence.

In this chapter, we begin our discussion of cloud-native patterns. We will discuss the patterns that provide the foundation for creating bounded isolated components. We eliminate all synchronous inter-component communication and build our foundation on asynchronous inter-component communication, replication, and eventual consistency. We will cover the following foundation patterns:

- Cloud-Native Databases Per Component
- Event Streaming
- Event Sourcing
- Data Lake
- Stream Circuit Breaker
- Trilateral API

Cloud-Native Databases Per Component

Leverage one or more fully managed cloud-native databases that are not shared across components and react to emitted events to trigger intra-component processing logic.

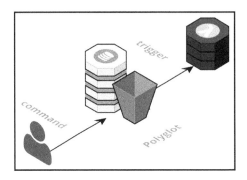

Context, problem, and forces

With cloud-native systems, we want to enable everyday companies and empower self-sufficient, full-stack teams to rapidly, continuously, and confidently deliver these global-scale systems. Modern high performance, horizontally scalable, sharded databases are critical to achieving global scalability. These databases come in many variations that are specialized for particular workload characteristics. Cloud-native systems are composed of many bounded isolated components. Each component has its own workload characteristics, which necessitates the use of polyglot persistence whereby many different types of databases are employed to support these characteristics.

To be truly isolated, cloud-native components need to control their own persistence. Each bounded isolated component needs to have its own dedicated databases to ensure proper bulkheads. Proper data level bulkheads help ensure that user interactions with components are responsive, that components are resilient to failures in upstream and downstream components, and that components can scale independently. Individual components, not just systems, can benefit from polyglot persistence. Thus, components need more than just their own dedicated database; each component may need multiple, dedicated databases. Mature cloud-native systems are also multi-regional and replicate data across regions. Data life cycle management is also necessary. For example, components that provide **online transaction processing** (**OLTP**) features benefit from continuously purging stale data to keep their databases lean. Furthermore, as the data in system ages and moves through different life cycle stages, it needs to propagate across components and across different types of databases.

Achieving the proper level of database isolation, though critical, is extremely complicated. Running a single database in the cloud across multiple availability zones is complex, running a sharded database in the cloud across availability zones is super complex, and running multiple sharded databases in the cloud can simply require more effort than most companies can afford. Going further, running many sharded databases, multiplied by many components, can seem unattainable. At this point in the typical discussion, there is literally no point in piling on the critical regional replication dimension. The workforce costs and the runtime cost of all these dimensions have the potential of being astronomical. Altogether this is a significant barrier to entry for proper data level bulkheads. This tends to force teams into a shared database model, despite the significant and potentially catastrophic pitfalls of the shared model.

What is worse is that the shared database model actually appears to be successful at first, at least for the initial components that use these resources. However, as more and more components leverage these shared resources, the responsiveness and scalability of all the components suffer and the impact of failure becomes more significant. These shared databases also tend to grow and grow because teams are not responsible for the full stack. Centralized operations teams own these shared databases. As a result, component teams neglect data life cycle concerns and the operations team lacks the functional knowledge to archive unneeded data, leading to even worse performance.

Vendor lock-in is a classic database concern. In traditional monolithic applications, object-relational mapping tools are leveraged to make applications database agnostic. In cloud-native systems, the startup overhead of these tools can be too much for short-lived component instances. Instead, the tendency is to leverage open source databases that can be deployed across multiple cloud providers. However, the learning curve for operating these databases is significant. Each database product has the potential to add a good 6 months or more to a project before a team can be confident in their ability to run these workloads in production. This further increases the tendency to leverage a shared database model. The effort required to move up the learning curve also tends to lock systems into the database technology decisions that were made early on in the system design, even after there is ample evidence that there are better alternatives.

The lack of distributed transactions based on two-phase commits is another concern. As a matter of course, modern databases favor the BASE model for distributed transactions: Basically Available, Soft state, Eventually consistent. The individual writes to each database follow the traditional ACID model, but a mechanism to achieve eventual consistency across databases is needed.

Solution

Leverage your cloud provider's fully managed cloud-native database services. Employ multiple database types within a component, as needed, to match the component's workload characteristics. Choose the database type, such as document store, blob storage, or search on a table-by-table basis. Each database is dedicated to a specific component and not shared across components. Use the change-data-capture and life cycle management features and react to the emitted events to trigger intra-component processing logic. Use the regional replication features to create multi-regional deployments, as needed.

Resulting context

The primary benefit of this solution is that proper data level bulkheads are achieved in a realistic and cost-effective manner. The shared responsibility model of the cloud allows teams to delegate the undifferentiated tasks of database management to the cloud provider and benefit from the cloud's economies of scale. The learning curve to get up and running with these value-added cloud services is short, which enable teams to focus on the value proposition of their components. Teams take full control of their stack and provision the exact resources need for their components. This isolation makes components *responsive* because they are not competing for database resources and those resources are optimized for their specific workloads; *elastic* because the load of the system is spread across many database instances; and *resilient* because database failures are contained within a component.

One drawback of this solution is that these services tend to be the source of regional outages. As discussed in `Chapter 2`, *The Anatomy of Cloud Native Systems*, these outages do not happen frequently, but when they do they can have a dramatic impact on systems that are not prepared for their eventuality. However, these outages are contained to a single region and systems that run in multiple regions are resilient to these outages. We have also discussed that mature cloud-native systems are multi-regional, which provides a more responsive experience for regional users, in addition to active-active redundancy to withstand these outages. To facilitate multi-regional deployments, cloud-native databases provide regional replication features. These features are becoming more and more turnkey, thanks to competition between cloud providers.

Change data capture (CDC) is one of the most important features provided by these databases. As we will see in the *Event Sourcing* pattern, this feature is critical in implementing transactionally sound eventual consistency across components. In the example ahead, we will see that change data capture is also instrumental in implementing intra-component asynchronous processing flows. Life cycle management features are complementary to change data capture. For example, in addition to keeping a database lean, a time to live feature will result in a delete event that can be leveraged to generate interesting and valuable time-based event-driven processing logic, over and above just propagating data through its life cycle stages. Versioning and archiving features are also typical of blob storage services.

Query limitations are a perceived drawback of this solution. We are not able to join data across components because they are in different databases. Now, even within a component, each table is isolated and cannot be joined. Plus, the query APIs of these databases tend to lack some of the features we are accustomed to with SQL. The new trend towards multi-model databases is changing this last issue. However, in general, this perceived drawback is rooted in our expectations set by monolithic general-purpose databases. We are accustomed to asking these general-purpose databases to do more work than we should. Ultimately, this resulted in inefficient utilization of scarce resources. Traditionally, we have isolated OLTP databases from OLAP databases for this exact reason. The nature of their performance and tuning characteristics are orthogonal, thus they need to be isolated.

The disposable nature of cloud infrastructure, and specifically cloud-native databases, enables us to take this isolation to the most fine-grained level. This is where the Event Sourcing and CQRS patterns come into play. In those patterns, we will be discussing how they come together with the *Event Streaming* pattern and eventual consistency to create materialized views that not only overcome this perceived query limitation through the pre-calculation of joins, but actually result in a more responsive, resilient, and elastic solution. I mentioned previously that this is where much of the rewiring of our engineering brains are needed.

Cloud-native databases do not hide many of the details that were encapsulated in relational databases. This is both a good thing and a bad thing. It is bad in that you need to be aware of these details and account for them, but it is good in that these details are easily within your control to optimize your solution. For example, it is a surprise at first that we need to account for all the various details of indexing and that indexes are explicitly priced. However, there was always an implicit price to indexes that was typically ignored at our own peril. *Hot shards* is another topic of concern that we will address in the example ahead, but essentially you must take care in the modeling of your partition hash keys. Cloud-native databases free us from the limitations of database connection pools, but they introduce capacity throttling. In the Stream Circuit Breaker pattern, we will discuss throttling and retries and so forth. For now, know that some of this logic is handled within the cloud provider SDKs. And while database monitoring is nothing new, the focus will be placed on throttling statistics to determine if and when the capacity settings and auto-scaling policies need to be adjusted.

And finally, the most commonly perceived drawback of this solution, vendor lock-in, brings us around full circle to the primary benefit of the solution. In `chapter 1`, *Understanding Cloud Native Concepts,* we discussed how vendor lock-in is rooted in monolithic thinking and that we need to embrace disposable architecture, which is afforded to us by disposable infrastructure and bounded isolated components. The primary drawback of other solutions is that they are difficult and costly to manage and ultimately increase the time to market and drive us to a shared database model that eliminates proper bulkheads. Their complexity and learning curve also leads to their own form of vendor lock-in. Instead, the cloud-native solution empowers self-sufficient, full-stack teams to embrace disposable architecture, which accelerates time to market. Once a component has been proven valuable and if its implementation is lacking, then the team can revisit its design decisions, with the confidence that the previous design decision was the cost of the information that led them to their current level of understanding. In the Data Lake pattern, we will discuss how events can be replayed to seed the data in new and improved implementations of components and thus help alleviate concerns over disposable architecture.

Each cloud provider has its own implementation of the most common database types. AWS has DynamoDB for key-value and document storage, S3 for blob storage, and both Solr and Elastic search are options for implementing search engines. Azure has CosmosDB for key-value, document, and graph storage, Azure Blob Storage, and Azure Search. Cloud providers compete on these offerings, thus a niche database offering can be the impetus for welcoming polyglot cloud. We can expect this competition to drive a great deal of innovation in the coming years.

Example – cloud-native database trigger

This typical example demonstrates the basic building blocks that can enable multiple cloud-native databases within a component to collaborate asynchronously to create a cohesive persistence solution. As depicted in the following diagram, data is atomically put into a DynamoDB table (document store), this, in turn, triggers a function that will atomically store the data in an S3 bucket (blob storage), and this could trigger another function. This pattern can repeat as many times as necessary until the data within the component is consistent and then ultimately publish an event to downstream components, as we will discuss in the Event Sourcing pattern.

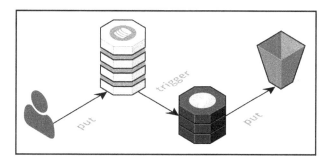

The following is a fragment of an AWS CloudFormation resource from a Serverless Framework `serverless.yml` file. In Chapter 6, *Deployment*, we will discuss how this fits into a continuous integration and deployment pipeline. What is important to note here is that provisioning cloud-native database resources are completely declarative and largely boilerplate and thus has a very low barrier to entry. Here we provide an AWS S3 bucket and an AWS DynamoDB table.

```
Resources:
  Bucket:
    Type: AWS::S3::Bucket
    Properties:
      BucketName: ${opt:stage}-${opt:region}-${self:service}-b1
  Table:
    Type: AWS::DynamoDB::Table
    Properties:
      TableName: ${opt:stage}-${self:service}-t1
      AttributeDefinitions:
        - AttributeName: id
          AttributeType: S
      KeySchema:
        - AttributeName: id
          KeyType: HASH
      ProvisionedThroughput:
```

```
        ReadCapacityUnits: 1
        WriteCapacityUnits: 1
      StreamSpecification:
        StreamViewType: NEW_AND_OLD_IMAGES
```

Next, we have a JavaScript fragment that uses the AWS-SDK to put an item into DynamoDB. Let me first point out that while our objective is to eliminate synchronous inter-component communication, synchronous intra-component communication is expected. Sooner or later there has to be synchronous communication. Our goal is to limit these synchronous calls to just the interactions with the highly available cloud-native databases and the cloud-native event stream. To support atomic transactions, we also want to limit these interactions, in general, to a single write to a single data store within a single request or event context. A version 4 UUID is used for the item ID because it is based on a random number, which will help evenly distribute the data across shards and minimize the possibility of hot shards that decrease performance.

```
const item = {
  id: uuid.v4(),
  name: 'Cloud Native Development Patterns and Best Practices',
};

const params = {
  TableName: process.env.TABLE_NAME,
  Item: item,
};

const db = new aws.DynamoDB.DocumentClient();
return db.put(params).promise();
```

The following fragment from a Serverless Framework `serverless.yml` file demonstrates provisioning a function to be triggered by a cloud-native database, such as AWS DynamoDB, and shows that this is completely declarative and largely boilerplate as well:

```
functions:
  trigger:
    handler: handler.trigger
    events:
      - stream:
          type: dynamodb
          arn:
            Fn::GetAtt:
              - Table
              - StreamArn
    environment:
      BUCKET_NAME:
        Ref: Bucket
```

Next, we have an example of a trigger function itself. This example is kept very basic to demonstrate the basic building blocks. Here we put the object to an S3 bucket so that it could potentially be accessed directly from a CDN, such as CloudFront. Another option could be to put image files directly into S3 and then trigger a function that indexes the image file metadata in DynamoDB to allow for queries in a content management user interface. The possibilities for combining multiple cloud-native databases to achieve efficient, effective, highly available, and scalable solutions are plentiful. We will discuss many throughout all the cloud-native patterns.

```
export const trigger = (event, context, cb) => {
  _(event.Records)
    .flatMap(putObject)
    .collect().toCallback(cb);
};

const putObject = (record) => {
  const params = {
    Bucket: process.env.BUCKET_NAME,
    Key: `items/${record.dynamodb.Keys.id.S}`,
    Body: JSON.stringify(record.dynamodb.NewImage),
  };

  const db = new aws.S3();
  return _(db.putObject(params).promise());
};
```

Event Streaming

Leverage a fully managed streaming service to implement all inter-component communication asynchronously, whereby upstream components delegate processing to downstream components by publishing domain events that are consumed downstream.

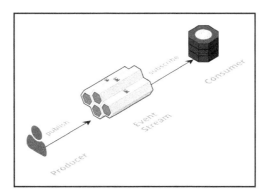

Context, problem, and forces

With cloud-native systems, we want to enable everyday companies and empower self-sufficient full-stack teams to rapidly, continuously, and confidently deliver these global scale systems. Following the reactive principles, these systems should be responsive, resilient, elastic, and message-driven. To this end, cloud-native systems are composed of many bounded isolated components that communicate via asynchronous messaging to increase responsiveness by delegating processing and achieve eventual consistency through the propagation of state change events. Stream processing has become the de facto standard in the cloud for implementing this message-driven inter-component communication.

To create responsive, resilient, isolated components our primary objective is to eliminate all synchronous inter-component communication. Synchronous, request, and response-based communication creates tightly coupled and brittle systems. The requesting component may not be coupled to the specific component that is servicing the request, but there must be some component available to respond to the request in a timely manner. Otherwise, at best, the request is fulfilled with high latency or, at worst, the request fails and the error propagates to the end user. Furthermore, the requester must discover a service instance that can fulfill the request. Service discovery adds significant complexity to systems based on synchronous communication.

Instead, we strive to limit synchronous communication to only intra-component communication with cloud-native databases and to the cloud-native streaming service. These are extremely high availability services with well-defined endpoints, which simplifies discovery and minimizes availability issues. With message-driven systems, location transparency between producers and consumers is accomplished via loosely coupled subscriptions. Through this mechanism, eventual consistency is achieved by publishing data change events, so that all interested consumers can eventually process the events. When the system is operating normally, eventual consistency happens in near real-time, but degrades gracefully when anomalies occur. In `Chapter 4`, *Boundary Patterns*, we discuss patterns that further shield end users from the anomalies.

It must be recognized that an event streaming system is an append-only, distributed, sharded database. As such, refer to the *Cloud Native Databases Per Component* pattern for the justifications for leveraging value-added cloud services and embracing disposable architecture in the context of event streaming as well. One thing that is different is that a database is owned by a single component, whereas an event stream is shared between components. But this does not mean that a single streaming cluster is shared across all components, as that would mean a catastrophic failure in that cluster would impact the whole system. Thus, we need to create bulkheads for our streams as well, by strategically segregating the system into cohesive groups of components, where each produce events to one stream in a topology of many independent streams.

We must also create a rational system of events as well. In the *Trilateral API* pattern, we will discuss how components should properly document the definitions of the events they produce and consume as part of their published interface. However, here we need to address event definitions at a more fundamental level. Streaming technology is part of the dumb pipes and smart endpoints generation. As such, stream consumers will ultimately receive events that they do not recognize and they must be able to treat these events in a consistent manner, so that they can be filtered out.

Solution

Leverage your cloud provider's fully managed streaming service to implement all inter-component communication asynchronously, whereby upstream components delegate processing to downstream components by publishing domain events that are consumed downstream. Define cohesive groupings of producer components and provision a separate stream for each producer group. Consumers will subscribe to one or more streams as appropriate. Define a standard event envelope format that all events extend, so that all consumers can handle all events in a consistent manner. For example, all events could have the following fields: id, type, timestamp, and tags; and all other fields will be specific to the type of event. Leverage your cloud provider's function-as-a-service offering as the de facto standard approach for implementing stream processors.

Resulting context

The primary benefit of this solution is that we facilitate our goal of creating an asynchronous, message-driven system while delegating the heavy lifting of running both an append-only, sharded database and stream processing clusters to the cloud provider. This in turn allows the team to focus on architecting an appropriate topology of streams to ensure proper bulkheads. When defining your stream topology, you should consider creating separate streams for different user communities. For example, a front-office stream would ensure customers are not impacted by a failure in the back-office stream used by employees.

Event Stream services are typically regional and do not support regional replication. This is actually a good thing, as a replicated event would ultimately be processed in multiple regions and most likely produce unintended results. It is the results of event processing that we want to replicate and this replication is handled per each cloud-native database as appropriate. Instead, we just want to embrace eventual consistency and know that any events currently in the stream of the affected region will eventually be processed. In all actuality, during an outage these events will likely be making their way through the system in fits and spurts as the region recovers. All new user interactions and thus new events would have failed over to another region. A user experience that is naturally designed for eventual consistency would not distinguish between different causes of inconsistency, such as intermittent latency, regional outage, or a component failure. In `Chapter 4`, *Boundary Patterns*, we will discuss such topics.

This leads to some of the interesting challenges of stream processing. Streams typically support at-least-once delivery, which means the smart endpoints need to be idempotent to account for multiple deliveries. Events will inevitably arrive out of order, such as when there is a fault and events are delegated to another component for error handling and eventually resubmitted. When target databases begin to throttle, we need to apply backpressure to reduce wasted processing. These topics, along with the benefits of micro-batches and functional reactive stream processing, are covered in the *Stream Circuit Breaker* pattern.

It needs reiterating that while producers are not coupled to specific consumers, the consumers are coupled to the event definitions. Thus it is important to have stable, published interfaces for the event definitions that are produced and consumed by each component. A standard event envelope format needs to be extended by all event types to allow for consistent processing of all events by all consumers. In the *Trilateral API* pattern we will discuss publishing and testing these interfaces. At a minimum, keep in mind that changes to these interfaces need to be backwards compatible in the same ways as synchronous interfaces.

It is recommended that you do not equate event types to topics, one for one. In some services, this is not even possible because in these services a stream is just a single pipe or channel with no concept of topics. While other services do have a distinct concept of a topic. In all the messaging systems I have ever used, I have always multiplexed event types through an architected topology consisting of a controlled number of channels or topics. This kind of inversion makes message-driven systems more manageable. For example, a system can easily have dozens, potentially hundreds, of event types. If we treat each event type as a physical construct that must be provisioned then this can easily get out of hand. In practice, event types are logical concepts that naturally coalesce into cohesive groups that should flow through a specific channel. So if your cloud provider's streaming services does not have a concept of topics then that is not a problem. If your streaming service does have topics then take care to utilize them as a grouping construct. In all cases, we want to provision multiple, distinct, and separate streams at a sufficiently coarse level to ensure that we have proper bulkheads, as mentioned previously. Producers should preferably emit all their events to just one of these streams. Consumers will need to process events from one or more streams, but typically not all of the streams. The data lake, as we will discuss in its own pattern, is one consumer that does consume from all streams.

One particular way that cloud-streaming services differ from self-managed solutions is in storage capacity. Cloud-streaming services manage the storage for you and the limit is a factor of the ingestion limits over typically one to seven days. This is important to note because after the specified number of days, the events are purged. Self-managed solutions obviously do not have storage limits and the typical practice is to keep events forever. The stream database itself becomes the data lake. This has some significant and obvious operational implications and risks. The cloud-streaming service approach is the much more manageable and low-risk solution when combined with the Data Lake pattern discussed later in this chapter. For now, know that the *Data Lake* pattern will consume all events from all streams and storage events in extremely durable blob storage in perpetuity. There is also a concern with cloud-streaming's fixed storage duration in the context of error handling and the potential for losing events when errors are not handled in a timely manner. We will discuss this topic in the *Stream Circuit Breaker* pattern, but keep in mind that the fail-safe is that all events are stored in the data lake and can be replayed in the case of an unforeseen mishap.

A perceived way that cloud-streaming services differ from self-managed solutions is in the number of supported concurrent reads per stream. Cloud-streaming services will throttle concurrent reads over a specified limit. The same thing happens in a self-managed solution, when the cluster is underpowered, but in a much more subtle, yet no less significant way. However, cloud-streaming services are priced and provisioned based on throughput, not on cluster size. Thus, their throttling limits are explicit. Unfortunately, too much emphasis is placed on these throttling metrics. They are an important indicator, with regard to ingress throughput, as to whether or not additional shards should be added. However, they are misleading with regard to egress throughput. In fact, read throttling tends to increase when ingress throughput is low and decrease when ingress throughput is high. This is because at low ingress, the reader's polling frequencies tend to line up and produce a sort of tidal wave of requests that exceed the limits. Whereas at higher ingress, the natural processing latency of the individual consumers tends to cause the polling of the consumers to weave below the limits.

Instead, for each consumer it is better to monitor its iterator age. This is a measure of how long a consumer is leaving events in the stream before processing them. The iterator age is generally more a factor of the combination of batch size, processing latency, and shard count than the result of any latency caused by read throttling. The vast majority of use cases are designed to assume eventual consistency, thus the potential for hundreds of milliseconds or even several seconds of additional intermittent latency is insignificant. When there are use cases that are sensitive to any latency, then these should be accounted for when architecting the stream topology and receive dedicated streams.

Each cloud provider has its own event streaming implementation, for example, AWS Kinesis, and Azure EventHub. Each is integrated with the provider's function-as-a-service offering, such as AWS Lambda and Azure Functions. More and more value-added cloud services emit their own events and integrate with function-as-a-service. We will discuss how to integrate these services into the event stream in the *External Service Gateway* pattern in `Chapter 4`, *Boundary Patterns*.

Example – stream, producer, and consumer

This example demonstrates the basic building blocks for implementing event streaming by leveraging cloud-native services. As depicted in the diagram at the top of the pattern, a producer publishes events to the stream (AWS Kinesis) and stream processors (AWS Lambda) consume and process the events. The following is a fragment of an AWS CloudFormation resource from a Serverless Framework `serverless.yml` file. In Chapter 6, *Deployment*, we will discuss how this fits into a continuous integration and deployment pipeline. This demonstrates that provisioning a cloud-native event stream, such as AWS Kinesis, is completely declarative and boilerplate and thus has a very low barrier to entry.

```
Resources:
  ExampleStream:
    Type: AWS::Kinesis::Stream
    Properties:
      Name: exampleStream
      RetentionPeriodHours: 24
      ShardCount: 1
```

The following example producer code publishes an `item-submitted` event to an AWS Kinesis stream. The domain entity is wrapped in a standard event envelope that at a minimum specifies an `id`, `type`, and `timestamp`. Then the event is wrapped in the parameters needed for the cloud provider's SDK and published.

```
const item = {
  id: uuid.v4(),
  name: 'Cloud Native Development Patterns and Best Practices'
};

const event = {
  id: uuid.v1(),
  type: 'item-submitted',
  timestamp: Date.now(),
  item: item
};

const params = {
  StreamName: process.env.STREAM_NAME,
  PartitionKey: item.id,
  Data: new Buffer(JSON.stringify(event)),
};

const kinesis = new aws.Kinesis();
return kinesis.putRecord(params).promise();
```

There are several important things to note here. First is the use of two types of UUIDs. The domain entity uses a version 4 UUIDs while the event uses a version 1 UUID and the domain entities ID is used as the partition key when sending the event to the stream. Version 1 UUIDs are based on a timestamp, while version 4 UUIDs are based on a random number. Events are unique facts that occurr at a specific point in time. Therefore, a timestamp-based UUID makes the most sense. This also means that event IDs will have a natural sort order, which will be beneficial when storing and indexing events in a search engine, as we will discuss in the *Data Lake* pattern. However, the same does not hold true when storing events in a stream. Instead, we use the domain entities random number-based UUID as the partition key. This helps increase the likelihood that we have an even distribution of events across the shards of the stream.

Conversely, if we used a timestamp-based UUID for the partition key then all the events in a time period would hash to a single hot shard. Each shard will be paired with an instance of a function. We maximize throughput by evenly distributing the events across the shards, which will invoke multiple function instances in parallel. Furthermore, we use the ID of the domain entity to ensure that all events for a given domain entity are processed by the same shard in the order in which they arrive. This example sends a single event to the stream at a time. We will typically publish events in batches to increase throughput.

The following fragment from a Serverless Framework `serverless.yml` file demonstrates that provisioning a consumer function is completely declarative and largely boilerplate and thus lowers the barrier to entry for stream processing. The batch size is one of the main dials for tuning stream processing. We ultimately want to tune the batch size in the context of the stream processing logic, the memory allocation, and the function timeout.

```
functions:
    consumer:
      handler: handler.listen
      events:
        - stream:
            type: kinesis
            arn:
              Fn::GetAtt:
                - ExampleStream
                - Arn
            batchSize: 100
            startingPosition: TRIM_HORIZON
```

Next, we have an example of a stream processor itself. This example is kept very basic to demonstrate the basic building blocks, but we can implement some very interesting logic in stream processors. The first thing to note is that we are using the functional reactive programming model because it matches well with the fact that we are processing micro-batches of events. Our batch size is set to 100, so we will receive up to 100 events in a single function invocation. If there are less than or equal to 100 events in the stream, then the function will receive all the events currently in the stream; otherwise, if there are more than 100 events in the stream, then the function will only receive 100 events. The main block of code sets up a pipeline of multiple steps, which the micro-batch of events contained in the event.Records array will flow through individually. The first step parses the event object from the record. Next, we filter out all events except for the item-submitted events. The streams will contain many different types of events and not all consumers will be interested in all events. Thus, these smart endpoints will weed out unwanted events upfront. Finally, we just print the event to the log, but ultimately a stream processor saves its results to a cloud-native database or produces more events. The function callback is invoked once all the events in the micro-batch have flowed through the pipeline. We will discuss error handling and other advanced stream processing features in the *Stream Circuit Breaker* pattern.

```
export const consume = (event, context, cb) => {
  _(event.Records)
    .map(recordToEvent)
    .filter(forItemSubmitted)
    .tap(print)
    .collect().toCallback(cb);
};

const recordToEvent = r =>
  JSON.parse(new Buffer(r.kinesis.data, 'base64'));
const forItemSubmitted = e => e.type === 'item-submitted';
const print = e => console.log('event: %j', e);
```

Event Sourcing

Communicate and persist the change in state of domain entities as a series of atomically produced immutable domain events, using Event-First or Database-First techniques, to drive asynchronous inter-component communication and facilitate event processing logic.

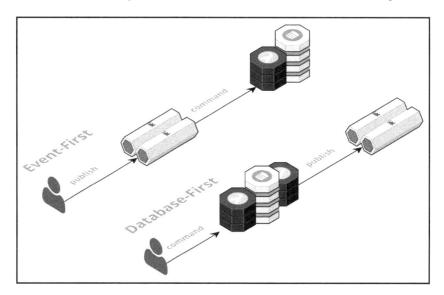

Context, problem, and forces

Our cloud-native, reactive systems are composed of bounded isolated components, which provide proper bulkheads to make the components responsive, resilient, and elastic. The isolation is achieved via asynchronous, message-driven, inter-component communication. Components communicate by publishing events to an event stream as their state changes. We have chosen to leverage value-added cloud services to implement our event streaming and our databases. This empowers self-sufficient, full-stack teams to focus their efforts on the requirements of their components and delegate the complexity of operating these services to the cloud provider. Modern database and messaging technology has abandoned **two-phase commit** (**2PC**) distributed transactions in favor of eventual consistency. 2PC does not scale globally without unrealistic infrastructure costs, whereas eventual consistency scales horizontally to support systems of all scales. Event streaming is the mechanism for implementing eventual consistency.

In an eventually consistent system, we need an approach to atomically publish events to the stream as the state in the database changes, without the aid of 2PC. We also need a historical record of all the events in the system for auditing, compensation, replay, and resubmission. Furthermore, in high volume, highly contentious systems, we need an approach for atomically persisting state changes.

The state or data in a system for all practical purposes originates with user interactions. At the beginning of any value stream, data must be entered into the system. Traditionally, this CRUD interaction only stores the current state of the data and thus the history or audit trail of the data is lost. Traditional event sourcing solutions persist the data as a series of data change events. This requires the system to recalculate the current state before presenting the data to the user, which is inefficient. Alternatively, the system can use the CQRS pattern to persist the current state in a materialized view as well, which can overly complicate the implementation of usually straightforward CRUD implementations. We will instead use CQRS at the opposite end of the value stream, as discussed in `Chapter 4`, *Boundary Patterns*. Furthermore, the traditional approach for turning these event records into events on a stream still requires 2PC to flag event records as published.

Downstream components in a chain of interactions need to capture events, perform some logic on the events, and store the results. For high volume processing, we want to avoid the contention of updates, which causes errors and increases retries and thus impedes throughput. We also need to recognize that event streaming only guarantees at-least-once delivery and that the events are delivered in the order in which they were received. We will see in the *Stream Circuit Breaker* pattern that there are various reasons that events will be delivered more than once and that the order received is not always the order that is important for the business logic. The ACID 2.0 transaction model (Associative, Commutative, Idempotent, and Distributed) recognizes these realities and can be combined with event sourcing in downstream components to implement logic that is tolerant of these conditions.

Solution

Communicate and persist the change in state of domain entities as a series of atomically produced immutable domain events to drive asynchronous inter-component communication and facilitate event processing logic. Strictly adhere to a policy that a command must perform one and only one atomic write operation against a single resource, either a stream or a cloud-native database, and then rely on the asynchronous mechanism of the resource to chain commands together. There are two compatible variations on this solution that are inevitably used together to form these chains: Event-First and Database-First.

Event-First Variant

An event-first command will not write any data to a database. The command will wrap the data in a domain event and publish it to one and only one stream. The stream acts as a temporal database that will durably store the event until it expires from the stream. One or more downstream components will consume the event from the stream. Each component will trigger a command to atomically write the data to one and only one database as needed.

Database-First Variant

A database-first command will write the data to one and only one cloud-native database. The CDC feature of the cloud-native database will trigger another command. The command will transform the insert, update, or delete database event to an appropriate domain event, and publish it to one and only one stream.

Resulting context

The primary benefit of this solution is that we are leveraging the asynchronous mechanisms of value-added cloud services to reliably chain together atomic operations to achieve eventual consistency in near real-time. When a write operation encounters an error, it returns control to its caller. The caller is responsible for performing a retry. When the write is successful, the cloud service is responsible for delivering the database or domain event and triggering the next command in the chain. This simple pattern is repeated as many times as necessary to chain together the desired functionality.

It is important to note that an atomic write operation can be a batch operation. Batch operations are critical to improving throughput. Write operations will also execute in the context of a stream processor command that is processing a micro-batch of events from a stream. Each atomic write in a stream processor is its own logical unit of work that must succeed or fail together. However, in a stream processor, a successful write can be followed by an unsuccessful write. We will discuss these scenarios in the *Stream Circuit Breaker* pattern.

The Event-First variant is appropriate in fire-and-forget scenarios. One example is a click-stream, where we want to track user actions in a browser, but it is not important to record a click locally before producing the event. Another example is a complex-event-processing algorithm that is evaluating many events over a time window and raising a higher order event when a condition is met. In both cases, it is assumed that downstream components will be capturing and storing these events. The benefit of just publishing the events is that it is very low latency and high throughput action. The downstream components will often be implementing the CQRS pattern that we will cover in Chapter 4, *Boundary Patterns*.

The Database-First variant is appropriate when we want to record the data locally before producing the event. The component may record each event individually, but we can actually have the best of both worlds, in that the component can record only the current state and rely on the CDC feature to emit the history. This allows for more traditional CRUD implementations that can easily query the database for the current state without relying on the CQRS pattern. One issue with this variant is that we typically need to include additional metadata in the database record, such as status and lastModifiedBy so that the database event can be transformed into a domain event. The status typically translates into an event type and the other metadata provides valuable context information to the event. We see a slight variant of this variant in the example presented in the *Cloud Native Databases Per Component* pattern. A component can chain together the CDC of each of its multiple databases, to achieve internal eventual consistency, until the last database in the internal chain produces a domain event.

This cloud-native version of the popular event-sourcing pattern is conspicuously missing an event storing mechanism. This is in part because we are leveraging value-added cloud services that are focused on their single responsibility, but ultimately because separating this concern provides more flexibility and provides for proper bulkheads. Instead, we use different mechanisms for different stages of the event life cycle. Initially, the event stream acts as a temporal event store that persists the events for consumption by consumers, until the events expire. The data lake, as we will discuss in the *Data Lake* pattern, is just another consumer that provides the perpetual event store to support replay, resubmission, and analytics. Furthermore, a great deal of flexibility and scale comes from any given components capturing its own micro event store in its own cloud-native database to perform its own logic. In Chapter 4, *Boundary Patterns*, in the *Command Query Responsibility Segregation (CQRS)* pattern, we will discuss how a component may store events to provide ACID 2.0 style logic to calculate materialized views. In Chapter 5, *Control Patterns*, in the *Event Orchestration* pattern we will discuss how a component can store events to help calculate process transitions, such as joins.

Notice how the last part of the event-first variant is the beginning of the database-first variant and the last part of the database-first variant is the beginning of the event-first variant. This is exactly why we are able to chain these together to solve sufficiently complex problems. However, for any given processing flow, it is best to discuss and document the entire flow from one perspective only. If the flow starts with a user invoking a command that produces an event, then stick with the database-first perspective. If the flow starts with a user producing an event that triggers a command, then stick with the event-first perspective. Switching between these perspectives in a single flow can lead to confusion and a sort of Abbott and Costello Who's On First comedy routine. Yet, keep in mind that every exit is an entrance when discussing flows across teams. From the perspective of an upstream component, an event is the result of its logic, whereas to a downstream component, an event is the beginning of its logic. Thus, switching between perspectives may be inevitable and just needs to be recognized.

Note that the Event Sourcing pattern is distinct from the lesser known Command Sourcing pattern. The Command Sourcing pattern records the inputs to a command, whereas the Event Sourcing pattern records the results of the execution of a command, aka the event. I mention this because I specifically named the second variant database-first to avoid any confusion with the Command Sourcing pattern.

Event sourcing is an instrumental pattern. It builds on its predecessor patterns, Cloud-Native Databases Per Component and Event Streaming, to facilitate its successor patterns, Data Lake and CQRS, which in turn power the higher order patterns, Backend For Frontend, External Service Gateway, Event Collaboration, Event Orchestration, and Saga.

Example – database-first event sourcing

This example builds on the cloud-native database and event stream examples and pieces them together to demonstrate the publishing side of the Database-First Variant. As depicted in the diagram at the top of the pattern, a command writes to the database (AWS DynamoDB) and a stream processor (AWS Lambda) consumes the database events, transforms them to domain events, and then publishes the domain events to the event stream (AWS Kinesis). The following fragment from a Serverless Framework `serverless.yml` file demonstrates provisioning a function to be triggered by a cloud-native database, such as AWS DynamoDB. It is very similar to consuming from an event stream. This also shows configuring environment variables, such as the target event stream name, to parameterize the execution of the function.

```
functions:
  trigger:
    handler: handler.trigger
    events:
```

```
      - stream:
          type: dynamodb
          arn:
            Fn::GetAtt:
              - Table
              - StreamArn
          batchSize: 25
          startingPosition: TRIM_HORIZON
      environment:
        STREAM_NAME:
          Ref: Stream
```

Next, we have the example of the stream processor itself. This example builds on the example in the event streaming pattern and leverages the functional reactive programming model to process a micro-batch of cloud-native database events. First, we map the database event to a domain event that can be published downstream without exposing the details of how the component is implemented. Thus, we can change our design decisions and dispose of the internal architecture of a component without effecting downstream components. We also include all the available context information in the event, such as the old and new versions of the data, so that consumers have the optimal amount of information to work with. We also use the entity's ID, which is a version 4 UUID, as the partition key, for the scalability reasons discussed in the Event Streaming pattern. Next, we wrap and batch the events for publication to the stream. Finally, the function callback is invoked once all the events in the micro-batch have flowed through the pipeline. If the function fails, it will retry to ensure that our database transaction ultimately results in the domain event being atomically published to the stream. We will discuss error handling in the *Stream Circuit Breaker* pattern.

```javascript
export const trigger = (event, context, cb) => {
  _(event.Records)
    .map(toEvent)
    .map(toRecord)
    .batch(25)
    .flatMap(publish)
    .collect().toCallback(cb);
};

const toEvent = record => ({
  id: uuid.v1(),
  type: `item-${record.eventName.toLowerCase()}`,
  timestamp: record.dynamodb.ApproximateCreationDateTime,
  partitionKey: record.dynamodb.Keys.id.S,
  item: {
    old: record.dynamodb.OldImage,
    new: record.dynamodb.NewImage,
  },
```

```
  });

  const toRecord = event => (      {
    PartitionKey: event.partitionKey,
    Data: new Buffer(JSON.stringify(event)),
  })

  const publish = records => {
    const params = {
      StreamName: process.env.STREAM_NAME,
      Records: records
    };

    const kinesis = new aws.Kinesis();
    return _(kinesis.putRecords(params).promise());
  }
```

Data Lake

Collect, store, and index all events in their raw format in perpetuity with complete fidelity and high durability to support auditing, replay, and analytics.

Context, problem, and forces

In our cloud-native system, we have chosen to leverage value-added cloud services to implement our event streaming and our databases. This empowers self-sufficient, full-stack teams to focus their efforts on the requirements of their components and delegate the complexity of operating these services to the cloud provider. We have also architected a topology of multiple event streams to connector our producer components to our consumer components in a well-reasoned manner, which provides proper bulkheads to ensure that a disruption in one stream does not impact the entire system. One side effect of using a cloud-streaming service is that these services only retain events in the stream for a short period of time, usually one to seven days.

In a reactive, cloud-native system, we are effectively turning the database inside out and leveraging the stream of events that are emitted by components as the ultimate transaction log and system of record for the entire system. As such, we need to maintain a complete record of all events ever emitted by the components of the system. There can be no loss of fidelity in the event information, the storage must be highly durable with replication for disaster recovery, and the data must be reasonably accessible for analysis and replay.

The components of the system are designed to consume events from the streaming service. With the historical events no longer in the streams, there will need to be another mechanism to allow events to be replayed from the data lake as opposed to from a stream. Furthermore, the hand-off from the streams to the data lake is extremely important to system integrity and thus cannot drop a single event. The single data lake should also track the events from all the streams in the topology so that there is only one source of truth for all events in the system.

As the system of truth, it is also critical that the data is stored securely and that the data is cataloged, indexed, and searchable. The data lake is the source of knowledge that can be leveraged to replay events to repair components, populate new components, and support data science activities. But with this power comes the responsibility of properly controlling access to this wealth of knowledge and protect privacy.

Solution

Implement one or more consumers that in aggregate consume all events from all streams and store the unaltered, raw events in highly durable blob storage. The consumers are optimized to store the events in batches. Batching increases throughput to ensure that the consumers keep pace with event volumes, it minimizes the potential for errors that could result in the loss of data, and it optimizes the objects for later retrieval. The objects are stored with the following path: `stream-name/yyyy/mm/dd/hh`.

It is critical to monitor these consumers for errors, alert on their iterator age, and take timely action in the case of an interruption. These consumers are all important, as any other consumer can be repaired from the events in the data lake so long as the data lake has successfully consumed the events. The data lake's blob storage should be replicated to a separate account and region for disaster recovery.

Create a program to replay events to a specific consumer. A generic program would read the events from a specified path, filter for specified event types, and send the events to the specified consumer. Specialized programs can be created as needed.

Optionally, implement consumers to store events in a search engine, such as Elasticsearch, for indexing and time series analytics. The index can be leveraged to perform ad hoc analysis, such as investigating an incident, which is usually a precursor to replaying a specified set of events. The index can also be used to create analytics dashboards.

Resulting context

The primary benefit of this solution is that we are not relying on a self-managed streaming cluster to retain a history of all events and double as a data lake. Managing this level of disk storage takes a great deal of effort and can expose a system to the risk of significant data loss if not managed properly. Instead, this solution enables teams to leverage value-added cloud-streaming services so that they can focus on the functional requirements of their components. The data lake is responsible for the long-term durable storage of all the events, while the streams run lean and just retain the most recent events. This ultimately helps ensure that we have proper bulkheads for the streams, instead of the tendency to have one large monolithic streaming cluster. Leveraging blob storage also has the added benefit of life cycle management to age events into cold storage and replicate to another region and account for disaster recovery.

One of the primary purposes of a data lake is to act as a safety net. Because the data lake collects, stores, and indexes all events, we can leverage it to repair components by replaying events. If a component drops events for some reason, we can replay those events; if a component has a bug that improperly performs calculations against the event stream, we can fix the bug and replay the events; and if we have enhanced a component, we can replay events as well. We can also replay events to seed a new component with data. And as we will discuss in the *Stream Circuit Breaker* pattern, components will emit fault events when they cannot process a given event or set of events. Once the cause of the fault is resolved, we can resubmit the events that caused the fault.

When replaying or resubmitting events, there are various considerations to keep in mind. First, replaying or resubmitting an event is not the same as publishing an event. When we publish an event, it is broadcast to all consumers. When we replay or resubmit an event, we are sending the event to a very specific consumer. When we replay an event, we need to consider the side effects of replaying the event. For example, will the specific component emit events as a result of receiving the replayed events and if so, is that desirable or not? Is the component idempotent and are the downstream components idempotent, or will replay cause double counting, or duplicate email notifications or similar improper logic? We will discuss idempotence in the *Stream Circuit Breaker* pattern. On the other hand, when we resubmit an event or group of events that caused a fault, then we typically do want the side effects. However, idempotency can still be important for resubmit as well when the events may have partially processed before the fault. Backwards compatibility is another concern when replaying older events. The component will need to properly handle the older formats. Otherwise, you should only replay events with the supported formats. The bottom line in all cases is to strive for idempotence and understand the impacts and side effects of replay and resubmission.

One drawback to this solution is the fact that the consumers cannot replay events by simply resetting their checkpoint on the stream and reprocessing those events from that point forward directly from the stream. A program must be implemented that reads events from the data lake and sends them to the consumer. It is preferable that the consumers do not have to support multiple entry points to support the normal stream flow plus replay and resubmission. This is straightforward when the consumer is implemented using function-as-a-service because functions can be invoked directly. The replay and resubmission programs just need to impersonate the stream by formatting the messages so that they look like they came from the stream itself. This is easily accomplished by storing the full stream message wrapper in the data lake as well.

Another drawback is the potential, no matter how small, that the consumers populating the data lake could fail to process the events from the stream before they expire. Therefore it is critical that the consumers are implemented with simple logic that is focused on storing the events in the data lake without any additional processing logic. It is also imperative that proper monitoring is implemented to alert the team when processing is in error or falling behind so that corrective measures can be taken. We will discuss monitoring in `Chapter 8`, *Monitoring*. Note, that in the event that some data is dropped, that data could potentially be recovered from the search engine.

The security and privacy of the data in the data lake are of the utmost importance. Security By Design is the first principle; we must design security up front. We will discuss security extensively in `Chapter 9`, *Security*. With regard to the data lake, we are concerned about access permissions and encryption. When we are designing the stream topology for the system, we should also be considering the security implications of the topology. The data lake should be organized by stream name, which means we can grant access to the data lake by stream name. With this knowledge in mind, we can design a topology whereby the events flow through the proper secure channels. With regard to encryption, it is never sufficient to rely on storage encryption. It is also not realistic to have the data lake encrypt specific data elements as the data flows into the data lake. Instead, the event producers are the most appropriate source for encrypting the appropriate elements. The design of each producer should account for the security requirements of the data it emits. For example, a producer of PCI data would tokenize the card data and a producer of HIPAA data would encrypt and/or redact the data along multiple dimensions.

The data lake is an excellent source of knowledge and it is equally important to use it as a source for analytics. Data warehouses will be typical consumers of the events flowing through the system and data scientists will leverage the data lake for performing big data experiments. As an example, a team may have a hypothesis that a specific change to an algorithm would yield better results. An experiment could be devised that loads several years of historical events from the data lake and processes the events through the new algorithm to validate whether or not the algorithm is better. The future uses of the data in the data lake are unpredictable. This is why it is important to collect, store, and index all the events of the system with no loss of fidelity.

Example – Data Lake consumer component

On AWS, the Kinesis Firehose service provides the essential components for processing a stream and storing the events in an S3 bucket, an Elasticsearch instance, or a Redshift instance. The following fragment from a `serverless.yml` file shows an example of connecting a Kinesis stream to an S3 bucket via Firehose. The entire solution can be configured declaratively as CloudFormation resources. In this example, a basic S3 bucket is defined to hold the data lake. Life cycle management and replication configurations are excluded for brevity. Next, a Firehose delivery stream is defined and connected to the Kinesis stream source and the S3 bucket destination. All of the necessary roles and permissions are also assigned, though the details are excluded for brevity. In this example, a compressed object will be written to S3 when the object size reaches 50 megabytes or after an interval of 60 seconds. To account for multiple streams, a delivery stream would be defined for each stream in the system's topology. Configuring a delivery stream for Elasticsearch or Redshift is virtually identical.

```
resources:
  Resources:
    Bucket:
      Type: AWS::S3::Bucket
      Properties:
        BucketName: ${opt:stage}-${opt:region}-${self:service}-datalake
    DeliveryStream:
      Type: AWS::KinesisFirehose::DeliveryStream
      Properties:
        DeliveryStreamType: KinesisStreamAsSource
        KinesisStreamSourceConfiguration:
          KinesisStreamARN:
            Fn::GetAtt:
              - Stream
              - Arn
          RoleARN:
            Fn::GetAtt:
              - KinesisRole
              - Arn
        ExtendedS3DestinationConfiguration:
          BucketARN:
            Fn::GetAtt:
              - Bucket
              - Arn
          Prefix: stream1/
          BufferingHints:
            IntervalInSeconds: 60
            SizeInMBs: 50
          CompressionFormat: GZIP
          RoleARN:
```

```
Fn::GetAtt:
  - DeliveryRole
  - Arn
```

Stream Circuit Breaker

Control the flow of events in stream processors so that failures do not inappropriately disrupt throughput by delegating the handling of unrecoverable errors through fault events.

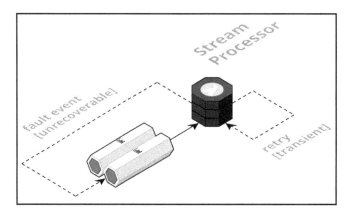

Context, problem, and forces

Our reactive, cloud-native systems are composed of bounded isolated components which rely on event streaming for inter-component communication. We have chosen to leverage value-added cloud services to implement our event streaming and stream processors. This empowers self-sufficient, full-stack teams to focus their efforts on the requirements of their components, but stream processor logic will still encounter bugs because developers are human. We endeavor to eliminate all inter-component synchronous communication, but stream processors ultimately need to perform intra-component synchronous communication to component resources. These resources can become unavailable for brief or extended periods.

Stream processors consume and process events in micro-batches and create checkpoints to mark their progress through the stream of events. When an unhandled error is encountered, a stream processor will not advance the checkpoint and it will retry at the same position in the stream until it either succeeds or the bad event expires from the stream. For intermittent errors, this is likely appropriate behavior because it affords the failing resource time to self-heal and thus minimize manual intervention. Even if the resource frequently produces intermittent errors, the processor will at least be making forward progress, provided the volume can still be processed before the events expire. However, if the error is unrecoverable, such as a bug, then the problem will not self-heal and the processor will retry until the event expires after one to seven days. At this point, the consumer will drop the failing event along with any other events that expire before the processor is able to catch up. Now keep in mind that the data lake will be recording all events so the events are not lost. But the processing of legitimate events is significantly held up and manual intervention is necessary to replay all the dropped events.

Errors usually occur at the most inopportune time. When processing a micro-batch, some events in the batch will process successfully before a later event in the batch fails. In this case, if the error goes unhandled, then the entire batch will be retried. This means that those events which were processed successfully will be reprocessed again and again until the problem is resolved and the checkpoint is advanced. There are plenty of approaches to minimize the probability of this situation, such as tuning the batch size, but none guarantees that this situation will not occur; many make the code overly complex and most have a negative impact on throughput.

Solution

Delegate events with unrecoverable errors to another component for handling so that they do not block legitimate events from processing. Publish these errors as fault events, along with the affected events and the stream processor information, so that the events can be resubmitted when appropriate. Monitor and alert on these fault events so that the team can react in a timely manner. Provide the necessary utilities to resubmit the affected events from the data lake to the component that emitted the fault event.

Implement the stream processor logic so that it is tolerant of events that are received out of order and idempotent when it receives and processes events more than once. Optionally, leverage a traditional synchronous circuit breaker on resource calls so that faults can be produced immediately when a failure threshold is reached, and periodically test to see if the resource has healed. Leverage a functional reactive stream programming paradigm for implementing stream processors. It is a very natural fit for stream processing and its pull-based model provides for backpressure that helps control the speed of the processing flow so that resources do not get overwhelmed with too many calls.

Resulting context

The primary benefit of the solution is that unrecoverable events, which are usually caused by bugs, will not delay the processing of legitimate events. Stream processors handle many different types of events. Some are of no interest to a specific processor and will be ignored and advance the checkpoint. Other events follow a different processing path that does not encounter an issue, while others follow the same path but the events themselves are valid. This increases stability and resilience because stream processors are able to continue to make forward progress in the face of failures and potentially self-heal.

One drawback is that a large number of fault events can be produced that will require manual intervention and resubmission. In some cases, this may be the best course of action, while in other cases retry may be a better option. Unfortunately, it is not always obvious in advance how errors will manifest themselves. Therefore, these interactions need to be tuned over time. Initially, it is best to take a conservative approach and have every error to produce a fault. Early on, as the processing logic is still evolving and unstable, many, if not most, errors will be bugs that are unrecoverable. The fault events will also be a good source of information for investigating and learning which types of errors should be retried instead.

Monitoring must also be set up to send out alerts when faults occur. These alerts are a critical tool that helps self-sufficient, full-stack teams respond to errors quickly and minimize the time needed to recover from errors. We will be discussing this in more detail in `Chapter 8`, *Monitoring*. In addition to monitoring for fault events, it is necessary to monitor the iterator age of each stream processor. For any errors that are not handled, the stream processor will retry until the error corrects itself or the event expires. When we properly choose to retry a transient error, then the error should recover in a short time period. However, if we make the wrong decision or if the recovery is taking abnormally long, then we need a way to be alerted to this condition. The iterator age is the metric that provides us this information. It is a measure of how long a processor is leaving events on the stream before successfully processing them. This metric serves two main purposes. First, it may be an indicator that event volumes are too high, causing the processor to fall behind and thus additional shards need to be added. Alternatively, as in this context, it could be an indication that there is a significant error and the stream processor is stuck in a retry loop. In either case, it is important to be alerted to the fact so that timely, corrective measures can be taken.

Event streaming guarantees that it will deliver events at least once and in the order that they were received. This is a good start, but it means that we have to account for the other possibilities. When a stream processor encounters an unhandled error it will retry and any events in the batch that successfully processed prior to the error will be processed more than once. When we set aside a fault event and later resubmit the affected events, those events will no longer be in order, as other events will have since processed. Neither of these are reasons to abandon stream processing because this is indicative of all messaging systems and of real life. Our stream processors simply have to handle these anomalous scenarios. Consider the fact that producers, particularly offline-first producers, may not even submit events in the correct order. In these cases, there is nothing that the messaging system can do to compensate for this. Therefore, we need to implement stream processors to be idempotent and order-agnostic. When we receive the same event more than once, the resulting calculation should not double count the event. When we receive events out of order, older events should not nullify newer events.

One solution to the issue is what I refer to as the **inverse optimistic lock**. Traditional optimistic locks will throw an error when an update is performed with stale data and force the logic to retrieve the latest data and retry. The inverse oplock will just ignore events that are received out of order. This works fine when we only want to record the latest and greatest event. When we need to calculate a result based on the aggregation of all the events, then Event Sourcing and the ACID 2.0 transaction model may be the correct solution. We will cover this in more detail in the *Command Query Responsibility Segregation (CQRS)* pattern in `Chapter 4`, *Boundary Patterns*. For now, keep in mind that events are immutable and have a unique identifier, thus we can save them over and over again and the result is the same. We can also receive and store events in any order and trigger a recalculation based on the new set of events.

Take care to perform validation on the data received in events and raise a fault event for invalid data. In the *Trilateral API* pattern, we discuss the need to publish component's asynchronous interfaces and perform contract testing. However, it is prudent not to solely rely on specifications and contract testing. Do not validate all the events in a micro-batch up front, as this can slow down throughput. It is typically more efficient to validate events as they flow through.

Networks are not reliable, thus it is necessary to retry synchronous calls to avoid throwing unnecessary errors. Most libraries have long default timeouts, so it is important to explicitly set the timeout to a reasonably short value, preferably less than 1,000 ms. The logic should retry at least once quickly to account for network hiccups and perform an exponential backoff for additional retries. Most cloud SDKs already perform this logic by default and it is only necessary to configure the timeout and the number of retries. Make certain that the accumulative total of timeouts and retries is less than the timeout set for the stream processor. Note that there is a correlation between the machine instance size and network throughput. Thus, if you experience frequent timeouts, you may need to increase to a larger instance.

Our objective is to limit synchronous communication to the cloud-native resources within a component. These resources have high availability standards, but they also implement throttling. Therefore, it is necessary to exert back pressure on the stream so as not to overwhelm the resource and cause throttling. Backpressure is a natural byproduct on the functional reactive stream programming model. Data is pulled through the pipeline by successive steps when they are ready to process more data. Traditional procedural programming, on the other hand, simply loops over data as fast as possible and ultimately overwhelms the target systems. In addition to natural backpressure, it is possible to add explicit rate-limiting steps to further avoid throttling and parallel steps to take full advantage of asynchronous non-blocking I/O. Regardless, it is still necessary to handle throttling errors and retry with an exponential backoff, similar to network timeouts. Make certain that the rate-limiting parallel configurations are compatible with the capacity allocated to a resource. If auto-scaling is configured for a resource, then it may be necessary to fail a stream processor and allow it to retry in order to give the auto-scaling policy time to take effect.

Leverage batch or bulk APIs whenever possible to minimize the number of network calls and thus improve throughput. However, these APIs can be more complicated to use if they allow the individual items in the batch to succeed or fail on their own. In these cases, it is necessary to check the status of each item and only retry those that failed. This can significantly increase the complexity of the code. Therefore, it may make sense to iterate towards the use of these APIs to make certain they are worth the additional effort. It may also be possible to batch the processing of events without leveraging a batch API. For example, a micro-batch of events received from the stream may contain related events that should be grouped together to calculate an aggregate result that involves a single database update. In these cases, it is critical to treat the group of events as a unit of work that will succeed or fail as a group. When raising a fault event for a group of events, make certain to include all the events in the fault so that they can be resubmitted together.

In some cases, it might make sense to wrap a resource with a traditional circuit breaker library. When the circuit is open, a fault event will automatically be generating instead of going through the protracted retry flow over and over again. Cloud-native resources are highly available; thus the need for this complexity is lowered. However, in the case of a regional disruption, this might be advantageous for some workloads. During a regional disruption, the most upstream component typically a boundary component, that initiates a flow of events, would failover to another region, at which point all new events would flow in the other region. All event flows that remain in the disrupted region will now take longer to become eventually consistent.

The default behavior would be to let those events continue to retry over and over until the region recovers. In the meantime, some events will trickle through as the region recovers. Once the region fully recovers, the stream processors would proceed at full capacity until they catch up with the backlog of events, which should be a reasonable size assuming that the failover occurred properly and promptly. If a processor were not able to catch up, then it would be necessary to replay the dropped events from the data lake. For some workloads, such as those with very high volumes, it may make sense to siphon off the events proactively as faults and just resubmit those fault events after the region recovers. This is an advanced alternative that you can evolve to when a specific processor so warrants.

Sooner or later your team will have to deal with a stream processor that drops events. Keep in mind that the data lake is the source of record and one of its main purposes is to account for just this situation. Investigate the problem, determine the range of missing events, understand the impacts and implications of replaying those events, and then move forward. Do not treat replay as a crutch, but definitely leverage it as a safety net so that you feel empowered to experiment and evolve your stream processing logic.

Example – stream processor flow control

The following example is an AWS Kinesis stream processor running as an AWS Lambda function. The code is implemented using the functional reactive programming paradigm supported by the `Highland.JS` streaming library. Similar functionality can be implemented with libraries such as RxJS. This main block of code sets up a pipeline of multiple steps, which the micro-batch of events contained in the `event.Records` array will flow through. This stream processor is responsible for capturing Item Created and Item Updated events and storing the data in DynamoDB. It demonstrates validation errors, unexpected errors, resource errors, and the handling of these errors.

```
export const consume = (event, context, cb) => {
  _(event.Records)
    .map(recordToUow)
    .filter(forItemCreatedOrUpdated)
    .tap(validate)
    .tap(randomError)
    .rateLimit(3, 30) // 3 per 30ms
    .map(save)
    .parallel(3)
    .errors(errors)
    .collect().toCallback(cb);
};
```

Each record is parsed into a **unit of work** (**uow**) that must succeed or fail together. In this example, the uow is a single event. However, many processors will group events together in various ways based on the contents of the events. In these cases, the uow will wrap all the events. Next, we filter for the events of interest. All other events are ignored. Note that this processor is interested in multiple types of events. It is typical that different event types will encounter different types of errors. The primary benefit of this pattern is that one event type will not prevent other events, types from processing when it is experiencing problems. This is in effect a micro bulkhead.

```
const recordToUow = rec => ({
  record: rec,
  event: JSON.parse(new Buffer(rec.kinesis.data, 'base64'))
});

const forItemCreatedOrUpdated = uow =>
  uow.event.type === 'item-created' || uow.event.type === 'item-updated';
```

Just as in any other type of program, it is important to assert that the input data meets the expected criteria. However, validation errors are unrecoverable because the event is already in the stream, so the processor will need to let the event pass through. When an event in a stream is invalid, it is an indication that there is likely a bug in an upstream component. The event will need to be set aside and resolved out of band and then resubmitted as needed. In this example, we throw a validation error when the required fields are not provided. When we manually create errors, we adorn the uow to indicate to the error handler that this is a handled error.

```
const validate = uow => {
  if (uow.event.item.name === undefined) {
    const err = new Error('Validation Error: name is required');
    err.uow = uow; // handled
    throw err;
  }
}
```

The following is a simulation of an unexpected transient error. These unhandled errors do not generate fault events and will cause processing to stop and the function to retry, until either the event goes through or it expires. Retry can be a good thing for transient errors, as it gives the source of the error the chance to self-heal and the stream processor will make forward progress once the problem corrects itself.

```
const randomError = () => {
  if (Math.floor((Math.random() * 5) + 1) === 3) {
    throw new Error('Random Error'); // unhandled
  }
}
```

The following is a basic example of catching a resource error. First, we initialize the timeout to a reasonably short value and we will rely on the SDK to retry several times with an exponential backoff. If an error still occurs after the retries, then we catch the error, adorn the uow, and rethrow the error. This is a good starting point for any stream processor. All errors will be handled and produce faults, thus allowing the stream to continue processing. As we learn which types of errors can self-heal and which cannot, we can tune the logic, based on the status code and content of the error, to allow the self-healing errors to fall through, cause the processing to stop and the function to retry. This is also the place where we could optionally leverage a traditional circuit breaker. When the circuit is already open, an error would automatically be thrown, without the overhead of calling the resource and waiting on multiple retries. The same logic would apply regarding whether the error causes a fault or a retry. This decision will often depend on whether the resource is a cloud service or an external service. If a cloud service is failing then we will most likely be failing over to another region and thus it might be appropriate to flush all the events through as faults and resubmit them after the region recovers. If an external service is failing, then it may be best to continue to retry.

```
const save = uow => {
  const params = {
    TableName: process.env.TABLE_NAME,
    Item: uow.event.item,
  };

  const db = new aws.DynamoDB.DocumentClient({
    httpOptions: { timeout: 1000 }
  });

  return _(db.put(params).promise()
    .catch(err => {
      err.uow = uow; // handled
      throw err;
    }));
}
```

This is the actual error handler. When an error is thrown from a step in the stream pipeline, it will pass over all the remaining steps until it hits an error handler or the end of the pipeline. If the error hits the end of the pipeline, then the processing will stop and the function will retry. Here the error handler inspects the error to determine if it is adorned with a uow. If there is no uow, then the error is considered unhandled and it is rethrown to stop the processing. Otherwise, an error with a uow is considered handled and it will publish a fault event and allow processing to continue. The fault event contains the error information, the unit of work, and the name of the processor that raised the fault. This information serves two purposes. First, it provides the necessary context for investigating the root cause of the fault. Second, all the events contained within the uow can be resubmitted to the specified processor by the resubmission tool if deemed necessary.

```
const errors = (err, push) => {
  if (err.uow) { // handled errors
    push(null, publish({
      type: 'fault',
      timestamp: Date.now(),
      tags: {
        functionName: process.env.AWS_LAMBDA_FUNCTION_NAME,
      },
      err: {
        name: err.name,
        message: err.message,
        stack: err.stack,
      },
      uow: err.uow,
    }));
  } else { // unhandled errors
    push(err); // rethrow
  }
}
```

Here we are publishing the fault event to the stream. The data lake will consume the fault event, as a fault is an event like any other. The monitoring system should also consume and alert on fault events. When deemed necessary, the events in the uow can be resubmitted from the data lake to the source function.

```
const publish = event => {
  const params = {
    StreamName: process.env.STREAM_NAME,
    PartitionKey: uuid.v4(),
    Data: new Buffer(JSON.stringify(event)),
  };

  const kinesis = new aws.Kinesis({
    httpOptions: { timeout: 1000 }
```

```
    });

    return _(kinesis.putRecord(params).promise());
}
```

Trilateral API

Publish multiple interfaces for each component: a synchronous API for processing commands and queries, an asynchronous API for publishing events as the state of the component changes, and/or an asynchronous API for consuming the events emitted by other components.

Context, problem, and forces

We are building reactive, cloud-native systems composed of bounded isolated components which rely on event streaming for inter-component communication. Therefore, a large portion of the system functionality does not communicate over RESTful interfaces. There are few, if any, tools for documenting asynchronous interfaces in a standardized way. One team owns each component, a team may be responsible for multiple components, but a single team rarely owns all of the components.

We need to recognize and acknowledge that reactive, cloud-native systems are different and require a different way of thinking about systems. We no longer communicate via just a synchronous API, such as REST and/or GraphQL. We now have an asynchronous API for publishing events and another asynchronous API for consuming events, as well. We actually strive to eliminate any inter-component communication via a synchronous API. As we will discuss in `Chapter 4`, *Boundary Patterns*, we are limiting the use of synchronous APIs to the interactions with a frontend and with external systems. This difference permeates how we develop the system, test the system, and deploy the system, and how we interact with the other, upstream and downstream, teams involved in the system.

Bounded isolated components are loosely coupled in that they are unaware of their actual upstream and downstream counterparts, but these components are still dependent on the formats of the messages they exchange. These components form natural bulkheads, which implicitly shield them from failures in downstream components. As discussed in the *Stream Circuit Breaker* pattern, components still need to explicitly shield themselves from invalid messages produced by upstream components. And even though bounded isolated components are resilient to failures in other components, the system as a whole is not working properly when any component is misbehaving. Therefore, we still need to take proper steps to ensure we can deploy changes with confidence. We need to define how we will test these asynchronous interactions.

Each of these APIs has different deployment and scaling requirements. The synchronous API is the most traditional. The consuming API will be processing events from one or more streams, each with one or more shards. The publishing API, when following the Event-First variant of the Event Sourcing pattern, will publish directly from one of the other deployment units. However, when it follows the Database-First variant, it will have its own deployment, similar to the consuming API. In each of these cases, there are deployment alternatives, such as various container schedulers and/or function-as-a-service. We also have to ensure we have proper bulkheads at the cluster level, so that we are not sharing one monolithic cluster across too many components and certainly not across all components.

Solution

Teams must publish the Trilateral API of each of their components. This not only includes documenting the APIs, but also understanding that published interfaces, when they are changed, must be backwards compatible. To this end, all APIs must have consume-driven contract tests. We will discuss contract testing in `Chapter 7`, *Testing*. Teams must understand the implications of their choice of deployment options. We will discuss these topics in `Chapter 6`, *Deployment*.

Document the event stream topology of the system. For each stream, document its purpose and any guidelines for producers and consumers. Provide a diagram of the stream topology with at least the major components included. Document the base event type envelope format that all events must conform with, as was discussed in the *Event Streaming* pattern. Events are typically formatted as JSON documents. As such, it is a good idea to document event types using TypeScript interface syntax, regardless of what language is used by producers and consumers.

Each team should create a diagram for each of its components, similar to the one discussed earlier, that identifies all the internal resources of the component. Document all the APIs of each component and make the documentation part of each component's git repository so that it is easily accessible by all teams. Use the preferred specification tool, such as Swagger, Raml, or GraphQL, for the synchronous API. For the asynchronous APIs, document all the event types that are produced and/or consumed, as TypeScript interfaces. Document the consumed events from the consumer perspective, to highlight the fields that the consumer depends on. For produced events, include all the available context information in the event.

It is impossible to predict what information future consumers might need, so it is more flexible to include additional information than to not have the necessary information. Events are a record of history, thus context information is an important part of understanding an event. Do not go out of the way to retrieve additional information, but do not exclude information that is readily available. Downstream components can adorn additional information as necessary, but they should not have to re-retrieve information that was present at the time of the event. In many cases, the consumer will actually want to work with a snapshot of the data at the time of the event.

Resulting context

The primary benefit of this solution is that it helps teams recognize the first order importance of asynchronous inter-component communication in cloud-native systems. In Chapter 4, *Boundary Patterns*, it will become clearer how critical a role asynchronous communication plays in cloud-native systems. Asynchronous communication is nothing new, but generally it has not been the primary form of communication and thus tends to not receive the proper attention. Instead, thinking about bounded isolated components in terms of their Trilateral API and how these touch points can fit together, helps simplify and compartmentalize the complexity of reactive systems.

It is hard to perform integration and end-to-end testing on distributed systems because so many components have to be coordinated. It is hard to automate test asynchronous systems, regardless of size, because the tests have to poll for messages within a reasonable amount of time. Thus, testing asynchronous distributed systems is extremely difficult when employing traditional testing techniques. In Chapter 7, *Testing*, we will discuss how consumer-driven contract testing addresses this complexity, with what I refer to as transitive integration and end-to-end testing, without the need for all components running at the same time. What is important now, in the context of this discussion, is that this enables teams to know immediately when they have made an API change to an event type definition that is not backward compatible.

Documentation improves communication across teams and increases confidence, as the stream topology and the event type definitions align with the various bounded contexts and the ubiquitous language of the system. The upstream and downstream dependencies of the system should be well defined. This, in turn, identifies the necessary consumer-driven contract testing, which helps ensure backwards compatibility. Understanding the various APIs and the required resources for each component helps teams ensure they have the proper technology bulkheads. Altogether this helps teams to continuously deliver with a higher degree of confidence.

Example – asynchronous API documentation

The following is an example of documenting the event types that have been used throughout the examples in this chapter. TypeScript interfaces are a concise way to document the structure of JSON payloads. These can be leveraged in the code itself when using Node.JS to implement components, but they are useful on their own, regardless of the implementation language. Notice that the ItemChangeEvent format includes both the old and new image of the data. This information is usually provided by a cloud-native database's change data capture feature. Both images are included, in the spirit of including all available context information, so that consumers can calculate deltas if need be.

```
// Event Envelope Definition
export interface Event {
    id: string;
    type: string;
    timestamp: number;
    partitionKey: string;
    tags: { [key: string]: string | number };
}

// Item Domain Entity Definition
export interface Item {
```

```
    id: string;
    name: string;
    status: Status;
    description: string;
}

export enum Status {
    Wip = 'wip',
    Submitted = 'submitted',
    Approved = 'approved',
    Published = 'published',
}

// Item Event Definitions
export interface ItemEvent extends Event {
    item: Item
}

export interface ItemChangeEvent extends Event {
    item: {
        old?: Item,
        new?: Item,
    }
}

// Valid Event Types
export const ITEM_CREATED_EVENT = 'item-created';
export const ITEM_UPDATED_EVENT = 'item-updated';
export const ITEM_DELETED_EVENT = 'item-deleted';
export const ITEM_SUBMITTED_EVENT = 'item-submitted';
export const ITEM_APPROVED_EVENT = 'item-approved';
export const ITEM_PUBLISHED_EVENT = 'item-published';
```

Example – component anatomy

The following example shows how the component in the diagram at the beginning of this pattern could be configured and deployed using function-as-a-service, following the patterns discusses throughout this chapter. There is a function for publishing events following the Database-First Event Sourcing variant, a function for consuming events, and two RESTful functions for implementing a command and a query. Each function is its own independently scalable deployment unit, yet they are conveniently managed together as a whole. We will recognize this pattern as we dive into the higher-order patterns in Chapter 4, *Boundary Patterns* and Chapter 5, *Control Patterns*.

```
functions:
  command:
    handler: handler.command
    events:
      - http:
          path: items
          method: post
      - http:
          path: items/{id}
          method: put
    environment:
      TABLE_NAME:
        Ref: Table
  query:
    handler: handler.query
    events:
      - http:
          path: items/{id}
          method: get
    environment:
      TABLE_NAME:
        Ref: Table
  publish:
    handler: handler.publish
    events:
      - stream:
          type: dynamodb
          arn:
            Fn::GetAtt:
              - Table
              - StreamArn
          batchSize: 100
          startingPosition: TRIM_HORIZON
    environment:
      STREAM_NAME:
```

```
        Ref: Stream
    subscribe:
      handler: handler.consume
      events:
        - stream:
            type: kinesis
            arn:
              Fn::GetAtt:
                - Stream
                - Arn
            batchSize: 100
            startingPosition: TRIM_HORIZON
    environment:
      STREAM_NAME:
        Ref: Stream
      TABLE_NAME:
        Ref: Table
```

Summary

In this chapter, we discussed the foundational patterns of reactive, cloud-native systems. We learned how leveraging fully managed cloud-native databases and event streaming empowers self-sufficient, full-stack teams to rapidly, continuously, and confidently deliver global scale systems by delegating the complexity of operating these services to the cloud provider so that they can focus on the value proposition of their components. With Event Sourcing, we communicate state changes between components as a series of atomically produced immutable events and the data lake collects, stores, and indexes all events in perpetuity with complete fidelity and high durability. These events act as the source of record and support the replay and resubmission of events, to repair existing components, populate new components, and support data science activities. The Stream Circuit Breaker pattern leverages functional reactive programming to control the flow of events in stream processors and achieves fault tolerance by delegating unrecoverable errors for resolution so that failures do not inappropriately disrupt throughput. Finally, in the Trilateral API pattern, we discussed the need to publish multiple interfaces for each component, which highlights that cloud-native components have more than just synchronous APIs and facilitates understanding of the system as a whole.

4
Boundary Patterns

In the previous chapter, we began our discussion of cloud-native patterns with foundation patterns. We leverage fully managed cloud-native databases and event streaming services to empower self-sufficient, full-stack teams to create globally scalable systems composed of bounded isolated components, which, following Reactive principles, are responsive, resilient, elastic, and message-driven. All inter-component communication is performed via asynchronous event streaming, which is typically triggered using the Database-First variant of the Event Sourcing pattern. With these bounded isolated components, we create proper functional and technical bulkheads, such that teams can continuously deliver innovation with confidence.

In this chapter, we will continue our discussion of cloud-native patterns. We will build on the foundation patterns and discuss the patterns that operate at the boundaries of cloud-native systems. The boundaries are where the system interacts with everything that is external to the system, including humans and other systems. We will cover the following boundary patterns:

- API Gateway
- Command Query Responsibility Segregation
- Offline-First Database
- Backend For Frontend
- External Service Gateway

API Gateway

Leverage a fully managed API gateway to create a barrier at the boundaries of a cloud-native system by pushing cross-cutting concerns, such as security and caching, to the edge of the cloud where some load is absorbed before entering the interior of the system.

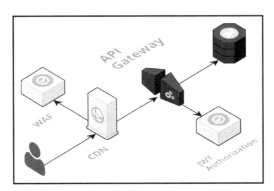

Context, problem, and forces

Cloud-native systems are composed of bounded isolated components, which are responsive, resilient, elastic, and message-driven. All inter-component communication is performed asynchronously via event streaming. Components publish events to downstream components and consume events from upstream components. We strive to limit synchronous communication to only the intra-component cloud-native databases and to the cloud-native streaming service. Yet, sooner or later, we have to implement synchronous communication at the boundaries of the system. At the boundaries, the system interacts with users via mobile apps and single page web applications and with external systems via Open APIs.

First and foremost, these public endpoints must be secured. We must form a perimeter at the boundaries of the system to govern access to the system. The perimeter minimizes the attack surface and controls the blast radius of an attack by providing a bulkhead, which absorbs unwanted traffic. These public endpoints must also be highly available. Yet, we strive to minimize synchronous communication, because implementing highly available synchronous communication is undifferentiated and cumbersome work, which distracts self-sufficient, full-stack teams from the value propositions of their specific components.

These cross-cutting concerns should be decoupled from the functionality of the system to facilitate responsiveness, resilience, elasticity, and global scalability. Intrusions should be stopped at the edge and not permeate the internal components where they will consume valuable resources and impact responsiveness. This reverse proxy layer should run on its own separately scalable infrastructure and support regional load-balancing and regional failover. In addition, this layer should provide caching at the edge to further attenuate load on the internal components and provide monitoring to help complete the overall performance picture. Finally, this capability should not be overly ambitious. It should be easy to use, a relatively dumb pipe that is focused on these responsibilities. There should be no incentive to code business logic in this layer.

Solution

Leverage your cloud provider's API gateway service, to allow teams to be self-sufficient and control their full-stack so that they can focus on the value proposition of their components. These fully managed services provide the ability to create a secure and scalable perimeter around boundary components. Throttling and Access Token Authorization are essential features. Deliver your endpoints through your cloud provider's **Content Delivery Network** (**CDN**) for additional security and performance benefits. Add a **Web Application Firewall** (**WAF**) for additional security features as needed. Teams should leverage their cloud provider's function-as-a-service offering as the de facto standard approach for implementing synchronous operations.

Resulting context

The primary benefit of this solution is that it provides a fully managed, **global scale perimeter** around the system that allows self-sufficient, full-stack teams to focus on their value proposition. The perimeter acts as a **bulkhead** to protect the internals of the system from attacks at the boundaries of the system. These cross-cutting concerns no longer permeate the business logic, which makes that code easier to maintain and removes the need to allocate resources to support processing that logic. The dedicated infrastructure of the API gateway automatically scales elastically.

Security is performed at the edge of the cloud. We typically only consider CDNs for their ability to cache static content at the edge. However, cloud providers recommend the use of their CDNs for all traffic: PUT, POST, DELETE, GET, and so forth, because network level **Distributed Denial of Service** (**DDOS**) attacks are handled by the CDN at the edge before they penetrate an availability zone and your system. Thus we limit the attack surface of the system by passing all traffic through the CDN. The API gateway itself provides throttling to protect the system at the application level. Further confidence can be attained as needed by leveraging the cloud provider's WAF that is already integrated with the CDN. Following our cloud-native, reactive architecture, we can process internal and external sources, such as access logs and third-party reputation lists, to continuously and dynamically manage rules, such as denying access based on IP address and mitigating OWASP Top 10 web application vulnerabilities. A self-sufficient, full-stack team would own the components that perform this processing, per usual, while the resulting rules would be leveraged across all services.

Implementing and scaling OAuth 2.0 and OpenID Connect for authorization and authentication, respectively, is a non-trivial exercise. Authentication is best delegated to a third party, such as AWS Cognito, Azure AD, or Auth0. Once a user receives a **JSON Web Token** (**JWT**), it is still necessary to authorize these bearer tokens when a service is invoked. An API gateway will perform this authorization at the edge and only pass down valid tokens to the business layer, which greatly simplifies the lower layers. The authorization results are also cached for a time to live to improve responsiveness. Integration with the cloud provider's authentication service is usually a turnkey solution, while implementing custom authorizers is also supported. It is common to use multiple authentication providers, each for a different user base, and implement an authorizer for each as needed. We will discuss user base focused components in the Backend For Frontend pattern.

There are several *performance benefits*, in addition to being fully managed and auto scaling. The cloud provider's CDN typically has optimized transfer rates between the edge and an availability zone, which improves all traffic, not just GET requests. An API should leverage cache-control headers, even for as little as a few seconds, to absorb some load before it reaches the API gateway. Traffic can be balanced across regions when components are deployed in a multi-region, active-active configuration in order to improve latency for regional users. This same feature provides failover when there is a regional outage. Implementing multi-regional components is a realistic objective when they are implemented using an API gateway, function-as-a-service, and cloud-native databases. Monitoring at the API gateway layer also helps provide a realistic performance picture of users' end-to-end digital experience.

Not all API gateway services are created equal. Some provide many more features than may be necessary for many components, such as a turnkey developer's portal. These features may be worth the added expense for a monetized open API, which you are providing as-a-service to your customers. However, for internal APIs, such as those we discuss in the Backend For Frontend pattern, these features are not necessary and they should not incur the often significant added cost. Other features, such as complex routing, transformation, fan-out, fan-in, and the like, should be avoided, as coding in the API gateway ought to be considered an anti-pattern. You should focus your API gateways on the single responsibility of providing a perimeter around your system's boundaries. Monetization features are great for the components that need them.

Finally, it is not necessary to run all interactions through an API gateway. Third-party services, such as authentication or an offline-first database, will provide their own perimeter and you will just integrate with and leverage those services, as we discuss in the External Service Gateway and Offline-First Database patterns. In addition, some content is dynamic, but not dynamic enough to warrant the use of the full technology stack. Instead, this content can be stored as a materialized view in blob storage and served through the CDN and mapped to the same RESTful resource path to encapsulate the implementation. A `PUT` to the blob storage would trigger invalidation on the CDN to indicate when the data does actually change. This technique works best for public data, can take a significant load off the API gateway and the internals of the system, and provides extremely high availability.

Example – CRUD service

This example demonstrates creating a simple and secure RESTful CRUD service, using the AWS API Gateway along with AWS Cognito, AWS Lambda, and AWS DynamoDB. The following Serverless Framework `serverless.yml` file fragment defines an API Gateway with a RESTful resource to `PUT`, `GET`, and `DELETE` items. Each of these HTTP methods is mapped to a Lambda function: save, get, and delete, respectively. We also enable **Cross-Origin Resource Sharing** (**CORS**) support so that the resource can be accessed from a web application, usually written in React or Angular. To add OAuth 2.0 support, we provide the **Amazon Resource Name** (**ARN**) for the AWS Cognito User Pool that is used to authenticate the users. Throttling is provided by default and can be overridden as needed. Finally, we declare an environment variable for the table name, so that it is not hardcoded in the functions and can change based on the deployment stage.

All of this is completely declarative, which frees the team to focus on the business logic. There are additional settings, such as API Keys and Usage Plans, but most components will use these example settings as is, other than the specific resource paths. The API Gateway will automatically run behind an AWS CloudFront distribution, which is the AWS CDN service. However, it is common to manage your own CloudFront distribution in front of the API Gateway to access the full power of CloudFront, such as WAF integration and caching support. As an alternative to AWS Lambda, the API Gateway could proxy to an application load balancer, which fronts an AWS ECS cluster running Docker containers. However, I recommend starting with the disposable architecture of AWS Lambda to empower teams to experiment with functionality more quickly.

```
custom: # variables
  authorizerArn: arn:aws:cognito-idp:us-east-1:xxx:userpool/us-east-1_ZZZ

# configure CRUD functions for api gateway and cognito jwt authorizer
functions:
  save:
    handler: handler.save
    events:
      - http:
          path: items/{id}
          method: put
          cors: true
          authorizer:
            arn: ${self:custom.authorizerArn}
  get:
    handler: handler.get
    events:
      - http:
          path: items/{id}
          method: get
          cors: true
          authorizer:
            arn: ${self:custom.authorizerArn}
  delete:
    handler: handler.delete
    events:
      - http:
          path: items/{id}
          method: delete
          cors: true
          authorizer:
            arn: ${self:custom.authorizerArn}
```

Next, we have example code for the `save` function. Note that this is the first synchronous code example we have covered. All other code examples have been for asynchronous stream processors, because our objective is to perform most logic asynchronously. But ultimately, some data enters the system manually through synchronous human interaction.

The path parameters, relevant context information, and the message body are merged together, saved to the database and the status code and appropriate headers are returned. The complex domain object is transported as a JSON string and stored as JSON; thus there is no need to transform the object to another format. We do adorn the object with some contextual information. The API Gateway decodes the JWT token and passes the valid values along with the request. We can store these values with the object to support event streaming. We are leveraging the DynamoDB Stream to perform Database-First Event Sourcing. Therefore we only need to store the current state of the object in this source database. We will discuss the idea of source/authoring components in the Backend For Frontend pattern.

This example only includes the bare essentials to keep it simple and not hide any moving parts. I will usually add some very lightweight layers to reuse common code fragments and facilitate unit testing with spies, stubs, and mocks. I normally wrap the data access code in a simple connector and add data validation utilities along with error handling. GraphQL is also a recommended tool, as we will discuss in the Backend For Frontend pattern.

```
// PUT items/{id}
export const save = (event, context, callback) => {
  const params = {
    TableName: process.env.TABLE_NAME,
    // merge the id and username with the JSON in the request body
    Item: Object.assign(
      {
        id: event.pathParameters.id,
        lastModifiedBy:
          event.requestContext.authorizer.claims['cognito:username'],
      },
      JSON.parse(event.body)
    )
  };

  const db = new aws.DynamoDB.DocumentClient();

  // insert or update the item in the database
  db.put(params).promise()
    .then((result) => {
      // return a success response
      callback(null, {
          statusCode: 200,
```

```
        headers: {
          'access-control-allow-origin': '*', // CORS support
          'cache-control': 'no-cache',
        },
      });
    }, (err) => {
      // return an error response
      callback(err);
    });
  };
```

Finally, we have example code for the `Get By ID` function. The path parameter is used as the key to retrieve the object from the database. The object is stored as JSON, so there is no need to transform the object for the response. We are leveraging the DynamoDB Stream to perform Database-First Event Sourcing. Therefore, there is no need to calculate the current state of the object from the events because only the current state is maintained in this table. This greatly simplifies the development experience.

This is also an example of the level of complexity we want to have in our user- facing synchronous boundary components. We will discuss this in detail next, in the CQRS pattern. We do not want components synchronously calling other components, much less multiple components. A query should make a straightforward synchronous call to its own cloud-native database and return the data, as it is stored in the database. All complex join logic is performed when the data is inserted into the materialized view.

```
// GET items/{id}
export const get = (event, context, callback) => {
  const params = {
    TableName: process.env.TABLE_NAME,
    Key: {
      id: event.pathParameters.id,
    },
  };

  const db = new aws.DynamoDB.DocumentClient();
  // retrieve the item from the database
  db.get(params).promise()
    .then((data) => {
      // return a success response
      callback(null, {
        statusCode: 200,
        headers: {
          'access-control-allow-origin': '*', // CORS support
          'cache-control': 'max-age=3',
        },
        body: JSON.stringify(data),
```

```
    });
}, (err) => {
    // return an error response
    callback(err);
});
};
```

Command Query Responsibility Segregation (CQRS)

Consume state change events from upstream components and maintain materialized views that support queries used within a component.

Context, problem, and forces

You are building a reactive, cloud-native system that is composed of bounded isolated components. Each component leverages value-added cloud services to implement one or more cloud-native databases that are exclusively owned by each component. This isolation empowers your self-sufficient, full-stack team to rapidly and continuously deliver innovation with confidence.

This isolation also makes it challenging to work with data across components. First, making synchronous requests between components to retrieve data is problematic. Second, making multiple synchronous requests to retrieve and join data from multiple components is even more problematic. Inter-component synchronous requests increase latency and reduce responsiveness because of the additional overhead required to traverse the layers of a component to retrieve its data. Latency and responsiveness are further impacted when we have to join data across multiple components.

Leveraging asynchronous, non-blocking I/O to make these requests in parallel minimizes the impact, but it is still necessary to process the responses and stitch them together to achieve the desired join. This response processing logic is repeated over and over again regardless of whether or not the response has changed. The typical solution is to add a caching layer to each consuming component, but this approach has significant drawbacks. We have the added headache of maintaining the additional caching infrastructure, such as Redis or Memcached, plus the added logic to check the cache for hits and update the cache on misses. We need to avoid stale cache as the data does change and incur added latency for cache misses and cold starts. All in all, caching adds a lot of complexity to an already complex situation.

Synchronous inter-component communication also increases coupling and reduces resilience. At its worst, synchronous inter-component communication is coupled to the availability of the component being called. A component may be highly available most of the time, but when it experiences an outage, then the requesting components will need to handle this condition appropriately. The problem is further complicated when we are aggregating or joining requests across multiple components. We must account for the failure of any single request and include compensation logic for each and every request. This logic can easily become a maintenance issue. Service Discovery and Circuit Breakers are common tools for handling some of these issues with synchronous communication. However, much like caching, these tools add their own complexity and their own issues.

At its best, synchronous inter-component communication is subject to competition for what amounts to a shared resource. This is the same problem we have at the database level, where we want to eliminate shared database clusters because they do not provide proper bulkheads. Here we have just moved the problem up to the component level, but the end result is similar. At the component level, this will manifest itself as throttling errors. The shared component will ultimately protect itself by implementing throttling that is consistent with its available capacity. Certainly, the capacity of a shared component can be increased and auto-scaled, but the allocation of capacity and throttling is not within the direct control of the consuming teams.

The scalability of synchronous inter-component communication also comes into question. With multiple components competing for the resources of a shared component, that shared component becomes a bottleneck that can impact all the dependent components. It most certainly is possible to sufficiently scale shared components, but at what cost and what complexity? The synchronous solution is certainly inefficient because we are repeating the same requests over and over again. We also need to increase team collaboration to communicate capacity requirements. Collaboration is generally not a bad thing, but we want to empower self-sufficient, full-stack teams, not impede them. Ultimately, bounded isolated components that communicate synchronously are in fact not actually isolated. The bottom line is that synchronous inter-component communication is best avoided.

Solution

Segregate upstream producer (that is, command) components from downstream consumer (that is, query) components by eliminating all synchronous inter-component communication. Originate data in upstream components, which typically apply the Database-First variant of the Event Sourcing pattern to atomically deliver events to the stream. This enables an upstream component to easily query its own table for the current state.

Downstream components consume the events and maintain their own materialized views that are optimized for each component's specific needs. Each component employs polyglot persistence and chooses the appropriate cloud-native database type for each view. A downstream component is then free to perform natural, synchronous intra-component queries against its own materialized views.

Resulting context

The primary benefit of this solution is that it provides proper bulkheads between components to make downstream components *resilient to failures in upstream components*. If an upstream becomes unavailable then it will have zero impact on downstream components. Queries will continue to return results from the *materialized views*. If an upstream component deploys a bug that produces invalid events, then the Stream Circuit Breaker pattern will handle these faults and the materialized views will continue to return the last known values. The data will eventually become consistent once the issue is resolved.

Materialized views are highly responsive. They are tuned to exactly the needs of the component and deployed using the most appropriate polyglot persistence. The performance of queries is not impacted by the calculations for joining data from multiple events because the *calculations are only performed when the data changes* and the result is stored in the view. A materialized view acts as a local cache that is *always hot and always up to date* with the last known values. It is still advised to set an appropriate cache-control header on the response of every query. The materialized view is a local resource that is owned by the component and thus no unnecessary layers must be traversed to retrieve the data. Retries due to capacity throttling are minimized since there is no inter-component competition for these resources, as they are not shared with other components.

Self-sufficient, full-stack teams are not reliant on other teams to define capacity requirements. A team is in full control of allocating the capacity for each and every one of its materialized views. Furthermore, as each materialized view is an independently provisioned cloud-native database, each view is tuned independently. A team must monitor and tune its capacity, but it is at liberty to do so.

Materialized views are the primary facilitator of global scalability. No matter how well we improve our ability to scale the other layers of a system, retrieving data from a database always has the final word on performance and scalability. For the longest time, we have only treated the symptoms by compensating at the higher layers with multiple layers of caching and through coarse-grained, database-wide replication. With cloud-native databases and materialized views, we are treating the root cause by *turning the database inside out* and ultimately *turning the cloud into the database*.

We are in essence scaling by *replicating data at the fine-grained level of individual query definitions*. This is actually pretty amazing when you stop and think about it, especially considering it is also cost effective. Each query definition leverages the most appropriate database type and has its own dedicated capacity that is not shared across components. It is updated with changes in near real time and its joins are pre-calculated, and it is further replicated across regions for optimized latency and regional failover.

A common complaint about some cloud-native databases and the use of materialized views is that the expressiveness of the queries is too limited and that managing the materialized views is too cumbersome. It is true that generic, monolithic databases, by design, make development easier. We can focus on getting the data into the database and then lazily create queries as we need them. However, this is what gets us into trouble. Queries have performance implications and each additional query begins to add up. Of course, there is a need to support ad hoc queries, but this should be the responsibility of specific analytics-oriented components. Individual components, however, have very specific query requirements. We, in essence, want to apply the single responsibility principle to each query definition. From the consumer's standpoint, a component-specific query should be responsive and provide simple filters. All the expressiveness of joins and groups should be pre-calculated. Our event streaming architecture provides the foundation for performing these calculations and creating materialized views. Next, we will cover some examples of techniques for joining and grouping events and handling events out of order.

Example – inverse oplock

This example demonstrates the most common form of the materialized view and the basic building blocks. We need to store the latest version of a select set of fields from a specific domain entity. We also need to account for events arriving out of order. On the authoring side of the equation, we typically need to account for multiple users updating the same record simultaneously and one transaction overwriting another. Optimistic locking is the typical solution to this problem. We store a timestamp or sequence number on each record and update this value with each successful update, so long as the current value in the database is equal to the value that was previously retrieved before the update. We throw an error when the assertion fails and delegate the handling of the specific scenario to the user.

On the consumer side of the equation, the events are facts that represent the history of an instance of a domain entity. We are not concerned with concurrency. We want to make certain that we do not overwrite newer events with older events. We still assert on an optimistic lock value; however, our reaction to the failure of the assertion is the opposite on this end of the equation. We can simply ignore older events when they arrive after newer events.

The following is a fragment from a Serverless Framework `serverless.yml` file, which defines the AWS DynamoDB table that is used to store the materialized view. It is no different from most DynamoDB table definitions, which means that from the query perspective, this materialized view works just like any other DynamoDB table. The developer experience is the same. A typical alternative is to store the materialized view in a search engine. The query requirements will usually drive the decision regarding which database type is the most appropriate. For example, a search engine is usually the best choice for geospatial and natural language queries. When we only ever access an object by its identifier, then it may be appropriate to persist the view in blob storage. This is often used in conjunction with a search engine for the query fields and blob storage for the record details.

```
View:
  Type: AWS::DynamoDB::Table
  Properties:
    TableName: ${opt:stage}-${self:service}-view
    AttributeDefinitions:
      - AttributeName: id
        AttributeType: S
    KeySchema:
      - AttributeName: id
        KeyType: HASH
    ProvisionedThroughput:
      ReadCapacityUnits: 1
      WriteCapacityUnits: 1
```

Next, we have the code to save the data in the view. It is a stream processor like the others we have discussed and leverages the functional reactive programming paradigm. The logic maps the required fields, sets up the conditional expression for the optimistic locking logic, and puts the data in the table. It catches and ignores `ConditionalCheckFailedException`. For all other exceptions, this example produces a fault based on the Stream Circuit Breaker pattern. In this example, `oplock` is based on the event `timestamp`. An alternative is to use the sequence number provided by the stream. This is useful when the `timestamp` may not be unique because it is too coarse-grained. However, if the events are not published to the stream in the correct order, then the sequence number will not be appropriate. In which case, if it is not unique, then the event sourcing approach may be the proper solution.

```
export const consumer = (event, context, cb) => {
  _(event.Records)
    .map(recordToUow)
    .filter(forItemCreateOrUpdated)
    .flatMap(save)
    .collect().toCallback(cb);
};

const save = uow => {
  const params = {
    TableName: process.env.TABLE_NAME,
    Item: {
      // map the identifier
      id: uow.event.item.id,

      // map the fields needed for the view
      name: uow.event.item.name,
      description: uow.event.item.description,

      // include the timestamp or sequence number
      oplock: uow.event.timestamp,
    },

    // define the oplock logic
    ConditionExpression: 'attribute_not_exists(#oplk) OR #oplk < :ts',
    ExpressionAttributeNames: {
      '#oplk': 'oplock'
    },
    ExpressionAttributeValues: {
      ':ts': uow.event.timestamp
    },
  };

  const db = new aws.DynamoDB.DocumentClient();
```

```
    return _(db.put(params).promise()
      .catch(err => {
        // check if we can ignore the error
        if (err.code !== 'ConditionalCheckFailedException') {
          // otherwise raise a fault
          err.uow = uow;
          throw err;
        }
      })
    );
  }
```

Example – event sourced join

In this example, we leverage Event Sourcing and ACID 2.0 to create views that join and group data from multiple event types emitted by multiple components. These events can arrive out of order and the logic is idempotent. In this example, we want to asynchronously join the user-created, user-loggedIn, and order-submitted event types and produce a view which aggregates the user ID, username, last logged in timestamp, and the count of recent orders.

This approach leverages two tables: a view table and an event store table. The view table is the same as the one in the preceding inverse optimistic lock example, so it is excluded for brevity. The following is a fragment from the `serverless.yml` file, which defines the AWS DynamoDB table that is used to create a component-specific event store for performing the desired join. The ID attribute is the hash key, which contains the concatenation of the field values from the events of interest that effectively form the where or group by clause. In this example, we are joining the events based on user ID. The sequence attribute is the range key, which is unique within the hash key. This will typically be the sequence number created by the stream or the timestamp of the individual events. The database stream is initialized so that we can use the trigger to calculate the view as events are captured.

```
    Events:
      Type: AWS::DynamoDB::Table
      Properties:
        TableName: ${opt:stage}-${self:service}-event-store
        AttributeDefinitions:
          - AttributeName: id
            AttributeType: S
          - AttributeName: sequence
            AttributeType: S
        KeySchema:
          - AttributeName: id
```

```
            KeyType: HASH
         - AttributeName: sequence
            KeyType: RANGE
       ProvisionedThroughput:
         ReadCapacityUnits: 1
         WriteCapacityUnits: 1
       StreamSpecification:
         StreamViewType: NEW_AND_OLD_IMAGES
```

Next, we have the code for the stream processor, which consumes the desired events from the inter-component stream and stores them in the event store table. In this example, we are interested in the user-created, user-loggedIn, and order-submitted event types. When inserting each event in the event store table, the user ID of each event type and the stream sequence number form the key. This key solves two problems. First, it makes the save operation idempotent. Events are immutable, thus if we save the same event multiple times, it only overwrites the row with the exact same values. This is an important aspect of Event Sourcing. Second, it groups related events together based on the hash key. In this example, all events for a specific user are grouped together, effectively joining the events of interest together.

```
export const consumer = (event, context, cb) => {
  _(event.Records)
    .map(recordToUow)
    .filter(byType)
    .flatMap(saveEvent)
    .collect().toCallback(cb);
};

const byType = uow =>
  uow.event.type === 'user-created' ||
  uow.event.type === 'user-loggedIn' ||
  uow.event.type === 'order-submitted';

const saveEvent = uow => {
  const params = {
    TableName: process.env.EVENT_STORE_TABLE_NAME,
    Item: {
      id: uow.event.user ? uow.event.user.id : uow.event.order.userId,
      sequence: uow.record.kinesis.sequenceNumber,
      event: uow.event,
    }
  };

  const db = new aws.DynamoDB.DocumentClient();
```

```
  return _(db.put(params).promise()
    .then(() => uow)));
}
```

Finally, we have the code for the trigger stream processor. This code is invoked each time an event is inserted into the event store table. The processor retrieves all the events from the table based on the given hash key that was just inserted. This returns all the events that are related to this newest event. In this example, it will return all the events for the specific user ID. Now we can calculate the fields for the desired view. We want the username, the last login time, and the count of recent orders. We reduce the list of events into a dictionary keyed by event type. We can rely on the fact that the events are returned in the order of the range key to simplify the logic. We only need to retain the last known last user-loggedIn event and there will be at most one user-created event. We accumulate all the order-submitted events to arrive at the count. Default values are provided to account for any missing events.

This approach solves the problem of receiving events out of order. Every time an event is inserted, we recalculate the view based on the new set of events. When the related events are retrieved, they are returned in the proper order. If an older event is received after new events, that event may or may not change the result of the calculation. In the case of the user-loggedIn event, the older event will be ignored. When a user-created event is received out of order, the view will miss the name until it arrives. For older order-submitted events, they will just accumulate in the total count. Thus as each additional event arrives, the view becomes more up to date, as shown in the following code.

```
export const trigger = (event, context, cb) => {
  _(event.Records)
    .flatMap(getRelatedEvents)
    .map(view)
    .flatMap(saveView)
    .collect().toCallback(cb);
};

const getRelatedEvents = (record) => {
  const params = {
    TableName: process.env.EVENT_STORE_TABLE_NAME,
    KeyConditionExpression: '#id = :id',
    ExpressionAttributeNames: {
      '#id': 'id'
    },
    ExpressionAttributeValues: {
      ':id': record.dynamodb.Keys.id.S
    }
  };
```

```
      const db = new aws.DynamoDB.DocumentClient();

      return _(db.query(params).promise()
        .then(data => ({
          record: record,
          data: data,
        }))
      );
    }

    const view = (uow) => {
      // create a dictionary by event type
      uow.dictionary = uow.data.Items.reduce((dictionary, item) => {
        // events are sorted by range key
        item.event.type === 'order-submitted' ?
          dictionary[item.event.type].push(item.event) :
          dictionary[item.event.type] = item.event;

        return dictionary;
      }, { // default values
          'user-created': { user: { name: undefined } },
          'user-loggedIn': { timestamp: undefined },
          'order-submitted': []
        });

      // map the fields
      uow.item = {
        id: uow.record.dynamodb.Keys.id.S,
        name: uow.dictionary['user-created'].user.name,
        lastLogin: uow.dictionary['user-loggedIn'].timestamp,
        recentOrderCount: uow.dictionary['order-submitted'].length,
      };

      return uow;
    }

    const saveView = (uow) => {
      const params = {
        TableName: process.env.VIEW_TABLE_NAME,
        Item: uow.item,
      };

      const db = new aws.DynamoDB.DocumentClient();
      return _(db.put(params).promise());
    };
```

Offline-first database

Persist user data in local storage and synchronize with the cloud when connected so that client-side changes are published as events and cloud-side changes are retrieved from materialized views.

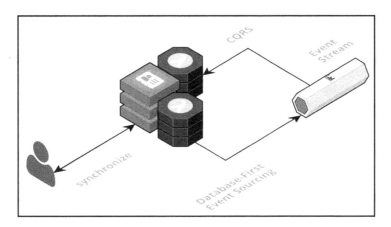

Context, problem, and forces

In cloud-native systems, the presentation layer lives on the client and the client device is more and more mobile. Users have more than one device, including phones and tablets and, to a decreasing degree, traditional desktops. The presentation layer must communicate with the backend component to send and receive data and perform actions. Mobile users frequently experience spotty connectivity, which increases latency and often leaves them completely disconnected.

The CAP theorem states that in the presence of a network partition, one has to choose between consistency and availability. In the context of modern consumer facing applications, even a temporary increase in latency is considered to be equivalent to a network partition because of the opportunity cost of lost customers. Therefore, it is widely preferred to choose availability over consistency and thus design systems around eventual consistency and session consistency.

With these realities in mind, we need to architect customer-focused user experiences with an offline-first mindset. At a minimum, some critical features should be reasonably available when the device is disconnected. Crucial information can be cached on the device to enable users to perform and securely store important actions until connectivity is restored. This same information should also synchronize across devices.

Solution

Leverage the cloud provider's offline-first database service to store data locally and synchronize with the cloud and across devices. Calculate user-specific materialized views, as discussed in the CQRS pattern, and synchronize the views to the device. This allows users to always access the latest known information. Store user actions and inputs locally and synchronize to the cloud when connected. This allows users to proceed with their intentions even when disconnected. The application should synchronize on explicit actions when possible, but otherwise synchronize in the background when connectivity is intermittent. The user experience should be designed such that the user understands when data may be stale or when actions may be pending because of limited connectivity, and informed when connectivity issues are resolved. On the backend, the system leverages Database-First Event Sourcing when synchronization occurs, to produce events based on state changes and user actions.

Resulting context

The primary benefit of this solution is that it provides extremely high availability and responsiveness for important user interactions. Users perceive the system as responsive and available even when connectivity is intermittent. The data is stored and accessed locally, thus it is always available when needed and the load on backend resources is reduced. The data has the potential to be stale when connectivity is intermittent, but that is the best alternative among bad alternatives. When connectivity is restored, the data is synchronized with the cloud storage and ultimately across devices, creating a resilient solution.

It is important to be upfront with the user about the eventual consistency of the data. Some solutions strive to be completely transparent, such that the user would not know the difference between being connected and not. This may be reasonable for certain applications, but most have diminished capabilities when disconnected. For example, an e-commerce app could show your recent history when disconnected but not allow for the execution of new searches. Therefore, it is important to provide clues to the user about the accuracy of the cached data. For example, a visible *as of* timestamp may accompany data in a materialized view or a pending status may be provided for outgoing actions. We all experience this kind of functionality in the email applications on our smartphones every day. This approach lends itself best to user-specific data such as preferences or work in progress like a shopping cart or a draft document, and transaction status information such as the status of an order or a review process. It is important to all parties that the data is not lost.

This solution is essentially a client-side extension to the Event Sourcing and CQRS patterns. User actions are stored on the client-side using Database-First Event Sourcing and the changes are eventually synchronized to cloud storage where the cloud-side CDC mechanism triggers the logic to publish a domain event downstream. Materialized views are created just as we discussed in the CQRS pattern, only the view is stored in the cloud storage of the offline-first database and eventually synchronized to the devices.

An interesting aspect of this solution is that there is no need to implement a synchronous interface for the component. The synchronous interface is provided by the fully managed third-party service and only needs to be configured. On the client-side, an SDK is used to access the API and hide many of the details, such as the security model. Examples of these services include GCP Firebase and AWS Cognito.

Example – offline-first counter

This example demonstrates the essentials for storing and synchronizing data on the client side. I have kept the example simple to focus on the plumbing. The example is implemented as a React application that leverages an AWS Cognito Dataset to store a counter and the square of the counter. The user increments the counter and it is stored locally. When the user presses the synchronize button the counter-updated event is published to the event stream. The consumer of this event calculates a materialized view that is the square of the counter and stores the value on the cloud side for synchronization back to the client. This example can easily be mapped to an e-commerce application, which stores the cart (that is, the counter) and order status (that is, the square) on the client or a customer survey application that stores answers locally until the survey is completed.

First, we have the React application that displays the counter and its square and renders the `Increment` and `Synchronize` buttons. `Synchronize` would typically happen in the background on load, periodically and/or on specific user actions.

```
class App extends React.Component {
  constructor(props) {
    super(props)
    this.state = { count: 0, squared: 0 };
  }

  componentWillMount() { ... }
  increment() { ... }
  synchronize() { ... }
  render() {
    return (
      <div>
        <h1>Counter: {this.state.count}</h1>
```

```
      <h1>Squared: {this.state.squared}</h1>
      <button onClick={this.increment.bind(this)}>Increment</button>
      <button onClick={this.synchronize.bind(this)}>Synchronize</button>
    </div>
  );
  }
}

ReactDOM.render(
  <App />,
  document.getElementById('root')
);
```

Next, we have the `componentWillMount` method, which is part of the React standard component life cycle. This method initializes the Cognito client, retrieves the data from local storage, and sets the values in the component's state, which triggers re-rendering. In this example, the user is unauthenticated. If the user previously accessed the identity pool, then credentials will be present in local storage; otherwise, a new user is created and the dataset is initialized with zeros.

```
componentWillMount() {
  AWS.config.region = 'us-east-1';
  AWS.config.credentials = new AWS.CognitoIdentityCredentials({
    IdentityPoolId: 'us-east-1:xxxxxxxx-xxxx-xxxx-xxxx-xxxxxxxxxxxx',
  });
  AWS.config.credentials.get(() => {
    const syncClient = new AWS.CognitoSyncManager();
    syncClient.openOrCreateDataset('counter', (err, dataset) => {
      dataset.get('count', (err, value) => {
        this.setState({
          count: value ? Number(value) : 0
        });
      });
      dataset.get('squared', (err, value) => {
        this.setState({
          squared: value ? Number(value) : 0
        });
      });
      this.dataset = dataset;
    });
  });
}
```

The `increment()` method just adds one to the current counter value, saves it in local storage, and updates the components state to trigger re-rendering. This is analogous to an add to cart method that stores the cart as a JSON string.

```
increment() {
  const val = this.state.count + 1;
  this.dataset.put('count', String(val), (err, record) => {
    this.setState({
      count: val
    });
  });
}
```

The `synchronize()` method sends state changes from local storage to the cloud and retrieves state changes from the cloud. The component's state is once again updated to re-render the screen. In an e-commerce example, this could be analogous to the final submission of an order in a checkout flow. The cart has been transformed to an order and stored locally with a submitted status.

```
synchronize() {
  this.dataset.synchronize({
    onSuccess: (data, newRecords) => {
      this.dataset.get('squared', (err, value) => {
        this.setState({
          squared: value
        });
      });
    }
  });
}
```

This is an example of a stream processor that is performing Database-First Event Sourcing logic on the changes streaming from AWS Cognito as the result of a synchronization. A counter-updated event is published when a count sync is found. Continuing our e-commerce analogy, this could be reacting to a sync for an order with a submitted status and publish an order-submitted event. In a customer survey system, this would be looking for a survey completed status.

```
export const trigger = (event, context, cb) => {
  _(event.Records)
    .flatMap(recordToUow)
    .filter(forCountSync)
    .map(toEvent)
    .flatMap(publish)
    .collect().toCallback(cb);
};
```

```
const forCountSync = uow => uow.sync.key === 'count';

const toEvent = uow => {
  uow.event = {
    id: uuid.v1(),
    type: `counter-updated`,
    timestamp: uow.sync.lastModifiedDate,
    partitionKey: uow.record.kinesis.partitionKey,
    tags: {
      identityPoolId: uow.data.identityPoolId,
      identityId: uow.data.identityId,
      datasetName: uow.data.datasetName
    },
    record: uow.sync
  }
  return uow;
}
```

This is an example of a stream processor that is calculating a materialized view for a specific user that is stored in an AWS Cognito Dataset instead of a DynamoDB table, a search engine, or an S3 bucket. This example is calculating the square of the latest counter value. AWS Cognito requires a read (listRecords) operation prior to a write (updateRecords) operation. This allows for retrieving the syncCount values, which act as optimistic locks. These values could be leveraged to perform an Inverse OpLock. We could also leverage the Event sourced join technique as well. The point being that this is just a materialized view that is user-specific and will ultimately be synchronized to that user's devices. Continuing the e-commerce analogy, this would be consuming events from order-fulfillment components that are publishing order status updates. Any data can be streamed to a specific client using this approach.

```
module.exports.consumer = (event, context, cb) => {
  _(event.Records)
    .map(recordToUow)
    .filter(forCounterUpdated)
    .flatMap(saveSquare)
    .collect().toCallback(cb);
};

const forCounterUpdated = uow => uow.event.type === 'counter-updated';

const saveSquare = uow => {
  const db = new aws.CognitoSync();

  uow.params = {
    IdentityPoolId: uow.event.tags.identityPoolId,
    IdentityId: uow.event.tags.identityId,
```

```
        DatasetName: uow.event.tags.datasetName
    };

    return _(db.listRecords(uow.params).promise()
        .then(data => {
          uow.params.SyncSessionToken = data.SyncSessionToken;
          uow.params.RecordPatches = [{
            Key: 'squared',
            Value: String(Math.pow(Number(uow.event.record.value), 2)),
            Op: 'replace',
            SyncCount: data.DatasetSyncCount
          }];

          return db.updateRecords(uow.params).promise()
        }));
}
```

Backend For Frontend

Create dedicated and self-sufficient backend components to support the features of user-focused frontend applications.

Context, problem, and forces

Cloud-native, Reactive systems are composed of bounded isolated components, which provide proper bulkheads to enable the components to be responsive, resilient, and elastic. All inter-component communication is accomplished via asynchronous event streaming and components leverage materialized views to cache upstream data locally. To increase availability for an increasingly mobile user base, we leverage an offline-first database to store data on devices and synchronize with the cloud. The boundary components leverage an API gateway to expose a synchronous interface, which is used to interact with a user interface. Cloud-native systems typically have multiple user bases with different user experiences, delivered over multiple channels and to multiple device types.

Our overarching objective with cloud-native is to empower self-sufficient, full-stack teams to rapidly and continuously deliver innovation with confidence. To achieve this goal, we must ensure we have proper bulkheads between system components. However, with so many user experience, channel, and device permutations, it can be difficult to strike the right balance with regard to the composition of backend components needed to support the frontends. The classic solution is to create a generic backend, which attempts to support all the permutations. However, this solution tends to implode, as the logic becomes tangled, as a single team endeavors to support all the requirements of all the other teams. The single component becomes the bottleneck to all advancement and a single point of failure, as there are no functional bulkheads between all the competing requirements.

At the other end of the spectrum, we create a separate backend component for each and every permutation. This can quickly become unmanageable as the number of permutations increases. It also tends to create a level of duplication that is hard to justify, even though duplication is not necessarily a bad thing; just as reuse is not always a good thing either. Reuse is synonymous with coupling, which limits flexibility and creates single points of failure. The generic backend component is the extreme example of the fallacies of reuse. Somewhere in the middle of the spectrum, we create smaller shared components, which each support a specific feature, and then we wrap them in fewer frontend-specific backend component layers. These layers reintroduce the synchronous inter-component communication that we aim to eliminate and reestablish coupling between teams. It is a difficult balancing act and over and over again I hear teams say they would lean the opposite way on the spectrum if they had the opportunity for a redo.

Solution

To fully empower self-sufficient, full-stack teams, a single team needs to own a frontend feature and its supporting backend. This BFF component must be self-sufficient in that it employs the CQRS pattern to create materialized views for all upstream dependencies and produces events to all downstream dependencies following the Event Sourcing pattern.

Architecture the user experience as a set of many independent experiences, each supporting a distinct user base and a distinct and cohesive set of features. Each experience is implemented as an independently deployed frontend application, which in turn is composed of multiple independent feature-oriented frontends. Each experience will dictate whether or not multiple flavors of the application must be written for different channels and device types.

Consider the following options and guidelines when deciding whether to merge or split BFF components. Leverage a client-directed query approach, such as GraphQL, to reasonably support multiple device formats in a single BFF. Do not merge components with different security models, such as authenticated and unauthenticated. Integrate shared components in the frontend, which naturally expects synchronous communication. Embrace disposable architecture and experiment to find the proper balance of BFF components.

Resulting context

The primary benefit of this solution is that it heeds Conway's Law that *"organizations are constrained to produce application designs which are copies of their communication structures"*. We are giving teams full control over their feature across the full-stack. The user experiences are decoupled and each is owned by a single team, which owns the synchronous interface that supports the frontend, owns the materialized views that both shield the component from and integrate it with upstream components, and owns the asynchronous outbound interface that produces events to delegate to downstream processing. The only upstream and downstream coupling is limited to event content. This empowers teams to press forward, independent of other teams, with confidence that their feature is functioning properly so long as the changes are backwards compatible.

The client-directed query approach can be very useful in reducing redundancy by supporting multiple variants of the same user experience across multiple device form factors within the single backend component. It is preferable that this is leveraged when the same team owns the development across the form factors, but it can reduce the complexity of shared components as well. When redundancy is necessary to support differences across device experiences, it is useful to recognize that this redundancy is a form of replication, which improves scalability. For example, Android users and iPhone users would interact with different components and materialized views and thus spread the capacity requirements. There is potential for this to lead to the need for bidirectional synchronization between components.

Decomposing the user experience into many independently deployable frontend applications and frontend features is crucial for all the same reasons that we decompose the backend components into bounded isolated components. First and foremost is that it provides the proper bulkheads needed to empower self-sufficient teams to innovate and continuously deploy the frontend with confidence as well. Next, not all user experiences warrant support for multiple channels and device types. Many can be implemented as a bounded isolated app that performs a specific function in an overall value stream. This user experience decomposition also leads to a naturally responsive, resilient, elastic, and globally scalable component topology when combined with the BFF pattern. In the examples, we will discuss four different categories of your experiences: Authors, Workers, Customers, and Managers, which apply the same patterns in different variations and combinations to implement very different BFF components.

It is inevitable that certain key components are used across multiple channels and device types. These features are often the main value proposition and have a significant code base, which would be unreasonable to duplicate. Likewise, wrapping these components in an additional BFF proxy layer adds little value but significant complexity. Instead, evolving micro-frontend approaches integrate these components in the presentation layer by composing multiple micro-frontend fragments into a single experience. The feature team of a shared component would own the frontend fragment, which is composed with the whole experience.

Finally, achieving an optimal balance of BFF components to support the permutations of channels and device types is an iterative process. Leverage disposable architecture to facilitate experiments, which allow teams to easily pivot and change their approach midstream. Disposable architecture also enables a polyglot approach across components.

Example – Author BFF

In `Chapter 2`, *The Anatomy of Cloud Native Systems*, we discussed how the data life cycle is a useful strategy for decomposing a system into bounded isolated components. As the data in the system ages, its storage requirements will change and thus the component that owns the storage changes as well. The users who interact with the data will also change over the data life cycle and thus so do the frontend applications used over the data life cycle. In a reactive, cloud-native system, a great deal of data is automatically created as events flow through the system. However, an event chain has to start somewhere. If it doesn't start in an external system, then it starts when a user creates it. This is where the Author user experience comes into play. Examples could include any data entry intensive user interaction, such as authoring content for an e-commerce site, creating records in a case management system, managing reference data in virtually any system, and so on.

As depicted in the following figure, an Authoring BFF component generally consists of two out of the three APIs in the Trilateral API pattern. An Authoring BFF has a synchronous API with commands and queries to create and retrieve domain entity data and an asynchronous API to publish events as the state of the entities change. The API Gateway pattern is leveraged for the synchronous interface, the Cloud Native Databases per Component pattern is followed for storing the data in the most appropriate polyglot persistence, and the Database-First Event Sourcing pattern variant is utilized to publish events.

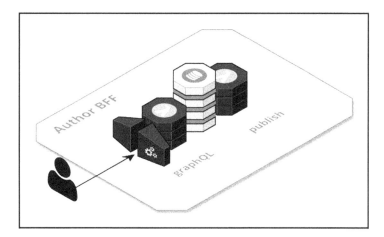

A RESTful CRUD implementation of the synchronous interface is suitable for a simple domain model. However, a GraphQL implementation is a good choice for more complex domain models, as it provides for a very structured implementation pattern. We will discuss this in more detail shortly. GraphQL is also client-oriented in that the client directs the format of query responses and the invocation of mutations. The server-side logic naturally conforms to Postel's Law (aka the Robustness Principle): *be conservative in what you send, be liberal in what you accept*. Thus, GraphQL is also a good choice if users author the data across multiple device types. For example, a case agent might enter essential information while on the go and double back later to complete the remaining details from a desktop.

Each aggregate domain entity is typically stored as a JSON document in a cloud-native document store, such as AWS DynamoDB, with references to related aggregates in other tables. GraphQL excels at stitching these relationships together for query responses and when publishing events. The published events consist of created, updated, and deleted events for each aggregate domain with the before and after snapshot of the instance. There are usually one or more primary aggregates that are the focal point of the business activity. These will contain a status field that is used to publish more concrete domain events, such as submitted, approved, rejected, completed, and so forth. A Search BFF component usually accompanies an Authoring BFF. The Search BFF implements the CQRS pattern to react to the events of the Authoring BFF and store the aggregate domain entities in a search engine.

A question often arises regarding the Authoring BFF and the single responsibility principle. There is a tendency to create a component per aggregate domain entity. This can lead to a lot of small components that must interact at the relationships between the aggregates, either via synchronous inter-component communication or via data synchronization. Of these choices, we definitely prefer data synchronization. However, the value of all these smaller components is limited at best, because our aim is to avoid shared components and synchronous inter-component communication in favor of turning the database inside out with materialized views.

Instead, the act of authoring is the single responsibility. It is perfectly reasonable to author all the domain entities of a complex domain model within a single component provided that the team can continuously deliver changes to the component with confidence. To achieve this confidence, the context of the domain model must certainly be bounded and cohesive. The code for the component must also follow a very predictable pattern. This is where the structure of GraphQL code also excels. Following best practices, the code for each domain entity in a GraphQL schema has the same structure: schema fragment, resolvers fragment, model class, validation rules, and pluggable connectors. The following is a typical schema fragment.

```
export const schema = `
  type Item {
    id: ID
    name: String!
    description: String
  }

  extend type Query {
    item(id: String!): Item
    itemsByName(name: String!, limit: Int, cursor: String): [Item]
  }

  extend type Mutation {
    saveItem(
      input: Item
    ): Item
    deleteItem(
      id: ID!
    ): Item
  }
`;
```

It is very easy to reason about the logic of many domain entities in a single Authoring BFF because the code follows a predictable pattern and it is solely focused on the act of data entry. Deviations from the pattern are quickly spotted in the code review. A Search BFF is implemented as a separate component precisely because its code follows a different pattern. Thus a single search BFF can support multiple domain entities as well. Still, all of this is cohesive within a bounded context and the user activity is scoped to a particular user base. In the following user experience categories, we will see where other responsibilities reside.

Example – Worker BFF

As an aggregate domain entity moves through its life cycle, users with different roles and skillsets will need to perform work in relation to an entity as part of a larger business process. This work often involves the use of a specialized user experience and work often dictates a specific device form factor: phone, tablet, or desktop. These are usually standalone, task-oriented applications. Examples include fieldwork, such as truck roll and sales calls; warehouse tasks, such as order fulfillment; or team activities, such as reviewing and contributing to content.

As depicted in the following figure, a **Worker BFF** component consists of all three APIs in the Trilateral API pattern. A **Worker BFF** has an asynchronous API to consume events related to task assignments, a synchronous API with queries and commands to interact with tasks, and an asynchronous API to publish events regarding the status of work. The CQRS pattern is employed to create the task view, the API Gateway pattern is leveraged for the synchronous interface, and the Database-First Event Sourcing pattern variant is utilized to publish status events.

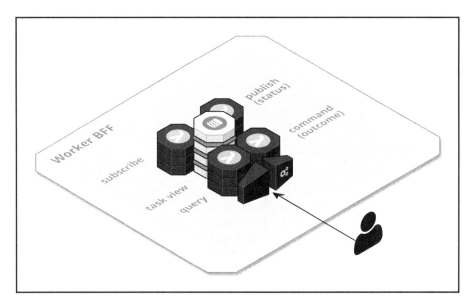

A task is typically stored as a JSON document in a cloud-native document store, such as AWS DynamoDB, and contains all the necessary information needed to direct the work. The necessary information should be available in the event which triggered the creation of the task. The **Worker BFF** is related to the *Event Orchestration* pattern, which is covered in `Chapter 5`, *Control Patterns*. One or more specific **Worker BFF** components are often associated with a specific business process component. The business process component produces the events which trigger the **Worker BFF** components and consume the status events of the **Worker BFF** to further direct the business process. Once a business process is complete, the tasks can be purged from the task views after a time to live. All the events related to the tasks should be archived with the aggregate domain entity instances.

Example – Customer BFF

The efforts of authors and workers, in most cases, are ultimately directed towards the purpose of delivering capabilities to customers in a customer- specific user experience. The customer experience is usually delivered through multiple channels. To simplify this example, we will focus on the web channel, as the concepts are applicable to the other form factors.

Modern websites are built as a collection of multiple, mobile-first, single page applications that are delivered from the CDN. These frontend applications will typically include a home page application, a search application, a product application, a sign up application, a checkout application, and a customer account application. Each frontend application may be further decomposed into independently deployed micro-frontend applications that provide fragments to the parent application. As an example, the product application would interact with the checkout application to display the add-to-cart button on the page and the cart button on the banner. The details of modern user interface development, however, are not the purview of this book. Instead, we want to focus on how to carve out cloud-native backend components for modern frontend applications.

First and foremost, the customer experience is a different stage in the life cycle of the system's data. The requirements to scale the data to potentially millions of users versus hundreds or thousands of authors and workers are very different. As depicted in the following figure, Customer BFF components make heavy use of the CQRS and Offline-First Database patterns. Authored content, such as products, is replicated to a Search BFF where it is stored in a search engine as well as blob storage for the product details that are delivered via the CDN. The user's cart is owned by the Checkout BFF and stored in the offline-first database. An Account BFF owns the user's order history, which is a materialized view stored in the offline-first database, as well as the user's preferences and wish list, which are also stored offline-first.

Note that the frontend is composed of multiple independent pieces and thus the backend is as well. The team responsible for each frontend also owns the backend that supports it and the data as well. All data that is created or generated by the user is published downstream as well to further support the data life cycle. It is also important to recognize that each frontend application has it own security context in that some parts of the user experience require authentication while others do not. The security model of the backend should match that of its frontend. It is usually easier to reason about a single BFF when all its resources either require authentication or do not. Unintended security gaps can slip in when we mix and match security models.

Example – Manager BFF

In any business, it is important to measure and track the work that is performed so that the results can be evaluated against objectives and course corrections made as necessary. **Key performance indicators** (**KPI**) are often made available in a manager application.

As depicted in the following figure, a **Manager BFF** component consists of two out of the three APIs in the Trilateral API pattern. A **Manager BFF** has an asynchronous API to consume events related to key performance indicators and a synchronous API with queries to retrieve the KPIs and their history. The CQRS pattern is employed to create the metrics materialized views and the API Gateway pattern is leveraged for the synchronous interface.

The key performance indicators are typically stored in a cloud-native key-value store, such as AWS DynamoDB, or a time series database. The CQRS Event Sourced Join technique can be employed to capture and aggregate the metrics and feed the materialized views. The metrics are usually aggregated by day, week, month, and year. The detailed events can be purged periodically as the days are rolled to weeks and months and years. Note that this user experience is different from that of an ad hoc analytics tool that would be supported by its own BFF and different from the work of a data scientist. This user experience delivers answers to a prescribed set of questions. The outcomes of ad hoc analytics and data science may drive the requirements of a **Manager BFF** as new indicators and algorithms are identified.

External Service Gateway

Integrate with external systems by encapsulating the inbound and outbound inter-system communication within a bounded isolated component to provide an anti-corruption layer that acts as a bridge to exchange events between the systems.

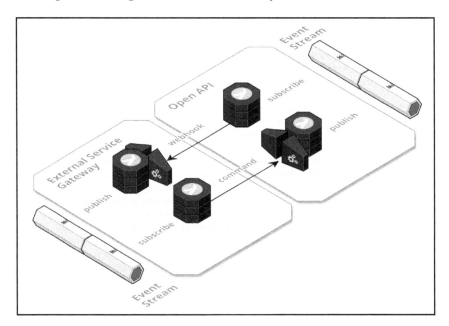

Context, problem, and forces

Systems often need to integrate with an external system, such as Stripe for payment processing, SendGrid for transactional emails, AWS Cognito for user authentication, or a custom system. Our cloud-native systems are composed of bounded isolated components, which provide proper bulkheads to make the components responsive, resilient, and elastic. The isolation is achieved via asynchronous inter-component communication. We aim to eliminate all synchronous inter-component communication. External systems provide an Open API for inbound and outbound communication with other systems.

Integrating with an external system is inherently risky because they are typically owned by a third party and thus not within your control. Some very popular services have simply gone out of business and left their customers scrambling for alternatives. They often change their pricing models, sometimes for the better but sometimes not. They strive to keep their APIs stable, but they are always evolving and the improvements are usually but not always backwards compatible. The data models of these systems, when they do overlap with yours, are usually different. Their security models are often different. They may state a service level agreement in terms of availability, but it is wise to hedge your bets. The inbound API for invoking commands is synchronous and the outbound **service provider interface** (**SPI**) is usually a webhook that will synchronously invoke an endpoint, which you will provide. To mitigate the risks and compensate for the differences, we need to encapsulate the use of an external system such that we can adapt to the semantic and syntactic differences, be resilient to failures in the external system, and allow for easily plugging in a different provider when a switch is needed. It is also not unusual for a system to have the requirement to support multiple providers of the same capability such that a specific provider is dynamically selected based on the details of any given business transaction.

Solution

Treat external systems like any other bounded isolated component. Create a component for each external system that acts as a bidirectional bridge for transmitting events between the systems.

Outbound communication

The component consumes internal events and invokes the appropriate commands on the external system. This interaction follows the Event-First variant of the Event Sourcing pattern and the external system represents the database that will persist the results of the commands. The internal events are transformed to meet the requirements of the external system. The component may employ the Event Sourcing and CQRS patterns to capture and cache additional events as needed to adorn missing information.

Inbound communication

The component consumes events from the external system and re-publishes them to the internal event stream to delegate processing to downstream components. The internal event contains the raw contents of the external event for auditing and a transformed version of the content for internal consumption. This interaction follows the Database-First variant of the Event Sourcing pattern and the external system represents the database that is emitting state change events. The component typically leverages the API Gateway pattern to create a RESTful service that can be registered with the external system's webhooks. Alternatively, when the cloud provider offers the external system, the component registers functions with the SPI of the cloud resource.

Resulting context

The primary benefit of this solution is that it establishes an anti-corruption layer between the systems because only the External Service Gateway components are coupled to their respective external systems. Upstream components are not required to produce events that can be consumed by the external systems. The gateway components are responsible for this transformation. For inbound communication, the raw version of the event is included, solely so that it can be captured by the data lake, where as the transformed version of the event is provided for consumption by downstream components. This enables the possibility of replacing an external system with another external system as needed or even supporting multiple external systems for the same functionality. It is recommended to consume and re-publish the external events even when there are currently no downstream consumers because the data lake will still capture the events. This can provide analytical information about what is happening in the external system as well as provide the ability to replay the events to seed any future downstream components.

This solution helps ensure that the communication between the systems is asynchronous. These components leverage the Event Sourcing pattern to encapsulate the necessarily synchronous communication at the boundaries of the systems and help ensure the atomic hand-off of the events between the systems. The inbound interaction makes a single call to publish the event to the stream following the Database-First variant of Event Sourcing to minimize the possibility of failure during the hand-off. The outbound interaction makes a single call to the external system following the Event-First variant of the Event Sourcing pattern along with the Stream Circuit Breaker pattern to help ensure a smooth hand-off.

We integrate with external systems because they provide valuable processing logic in some domain that is non-trivial to duplicate, not because they store a specific domain model. Therefore, it is important not to treat an external system as a database but instead think of it like any other bounded isolated component. Thus, we do not make synchronous calls to retrieve data from external systems; all inter-component communication is accomplished asynchronously via the event stream. Downstream components consume the re-published events to maintain materialized views per usual. Upstream components may also maintain a redundant data model to support their behavior and produce the events needed to drive the outbound interactions with external systems. To support the outbound interaction, the gateway component may need to maintain its own micro-event-store and materialized views to facilitate proper communication with the external system. We will discuss control flow logic of this type in `Chapter 5`, *Control Patterns*.

Security is another important aspect of this solution. External systems will often support a different communication security mechanism that we want to encapsulate within the gateway component. Even though most systems are converging on the use of JWT tokens, in all cases we need to establish a trust relationship between the systems to enable authentication and authorization. To establish a trust relationship, we securely exchange and store access tokens on each side of the integration. For example, when configuring a webhook, you will typically provide an access token that is stored in the external system and passed along in the authorization header on every invocation. As discussed in the API Gateway pattern, we delegate the crosscutting concern of token validation to the API Gateway. In `Chapter 6`, *Deployment*, we will discuss how components can be securely configured with an access token for an external system.

This solution is consistent with our aim to minimize synchronous interactions. However, some external systems, such as payment processors, require some synchronous interactions with the end user. In the case of payment processors, this is important because it isolates your system from PCI compliance requirements. In these cases, an external system gateway component would typically need to expose a simple RESTful endpoint that can be invoked from the presentation layer to proxy those requests to the external system and adorn encapsulated access token information. Keep in mind that the synchronous APIs may be the focal point of these external services, yet the bulk of the interactions with these external systems is still asynchronous.

Finally, this solution is not limited to use with just external systems that are owned by another company. You may have multiple cloud-native systems that you want to keep isolated, yet still have them integrated. Alternatively, you may have welcomed polyglot cloud and need events to flow across cloud providers. In either case, the external service gateway will simply provide a straightforward bridge between the event streaming services on either end. In the first case, the bridge may very well be joining homogeneous streaming services, whereas in the polyglot cloud case, the bridge will most certainly be across heterogeneous streaming services. Ultimately, this is a natural and mature extension and evolution of your streaming topology.

Example – user authentication integration

The following is an example of a bidirectional integration with a User Authentication system, such as AWS Cognito. The outbound communication demonstrates directing the external service to send an invitation to a new user. The inbound communication demonstrates re-publishing the external events for user sign-up and sign-in. In the case of an email system, this communication would entail sending emails and reacting to the likes of bounce and unsubscribe events, whereas for a payment processor we would process payments and react to disputes, refunds, and so forth. The following is a fragment from a Serverless Framework `serverless.yml` file, which demonstrates the configuration and registration of the functions.

```yaml
functions:
  trigger:
    handler: handler.trigger
    events:
      - cognitoUserPool:
          pool: UserPool
          trigger: PostConfirmation
      - cognitoUserPool:
          pool: UserPool
          trigger: PostAuthentication
    environment:
      STREAM_NAME:
        Ref: Stream
  consumer:
    handler: handler.consumer
    events:
      - stream:
          type: kinesis
          arn:
            Fn::GetAtt:
              - Stream
              - Arn
```

```
            batchSize: 100
            startingPosition: TRIM_HORIZON
        environment:
          USER_POOL_ID:
            Ref: UserPool
```

This is the trigger function that is registered with the Cognito SPI. This function will be triggered when new users sign up and when existing users authenticate. The external event is transformed to the internal event format and then published. No other interactions are performed in this function. This minimizes the chance of a failure and provides flexibility and extensibility by delegating all other possible actions to downstream components. For example, downstream the data lake component will collect the events, a security component may track logins, an email component may send a welcome email via another external service, and a user management BFF component will maintain a materialized view of all users so that it does not need to rely on the external service for this data. Alternatively, a payment processing system would typically emit events about disputes and subscriptions and an email service would emit events regarding a bounce or an unsubscribe. The external service gateway component will just bridge these events to the internal event structure and nothing more.

```
export const trigger = (extEvt, context, callback) => {
  const event = {
    id: uuid.v1(),
    type: extEvt.triggerSource, // PostConfirmation or PostAuthenitcation
    timestamp: Date.now(),
    partitionKey: extEvt.userName,
    raw: extEvt,
    user: {
      id: extEvt.request.userAttributes.sub,
      username: extEvt.userName,
      email: extEvt.request.userAttributes.email,
      status: extEvt.request.userAttributes['cognito:user_status']
    }
  };

  const params = {
    StreamName: process.env.STREAM_NAME,
    PartitionKey: event.partitionKey,
    Data: new Buffer(JSON.stringify(event)),
  };

  const kinesis = new aws.Kinesis();
  kinesis.putRecord(params).promise()
    .then(resp => callback(null, extEvt))
    .catch(err => callback(err));
};
```

It is important to reiterate this last point. Our bounded isolated components do not make inter-component synchronous calls to retrieve data. We instead leverage the CQRS pattern and maintain materialized views within components to maximize responsiveness, resilience, and elasticity. The CQRS pattern is even more important when interacting with an external service. These services are optimized for performing their value proposition, such as authentication, processing payments, sending email, and so forth. Their APIs will likely provide queries to retrieve data, but those operations are usually severely throttled, as they are not the value proposition. In essence, they are following the same reactive principles.

Continuing the BFF thread of this example, a user management component may interact with its materialized view and allow various actions to be performed that ultimately need to propagate back to the external system. In the case of user management, this could include assigning permissions, deactivation, or new invitations. These components would employ the Database-First variant of the Event Sourcing pattern to produce the events that must be consumed by an External Service Gateway component. The following is such an example of consuming a user invitation event and invoking the proper command on the external system. The external system would then take control of the business process until it produced another event via is SPI or a webhook.

```
export const consumer = (event, context, cb) => {
  _(event.Records)
    .map(recordToUow)
    .filter(forUserInvited)
    .flatMap(createUser)
    .collect().toCallback(cb);
};

const recordToUow = r => ({
  record: r,
  event: JSON.parse(new Buffer(r.kinesis.data, 'base64'))
});

const forUserInvited = uow => uow.event.type === 'user-invited';

const createUser = uow => {
  const userPool = new aws.CognitoIdentityServiceProvider();

  uow.params = {
    UserPoolId: process.env.USER_POOL_ID,
    Username: uow.event.user.id,
    DesiredDeliveryMediums: ['EMAIL'],
    UserAttributes: [
      { Name: 'name', Value: uow.event.user.name },
      { Name: 'email', Value: uow.event.user.email },
```

```
      { Name: 'email_verified', Value: 'true' },
    ],
  };

  return _(userPool.adminCreateUser(uow.params).promise());
}
```

Summary

In this chapter, we discussed the boundary patterns of reactive, cloud-native systems. Although we focus on asynchronous, event-driven inter-component communication, we ultimately need to implement synchronous communication at the boundaries where the system interacts with humans and external systems. The API Gateway pattern provides a secure and scalable foundation for synchronous communication. With the CQRS pattern, we leverage materialized views to decouple upstream dependencies in order to make the synchronous communication responsive, resilient, and elastic. The offline-first database pattern allows some synchronous interactions to operate locally by storing event and materialized view data in local storage and synchronizing with the cloud to increase the availability of the system from the user's perspective. The BFF is a higher-order pattern that pulls all these patterns together to create dedicated and self-sufficient components, which provide synchronous system boundaries to facilitate frontend features. The BFF components, in turn, interact with the rest of the system asynchronously. Finally, in the External Service Gateway pattern, we provide for bidirectional integration with other systems.

5
Control Patterns

In the previous chapter, we continued our discussion of cloud-native patterns with boundary patterns. Boundaries are where the system interacts with everything that is external to the system, including humans and other systems. We leverage a fully managed API gateway to provide secure and scalable synchronous communication. Materialized views are employed to decouple upstream components and make end-user interactions responsive, resilient, and elastic. Offline-first databases enable high availability for an increasingly mobile user base. End users interact with Backend For Frontend components to consume information and perform system functions. While External Service Gateway components provide for bi-directional integration with other systems.

In this chapter, we will conclude our discussion of cloud-native patterns. We will build on the foundation patterns and discuss the patterns that provide the flow of control for collaboration between the boundary components. It is with these collaborations that we ultimately realize the intended functionality of a system. We will cover the following control patterns:

- Event collaboration
- Event orchestration
- Saga

Event collaboration

Publish domain events to trigger downstream commands and create a reactive chain of collaboration across multiple components.

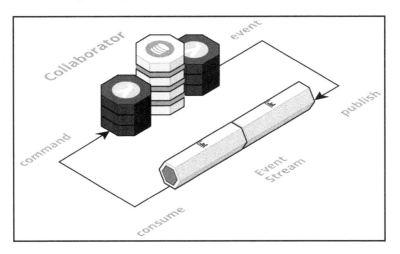

Context, problem, and forces

You are building a reactive, cloud-native system that is composed of bounded isolated components. The **Command Query Responsibility Segregation (CQRS)** pattern is leveraged to replicate data from upstream components to avoid performing non-resilient, synchronous inter-component communication to retrieve needed information. Each component leverages value-added cloud services to implement one or more cloud-native databases that are exclusively owned by each component. Data from upstream components is synchronized to these cloud-native databases to provide synchronous intra-component access to highly available data. This isolation enables downstream components to continue functioning even when their upstream dependencies are experiencing an outage. This empowers your self-sufficient, full-stack team to rapidly and continuously deliver innovation with the confidence that an honest mistake will not impact other components.

CQRS resolves the issues of synchronous inter-component communication with regard to queries; however, we still have similar problems when relying on synchronous inter-component communication for invoking commands on one or more collaborating components to perform higher-order business activities. When using traditional request-response collaboration, one component invokes another component and waits for a response and then invokes another component and so on. Promises or futures are leveraged when multiple calls can be performed in parallel to improve overall performance. If an error response is received then the calling component must handle the logic to reverse the impacts of any preceding and outstanding calls.

The code required to orchestrate the collaboration for the happy path is already complicated enough without error handling. In an effort to improve the probability of successful collaboration and account for typical availability issues, we have to add further complexity by employing service discovery and circuit breaker techniques. All the while, the responsiveness of the system is degraded and in the worst cases, users receive errors they can do nothing about. Adding insult to injury, once availability is restored, any transactions that were partially processed and reversed must be reprocessed from the beginning. Unfortunately, users may not return to complete their transactions when the system is restored and there may be no record that the collaboration occurred in the first place.

Testing is another common issue with request-response collaboration. One of the most common questions I encounter regarding microservice architecture revolves around how to effectively perform testing with so many moving pieces. We will discuss modern testing techniques in `Chapter 7`, *Testing,* and `Chapter 8`, *Monitoring*. However, instead of compensating for these problems, it is better to eliminate them in the first place by delegating them away from the end user.

Solution

Redesign the user experience to be eventually consistent. Replace synchronous inter-component communication with asynchronous inter-component communication by using the event stream to publish events which trigger downstream commands. Upstream components apply the Database-First variant of the Event Sourcing pattern to publish domain events that reflect changes in their state. Downstream components react to the domain events by performing a command and publishing a domain event to reflect the outcome of the command.

This cycle repeats through as many steps as are necessary to complete the activity. The cycle can fan-out to perform steps in parallel and then fan-in as well. Collaborators apply the CQRS pattern to avoid needing to synchronously retrieve relevant information. The CQRS Event Sourced Join technique can be used to implement fan-in. Ultimately, the outcome of the collaboration is revealed to the user.

Resulting Context

The primary benefit of this solution is that it eliminates synchronous inter-component communication. A collaborating component performs its command in reaction to an event, emits another event, and its work is done. One or more collaborating components, in turn, perform their command, emit their event, and so one. Any step can fail and retry independently by employing the straightforward Stream Circuit Breaker pattern. A third party can intervene to resolve an issue and resubmit an event without the need to rerun prior steps and without end-user participation. When the system is operating normally, eventual consistency happens in near real-time but degrades gracefully when anomalies occur. Combined with the Event Sourcing and CQRS patterns, we effectively eliminate all synchronous inter-component communication, for both upstream queries and downstream commands, and relegate synchronous communication to the boundaries of the system where it fits naturally.

Reasoning about the logic of each individual collaborator becomes easier as each is focused on a single responsibility. The collaborator has its input and output events and everything else is encapsulated. This also makes it possible to test components in isolation, because there is no synchronous communication to other components. In Chapter 7, *Testing*, we will discuss transitive integration and end-to-end testing, which enables complete testing of a collaboration in aggregate without all components running simultaneously.

A drawback of this isolation is that a collaborator applying the CQRS pattern could perform a command based on stale data. If this is an issue for a specific collaborator, one potential solution is to include the information in the event instead of relying on CQRS. Furthermore, Event Collaboration allows components to listen to the collaboration without participating. For example, the data lake listens to all events to create a complete audit trail. The audit trail can provide diagnostic information to facilitate corrective action.

Raw Event Collaboration is a great solution for reasonably sized scenarios but can become less manageable as scenarios grow in size. Each collaborator is explicitly coupled to the events it consumes. To account for multiple and larger scenarios, each collaborator must know and understand more events. Each additional event bloats the component and makes it more difficult to reason about. It is also difficult to see the overall end-to-end collaboration flow as each component only knows its part. For complex flows, raw Event Collaboration can limit flexibility, which impedes innovation. The Event Orchestration pattern can be layered on top of Event Collaboration to address these limitations.

Example – order collaboration

This example, as depicted in the following diagram, demonstrates choreographing the interactions of multiple components using the Event Collaboration pattern. The components are collaborating to implement a business process for ordering a product that must be reserved in advance, such as a ticket to a play or an airline reservation. The customer completes and submits the order, and then the reservation must be confirmed, followed by charging the customer's credit card, and finally sending an email confirmation to the customer.

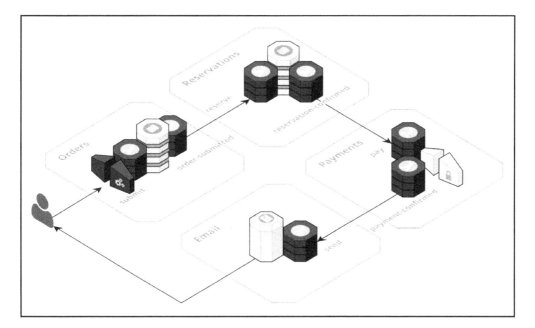

The **Orders** component is implemented following the Backend For Frontend pattern. The customer submits the order to the **Orders** component via an API gateway call to update the order in the database with a submitted status. The **Orders** component employs the Database-First variant of the Event Sourcing pattern to atomically publish the order-submitted event in reaction to the database update. The specific event to publish is determined based on the status field.

The **Reservations** component implements a stream processor that consumes the order-submitted event and reserves the product in the database. The **Reservations** component also leverages Database-First Event Sourcing to atomically publish the reservation-confirmed event. Again, the status of the reservation in the database is used to determine the correct event type to emit.

The **Payments** component is implemented following the External Service Gateway pattern. The component implements a stream processor to consume the reservation-confirmed event and invoke the external service to charge the customer's credit card. A webhook is registered to consume events from the external service. The component publishes a payment-confirmed event when it is notified by the external system that the charge was successfully processed.

The **Email** component is also implemented following the External Service Gateway pattern. The component implements a stream processor to consume the payment-confirmed event and then sends a confirmation message to the customer. In this example, there is no reason to consume events from the external email system.

The collaboration is initiated by a synchronous interaction with the end user at the boundary of the system. The other components atomically invoke a command when the desired event is received. They each atomically produce an event to reflect the change in state, thus triggering further action. A reasonably complex collaboration can be accomplished by simply chaining together multiple components following the Database-First variant of the Event Sourcing pattern.

Event orchestration

Leverage a mediator component to orchestrate collaboration between components without event type coupling.

Context, problem, and forces

You are building a reactive, cloud-native system that is composed of bounded isolated components. You are employing the Cloud Native Databases Per Component and Event Streaming patterns as well as the Event Sourcing and CQRS patterns to ensure that you have the proper bulkheads in place to make your components responsive, resilient, and elastic. This has increased the confidence of teams to deliver innovation and the system is growing rapidly. You have been successfully using raw Event Collaboration to choreograph the long-running behaviors of the system, but with the increasing complexity of the system, you are starting to outgrow this approach.

Event-driven architecture has the benefit of decoupling specific event producers from specific consumers. Producers emit events with no knowledge of what components will consume the events and consumers capture events with no knowledge of what component produced the event. Events also solve the availability issues of synchronous communication, because events are produced without the need for an immediate response from a consumer or any response at all in most cases. However, consumers are still coupled to the event types to which they subscribe, both in name and format. If an event type is no longer produced, then a subscribing component will no longer be triggered. If the event type name or format changes, then the consumers must also change. If new event types are added, then eventually some component will need to consume the event type, other than the data lake, if more behavior than auditing is desired.

Raw Event Collaboration explicitly couples consumer components to specific event types. From the perspective of a specific collaboration, this is a perfectly manageable solution for a reasonably sized scenario. From the perspective of a specific consumer, this solution is also reasonable, provided the consumer is only consuming a limited number of event types. However, raw Event Collaboration becomes less manageable, as the number of collaborations increases, as the complexity of collaborations increase, and as the number of event types increases.

Each collaborator is coupled to the event types it consumes. With each additional event type, more and more logic must be added to a component to process each event type. It is certainly possible to structure the code to minimize the impact, but there will still be code bloat and the ability to reason about the correctness of an individual component will decrease. A component may have a single core responsibility, but it also takes on part of the responsibility of each collaboration it participates in. As collaborations are added, changed, and removed, the collaborators must be modified as well. All this will eventually negatively impact a team's confidence in their ability to deliver changes to a component.

It is also difficult to see the overall end-to-end flow of a collaboration, as each component only knows its part and the parts are spread over multiple collaborators. For large scenarios, it is difficult to reason about the correctness of the overall flow as well as the individual parts. Each additional collaboration compounds the problem. Making changes to one flow can impact another flow at the steps where they share the components. Ultimately, teams will lose their confidence to evolve these collaborations and innovation will be impeded.

Solution

Create a component for each business process to act as a mediator between the collaborator components and orchestrate the collaboration flow across those components. Each component defines the events it will consume and publish independently of any business processes. The mediator maps and translates the published events of upstream components to the consumed events of downstream components. These mappings and translations are encapsulated in the mediator as a set of rules, which define the transitions in the collaboration flow.

The mediator consumes events from the stream based on these rules and emits transition events, following the Event-First variant of the Event Sourcing pattern, to trigger the necessary downstream components. Downstream components consume the events and perform the needed command. Each consuming component emits another event regarding the outcome of the command, usually following the Database-First variant of the Event Sourcing pattern. The mediator consumes the outcome events and the cycle repeats.

Resulting context

The primary benefit of this solution, over and above raw Event Collaboration, is that the collaborator components are completely decoupled. The business process component acts as a mediator to address the limitations of raw Event Collaboration while retaining the advantages. The collaborators have no knowledge of each other or the mediator component. The mediator defines the business process, thus only the mediator needs to change when the process evolves.

The full definition of a process flow is encapsulated in its mediator component. This makes it easy to reason about the whole flow as it is defined in a single place. Each mediator has a single responsibility for a single business process definition. The entire flow and all its transitions can be tested independently from the individual collaborators. The individual collaborator components are also easier to reason about because they have a single responsibility with a discrete set of input and output events. Each collaborator can be fully tested in complete isolation. In Chapter 7, *Testing*, we will discuss transitive integration and end-to-end testing, which enables complete testing of a collaboration in aggregate without all components running simultaneously.

The solution embraces the notion of dumb pipes and smart endpoints. A mediator has a single responsibility to a single process definition and within that process, it is only responsible for the state transitions of the process. The mediator delegates the responsibility of each step to the collaborator when it emits the transition event. A mediator may apply the CQRS pattern to accomplish its responsibility for these transitions. For example, additional information may be needed to map one event type to another event type. To accomplish this, the mediator would maintain a materialized view for the specific data. The Event Sourced Join technique can be used to support forks and joins in the process flow. Business processes usually support human interactions. In the Backend For Frontend pattern, we discussed the creation of Worker BFF components for just this purpose. These Worker BFF components can participate in a process flow just like any other collaborator. No other smarts should exist in a mediator component.

The solution does require the system to define more event types. In raw Event Collaboration, a collaborator consumes event types defined by other components. In this pattern, the consumers define their own input event type that will be emitted by the mediator in reaction to the upstream events. These additional event types are subtly different from most event types. It is generally accepted that events and commands are different. They may be two sides of the same coin, but commands are a request to perform some action, while events are a statement of fact that a command was performed and resulted in a change of state. In raw Event Collaboration, a collaborator subscribes to another component's event type and reacts by performing a command, which emits an event stating the fact the command was completed with a specific outcome.

These additional event types are defined by a component with the express purpose of triggering the invocation of its own command. Thus they feel more like command messages than like event messages and their names will naturally portray this. I call these transition events because they are emitted at the state transitions in the process definition. So from the perspective of the business process, they are classic event messages, but from the perspective of the collaborating component, they are command messages. With this nuance in mind, it is common to have a specific stream in the stream topology that is dedicated to command messages. This has the nice byproduct of putting all command messages into a separate location in the data lake since we include the stream name in the data lake path. This makes it easier to exclude these events during replay, as they can have unintended side effects. Another important by-product of these transition events is the audit record in the data lake that the process transitions occurred.

Finally, it is important to distinguish between transition events and the data events that a collaborator will consume. A collaborator component may also apply the CQRS pattern to cache data in materialized views to facilitate its own processing logic. We can call these data events. These data events are still defined by the upstream components. There is generally no need to mediate these event types because they are typically more stable than transition events.

Example – order orchestration

This example, as depicted in the following diagram, demonstrates mediating the interactions of multiple components using the Event Orchestration pattern. The components are assembled to implement a business process for ordering a product that must be reserved in advance, such as a ticket to a play or an airline reservation. The customer completes and submits the order, then the reservation must be confirmed, followed by charging the customer's credit card, and finally sending an email confirmation to the customer. This example builds on the example presented in the Event Collaboration pattern. The individual components are modified to be completely self-contained and a **Mediator** component is added to perform the orchestration.

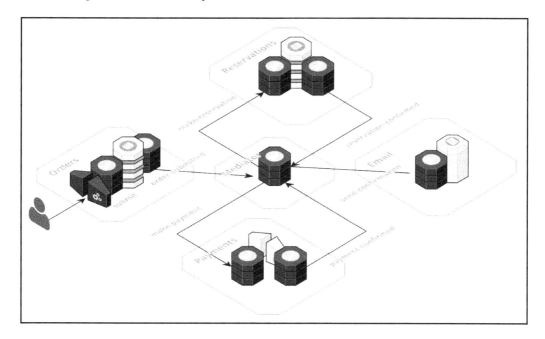

The **Orders** component is implemented following the Backend For Frontend pattern. The customer submits the order to the **Orders** component via an API gateway call to update the order in the database with a submitted status. The **Orders** component employs the Database-First variant of the Event Sourcing pattern to atomically publish the order-submitted event in reaction to the database update. The specific event to publish is determined based on the status field. It is important to note that this component is completely unchanged compared to the Event Collaboration pattern example. This means that many different business processes could be initiated, possibly based on the contents of the order, without coupling the **Orders** component to those processes.

The **Reservations** component implements a stream processor that consumes the make-reservation event and reserves the product in the database. The **Reservations** component also leverages Database-First Event Sourcing to atomically publish the reservation-confirmed event. Again, the status of the reservation in the database is used to determine the correct event type to emit. As compared to the Event Collaboration pattern example, this component is no longer coupled to the order-submitted event that is defined by an upstream component. The make-reservation event is defined by this component to support its specific needs.

The **Payments** component is also modified to consume an input event type that it defines and controls to suit its own needs, called make-payment. The component is still implemented following the External Service Gateway pattern. It implements a stream processor to consume the make-payment event and invoke the external service to charge the customer's credit card. A webhook is registered to consume events from the external service. The component publishes a payment-confirmed event when it is notified by the external system that the charge was successfully processed.

The **Email** component is also implemented following the External Service Gateway pattern. The component implements a stream processor to consume the send-confirmation event and then sends a confirmation email to the customer. Again, this new event type is completely controlled by the **Email** component to completely decouple it from upstream components.

Now that all the collaborators are decoupled, we need to add the mediator component that will conduct the orchestration. As shown in the preceding diagram, this component sits in between the other components, consumes an event from one component, and dispatches a different event to another component to perform the next step in the business process. The events are dispatched atomically following the Event-First variant of the Event Sourcing pattern. The mediator is essentially implemented as a stateless state machine, as all the necessary state information is contained in the events that are consumed. As mentioned previously, a mediator component could maintain information to adorn needed information to events or calculate joins, but these are non-essential for many processes.

The following code fragment provides the core implementation of the **Mediator** component's stream processor. The process consumes events from the stream and filters the events against a set of transition metadata to determine if there is a match. We will look at the metadata in detail shortly. For each matching transition, a new event is created based on the information contained in the triggering event. Finally, the new event is published to trigger the next step in the process.

```
export const consume = (event, context, cb) => {
  _(event.Records)
    .map(recordToUow)
```

```
      .filter(onTransitions)
      .flatMap(toEvent)
      .flatMap(publish)
      .collect().toCallback(cb);
};

const onTransitions = uow => {
  // find matching transitions
  uow.transitions = transitions.filter(t => t.filter === uow.event.type);

  // multiple transitions constitute a fork
  // can leverage event sourcing to implement process joins

  // proceed forward if there are any matches
  return uow.transitions.length > 0;
};

const toEvent = uow => {
  // create the event to emit
  // for each matching transition
  return _(uow.transitions.map(t => t.emit(uow)));
};
```

The following metadata defines the transitions in the state machine. Each transition defines the event type that will trigger the transition and a function to create a new event that will be emitted. For this example, I limited the metadata model to the bare essentials, but there is plenty of room for more flexibility. For example, the filter would typically support additional options, such as multiple event types, a function to perform arbitrary filtering against any content in the trigger event and/or a join count. As each mediator is its own bounded isolated component, the metadata model only needs to be as sophisticated as the requirements warrant.

```
const transitions = [
  { // transition order-submitted to make-reservation
    filter: 'order-submitted',
    emit: (uow) => ({ // translate
      id: uuid.v1(),
      type: 'make-reservation',
      timestamp: Date.now(),
      partitionKey: uow.event.order.id,
      reservation: {
        sku: uow.event.order.sku,
        quantity: uow.event.order.quantity,
      },
      context: {
        order: uow.event.order,
        trigger: uow.event.id
```

```
        }
      })
  },
  { // transition reservation-confirmed to make-payment
    filter: 'reservation-confirmed',
    emit: (uow) => ({ // translate
      id: uuid.v1(),
      type: 'make-payment',
      timestamp: Date.now(),
      partitionKey: uow.event.context.order.id,
      payment: {
        token: uow.event.context.order.token,
        amount: uow.event.context.order.amount,
      },
      context: {
        order: uow.event.context.order,
        reservation: uow.event.reservation,
        trigger: uow.event.id
      }
    })
  },
  { // transition payment-confirmed to send-confirmation
    filter: 'payment-confirmed',
    emit: (uow) => ({ // translate
      id: uuid.v1(),
      type: 'send-confirmation',
      timestamp: Date.now(),
      partitionKey: uow.event.context.order.id,
      message: {
        to: uow.event.context.order.submitter,
        from: process.env.FROM_ADDRESS,
        body: `Order: ${uow.event.context.order.id} is Confirmed`
      },
      context: {
        order: uow.event.context.order,
        reservation: uow.event.context.reservation,
        payment: uow.event.payment,
        trigger: uow.event.id
      }
    })
  },
];
```

For the most part, the emit functions are self-explanatory. Each event must have an ID, a type, and a timestamp. The partition key will ensure that all the events for a specific order ID will be processed through the same stream shard in the order received. Each event contains the information necessary to perform the desired command, as defined by the specific event type, such as the reservation, payment, and message information. The one piece that is not necessarily obvious is the context element in each event type. Each collaborator component is completely decoupled from the other collaborators and the mediator component as well. However, this doesn't mean that the collaborators do not have a responsibility to convey contextual information about the overall process. Each collaborator simply needs to retain the opaque context information from the trigger event and adorn it to the output event that it eventually produces. This information is used downstream to create the input events for additional steps and correlates the various steps.

As intended, the mediator component is essentially a dumb pipe that delegates the business logic of each step to the collaborator components. It is only responsible for the transition logic. It is interesting to point out the power of this transition logic. For example, if the business requirement changed, such that payment is required prior to reservation, then these steps could easily be flipped in the metadata, without changes to the collaborators. New steps could be inserted into the process as well, with just a metadata change.

Arbitrarily complex process flows can be created by assembling different components. Smart components can also play a role in the transition logic. In this example, the mediator component only determines at which step to make a reservation and produces the necessary event. However, because the transition is published as an event, multiple collaborator components could consume the event and determine whether or not it is applicable. For example, there could be multiple reservation components, which handle different product types and only react to orders with those product types. The point being that a very flexible solution can be implemented with event orchestration.

Saga

Trigger compensating transactions to undo changes in a multi-step flow when business rules are violated downstream.

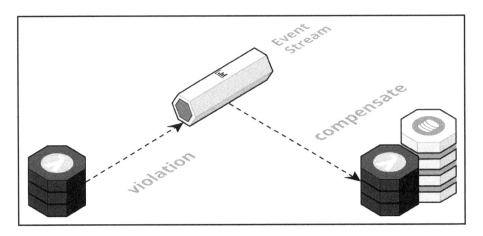

Context, problem, and forces

You are building a reactive, cloud-native system that is composed of bounded isolated components. You employ the Cloud Native Databases Per Component and Event Streaming patterns as the backbone of the system. You atomically produce events based on the Database-First variant of the Event Sourcing pattern and you leverage the CQRS pattern to isolate components from upstream failures and make them responsive, resilient, and elastic. You implement business processes based on the Event Collaboration and/or Event Orchestration patterns. The Data Lake pattern provides a system-wide audit trail of all events emitted by the system and, following the Stream Circuit Breaker pattern, your stream processors properly handle technical failures.

The Event Collaboration and Event Orchestration patterns provide the ability to leverage asynchronous inter-component communication to create arbitrarily long logic flows across many components and over long periods of time, while maintaining the responsiveness, resilience, and elasticity of the system. Even for complex flows the happy path is relatively straightforward to implement. The crux of the problem arrives when the flow encounters a business rule violation and must be abandoned and the system returned to the proper state.

Traditionally, a saga solves the problem of long-running transactions that lock too many resources for too long and therefore block other transactions from proceeding. As a result, the overall throughput of the system suffers. Their solution was to break a long-running transaction down into a series of short transactions and compensate for all preceding transactions when a later transaction fails. This solution still applies today, except that the context of the problem has changed dramatically.

In today's context, we have a distributed cloud-native system composed of bounded isolated components. Each component has its own databases and each database may be of a different type. As a matter of course, modern databases favor the BASE model for distributed transactions: Basically Available, Soft state, Eventually consistent. Modern database and messaging technologies have abandoned two-phase commit (2PC) distributed transactions. 2PC does not scale globally without unrealistic infrastructure costs, whereas eventual consistency scales horizontally to support systems of all scales. As a result, we must leverage the Event Sourcing pattern to atomically change the state of a component and produce an event reflecting that state change. Chaining these atomic units produces eventual consistency.

Eventual consistency allows for reduced contention and increased throughput because resources are not locked over the course of these logical transactions. This means that different logical transactions can potentially interlace and update the same resources. Therefore, we cannot simply rollback the state of a resource to the state before a specific logical transaction started. We must take into account all the additional updates that have been layered on top of the updates of the specific logical transaction that must be reversed. With this in mind, we need to maintain an audit trail of the series of updates that have interlaced to bring a resource to its current state. Reversing the effects of a specific update should be accomplished by another properly calculated update that is also accounted for in the audit trail. As always these updates must be idempotent. In some cases, delegating the reversal of a transaction to a manual activity may be perfectly legitimate.

Solution

Use compensating transactions to undo changes in a multi-step business process. Upstream components will publish domain events as they complete their steps to move a business process forward. A downstream component will publish an appropriate violation event when its business rules are violated to inform the upstream components that the process cannot proceed forward to completion. The upstream components react to the violation event by performing compensating transactions to undo the changes of the previous steps in the collaboration. The upstream components will, in turn, produce their own domain events to indicate the reversal has occurred, which may in turn trigger additional compensations. This cycle will continue until the system is eventually consistent.

Resulting context

The primary benefit of this solution is that it simply continues the theme of leveraging events to build the control flows of the system. Business violations are signaled as additional events and the compensations are the reactions to these specific events. All the same patterns and mechanisms are used to implement the compensation logic as a set of atomic actions, which in turn produce events per usual. No new techniques or tools must be learned or acquired. Only the context of each compensation must be understood.

As the context of each compensation is different, this solution does not try to force fit a generic solution where none exists. The industry has abandoned distributed two-phase-commit transactions because they do not scale. The use of polyglot persistence means that there are many different types of resources to account for. Plus, these resources are spread across and encapsulated within bounded isolated components. As such, each component has its own specific application logic, which must be accounted for in a compensation transaction. Thus, this solution embraces the design philosophy of dumb pipes with smart endpoints.

The Event Sourcing pattern is a prerequisite for the Saga pattern. Each step in a business process must be individually transactional. When the state of a component changes, it must publish a domain event to notify collaborators. This requirement is certainly not specific to this pattern. It is a prerequisite for eventual consistency in general. For a multi-step process, it is important to clarify that the transactionality of the overall process is predicated on the transactionality of the individual steps, including the compensating steps. A component can employ the Event-First variant or the Database-First variant of the Event Sourcing pattern to ensure that a step is transactional. Note that an individual step can be arbitrarily complex. A collaborator step could encompass several internal events, as it flows through its own polyglot persistence, before publishing the outcome of the step. A step could be a Worker BFF that is not complete until a user action is performed. A step could even trigger another event orchestration, which acts as a subordinate process.

Compensation is not equal to a rollback. The intent is not to erase the existence of the execution of a previous step. In fact, we want to have an audit trail that the step was completed and later reversed. In some domains, such as public accounting, this is a requirement. Public accounting is an apt analogy for compensating transactions because an accounting journal is maintained, adjustment entries are created as needed, and nothing is ever erased. The data lake will maintain an audit of all the events, but it is important for a component to reflect the proper history as well. Compensation is also important to keep in mind, with regard to eventual consistency, where the data in a previous step may have been subsequently updated by another activity. This intertwining of activities means that the subsequent change must be accounted for when performing the compensation. It is typically preferable to guard against these scenarios in the design, such as disallowing other changes when an object is in a specific status, but this may not always be realistic. Therefore, it is important to take this into consideration when designing the compensation for a specific step.

The processing order may or may not be important to a specific flow and therefore could be a useful tool. For example, some steps may be more likely to fail than others. If a step is more likely to fail and can be performed before other steps, then moving the step earlier in the flow could reduce the need to perform certain compensations. This could be the case for a set of steps that can logically be performed in parallel, but for technical reasons, we serialize a step ahead of the others. It may be advantageous to divide a step in two, such that a preliminary execution is performed before other steps to test the business rules and then a final execution is performed after the other steps to actually execute the change. The final execution would still test the business rules and may still fail, but the probability of the failure is reduced. Credit card processing is a typical example, where an authorization is performed up front. The order may or may not be important during the compensation phase as well. Sometimes the reversals must happen in the exact opposite order as they were originally executed and sometimes all compensations can be performed in parallel. Compensations are also eventually consistent, so these same ordering techniques may be applied as well.

It is important to distinguish between business rule violations and error handling. The Stream Circuit Breaker pattern is responsible for error handling, while the Saga pattern is responsible for business rule violations. In essence, the objective of the Stream Circuit Breaker pattern is to keep events flowing forward, versus the objective of the Saga pattern, which is focused on reversing the effects of previous events. These patterns need to work together. Violation events are handled by stream processors, just like any other event. Their execution is subject to the same transient errors, as well as code defects. When compensation experiences an error, we want to keep the compensation logic moving. We do not want to hold up compensations in other components just because another component is in error. The other compensations should complete and let the failing component eventually be corrected. This also highlights that compensation logic should be idempotent, like any other, such that retries and replays do not overcompensate.

Example – order collaboration with compensation

This example, as depicted in the following diagram, demonstrates using the Saga pattern in conjunction with the Event Collaboration pattern to compensate for the interactions of multiple components when a business violation occurs. The example builds on the example presented in the Event Collaboration pattern. The components are assembled to implement a business process for ordering a product that must be reserved in advance, such as a ticket to a play or an airline reservation. The customer completes and submits the order, and then the reservation must be confirmed, followed by charging the customer's credit card, and finally sending an email confirmation to the customer. However, in this example, the credit card charge is denied and the previous steps must be undone. The reservation and the order need to be canceled.

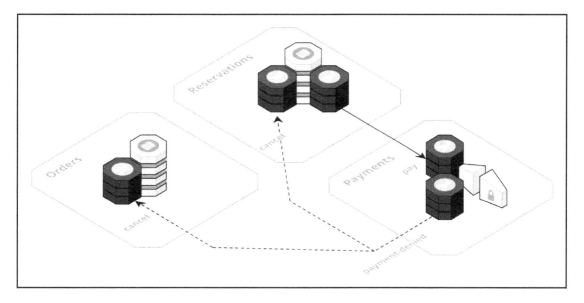

To highlight the compensation activity, the diagram depicts the flow starting with the triggering of the payment step after the reservation step. The dashed arrows represent the compensation flows, whereas the solid arrows are the normal flow. The **Payments** component is implemented following the External Service Gateway pattern. A webhook is registered to consume events from the external service. The component publishes a payment-denied event when it is notified by the external system that the charge was unsuccessfully processed.

In this specific example, it is assumed that all steps can be compensated in parallel. The payment-denied event has been published and all interested components will react to this single event. Both the **Orders** and **Reservations** components implement a stream processor that consumes the payment-denied event. The **Reservations** component removes the reservation and the **Orders** component sets the status of the order to canceled. The payment-denied event contains the context information, which identifies the specific reservation and order that must be updated. Although not depicted, the **Reservations** component will publish a reservation-canceled event and the **Orders** component will emit an order-canceled event.

As an alternative compensation flow, if the reservation needed to be canceled before the order, then the **Orders** component would consume the reservation-canceled event, instead of the payment-denied event. This highlights that the components are coupled based on the event types when using the Event Collaboration pattern. This simple variation in the flow requires a change to the **Orders** component. This is not the case in the next example that is based on the Event Orchestration pattern.

Example – order orchestration with compensation

This example, as depicted in the following diagram, demonstrates using the Saga pattern in conjunction with the Event Orchestration pattern to compensate for the interactions of multiple components when a business violation occurs. The example builds on the example presented in the Event Orchestration pattern. The **Mediator** component conducts a business process for ordering a product that must be reserved and paid for in advance. However, in this example, the credit card charge is denied and the previous steps must be undone. The reservation and the order need to be canceled.

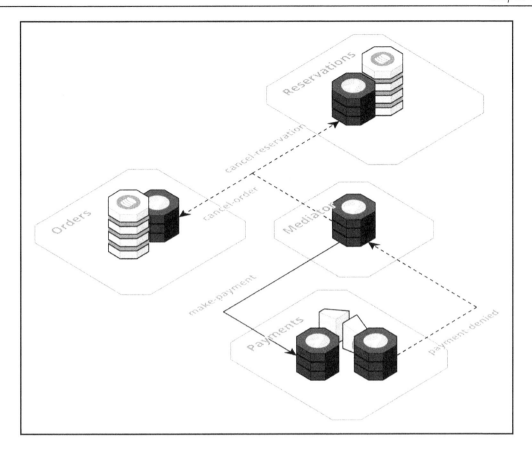

Once again, to highlight the compensation activity, the diagram depicts the flow starting with the triggering of the payment step after the reservation step. The dashed arrows represent the compensation flows, while the solid arrows are the normal flow. The **Payments** component is implemented following the External Service Gateway pattern. A webhook is registered to consume events from the external service. The component publishes a payment-denied event when it is notified by the external system that the charge was unsuccessfully processed.

In this specific version of the example, it is assumed that all steps can be compensated in parallel. The **Mediator** component consumes the payment-denied event and in turn emits two events: the cancel-reservation event and the cancel-order event. Both the **Reservations** and **Orders** components implement a stream processor that consumes their respective event. The **Reservations** component removes the reservation and the **Orders** component sets the status of the order to canceled. The following code fragment contains the two additional transitions that would be added to the **Mediator** component implemented in the Event Orchestration pattern example. Both transitions react to the payment-denied event. One emits the cancel-reservation event and the other emits the cancel-order event.

```
const transitions = [
  ...
  {
    filter: 'payment-denied',
    emit: (uow) => ({
      id: uuid.v1(),
      type: 'cancel-reservation',
      timestamp: Date.now(),
      partitionKey: uow.event.context.order.id,
      reservation: {
        id: uow.event.context.reservation.id,
      },
      context: {
        order: uow.event.context.order,
        reservation: uow.event.context.reservation,
        payment: uow.event.payment,
        trigger: uow.event.id
      }
    })
  },
  {
    filter: 'payment-denied',
    emit: (uow) => ({
      id: uuid.v1(),
      type: 'cancel-order',
      timestamp: Date.now(),
      partitionKey: uow.event.context.order.id,
      order: {
        id: uow.event.context.order.id,
      },
      context: {
        order: uow.event.context.order,
        reservation: uow.event.context.reservation,
        payment: uow.event.payment,
        trigger: uow.event.id
      }
    })
```

```
    },
  ];
```

The following diagram depicts an alternative flow where the compensation steps need to be performed sequentially. As the reservation needs to be canceled before the order, the **Mediator** only emits the cancel-reservation event in reaction to the payment-denied event. Next, it reacts to the reservation-canceled event and then emits the cancel-order event.

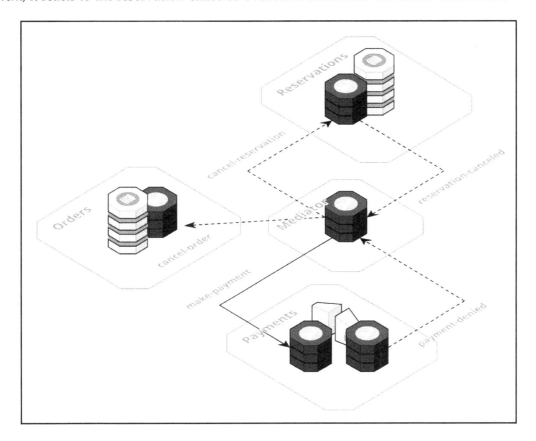

The following code fragment highlights the minor change that is needed to affect this alternate flow. The filter for the cancel-order event just needs to be changed from payment-denied to reservation-canceled. This demonstrates a major advantage of the Event Orchestration pattern over the raw Event Collaboration pattern.

```
const transitions = [
  ...
  {
    filter: 'payment-denied',
    emit: (uow) => ({
```

```
          id: uuid.v1(),
          type: 'cancel-reservation',
          timestamp: Date.now(),
          partitionKey: uow.event.context.order.id,
          reservation: {
            id: uow.event.context.reservation.id,
          },
          context: {
            order: uow.event.context.order,
            reservation: uow.event.context.reservation,
            payment: uow.event.payment,
            trigger: uow.event.id
          }
        })
    },
    {
      filter: 'reservation-canceled', // modified filter
      emit: (uow) => ({
        id: uuid.v1(),
        type: 'cancel-order',
        timestamp: Date.now(),
        partitionKey: uow.event.context.order.id,
        order: {
          id: uow.event.context.order.id,
        },
        context: {
          order: uow.event.context.order,
          reservation: uow.event.context.reservation,
          payment: uow.event.payment,
          trigger: uow.event.id
        }
      })
    },
  ];
```

Both the Event Collaboration and the Event Orchestration patterns, along with the Saga pattern, work well to create powerful control flows. Event Collaboration works best for simple scenarios and is a great approach to start uncovering system requirements without additional components. As the system evolves and scenarios become more complex, the Event Orchestration pattern results in the least coupling and the most flexibility.

Summary

In this chapter, we discussed the control patterns of reactive, cloud-native systems. The Event Collaboration pattern replaces synchronous communication with asynchronous domain events, which successively trigger commands in downstream components, to resiliently choreograph long-running collaborations between boundary components. In the Event Orchestration pattern, we improve on the Event Collaboration pattern by creating mediator components to orchestrate the collaboration between decoupled boundary components. Finally, in the Saga pattern, we provide a long-running transaction mechanism based on compensation to undo the successive steps in these collaborations when later steps encounter business rule violations.

6
Deployment

In `Chapter 1`, *Understanding Cloud Native Concepts*, we discussed the promise of cloud-native and the cloud-native concepts that help deliver on those promises. Cloud-native enables companies to rapidly and continuously deliver innovation with the confidence that the system will stay stable despite the rate of change and scale to meet demand. Then we took a deep dive into the architectural aspects of cloud-native systems, starting with the anatomy of cloud-native systems and continuing through the foundation, boundary, and control patterns. We focused heavily on how to create bounded, isolated components that are responsive, resilient, elastic, and message-driven.

Now we turn our attention to the human factors of cloud-native. We will delve into the best practices and methods that empower self-sufficient, full-stack teams, drive cultural change, and comprise the cloud-native product delivery pipeline. We will continuously deploy, test, monitor, and secure our bounded isolated components and disposable infrastructure.

In this chapter, we will shift deployments all the way to the left to help enable teams to continuously deploy changes to production and continuously deliver innovation to customers with confidence. We will cover the following topics:

- Decoupling deployment from release
- Multi-level roadmaps
- Task branch workflow
- Modern deployment pipelines
- Zero-downtime deployment
- Multi-regional deployment
- Feature flags
- Versioning
- Trilateral API per containers

Decoupling deployment from release

Let's start this chapter by posing three questions:

1. Did you notice that the *Deployment* chapter is before the *Testing* chapter?
2. Do you find the typical definitions of continuous delivery versus continuous deployment unsatisfying?
3. How can a company possibly perform multiple deployments each day and still have any confidence that the system will continue to function properly?

I placed the *Deployment* chapter before the *Testing* chapter to emphasize the fact that we are shifting the activity of deployment all the way to the left on the life cycle timeline of any given bounded isolated component. In fact, I advocate deploying a new component all the way into production on the very first day of its development. This first deployment is just a boilerplate stub created from a well-crafted template or it may even be just an empty stack. Regardless, the goal of this first task is to get the plumbing of the deployment pipeline up and running as the first order of business.

We are shifting testing all the way to the left as well. As we will cover thoroughly, testing is no longer a phase, but an integral part of the deployment pipeline. This initial deployment is tested. The stub generated from the template would certainly have generated test code. But even if this first deployment only created an empty stack, its successful deployment is the first test run of the deployment pipeline.

If you spend some time looking at job postings, you will see the terms continuous delivery and continuous deployment used seemingly interchangeably. If you search the web for their definitions, you will find a lot of contradictions, and you may notice that many postings on the topic are either dated or still based on monolithic thinking. My colleague, Steve Andrews, is adamant when he points out that customers simply do not care how often you deploy your software; they only care how timely you deliver the capabilities they require. Keep your customers in mind as I describe our cloud-native product delivery pipeline, as our context has evolved.

In the first chapter, we discussed the promise of cloud-native: to rapidly and continuously deliver innovation to customers with confidence. We need to perform timely experiments to determine what our customers really want out of our products. To perform these experiments, we need to make changes to the product, but we must ensure that the changes do not break proven features. We discussed how cloud-native concepts deliver on the promise. Disposable infrastructure and bounded isolated components increase both the quality and the pace of change while ensuring that we have proper bulkheads in place when an honest mistake is made. When we hit the jackpot on customer requirements, the system will scale globally. Embracing disposable architecture, leveraging value-added cloud services, and welcoming polyglot cloud enables self-sufficient, full-stack teams to focus on the experiments required to determine the right value proposition for the customer. All of this ultimately drives the cultural change that is needed to deliver on the promise.

Cloud-native concepts essentially align along two parallel threads: technical factors and human factors. Typical definitions of continuous delivery versus continuous deployment treat the two as a continuum. With cloud-native, we treat the two as interrelated parallel threads by decoupling deployment from release. A deployment is just the technical act of deploying a change to a component, whereas a release is a human act of delivering (that is, enabling) a capability for the customer. The two work in tandem. One is not an evolution of the other. We will now discuss using multi-level roadmaps to continuously deliver innovation to customers and continuously deploy changes to production.

This is how companies perform multiple deployments each day with confidence. A deployment is not a large monolithic activity. Each deployment is a small, focused, and controlled change to a single bounded isolated component that is performed by a self-sufficient, full-stack team. In this chapter, we will discuss how the process is governed by a task branch workflow and implemented as a modern deployment pipeline. Testing is not a separate phase in the development life cycle. In Chapter 7, *Testing*, we will discuss the modern testing techniques that act as an integral part of the pipeline. Operating the production environment is not a passive activity. In Chapter 8, *Monitoring*, we will show how deploying small changes and continuously testing in production allow us to focus on the mean time to recovery. A release is a marketing event, not a technical activity. We will leverage feature flags to perform dark launches whereby we enable targeted groups of users to participate in the experiments and provide valuable feedback regarding new features.

Multi-level roadmaps

We will be performing deployments much more frequently, but we do not perform deployments for the sake of performing deployments. Smaller batch sizes actually increase our confidence in any specific deployment. However, we must be very deliberate about each deployment. For example, the order in which related changes are deployed to multiple components may be very important. Therefore, fine-grained deployment roadmaps are a necessity, but these are activities directed towards a higher goal.

Release roadmaps

We are building or changing a system for a specific purpose. There is a product vision that we are trying to achieve. This vision is sliced into a series of experiments that teams will perform by implementing just enough of the vision to elicit the end user feedback needed to validate the hypothesis of the value proposition. These slices form a coarse-grained roadmap. The results of each experiment will drive the recalibration of the roadmap. Using another ship metaphor, we are charting a course for a destination, but as the winds and currents push us off course, we must perform course corrections.

The roadmap of experiments is important for several reasons. First, it means that there is a vision that is directing all the deployments. There is a goal that is guiding the contents of these tactical deployments. Next, the slices of functionality we are implementing also have a focused batch size. A controlled batch size once again helps increase our confidence in the correctness of what we are implementing and deploying. We can touch on the topic of correctness from several different perspectives. For example, we are performing experiments to arrive at the correct product. But within a specific experiment, we establish a focused set of assumptions that we want the end user to evaluate. Correctness from the perspective of an individual deployment is laser focused on whether or not we think the deployment will break existing functionality. The limited scope of an experiment or a deployment helps us reason about the correctness. Finally, individual teams will be crafting the deployment roadmaps just in time as we progress towards the vision. There is no need for an elaborate upfront deployment roadmap, as it will likely change.

Agile development methodology is not the focus of this course or even this chapter. There are plenty of great sources of information about Lean Thinking and the Kanban method. My goal here is threefold. First, I want to make it clear that the combination of Lean and Kanban is the right match for our cloud-native product delivery pipeline. Do not bother trying to use the structured cadence of sprints with cloud-native. There is a fundamental impedance mismatch between sprints and the frequency of cloud-native deployments. I will point out some analogs that do work. Second, I need to cover just enough methodology to put our cloud-native product delivery pipeline in context to get self-sufficient, full-stack teams out of the starting gate.

Finally, I think it is probably clear that this is where all the cultural change lies. Lean experiments and continuous deployment form a two-way street. From a grassroots level, I find that most teams are eager to start using these deployment techniques. But top-down buy-in on delivering functionality as a series of experiments tends to be a longer road. In Chapter 1, *Understanding Cloud Native Concepts*, I discussed how cloud-native drives this cultural change by first establishing trust from the bottom up. In Chapter 10, *Value Focused Migration*, we will discuss how to incrementally make the move to cloud-native. The first step is acknowledging the gap. User story mapping is a way to start to bridge that gap.

Story mapping

Story Mapping (http://jpattonassociates.com/wp-content/uploads/2015/03/story_mapping.pdf) is a technique I find useful for slicing a product vision into a series of experiments that can be incrementally released to specific groups of users. As the following diagram depicts, it is a visualization technique to help tell a story about how different users (blue cards) do something to reach a specific goal. It is important to have a user focus because we will be using feature flags to enable features for specific user groups. Thus, the user needs to be a fundamental delimiter in the roadmap. User tasks (green and yellow cards) are organized from left to right in the order you would describe the user tasks to someone else. User tasks are organized from top to bottom based on priority.

This is where we create our slices (grey arrows). The smallest number of tasks that enable a specific user type to accomplish a goal is a viable release to perform an experiment.

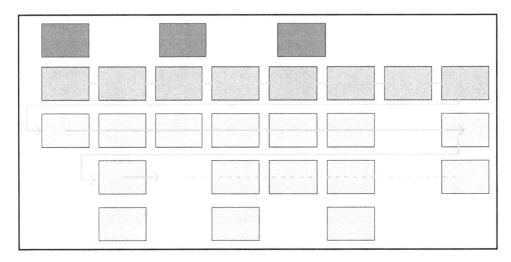

The first slice should be the walking skeleton (green cards). I mentioned earlier that I would point out analogs to scrum sprints that we can apply to Lean and Kanban. Milestones are one such analog. Obviously, a release (that is, a slice) is a milestone and the walking skeleton should be the first major internal milestone. Completing and validating the walking skeleton across the various user types is a major achievement. The backbone of the system is in production and access is flipped on for internal users to preview the release and provide initial feedback.

This first experiment sets the stage for everything that follows. From here, individual teams can perform experiments independently for different user types. It is interesting to point out that our cloud-native architecture facilitates these independent experiments. For example, a team can build a component in one experiment that sends events downstream to a component that may be built in a later experiment. The current component can still function properly for the experiment without the presence of the other component. When we do implement the other slice, we can replay the previous events from the data lake to seed the new component.

Deployment roadmaps

Within a slice, self-sufficient, full-stack teams will implement the specific user tasks. Each user task is a card (aka story) on the Kanban backlog. A single team owns a cloud-native bounded isolated component. That component may be a backend for frontend, and the full-stack team owns the frontend as well. As such, it is not unusual for a single team to own the majority of the stories in an experiment, particularly since upstream and downstream components can be implemented in separate experiments. The stories in our cloud-native product delivery pipeline tend to be much more coarse-grained than in typical scrum practices. A story covers the full-stack and a team will implement the full-stack concurrently. This is where we divide a story into individual tasks that define our individual deployment units of work.

When a team pulls a story in off the backlog, the first order of business is to divide the story up into the individual tasks that define the deployment roadmap. This activity is akin to a sprint planning session. It is not unusual, particularly in the early stages, for our coarse-grained stories across the full-stack to resemble a typical sprint duration. Instead of creating fine-grained stories, we are defining each individual task to be a small focused unit of deployable work that takes preferably less than a day to implement and test, but certainly no more than two days. It can be useful to think of a cloud-native story as a mini sprint. The story planning session would include all the typical three amigos activities. The completion of each story is another important milestone. When a story is done, there should be a demo; only the demo is performed in production, the feature being flipped on for the participants. When all the stories in a slice are done, we release the experiment to a controlled set of users. If you are screaming heresy, that's fine—just soldier on.

Task branch workflow

When discussing the topic of continuous deployment, it is understandable that you might conjure up the image of every single commit by every developer being automatically deployed to production. It is natural to find this concerning because there are too many human factors involved that can send this awry. There is also the notion that there are no manual gates, but this isn't really true either. What is true is that we want to make small and controlled changes that are automatically deployed to production. This is because it is much easier to reason about the correctness of small changes and it is much easier to diagnose a problem in production when it could only be the result of a small change.

To facilitate these small deployment units, we must decouple deployment from release and treat the two as separate, continuous threads working in tandem. We define a release roadmap that consists of a series of experiments that implement thin slices of functionality in an effort to validate the value proposition for a specific user base. Each slice is made up of a set of user stories. As a team pulls in a story, they decompose the story into an ordered set of tasks that constitutes the deployment roadmap for the specific story.

Each task is a self-contained unit of work that will ultimately be deployed to production. This unit of work includes coding the functionality, coding the tests, performing code review, executing the tests, testing the deployment, deploying to production, and asserting the stability of the system. To this end, we need a mechanism to govern this process. Our mechanism of choice is the Git Pull/Merge request. GitHub and others use the term Pull request because the first step is to pull code from a branch. GitLab uses the term Merge request because the last step is to merge the change into a target branch. The two are the same and the terms can be used interchangeably.

If you are still working on a monolithic system, it is likely that you are still using Subversion and doing trunk-based development. When making the transition from monolithic to cloud-native, it is critical to make the switch from Subversion to Git as well. Trunk-based development relies totally on the developer doing the right thing to not break the build, but we are all human and we make honest mistakes. Therefore, trunk-based development does not provide the stability we need.

In Git, a workflow defines a branching strategy. There are many different workflow strategies. For cloud-native, we want a very simple and straightforward workflow. We want very short-lived branches. The classic reason for short-lived branches is to avoid merge conflicts by performing continuous integration. We want this as well, but we also want to limit the batch size of our deployments. By limiting the scope of a branch to a small atomic unit of preferably less than a day of development, we can better accomplish both these goals.

The name task branch workflow implies a short-lived branch that is focused on a specific task. Issue branch workflow is another name that is often used for the same goal. Its name is derived from the idea that a branch is created for each issue in an issue-tracking system. With a task branch workflow, we will also create a branch per ticket (that is, issue) in the tracking system. However, not all tickets are created equal. A ticket might represent a task, story, feature, bug, or even an epic. The name task branch workflow, therefore, implies that we are creating branches only for issues that represent a task within a specific user story.

So how does it work? For starters, each deployable component lives in its own Git repository. Therefore, each task in the deployment roadmap will be focused on a single component in a separate repository. A developer creates a new branch and a pull request. It is best to create the pull request upfront as the pull request is where the code review will be performed. Starting the pull request immediately allows discussion to begin with the first push. The developer will implement the code for the functionality and the tests on the branch.

We will discuss testing in depth in the next chapter, `Chapter 7`, *Testing*. For now, it is important to understand that testing is not a phase and it is not a job title. Testing is an integral part of each task and it is a team effort. A task includes unit testing, integration testing, static analysis, code coverage, and so forth. This is always where I hear cries of heresy. How is it possible to do all this in a single task? The shortest answer is focus. We make each task very focused.

One tenet of the Kanban method is to eliminate waste. This essentially means do not write any code until you need it. But we find ourselves writing code all the time just because we might need it and we might as well get it in now. But this is monolithic thinking driven by coarse-grained deployments. Instead, we are deploying all the time. There will be ample opportunity to add code and deploy when we need it. When we do write code, we have to test it—all of it. Therefore, a focused task will have all the flavors of testing, but only a little of each because we only wrote a little bit of code that needs to be tested. The test suite will accumulate with each additional task.

When the developer is ready, the code is pushed to the origin repository. At this point, the code is automatically tested by the pipeline, as we will discuss shortly. The component will also be deployed to the staging environment to assert the correctness of the deployment. The code is also ready for code review in the pull request. Note that the code review is also quicker because less code is written in a focused task. Once everything is in order, the pull request can be manually approved, which will merge the code into the master branch and trigger the pipeline to deploy the component to production. Once the component is successfully deployed to production, the team will confirm that the continuous tests executing in production are all green and move on to the next task. These continuous tests are known as synthetic transaction monitoring, which we will cover in `Chapter 8`, *Monitoring*.

Another key governing aspect of the pull request is the timing of the manual approval. A task is specific to a deployment unit, such as a backend for a frontend component or the frontend itself. A single team will own both of these repositories and will likely work on related tasks for each in parallel. However, to ensure zero downtime, it will usually be necessary to deploy each unit in the specific order as the team noted in the deployment roadmap. Therefore, even when a pull request is ready to go, the team may hold off until another pull request is approved and deployed first. We will enumerate some scenarios in the *Versioning* section. A team may also hold off because it is late and it is best to wait until morning or wait until later in the day when system usage is lower. The point is that this manual gate is an important control tool.

Deployment pipeline

The deployment pipeline is governed by a Git pull request in the context of a task branch workflow. The short-lived branch helps control the batch size of the deployment; the focused change is tested, reviewed, and manually approved, and the deployments are fully automated. The pipeline is orchestrated by multiple tools. A modern CI/CD tool controls the overall flow, **node package manager** (**npm**) controls the individual steps, the cloud provider's infrastructure-as-code service provisions the cloud resources, and the Serverless Framework provides an important abstraction layer for the infrastructure-as-code service.

Modern CI/CD

The latest generation of continuous integration and deployment tools provides a much more simplified model than traditional tools. Configuration is streamlined, they are fully managed, and they are seamlessly integrated with hosted Git services. These tools include the likes of TravisCI, CircleCI, GitLabCI, and Bitbucket Pipelines.

Traditional tools have struggled to evolve from their continuous integration roots to meet the complex needs of modern pipelines. There is a tendency to leverage a shared infrastructure model, which impedes team independence. Too much coding is performed in the CI tool that cannot be shared and executed outside the tool.

With modern tools, a pipeline is defined in and versioned with each specific project. There is no need to work outside of a project to configure its pipeline. The configuration of a pipeline is declarative, and fine-grained details are delegated to external scripts, which can also be executed independently. The presence of the configuration YAML file in the root of a project will automatically trigger the pipeline at the specified points in the Git workflow. The outcomes of each pipeline instance are reported back to the pull request to enforce checks and balances.

The following is an example of a `.gitlab-ci.yml` configuration file. The presence of the file in a project's root folder enables the pipeline. The first line of the file specifies the Docker image that is used to execute the pipeline jobs. This pipeline defines three jobs: `test`, `staging-east`, and `production-east`. The test job is not associated with any specific branches, thus it will execute on all branches. This job effectively fulfills our need for traditional continuous integration. Every push to a branch will trigger the `test` job. This includes all task branches and the master branch. The job executes the unit tests, which includes lint and code coverage, followed by the transitive integration tests. We will cover testing in detail in `Chapter 7`, *Testing*.

```
image: node:6     # docker image

before_script:
  - npm install    # all dependencies

stages:
  - test
  - deploy

# continuous integration testing on all branches including master
# on all pushes and accepted pull requests
test:
  stage: test
  script:    # delegate to external scripts
    - npm test
    - npm run test:int

# deploy to staging when a task branch is tagged for deployment
staging-east:
  stage: deploy
  variables:
    AWS_ACCESS_KEY_ID: $STG_AWS_ACCESS_KEY_ID    # secure variables
    AWS_SECRET_ACCESS_KEY: $STG_AWS_SECRET_ACCESS_KEY
  script:
    - npm run dp:stg:e
  only:
    - tags
```

```
    except:
      - master

  # deploy to production when a pull request is accepted
  production-east:
    stage: deploy
    variables:
      AWS_ACCESS_KEY_ID: $PROD_AWS_ACCESS_KEY_ID
      AWS_SECRET_ACCESS_KEY: $PROD_AWS_SECRET_ACCESS_KEY
    script:
      - npm run dp:prd:e
    only:
      - master
```

The `staging-east` job will execute on all branches except for `master` (that is, task branches), so long as the branch has been tagged. It is good practice to push code early and often to elicit feedback in the pull request as soon as possible. However, the early pushes may not be ready for deployment to the staging environment. Therefore, to trigger a deployment, a tag, such as `deploy`, should be applied to the specific branch. This will test whether all the deployment scripts are working properly. The staging environment will also have synthetic transaction tests continuously executing to smoke test the system. We will cover continuous production testing in `Chapter 8`, *Monitoring*. Manual exploratory testing can be performed in the staging environment before a pull request is accepted if the specific change so warrants. The pipeline definition also manages the configuration of environment variables via global and job-specific variables. Secret variables, such as access keys, are stored securely.

The `production-east` job will only execute on the master branch after a pull request has been accepted. This job is associated with the `deploy` stage. Jobs are sequenced into stages and the `test` stage is defined to execute before the `deploy` stage. Thus, the production deployment will only proceed after the tests have passed on the master branch as well. Once in production, the deployment will be scrutinized by synthetic and real transactions, and alerts will be produced by the application performance monitoring system. The team must confirm that all is well before turning their attention to the next tasks.

npm

We do not want to write scripts in the CI/CD tool. The CI/CD tool is focused on orchestrating the pipeline and should delegate to external scripts that can also be executed manually. This allows developers to test deployments from their own machine. These scripts should use the most appropriate tools as dictated by the language and frameworks used in the specific project. However, the frontend applications of cloud-native systems are typically implemented as React and/or Angular JavaScript single-page applications. Therefore, npm will already be part of the ecosystem. As we will discuss shortly, I recommend using the Serverless Framework as a layer over a cloud provider's infrastructure-as-code service, regardless of whether or not function-as-a-service is being used, and it needs to be installed by NPM. NPM can also help handle differences between Linux and Windows scripts. Thus, NPM is a good choice for executing external scripts. This also enables developers to move from project to project and use standard commands, such as `npm test`, without immediate concern for the specific tools used.

The following is an example of an NPM `package.json` configuration file. Its main purpose is to manage dependencies and execute scripts. In this example, I have included the vast majority of dependencies leveraged when implementing a component in JavaScript; it is a surprisingly small number. All the scripts used by the pipeline are included, plus additional scripts used by the developers only.

```
{
  "name": "my-project",
  "scripts": {
    "test": "mocha ./test/unit/**/*.test.js",
    "test:int": "mocha ./test/int/**/*.test.js",
    "dp:lcl": "sls deploy -v -r us-east-1 --acct dev",
    "rm:lcl": "sls remove -v -r us-east-1 --acct dev",
    "dp:stg:e": "sls deploy -v -r us-east-1 -s stg --acct dev",
    "dp:prd:e": "sls deploy -v -r us-east-1 -s prd --acct prd"
  },
  "dependencies": {
    "bluebird": "latest",
    "debug": "latest",
    "highland": "latest",
    "lodash": "latest",
    "moment": "latest",
    "uuid": "latest"
  },
  "devDependencies": {
    "aws-sdk": "latest",
    "aws-sdk-mock": "latest",
    "chai": "latest",
    "mocha": "latest",
```

```
      "serverless": "latest",
      "serverless-offline": "latest",
      "serverless-webpack": "latest",
      "sinon": "latest",
      "supertest": "latest",
      "webpack": "latest"
  }
}
```

The example test scripts use the Mocha testing tool to execute all the unit tests and integration tests defined in the project. These tests will be executed on all branches via the CI/CD tool. A detailed discussion of testing practices is covered in `Chapter 7`, *Testing*. The `dp:stg:e` and `dp:prd:e` scripts delegate to the Serverless Framework to perform the deployments, as described in the next section. These specific scripts deploy to the eastern region. We will cover multi-regional deployments shortly. All task branches are automatically deployed to the staging environment in the development account. The `master` branch will be automatically deployed to the production account. In the next section, we will see how the `--acct` command-line option is used to select account-specific variables.

A developer can execute these scripts in the same manner as the CI/CD tool. For example, a developer can run the tests locally while implementing the code and test the deployment prior to pushing the change to the remote branch. A developer can also create a personal stack for development and testing purposes without stepping on the work of other developers. The developer would then remove the stack when it is no longer needed. As an example, I will use the following commands to deploy and remove my personal local stack. The `--stage` command-line option is a qualifier that the Serverless Framework includes in the stack name to make it unique:

```
$ npm run dp:lcl -- --stage john
$ npm run rm:lcl -- --stage john
```

Infrastructure as Code services

Each cloud provider offers an Infrastructure as Code service, such as AWS CloudFormation, Azure Resource Manager, and GCP Cloud Deployment Manager. These services provide a declarative template language that is used to provision a collection of related cloud resources. This collection of resources is typically referred to as a stack.

A stack is provisioned and updated as a unit in an orderly and predictable fashion. A stack maintains state about all of its resources. Resources that have been added to a template will be created, resources that have been removed from a template will be deleted, and resources that have been changed in the template will be updated. In addition, all these actions are performed in the appropriate order as determined by their interdependencies. When a stack is deleted, all the resources in the stack are also deleted. This housekeeping controls the clutter and drift that can form in an account if these resources are managed manually.

There are many different Infrastructure as Code tools available and everyone has their favorite. The cloud provider tools have the advantage that they manage the resource state and interdependencies automatically. They also facilitate governance and auditing because the service tracks the inventory of stacks and their components. The declarative nature of the templates can become cumbersome as a template grows in size; when used to manage our monoliths, they were definitely too unwieldy. However, these services are a very good match for bounded isolated components. If a template grows too large, it is an indication that the component may have grown too large and is likely no longer bounded or isolated. That said, there is still room for improvement, and this is where the Serverless Framework shines.

Serverless Framework

The Serverless Framework is arguably the de facto standard tool for managing Function-as-a-Service projects. It embodies a set of best practices and configuration-by-exception rules that eliminate a significant amount of boilerplate scripts and configurations. For example, the following 30-line example will generate a 275-line CloudFormation template. The tool supports multiple providers, including AWS, Azure, GCP, and more.

The Serverless Framework is the best tool I have found for managing AWS CloudFormation, regardless of whether or not Function-as-a-Service is being used. One such example of its ability can be seen when deploying a React or Angular single-page application. Those projects will employ this same pipeline pattern. The `serverless.yml` file will create the S3 bucket to hold all the static files, the CloudFront CDN to serve the files, and the Route53 RecordSet to define the domain, along with any other resources that may be needed. I also create a Serverless project for every AWS account that I create. These projects enable CloudTrail, defined IAM roles, groups, and policies, grant access to the deployment pipelines and the application performance monitoring service, create the Route53 hosted zone and certificates, and any other global, account-scoped resources used throughout the cloud-native system. Each account project also defines a similar deployment pipeline. The Serverless Framework helps unify the management of all these different project types.

The following is a full `serverless.yml` file example. We have already seen many examples of `serverless.yml` file fragments throughout the patterns chapters. For completeness, this example shows a simple function leveraging the AWS API Gateway, like we have seen before. The other features are of more importance in this discussion.

```
service: my-project    # base name of the stack and component

provider:
  name: aws
  runtime: nodejs6.10

plugins:
  - serverless-offline
  - serverless-webpack

custom: # account specific variables
  dev:
    v1: 123
  prd:
    v1: 789

functions:
  get:
    handler: handler.get
    events:
      - http:
          path: items/{id}
          method: get
    environment:
      V1: ${self:custom.${opt:acct}.v1} # recursive variable
```

```
resources:
# additional resources such as dynamodb tables
```

The Serverless Framework can also be extended via plugins. For example, the `serverless-offline` plugin simulates AWS API Gateway and AWS Lambda for local testing. The `serverless-webpack` plugin leverages the power of webpack to optimize the deployment size of the JavaScript Function-as-a-Service.

The Serverless Framework provides a very nice mechanism for variable substitution. Variables can be sourced from command-line options, environment variables, files, scripts, other stacks and the YML file itself. In this example, we use the `${opt:acct}` command-line option passed in from the NPM script to index into the account-specific variables that are defined in the custom section of the `serverless.yml` file. This demonstrates the ability to recursively reference variables. If there were many account-specific variables, then they could be decomposed into separate files. The account-specific variable in turn is used to store the configuration in the environment so that it can be easily accessed by the function code.

Any additional resources, such as streams, tables, buckets, CDNs, and so forth, can be managed in the resources section. We have seen many such examples in `Chapter 3`, *Foundation Patterns* and `Chapter 4`, *Boundary Patterns*.

Zero-downtime deployment

Cloud-native systems are always on, and they follow the sun. There is never an opportune time to take the system offline to perform maintenance and deployments. We must update the system while it is running and with zero user interruptions. To achieve this, the system components must be stateless, since a component may be changed out in the middle of user sessions. A new component must also be backwards compatible because it is not possible to change out all the components at the exact same time. No matter how well we test and prepare, sooner or later a deployment will go wrong because of honest human error. It is inevitable. When a deployment does go wrong, we want to limit the blast radius and we want to recover quickly. It is preferable to roll forward with a quick fix, but we need to have the option to roll back as well. There are a variety of approaches, including blue-green deployments, canary deployments, multi-regional deployments, and feature flags, plus other various useful combinations.

Blue-green deployment

Blue-green deployment is probably the most commonly sited approach to zero-downtime deployment. The general idea is to maintain two identical infrastructure environments named blue and green. At any given point in time only one environment is live. In the following diagram, **Blue** is the live environment. A new version is deployed to the **Green** environment and smoke tested via a private endpoint. When the new deployment is deemed ready then the **Green** environment is made live by switching all traffic from **Blue** to **Green**. If anything goes wrong, then the traffic can be routed back to the blue environment. Otherwise, the **Blue** deployment is retired and the next deployment will start in the **Blue**.

Ironically, this approach works much more easily with a monolith because there are fewer moving parts. A new deployment of the entire monolith is created and swapped out. With a cloud-native system, each component is deployed independently, thus each component needs to perform a blue-green deployment. If no infrastructure is shared between components, then the process is essentially the same. However, there is a strong tendency to share a container cluster across components. In this case, there are basically two options available to achieve blue-green deployments.

One option is to perform blue-green deployments within a single cluster. Each component would maintain a blue and a green definition in the cluster and alternate between the definitions by changing the image version and switching the targeting on the load balancer. This option can be tricky, and also requires additional headroom in the cluster to accommodate upwards of twice the number of container instances until the switch is fully completed. It also puts the single cluster at risk during the deployment.

The other option is to maintain a blue cluster and a green cluster. At any point in time, some components would be live in the green cluster while the other components would be live in the blue cluster. This approach still requires additional headroom during the switch, but this involves ramping up one cluster and later ramping down the other cluster. Overall, it is much easier to reason about the correctness of this approach, and the additional cluster provides a natural bulkhead. However, there is the additional overhead of managing twice as many clusters.

The blue-green approach does not take the database directly into account, and it is also an all or nothing solution regarding routing. We will discuss improvements with canary deployments.

Canary deployment

The canary deployment approach improves on the blue-green approach by routing only a portion of users to the new version, as shown in the following diagram, to ensure it is working properly before switching over all the traffic. The name comes from the mining practice of bringing a canary into the mine because the bird is more susceptible to toxic fumes and would provide an early warning sign to the miners when the bird stopped singing.

From an infrastructure standpoint, a canary deployment looks pretty much the same as the blue-green deployment. The major difference is with the database. Both the old and the new version of the components are used simultaneously. Therefore, it is not usually feasible to have two versions of the database running concurrently and keeping them in sync, to support rolling back to the previous version if the canary test fails. The same case can be made for blue-green deployments, which assumes a conversion prior to the switch in either direction.

Database versioning and versioning in general are important enough that we will cover the topic in its own section shortly. There is still room for improving the zero-downtime deployment approach and account for regional failover as well.

Multi-regional deployment

A major cloud-native theme that I repeat over and over is putting proper bulkheads in place to guard against inevitable failures and control the blast radius. In `Chapter 2`, *The Anatomy of Cloud Native Systems*, we discussed how cloud regions provide a natural and necessary bulkhead, as regional failures are inevitable. The following diagram depicts how running a multi-regional deployment intrinsically requires redundant infrastructure, replicates data between the regions, routes subsets of traffic to each region, and provides failover when a region is not operating properly. These are all the ingredients needed to perform zero-downtime deployment, as highlighted for blue-green and canary deployments. This is a great opportunity to fill two needs with one fell swoop.

With the multi-regional deployment approach, we stagger the deployment of the new version to each region after confirming the deployment in the previous region. If anything goes seriously wrong with the deployment to a region, then its traffic will failover to the nearest region. If there was a less significant problem with the deployment in a region, then the users of that region would be impacted until the deployment was either rolled forward or rolled back. To compensate for this, we could have the regional deployments follow the moon, so to speak, so that fewer users are actively using the system in a specific region. With synthetic transition monitoring in place, as we will discuss in `Chapter 8`, *Monitoring*, this continuous smoke testing would assert the success of the regional deployment.

To implement regional deployment, we simply add an NPM script and a CI job for each region. The regional deployment jobs could be triggered when a region-specific tag is applied to the master branch. Another approach is to have regional branches off the master branch and use a pull request to merge the master branch into each regional branch to trigger the regional jobs. There may be variations on these two options that suite a team's specific needs.

Value-added cloud services, such as cloud-native databases, Function-as-a-Service, and API Gateway services make multi-regional deployments both economical and much more manageable. Cloud-native database support for regional replication is becoming more and more turnkey. Function-as-a-Service and API Gateway services support versioning to facilitate rollback and incur no additional cost when deployed to multiple regions. The Serverless Framework and Infrastructure as Code services are already geared towards multi-regional deployment.

Probably the most important aspect of zero-downtime deployments is the batch size of the specific change. By decoupling deployment from release and leveraging a task branch workflow, we are significantly reducing the risk of each deployment. If a team's confidence level is still low, then this may be an indication that the batch sizes are still too large or that a component itself is too large and should be divided up. There is still room for improving the zero-downtime deployment approach by leveraging feature flags.

Feature flags

Our overarching deployment philosophy is to decouple deployment from release. We are slicing the delivery of features into incremental experiments and testing user reaction to the new capabilities to validate their value proposition. To accomplish each slice, we are continuously deploying small incremental changes all the way into production. These small batch sizes significantly reduce the risk of each deployment and increase the speed at which teams can recover from any deployment failure by rolling forward. These deployments accumulate in production until the slice is completed and the experiment is released to a select group of users. A release is accomplished by flipping feature flags to make the new features accessible.

A feature flag provides the ability to hide, enable, or disable a feature at runtime. The changes in each deployment are effectively turned off until they are explicitly enabled. In their simplest form, feature flags are implemented as flags in a database that are checked before performing a block of code. This approach has the disadvantage of polluting the code, and must be carefully removed when no longer needed. The preferred approach is to leverage the natural feature flags of a system, such as permissions and preferences.

Groups of users will be granted access to use new features in the same manner in which all permissions are granted. Internal users are granted access to perform demonstrations and exploratory testing, early adopters are granted preview access in exchange for feedback, and, ultimately, access is granted for general availability to all users. Users may be given the ability to opt-in for a feature via their preferences or by purchasing a feature.

Smart feature flags can be used to do A/B testing. A certain percentage of users may be presented with one option rather than another. Machine learning can be used to intelligently choose when to present a new feature. We are also seeing feature flags successfully offered by third party services.

Feature flags greatly reduce the complexity of zero-downtime deployment with regard to infrastructure. Small changes are deployed in place and control the risk of each deployment. Staggering regional deployments is certainly reasonable, but not a necessity, because new features are disabled. When staggering is employed, regional failover handles the worst-case scenarios. Still, multiple versions of the code are deployed to production concurrently and will ultimately be used concurrently by different groups of users. Therefore, care must be exercised when implementing and deploying these changes, and versioning requirements may greatly impact the deployment roadmap.

Versioning

The topic of versioning may immediately bring to mind the nightmares of managing multiple versions of a product with a branch per version, cherry picking fixes across branches, operating version-specific deployments, and wrangling with customers who refuse to upgrade. Fortunately, the topic of versioning in cloud-native systems, that are always-on and provided as-a-service, is an entirely different subject. Our cloud-native product delivery pipeline and the versioning implications is another area where we need to rewire the way we think about software development.

We are continuously deploying small batch sizes to production, staggered across multiple regions, and leveraging feature flags to hide new capabilities until they are ready for consumption. When new features are ready for consumption, we enable them incrementally for specific target audiences to elicit feedback. We may even implement A/B testing based on feature flags to test user reactions to different versions of a feature. The customer may not even notice that they are using a new version, much less even care, as it is no longer their responsibility to manage upgrades.

To continuously deploy small batch sizes to production, we must be confident that these deployments will not violate our requirement for zero-downtime deployments. Our confidence is largely derived from a well-crafted deployment roadmap. Versioning is the primary driving force behind a well-crafted deployment roadmap. On a story-by-story basis, a team comes together in the story planning session and defines a deployment roadmap that consists of a set of ordered tasks that will each deploy a backwards-compatible change to production. It is interesting to note that while small batch sizes reduce the risk of each deployment, it is the backwards compatibility requirement that drives the scope of each task to be even smaller.

Take a simple bug fix as a basic example. If the fix is contained within a single deployable unit, then the deployment roadmap for the fix could consist of a single task. However, if the backwards-compatible fix was in a shared library, then the roadmap would consist of a task to fix and deploy the library to the registry, followed by a task for each dependent component to increment the version of the library and follow its pipeline into production. It is important to point out that the deployment of the shared library would not automatically trigger the redeployment of its dependents. This kind of lack of transparency can lead to unintended consequences in a continuous deployment model, particularly when a dependent team is unaware of the change. Instead, it is critical that dependent components upgrade their dependencies when they are ready.

In this section, we will cover the various guidelines that a team should consider when crafting a deployment roadmap. In many scenarios, we will see that backwards-compatible changes may only need to live for a few hours, while others may be very long-lived and become a way of coding.

Synchronous API

There is a very direct dependency between a consumer of a synchronous API and the definition of the synchronous API. If the definition is changed and deployed before a consumer has been upgraded, then there will be an outage if that API is invoked. With an asynchronous API, there would be an error, but it can be corrected and resubmitted out of band with limited to zero impact on the consumer other than the overall latency of the downstream flow. Therefore, a backwards-incompatible change to a synchronous API is always an indication that care must be taken when defining the deployment roadmap for the specific story.

In our cloud-native systems, we strive to eliminate all synchronous intercomponent communication and relegate synchronous calls to the boundaries of the system. The **Backend For Frontend** (**BFF**) is one such pattern where we have a need for a synchronous API between the frontend and the backend. Fortunately, in this pattern, we prefer that the same team owns the backend and the frontend. This enables the team to implement the backwards-incompatible change with zero downtime, with the quick succession of multiple tasks.

As an example, let's take a case where a team wants to change the name of a field on the API of their BFF. The following deployment roadmap could be employed:

1. Create a task branch workflow in the BFF project to add the new field name while leaving the old field name in place.
2. Create a task branch workflow in the frontend project to change the code to use the new field name. This task could be implemented in parallel, but its pull request would not be accepted until after the BFF task was successfully deployed to production.
3. Create a follow-up task branch workflow in the BFF project to remove the old field name. This pull request would be accepted after the frontend had been successfully deployed and its caching policy expired, which could be a short or long time, depending on the frontend technology.

In this case, the single team could potentially complete all three tasks across the two projects in a matter of hours, resulting in three production deployments in a single day by a single team. In the case of a similar change to shared resources, then the same process would be followed, but would involve multiple teams. The overall process would only be as protracted as is necessary for all the teams to coordinate. The final task to remove the old field from the shared resources would occur after all dependent teams had completed their tasks.

The extreme case involves an open API that is exposed to the public. In this case, it is difficult to impossible to determine all the dependents. The typical solution is to implement a versioned endpoint. The *vN* endpoint would contain the new field name and the *vN-1* endpoint would still contain the old field name. The old endpoint would be updated to adapt to the new implementation as opposed to running many versions, where possible. A deprecation policy would also be announced for the old endpoint. GraphQL is emerging as an alternative solution to this problem, as the client directs the fields that are used. This increases the number of variations that the component can reasonably support.

Database schema

Database versioning in a cloud-native system is very different. Traditionally, we would perform a database conversion. However, conversions often require downtime. Furthermore, a batch-oriented conversion may not be reasonable in a cloud-native system because of the volume of data. Alternatively, an A/B feature flag may necessitate running concurrent versions.

Cloud-native databases are often schemaless. This eliminates a great deal of complexity that is traditionally required to deploy a new database or change a database schema. However, the data structure stored in a cloud-native database does have an implicit schema. Therefore, the code must be implemented to handle multiple versions of the implicit schema. Each row could potentially contain a different version of the data structure. New versions of the code must handle old data in a way that they adorn the new structure in a backwards-compatible way and lazily convert or initialize missing elements. Every version of the code should handle new versions of the data so that unrecognized data is not lost. As a result, the data will be gradually converted row by row, in a just-in-time fashion. This technique follows Postel's Law (aka the Robustness Principle): *Be conservative in what you send, be liberal in what you accept.*

When applying the CQRS pattern, it is not unusual to change the type of persistence that is used to implement the materialized view. The deployment roadmap for such a change might have the following tasks:

1. Deploy the new database alongside the existing database.
2. Implement a new listener to consume events and populate the new database.
3. Implement a feature flag in the BFF logic to flip between data sources.
4. Replay past events from the data lake to seed the new database. This step could be protracted if there is a large amount of historical data.
5. Deploy the change to switch to the new database.
6. Remove the old database and its listener.

This is another case where the story is owned by a single team. The BFF contract would not change and the upstream event type would not change. The team's confidence with the new database type would dictate how quickly these tasks could and should be rolled out. Tasks 1-4 could be rolled out quickly, while task 5 and 6 would proceed after a sufficient evaluation period.

Asynchronous API

Versioning of our asynchronous APIs is concerned with the backwards compatibility of the event type definitions. Upstream components must uphold their contract with downstream components. Meanwhile, downstream components may need to support legacy event type definitions. Fortunately, event type definitions are only used within the cloud-native system and not exposed to third parties. This means that reasonable changes can be enacted relatively quickly with timely team coordination.

The event type names are the critical link that enables downstream components to consume the proper events. Therefore, it is important not to change the names of the event types. This is analogous to changing the endpoint of a synchronous API in that it will immediately break the system, but with a couple of caveats. First, if an upstream component changes an event type name, nothing will produce an error. The new event type will be silently ignored by downstream components, which are still expecting the old event type. Therefore, this bug could go unnoticed for a while. Second, the typical approach with a synchronous API is to create a versioned endpoint. However, as previously mentioned, event types are only used internally. Therefore, there is no need to follow a similarly protracted approach of versioning the event type names. Instead, we will version the contents of the event types, which may allow some consumers to go unaffected if they are not dependent on the specific change. The only legitimate reason to change an event type name is if it is wrong, which ought to be caught early in the life cycle.

Following our common example, let's take a case where an upstream team wants to change the name of a field in the event type they produce. The following deployment roadmap could be employed:

- Each downsteam component that is dependent on the field will create a task branch workflow to add logic to conditionally handle the presence of the old or new field name. More on this in a bit.
- The upstream component creates a task branch workflow to change the name of the field. This pull request can be accepted once all the downstream components have been updated.
- Some downstream components may be able to create a task to remove the conditional logic once the upstream change has been deployed.

Note that downstream components need to support the replay of events. The content and format of historical events are immutable and should not be modified as they provide an audit trail of the events. Therefore, some downstream components may need to support multiple formats if they need to support the replay of those older events. This is another application of Postel's Law (aka the Robustness Principle). Generally speaking, there is no need for a specific version number field. Asserting the presence of a specific field should be sufficient for most changes. A more drastic change in an event definition may occur when a new upstream component is added to produce a specific event type.

When introducing a new upstream component that is producing a new version of an existing event type, it may make sense to have the new source initially emit events that are backwards-compatible. The new component would produce events that are an amalgamation of the old and the new format. This is useful when there are many consumers or when some consumers will be phased out as well. Once all consumers are either updated or retired, then the new producer will be cleansed of the old event type mapping logic.

Micro-frontend

In the examples of the *Backend For Frontend* pattern in `Chapter 4`, *Boundary Patterns*, we discussed the concept of the micro-frontend. The objective of the micro-frontend architecture is to avoid creating a monolithic frontend and enjoy the benefits of independently deployable frontend components. One of the examples was an e-commerce site where the checkout feature is one of several completely separate micro-frontend applications that work together to provide a complete user experience. The team responsible for the checkout micro-frontend application would also provide the micro-frontend add-to-chart widget that is leveraged by the product details micro-frontend application. Each of these pieces could be versioned independently and rely on a feature flag to control which version is presented to the user. Each team would be responsible for the versioning of the BFF, along with the frontend, as discussed earlier. The various teams would work together to create the deployment roadmap for the task branch workflows needed to put the feature flags in place at the various junction points in the user experience flow.

Trilateral API per container

In the *Trilateral API* pattern in `Chapter 3`, *Foundation Patterns*, we talked about how a cloud-native component can publish up to three different interfaces: a synchronous API for processing commands and queries, an asynchronous API for publishing events as the state of the component changes, and an asynchronous API for consuming the events emitted by other components. The synchronous API is usually published via the *API Gateway* pattern, as discussed in `Chapter 4`, *Boundary Patterns*. The asynchronous API for consuming events is usually implemented as a stream consumer, as discussed in the *Event Streaming* pattern and the asynchronous API for publishing events is usually implemented as a database stream consumer following the Database-First variant of the *Event Sourcing* pattern, as discussed in `Chapter 3`, *Foundation Patterns*. This means that a cloud-native component will also consist of multiple deployment units.

Containers are very important in cloud-native systems. They are lightweight, efficient, and start up very quickly. We use them to power our deployment pipeline. The first line of the preceding pipeline example uses a node:6 Docker image. The various Function-as-a-Service offerings from the various cloud providers are implemented on top of containers. Ultimately, a decision must be made whether to use Function-as-a-Service or to manage your own container clusters and craft your own container images.

Function-as-a-Service is a natural fit for cloud-native systems. They integrate seamlessly with a cloud provider's API gateway service, streaming service, and cloud-native database streams. They are fully managed and scale globally. They also embody disposable architecture. A self-sufficient, full-stack team can hit the ground running with these value-added cloud services. This empowers teams to focus on the value proposition of their components. If the experiments do not yield value, then the team is free to change course. The architecture is completely disposable. There is no vested interest in the architecture that would cause a team to stay the course because of the great effort applied in assembling the architecture. On the flip side, if a component does prove valuable, and if the chosen architecture proves lacking, then there is a business case to put additional effort into an alternative containerized solution. That being said, as a very early adopter, I have not found Function-as-a-Service to be lacking on any project.

When my customers choose to run their own container clusters, I recommend using the container service offered by their chosen cloud provider. This minimizes the heavy lifting that is needed to integrate all the various pieces with the cloud provider's other services. However, it is still important to understand what all this entails and the risks involved. The actual containers are only the tip of a very large iceberg. These details are where all the risk lies, and they are not portable across cloud providers.

The following diagram provides an example of the various services involved in running an AWS **Elastic Container Service** (**ECS**) cluster. The example is straight out of the AwsLabs project on GitHub. It provides a vanilla cluster deployment that can be assembled quickly, but will take time to tune for specific component requirements. First, the solution requires the creation of a **Virtual Private Cloud** (**VPC**) with public and private subnets across multiple availability zones and an Internet Gateway and multiple NAT Gateways to allow traffic in and out of the VPC. Next, the container cluster is created with an autoscaling group for creating multiple EC2 instances across the availability, which will ultimately run the containers. An application load balancer is added to route incoming requests. Finally, we get to the point of actually creating the container images and deploying them to the cluster as task definitions, and then connecting everything together with the load balancer via a service with listener rules and a target group.

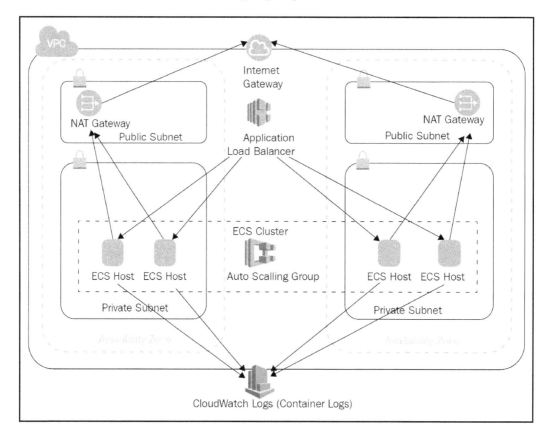

All of this is just for a single region. As we discussed in `Chapter 2`, *The Anatomy of Cloud Native Systems*, we do not want to use a shared cluster for all our components because it does not provide for sufficient bulkheads. Therefore, we need to define logical groupings of components and create separate clusters for each. There is an argument to be made for further dividing up clusters according to the three different trilateral API flavors. As you can see, this is not a very disposable architecture. A great deal of effort goes into maintaining a container cluster, and human nature does not see that effort as disposable.

Much of this may be very boilerplate at first, but there are a lot of little dials to tune, and this is where all the risk lies. For example, how much headroom (that is, unused capacity) should a cluster maintain to ensure there is always enough capacity available to scale out containers when they are needed? When there is not enough capacity, then new containers cannot be created and the system will appear unavailable to the user. The cluster's autoscaling policy will create additional hosts to add more capacity, but these do not come online as quickly as containers, hence the appeal of containers. These are the kinds of details that used to keep me up at night. Accounting for all the risks in a production environment can easily take months before reaching a reasonable level of confidence. All these risks act as a governor on a team's ability to deliver on the promises of cloud-native: its speed, safety, and scale.

My recommendation is to try to outgrow Function-as-a-Service as opposed to trying to grow into your own container cluster. There is plenty to learn about Function-as-a-Service as well, to get every last drop of performance out of it. But an unoptimized function will work and scale in spite of itself, and it will not impede a team from focusing on their value proposition.

As of writing this course, Azure Container Instances is in preview and AWS Fargate was recently released. These offerings are more or less serverless models for custom containers. You create the container image and ask the cloud provider to run it. This is a very interesting alternative that could potentially fill any discovered gaps, while still allowing teams to focus their energies on the business solution. We will have to see where this goes, but cloud providers are putting a great deal of effort into integrating Function-as-a-Service with all their various offerings.

Summary

In this chapter, we discussed how decoupling deployment from release allows self-sufficient, full-stack teams to shift deployments all the way to the left on the timeline. This helps to minimize risk and increase throughput by deploying small batch sizes, and ultimately delivers features by enabling feature flags for targeted groups of users. Decoupling deployment from release requires multiple levels of planning. The release roadmap defines how the desired functionality is divided into slices. Each slice is designed as an experiment to elicit feedback from customers about the correctness of the value proposition. A deployment roadmap defines the ordered set of tasks needed to implement a specific story as a series of task branch workflows. We discussed how a task branch workflow governs an individual instance of a deployment pipeline that is implemented using a modern, hosted CI/CD tool. A well-crafted deployment roadmap facilitates zero-downtime deployments because task ordering takes versioning into account, while feature flags hide incomplete features and staggered multi-regional deployments provide a variation on canary deployments. Ultimately, the Trilateral API pattern guides the proper use of Function-as-a-Service versus raw containers as the unit of deployment.

7
Testing

In the previous chapter, we began our deep dive into the human factors of cloud-native. We discussed how decoupling deployment from release by controlling batch size, shifting deployment all the way to the left, and leveraging dark launches helps mitigate risk and empowers self-sufficient, full-stack teams to rapidly and continuously deliver innovation with confidence. Deliberately planned release and deployment roadmaps facilitate this decoupling. Deployments are controlled by a task branch workflow and orchestrated by a modern CI/CD pipeline to help ensure zero-downtime deployments. Testing is no longer a phase—it is an integral part of the deployment pipeline.

In this chapter, we will continue to discuss the human factors of cloud-native. We will shift testing all the way to the left and weave it into the CI/CD pipeline to help enable teams to continuously deploy changes to production and deliver innovation to customers with confidence. We will cover the following topics:

- Shifting testing to the left
- Test engineering
- Isolated testing
- Transitive testing
- Manual testing

Shifting testing to the left

Cloud-native is a different way of thinking. In the first chapter, we discussed the need to approach cloud-native with an open mind, and that you need to be prepared and willing to rewire your software-engineering brain. There are plenty of *"what, really?! wow!"* moments, followed by *"how can we do more of this?"*. Testing is one arena that is significantly impacted by the contextual changes brought about by the promises and concepts of cloud-native. Cloud-native systems are not monolithic. Unfortunately, traditional testing practices are rooted in the context of the monolith. Many fundamental assumptions that drive traditional testing techniques no longer apply. Not only do they not apply, they are actually counterproductive and even impede quality. We must realign our testing strategies to provide the necessary confidence within the context of cloud-native.

Cloud-native promises speed, safety, and scale. The pace of innovation is significantly increased with cloud-native. Self-sufficient, full-stack teams are empowered by disposable infrastructure and value-added cloud services to focus on the value proposition, and respond to user feedback much more quickly. Yet how can teams be confident in the quality of the deliverable at this pace? The distributed nature of cloud-native systems allows for global scalability. However, the complexity of distributed systems presents significant testing challenges. In this context, how can we deliver on the promise of safety? How can we balance the requirement for rapid innovation and global scalability with the requirement for system stability? In short, how can we rapidly and continuously deliver innovation with confidence?

We garner much of this confidence from the cloud-native architecture itself. The automation of disposable infrastructure makes the deployment process predictable and repeatable. Leveraging value-added cloud services, such as cloud-native databases, event streaming, and function-as-a-service, mitigates the risks of implementing and operating these complex capabilities. Bounded isolated components, built on our Foundation, Boundary, and Control patterns, provide us the confidence that the necessary bulkheads are in place to limit the blast radius when a problem does arise. The limited scope of each component enables a team to better reason about the impacts of any given change and thus reduces the likelihood of a problem. When an incident does occur, the team can resolve the issue quickly.

Strategically, we gain confidence through experimentation. Cloud-native architecture facilitates speed, which allows us to iterate quickly and condense the feedback loop with end users. We purposefully forgo some level of accuracy to more quickly determine not whether the product is fit for purpose, but whether or not the purpose is fit for the customer. As we discussed in `Chapter 6`, *Deployment*, we slice the delivery of features into a series of controlled experiments to incrementally vet the value proposition. Each experiment is a test that is designed to help steer the product roadmap. Our confidence is derived from shifting this testing to the left on the timeline and validating our assumptions early and often.

In each slice, we build just enough functionality to support the experiment. This minimizes waste when the results of an experiment necessitate a change in direction. Experimentation and the disposable nature of cloud-native architecture complement each other. When all signs suggest a prudent change of direction, we are not inclined to stay the course to justify a larger sunk cost. Instead, we are at liberty to experiment precisely because we are confident that the limited scope of an experiment is disposable and is simply the cost of acquiring the necessary information to make further roadmap decisions.

Tactically, our confidence comes from decoupling deployment from release and controlling the batch size of each deployment. The scope of each slice (that is, release) is already focused. A slice may be composed of several stories across a few components. For each story, a team crafts a deployment roadmap, which establishes a deliberately ordered set of tasks that accounts for all inter-dependencies. Each task is focused on a specific backward-compatible change to a specific component. The batch size of these deployments includes only enough code for the task, and the code is completely tested.

Testing is no longer a phase—it is an integral part of the cloud-native product delivery pipeline. Testing is no longer a job title—it is a team effort. Testing is executed with every deployment. We are shifting automated testing all the way to the left on the development timeline and accumulating test coverage over the course of each release. Each task implements just enough code and all code that is written must be tested. This strict requirement to test all code in a deployment further drives down the batch size of each deployment because it places incentives on implementing only just enough code. This further increases our confidence in each deployment because of the limited scope.

Shifting testing all the way to the left, controlling the batch size, and stating that all code must be tested is not enough to instill full confidence. We need to change our perspectives on testing and change our testing techniques as well. For example, priority number one for the tests implemented in each task is not that the functionality is correct, but that the change does not break the features that are already released. This is a different perspective that involves more than just traditional regression testing. The new feature under development must be feature-flipped off, and thus there must be tests to ensure the feature flag is working. Another change in perspective is that testing is cumulative—it does not need to be implemented and executed all at once. With each task, we are accumulating a more and more comprehensive suite of tests. This spreads the testing effort across the development lifecycle. With each additional task, the assertion of correctness is strengthened until each story is done and a feature is enabled for use.

The testing effort is also spread across the components. Cloud-native systems are distributed systems with many components. Performing end-to-end testing across all the components for each deployment is not practical. Delaying deployments so that teams can coordinate an end-to-end test is counterproductive. In this chapter, we will cover techniques, such as transitive testing, that accomplish end-to-end testing without deploying the entire system. In Chapter 8, *Monitoring*, we will cover techniques, such as synthetic transaction monitoring, that continuously execute end-to-end smoke tests in staging and production.

Test engineering

The role of testers is changing. The key word here is "changing". Automation is eating the software world. Testing has traditionally been a largely manual effort. More often than not, unit testing has been the only testing that is automated and all other testing is performed manually. In this chapter, we will discuss how to reliably extend test automation all the way through end-to-end testing with a technique I call **transitive testing**. All this automation has the testing community wondering whether or not their jobs will disappear. I think it is fair to say that the traditional role of testers will disappear, but will be replaced with higher value responsibilities.

These new responsibilities do not include writing automated tests. Writing automated tests is a development task. Developers spend years honing their skills. Treating test automation as anything less than code and expecting testers to learn to code overnight is unrealistic. I know plenty of testers who love to code and are great coders. I also know plenty of great testers who love to test but hate coding. On the flip side, I think developers are more than happy to write test case code, over and above their unit tests, but they do not want to be responsible for defining the test cases. This makes sense, because if you write the code and define the tests, then your tests are more than likely to confirm the code you wrote and miss alternate paths. This highlights the fact that the engineering of test suites is an entirely separate skill that is honed by extensive testing experience.

The role of a tester is transforming into that of a test engineer. Testing is a team effort. Developers write the test code. When developers write the business logic, they do so based on the requirements provided by business analysts. When developers write test logic, they should do so based on the requirements provided by test engineers. This highlights the fact that we are actually building two different systems concurrently: the system under test and the test system. In all actuality, the test system dwarfs the system under test. If the test system is larger than the system under test then it stands to reason that the test system should be at least as well engineered as the system under test.

Test engineering largely revolves around architecting a shared understanding of the system as a whole. Yes, there are technical decisions that must be made about the test system, but the technical folks can aptly handle those decisions. And yes, the test system should consist of a well-balanced test portfolio that respects the notion of the test automation pyramid. Instead, the focus of test engineering should be on creating a test suite architecture that can be leveraged up and down the test automation pyramid, across teams, and throughout the system life cycle. The test suite architecture consists of a well-crafted set of personas and a representative set of supporting data for each persona.

The personas are leveraged to create consistent test cases through the layers of the test automation pyramid, such that each successive layer reinforces the lower layers. The personas are used across teams as part of the ubiquitous language of the system to reinforce the shared understanding of the system and to drive the end-to-end testing scenarios. The personas evolve as the system evolves, and emerge from story mapping and the formulation of the release roadmap of experiments. This shared understanding extends into production as the basis for implementing synthetic transaction monitoring and alerting on key performance indicators.

The high-value responsibilities of test engineering shift both to the left and to the right on the system life cycle timeline. Test engineering plays an important role in defining the experiments that assert the value proposition of the system. Test engineering supports the critical responsibility of asserting the health of the system in production. In all these responsibilities, the mindset and experience of a tester are crucial.

Isolated testing

Testing is no longer a phase—it is an integral part of the cloud-native CI/CD pipeline. We are decoupling deployment from release and controlling the batch size of each deployment so that we can minimize the risk of each deployment and thereby increase the pace of deployments to many times per day. To achieve the desired pace with confidence, the test suites must execute within the CI/CD pipeline without creating a bottleneck. In `Chapter 6`, *Deployment*, our modern CI/CD pipeline executes all tests on every push to a given branch. This includes both unit testing and integration testing. As we will discuss in the *Transitive testing* section, this effectively includes end-to-end testing as well.

To accomplish this objective, all testing must be isolated to the component under test. The CI/CD pipeline cannot rely on the presence of any resources outside the pipeline itself. The tests must be completely self-contained. Fortunately, our cloud-native systems are composed of bounded, isolated components, which are, following reactive principles, responsive, resilient, elastic, and message-driven. All inter-component communication is performed asynchronously via event streaming. All intra-component communication interacts with highly available, value-added cloud services, such as cloud-native databases. The natural isolation of our cloud-native components minimizes the number and variety of external resources that must be accounted for in our isolated testing.

The isolation of external resources is accomplished via test doubles. For unit testing and component testing, you can use the mocking library that is best suited to your programming language and frameworks. The examples here use the Sinon library. We will discuss isolating integration tests and end-to-end testing in the *Transitive testing* section. By holding all external factors constant, we can focus our attention on the component under test. When a test case fails, it is clear that external factors are not the cause, and that the problem lies within the component.

The testing portion of the CI/CD pipeline executes quickly because nothing needs to be deployed; test data is explicitly configured in the tests and test doubles, and no calls are made over the network. This fail-fast feedback loop helps provide teams with the confidence necessary to increase the pace of innovation.

We also need to isolate our tests in relation to time. To have confidence in our tests, they must be deterministic. The inputs and the context must be held constant, otherwise the assertions of the outputs are suspect, or worse, the tests could be flaky and randomly fail for not-so-obvious reasons. For example, twice a year in locations that observe daylight savings time, it is not uncommon to experience a testing fire drill where tests that worked the day before now produce errors. The functionality of the system may be working fine; instead, it is the test cases that are bad. Unfortunately, there often turns out to a bug in the system that doesn't account for daylight savings, and the tests are also broken because they did not uncover the bug.

The problem is that the tests are relying on the system time, which is different in every execution. For any logic that is time dependent, we need to mock out the system clock to return a deterministic value. There should also be test cases that account for daylight savings time and leap years. UUIDs are a similar problem. V1 UUIDs are time based and V4 UUIDs are random-number based. These should be deterministic as well. Holding time and identifiers constant will be critical for transitive testing, which we will discuss shortly. The following example uses the Sinon test-double library to mock identifiers:

```
sandbox.stub(uuid, 'v1').callsFake(() => {
  return '00000000-0000-0000-0000-000000000000';
});
```

Traditionally, unit testing and component testing are the focus of isolated testing. We will discuss those next. However, distributed systems pose significant challenges to performing integration and end-to-end testing, which can be addressed by isolation as well. We will discuss this in the context of transitive testing in the next section.

Unit testing

Unit testing verifies that the individual units within a component produce the desired behavior. The units are tested in isolation from each other and from external resources through the use of test doubles. Unit testing should account for the vast majority of automated test cases. In this day and age, unit testing should be a standard practice across all projects. I will merely highlight some interesting aspects of unit testing as they pertain to the context of cloud-native.

Cloud-native components are very focused with little if any code that is shared across components. As such, there is less reliance on frameworks, such as dependency injection and object-relational mapping. In fact, when implemented using function-as-a-service, these frameworks have a significant negative impact on performance. However, it is still a best practice to implement some lightweight layering within the code. For example, access to external resources, such as cloud-native databases and the event-streaming service, should be wrapped in simple connector classes. When using GraphQL, there is a resolver layer and usually a model layer and validators.

The value of these lightweight layers is most evident in testing. Unit tests should be implemented from the bottom layer up, with each layer isolated from the lower layers. The following example uses the Mocha test runner along with aws-sdk-mock to test a connector that wraps AWS DynamoDB. With this layer completely covered, all other layers can be tested without the complexity of mocking the database layer.

```
describe('connector.js', () => { // test suite
  it('should get the object by id', () => { // test case
    const ID = '00000000-0000-0000-0000-000000000000';
    const ITEM = { id: ID, name: 'thing0' };

    AWS.mock('DynamoDB.DocumentClient', 'get', (params, callback) => {
      expect(params).to.deep.equal({
        TableName: 't1',
        Key: { id: ID },
      });
      callback(null, { Item: ITEM });
    });

    return new Connector('t1').getById(ID)
      .then(data => expect(data).to.deep.equal(ITEM));
  });

  afterEach(() => AWS.restore('DynamoDB.DocumentClient'));
});
```

In addition to unit testing layer by layer, we should test function by function for components implemented using function-as-a-service and entity by entity when using GraphQL. The following example uses the Mocha test runner and Sinon test doubles to test a function that uses the connector layer tested earlier. This test stubs out the connector layer so that it can focus on testing the business logic:

```
describe('get.js', () => { // test suite
  beforeEach(() => {
    sandbox = sinon.sandbox.create(); // create cache for stubs
  });
```

```
it('should get the object by id', () => { // test case
  const ID = '00000000-0000-0000-0000-000000000000';
  const ITEM = { id: ID, name: 'thing0' };

  const stub = sandbox.stub(Connector.prototype, 'getById')
    .callsFake(() => Promise.resolve(ITEM));

  return new GetHandler().handle({ pathParameters: { id: ID } })
    .tap((response) => {
      expect(stub.calledWith(ID)).to.be.true;
      expect(response).to.deep.equal(...);
    });
  });
});

afterEach(() => sandbox.restore()); // remove all stubs
});
```

The first priority of testing in our continuous deployment pipeline is to ensure that the code changes in the current task branch workflow do not break the currently released functionality. Therefore, we need to ensure that all the new code is tested. The easiest way to know that we have at least covered all the new code is to maintain 100% code coverage. This goal is actually very easy to achieve with cloud-native components because we are implementing them as a series of ordered tasks. In each task, we implement only just enough code to accomplish the task and only just enough test code to ensure that the new code is properly tested. Conversely, any code that is not tested should not be included in the task. This is easy when we incrementally accumulate the code and the tests and maintain 100% coverage from the very beginning.

Yes, I agree that 100% coverage does not mean that the tests really test the functionality. But keep in mind that the first priority is not to break the existing functionality. As a self-sufficient team, if you break production, you fix production, at any hour of the night. The accuracy of the functional testing will accumulate with each additional task. By maintaining 100% coverage, we make it easier on ourselves to see where we have missed a line or branch that might bite us in the middle of the night. It is also an incentive to keep the batch size of each task down, which further reduces the risk of a deployment.

Static code analysis, such as **lint**, should be included at the unit-testing level. This has several benefits. Static analysis will identify potential errors in the code that may slip through the unit tests. It streamlines manual code review because essential rules and best practices are enforced at build time. For example, I use the `eslint-config-airbnb` rules for helping to teach teams proper ReactJS best practices. I remember turning these rules on shortly after starting to use ReactJS. It immediately and significantly improved the code. Many best practices, such as when to use a class component versus a stateless functional component, were baked in. Developers learn best practices simply by writing code and having Lint critique the code. Code reviews were immediately streamlined as well. Important security rules and best practices can also be enforced. Adding Lint to the build is so easy that there is no real reason not to add it. It should be part of the boilerplate templates used to initialize all new projects. These rules increase our confidence that the code has been properly reviewed when we are performing many deployments per day.

Component testing

Component testing verifies that the units within a component work together properly to produce the desired behavior while still isolating the component from external resources via test doubles. The need for component testing depends on the complexity of the component. In many cases, a bounded, isolated component can be sufficiently tested with just unit testing and integration testing, as covered in the next section. However, some components may perform complex calculations and logic with many permutations. These components will often have a strict set of acceptance tests that must be satisfied, in which case the tests may be implemented with a **behavior-driven development** (**BDD**) tool, such as Cucumber.

The line between component testing and unit testing has become a bit blurry because the testing environment is usually the same. It is less and less necessary to test cloud-native components in a full runtime environment. Simulating the execution environment locally has become very straightforward, particularly for components implemented using function-as-a-service. Tools such as serverless-offline and SAM Local simulate the deployment environment locally and within the CI/CD pipeline. This significantly increases the efficiency of the deployment pipeline and further tightens the feedback loop. We will see shortly that these same tools are leveraged to accomplish integration, contract, and end-to-end testing as well.

Transitive testing

In a traditional product-delivery pipeline, it is customary to execute integration and end-to-end test suites prior to performing a production deployment. This is a perfectly laudable practice, and one that we wish to retain for cloud-native systems. However, the traditional approach to accomplishing this testing effort is at odds with the practice of decoupling deployment from release and driving down batch sizes to minimize deployment risk and accelerate innovation. There is a fundamental impedance mismatch between traditional integration and end-to-end testing practices and the modern continuous deployment pipeline that produces an impenetrable bottleneck.

The traditional approach necessitates a large and expensive effort to coordinate, set up, and maintain a comprehensive testing environment with the correct versions of all the various system components installed. This comprehensive environment must also be reinitialized before each testing exercise. The complexity of this effort can grow exponentially as the number of components in the system increases. By definition, a distributed cloud-native system is composed of many components, which exacerbates the problem. Furthermore, once the environment is deployed, it can take a considerably long time to execute all the test suites.

As a result of the time, effort, and cost required, the natural tendency is to delay integration and end-to-end testing, and batch up changes into larger batch sizes. This is exactly the opposite of the objectives for a mature product-delivery pipeline. Larger batch sizes increase the risk of any given deployment. The delay lengthens the feedback loop and thus stifles the pace of innovation. Worse yet, these tests are often not performed at all because the effort is too great. Ultimately, these traditional testing practices actually reduce the quality of the system.

When we do put forth the effort to perform this traditional integration and end-to-end testing exercise, we find the results underwhelming. More often than not the tests prove to be flaky, brittle, slow, and unreliable. Distributed systems, such as cloud-native, perform a significant amount of intra-component and inter-component communication over the network. Unfortunately, we can count on the fact that networks are unreliable, which results in sporadic timeouts. In a cloud-native system, we must account for this fact in our everyday usage by adding reasonable timeouts, retries, and exponential back-offs.

In the context of integration and end-to-end testing, latency is extremely problematic. The purpose of these tests is not to test the retry mechanism. Anything that is not under test should be held constant, but, by definition, we cannot hold something constant that is unreliable. Inevitably, the latency will cause the tests themselves to time out. Many testing frameworks can be configured to retry as well, but this can lead to unexpected situations where the initial transaction did succeed in spite of the timeout. Again, we design cloud-native systems to be idempotent for this very reason, but the purpose of the test is not to exercise the idempotency mechanism. Ultimately, we set the test timeout settings extremely high, which can significantly protract the execution time of the tests, and they will still fail sporadically, regardless.

By design, in our reactive cloud-native systems, we strive to maximize the use of asynchronous inter-component communication to increase responsiveness, resilience, and elasticity. Much like latency issues, asynchronous systems present a challenge to integration and end-to-end testing. A test case will typically need to invoke an action that produces a message and then poll some other action to assert the desired behavior. As the system reacts to the message, latency can be encountered at any number of network hops in the logic flow under test. Therefore, the test must set a reasonably high polling interval and overall timeout as well. Furthermore, the act of polling can experience latency. Asynchronicity is an excellent architectural mechanism because humans are naturally asynchronous. However, it is very problematic for testing and results in unreliable tests with sporadic timing errors.

Flaky, brittle, slow, and unreliable tests obviously impede the progress of the deployment pipeline, but their real cost is paid for in team morale. I can attest to this fact. In the early phase of our cloud journey at Dante, we achieved an extremely high degree of automation with our monolith, as outlined in the first chapter. Our pipeline would recreate the entire testing environment for every execution and then execute the entire test suite. It was a major improvement over our manual testing practices that only tested a small fraction of the system. However, a significant portion of the team's day could be consumed chasing these red herrings, which hindered progress towards deadlines. Every failing test had to be attended to and reexecuted potentially multiple times until it succeeded. Nursing flaky tests was a major bone of contention at daily standups and periodic retrospectives. Some tests were ultimately reverted to manual tests executed just in time before a deployment go-no-go decision.

Traditional integration and end-to-end testing do not test components in isolation; therefore, it is often not immediately obvious as to which component is the root cause of a test failure. For example, did the client fail or did the requested component return a broken response? It can take a good amount of effort to triage a test failure to determine which side failed. This is obviously an inefficient use of time. Less obvious is the fact that interteam relationships can be strained if one team's issues continuously impact dependent teams. Frequently, this is another case where something that is not under test impacts a test and should be held constant, such as an incomplete enhancement by another team.

For our cloud-native systems, we want the best of both worlds. We want small batch sizes and frequent deployments along with full integration and end-to-end testing. We want the stability of isolated testing along with the confidence that components fit together properly. Fortunately, we can use multiple new techniques in combination to achieve what I refer to as transitive integration and end-to-end testing.

Integration testing

Integration testing verifies the interactions between the component under test and its external resources. For example, a cloud-native component performs synchronous intra-component communication with its cloud-native databases and the event streaming service, a frontend communicates with its backend-for-frontend component, and an external service gateway component communicates with the third-party service that it wraps. These tests are focused on the coverage of the communication pathways instead of the component's behavior.

When performing unit testing and component testing, these interactions are replaced with test doubles so that the component's behavior can be tested in isolation. These test doubles are implemented in the form of handcrafted mocks, stubs, and spies. These handcrafted objects serve their purpose of isolation well, but as they are handcrafted, we cannot be completely confident that they accurately represent the payloads exchanged in the interactions. Therefore, the integration tests need to interact with the real external resources. However, for all the reasons discussed earlier, we want to accomplish this with the same stability as the isolated tests.

VCR libraries provide test doubles that are able to record and play back the request and response payloads when making calls to an external resource. These recordings act as a permanent cache that is checked in with the test cases. When in record mode, these test doubles will forward a cache miss to the external resources and record the response for use in the next test run. When in playback mode, a cache miss will result in a test failure. There are often other modes, such bypass or partial bypass, that are helpful for debugging. There are many VCR libraries written in different languages and with support for different frameworks. They are all inspired by the original Ruby VCR library. The following diagram depicts an example of recording the interactions with a component's cloud-native database:

Here, the developer creates the desired test case with the VCR library initialized. If necessary, the database is set up with any required test data, either manually or via a separate script. The developer executes the test case, the database is accessed using the developer's access key, and the payloads are recorded. The test case and the recorded payloads are checked into the task branch, which triggers the test job in the CI/CD pipeline, as discussed in Chapter 6, *Deployment*. The pipeline executes the tests in playback mode so that it will fail when a matching recording is not found.

It is always important to ensure that test cases are deterministic, but it is critical when using a VCR library to ensure a match. If any values in the request payload change from execution to execution then the records will not match and the test will fail. Most libraries have the ability to adjust the filter criteria to exclude headers and so forth. The test case itself will need to mock any dates, UUIDs, and so on to ensure that the same values are produced for each execution.

This approach has many benefits. First and foremost, the external dependencies are not required when the tests execute in the CI/CD pipeline. No testing environment must be maintained. No setup and teardown are required. The test cases are implicitly initialized with the necessary test data for every run because the data is in the recordings. The effort of crafting and initializing the test data is only expended when implementing the test cases. What is equally important is that the tests are no longer flaky. They are stable, repeatable, and fast. The network has been removed from the equation. The successful recording of the payloads ensured that the communication is properly implemented. Each execution of a test case asserts the proper handling of the recorded payloads to ensure that the component has not changed in that regard. When a failure does occur, we can be certain that the problem is in the component under test and not in the external resource.

There is one glaring drawback with this approach. When running integration tests in isolation, it is not possible to detect when the external resource has changed and broken the contract. To address this problem, we need to implement contract tests. We can think of integration and contract tests as two sides of the same coin.

Contract testing

Contract testing ensures that a component has not broken its contract with its consumers. When we looked at the Trilateral API pattern, we highlighted that this contract includes both the component's synchronous interface and the event types that it publishes through its asynchronous outbound interface. The contract tests ensure that any enhancements to a component are at least backward compatible with its consumers.

An interesting twist with contract tests is that the component team does not implement them. Instead, these tests are implemented by the consuming team and then submitted to the component team as a pull request. This approach is referred to as consumer-driven contract testing. When creating a deployment roadmap in a story-planning session, the component team should be able to identify all its consumers by inspecting its contract tests and then craft an appropriate roadmap. However, if anything is overlooked, then these contract tests provide the early warning sign when a change to a component will break a specific consumer.

Once again, we cannot be confident that these tests will be accurate if they are handcrafted. The devil is always in the details. For example, the consumer and provider might agree on a specific field name, but not its contents or data type. Therefore, we want to use the recordings from the consumer-side integration tests to drive the contract tests on the provider side. A recorded request payload is passed as the input to a test case and the output response is asserted against the recorded response payload.

The following diagram depicts how this works for asynchronous interfaces, such as the contract between a frontend **single page application** (**SPA**) and its BFF component. An integration test is implemented in the project of the frontend application that records the payloads from the API gateway of a remote instance of the BFF component. The test and the records are checked into the frontend project as per usual. The specific payloads are also included in the pull request for the BFF project to drive the contract tests as well; thus, both sides of the interaction are accounted for. When either side is changed, the other side is held constant and the tests assert the side under test. This is shown in the following diagram:

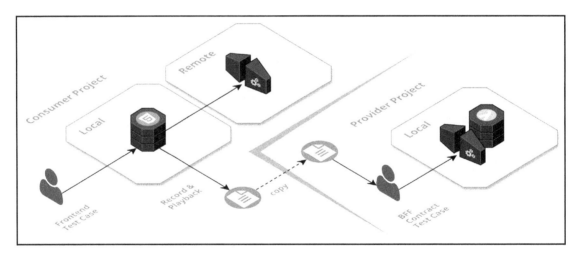

Asynchronous interactions present an interesting wrinkle in contract testing because the producer initiates the interaction instead of the consumer. The following diagram depicts how contract testing unfolds for asynchronous communication. The downstream (that is, consumer) team first creates an integration test in the upstream (that is, producer) project for its specific scenario. This test records the event payload published to the remote stream service. If the upstream team implements a backward-incompatible change, then this test enforces the contract because it will no longer find a match, and will fail. The downstream team copies the recording to its own project and implements a contract test that ensures that the recorded event payload is compatible with its stream-processing logic. This is shown in the following diagram:

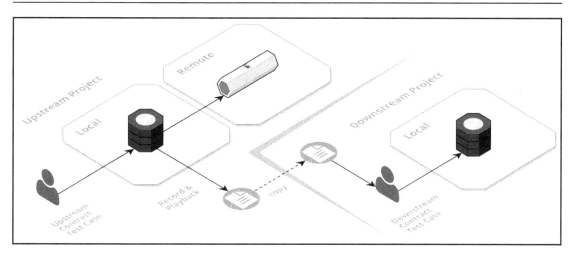

This approach solves the major drawback of VCR-based integration testing. By using contract testing in conjunction with integration testing, and using the recorded payloads on both sides, we can ascertain when a provider is breaking the contract with one or more of its consumers because of a backward-incompatible change. This approach solves an additional problem for asynchronous communication. It eliminates the need to poll for the outcome of an asynchronous message. The producer side simply asserts that the proper event is produced. The consumer side holds message delivery as a constant and asserts its logic from the point of receiving the message. We can expand on this approach to perform transitive end-to-end testing.

End-to-end testing

End-to-end testing asserts whether a specific flow of an application behaves as expected from start to finish. A flow may cross several tasks of a single user, cross multiple users, include autonomous steps, and take a long time. We have already discussed the drawbacks of the traditional end-to-end testing approach, which requires the maintenance of a comprehensive testing environment and is subject to the unreliability of network communication and the nature of asynchronous processing.

This complexity has lead to the adoption of modern testing techniques for performing integration testing and consumer-driven contract testing based on recorded communication payloads. We have also shown how we can use integration testing and contract testing in conjunction, like two sides of the same coin, while still executing each in isolation, by sharing the same recordings on each side.

We can take this a step further with the addition of strong test-engineering practices. Given a well-crafted end-to-end test case scenario, multiple teams can coordinate to chain together a series of integration and contract test interactions to create an arbitrarily long end-to-end test built entirely of isolated tests. I refer to this as transitive testing.

In the following diagram, we can see that the first component produces a payload recording. This recording is then shared with the next component, which produces another recording. This second recording is shared with a third component, which produces yet another recording. Borrowing from the transitive property of equality, if Component A produces Payload 1, which works with Component B to produce Payload 2, which works with Component C to produce the expected Payload 3, then we can assert that when Component A produces Payload 1, then ultimately Component C will produce Payload 3.

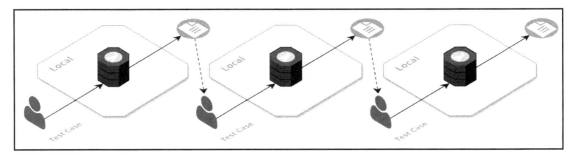

Borrowing from a relay race analogy commonly used in lean business practices, the change in the mental model here is to *watch the baton, not the runners*. The payloads are the *baton*, the value that the system produces. The runners are the components, which produce the value. With traditional end-to-end testing techniques, we spend an inordinate amount of time tending to the environment (that is, the runners) and very little time, in contrast, executing the tests (that is, moving the baton). Transitive testing turns this on its head. We focus a small amount of time implementing the tests (that is, the runners) and then the tests are executed over and over again in the deployment pipeline, producing and asserting the payloads (that is, the baton).

Another interesting property of this approach is that we can incrementally build out the end-to-end test flow without having to re-execute portions of the flow that have not changed. This works very well with the cloud-native practices of rapidly and continuously delivering slices of innovation. As we build up the layers of functionality, we can incrementally build out the end-to-end test flow without the need to repeatedly coordinate an end-to-end testing exercise. Only when a specific portion of the flow changes do we need to re-execute that leg of the end-to-end test.

Transitive testing gives us the best of both worlds and more. We have the stability of isolated tests, we have full integration and end-to-end coverage, we can build and execute the tests incrementally, and we can improve team efficiency. All while executing the tests more frequently for smaller batch sizes and ultimately increasing quality. Nevertheless, there is still some need for the traditional techniques, although with a cloud-native twist. We will discuss the topic of continuous synthetic transaction monitoring (that is, continuous smoke testing) in `Chapter 8`, *Monitoring*.

Manual testing

This chapter is all about confidence. Specifically, it is about how testing relates to our confidence in the cloud-native systems we build and particularly with regard to the pace at which we can build these systems. Our reactive cloud-native architecture gives us confidence that when an honest mistake is made, the blast radius will be controlled. Delivering features as a series of controlled experiments gives us confidence that we are not building too much functionality too fast before we have validated that we are building toward the correct value proposition. All our automated testing gives us confidence that we are building the system correctly and that there are no regressions, despite our rapid pace of innovation .

This last point is very important. Our automated testing does not give us confidence that we are building the correct system. It only gives us confidence that the system is properly coded and that it is not broken. As the saying goes, "garbage in, garbage out". We could be building the wrong system with perfect precision, but it is still the wrong system. This is exactly why we deliver functionality as a series of experiments. But this begs the question of how we validate the hypothesis of the experiment. The short answer is that we use the system. We manually use the system to see if it is what we thought it would be. In `Chapter 8`, *Monitoring*, we will discuss how we measure the usage of the system to provide quantitative information about the outcome of each experiment. But, ultimately, we put the system in the hands of the end user and react to their qualitative feedback.

Still, knowing that our automated testing cannot tell us if we are building the correct system, we would be wise to perform an appropriate level of internal, manual, exploratory testing before flipping a feature on for even the first set of beta users. In `Chapter 6`, *Deployment*, we covered the idea of the walking skeleton. This is the first slice of the system. It is an internal experiment that is intended to give the teams a chance to put their hands on the system as a whole to ensure that everyone is on the same page and build a shared understanding of the system. The system at this point consists of just the absolute bare essentials. There is no meat on the bones, so to speak. The functionality is very shallow, but the end-to-end flow of the system should be evident. The teams will perform exploratory testing to validate this experiment and make necessary course corrections.

The walking skeleton is neither the first nor the last time that internal, manual, exploratory testing is performed. We should attach screenshots of the user interface to the pull requests of the frontend projects. This is a great way to get quick feedback with minimal effort from the reviewers, and it brings nontechnical team members into the review process. Each task branch workflow is ultimately deployed to the staging environment before the pull request can be accepted. This is another opportunity to perform some quick manual testing to get a feel for the correctness of the trajectory of the current story. A manual demonstration should be performed in production once a story is completed. The product owner should be granted access to perform exploratory testing at this point as well. Exploratory testing will certainly be performed prior to the go-no-go decision to enable a feature for a new set of customers. Essentially, all milestones warrant manual exploratory testing and anywhere in between that builds confidence.

Example – end-to-end relay

Let's pull this all together with an end-to-end example of a typical ordering process of an e-commerce system. At the highest level, the system receives an order, forwards the order to a third-party order-management system, and receives order status updates. The system is built using our cloud-native patterns.

We have a **frontend** (**FE**) application that submits orders to its BFF component. The BFF component emits the order-submitted event type and consumes the order-received and order-fulfilled event types to track the order status. These two pieces are owned by the same team. Another team owns the **external service gateway** (**ESG**) component that encapsulates the interactions with the third-party order management system. This component consumes the fulfill-order event type and emits fulfill-order-received and fulfill-order-complete event types. A third team owns the order process event orchestration component (EO) that is responsible for orchestrating the events between the BFF and ESG components. These event flows are shown in the following sequence diagram:

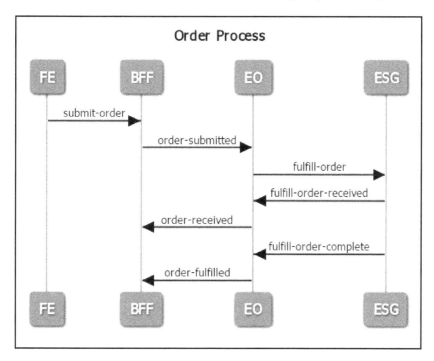

To enhance the example, the team responsible for building the ESG component is scheduled to start building the component well after the BFF team has completed their initial experiment. As a result, the EO team will initially simulate interaction with the ESG component for the time being. This demonstrates the power and flexibility of bounded isolated components and the incremental nature of transitive testing. When the ESG component is eventually added, only the EO component will need to be updated. The EO component will assert that its contract with the BFF component is still intact, but the BFF component will not need to be enhanced, nor its tests executed.

The test engineers of the various teams will coordinate to define the concrete set of end-to-end test scenarios that will be implemented by the teams. The teams will implement the scenarios incrementally as the functionality is implemented. Initially, the teams will implement the plumbing of the scenarios and then rerecord and distribute the payloads as the functionality evolves, and add additional scenarios as appropriate. The following examples demonstrate the plumbing. Again, as mentioned previously, focus on the baton, not the runners. The plumbing is fairly boilerplate; the real details are in the data payloads (that is, the baton) and the possibly numerous permutations. Following the guidance of the test automation pyramid, all the permutations will be tested at the unit level. At the end-to-end level, we only need enough coverage to have sufficient confidence that the components are working together properly.

Submit order leg

The first leg of an end-to-end scenario is often initiated by a user interaction. In this example, the user submits an order from a website that may be implemented in Angular or React. The scenario could include a Selenium test, implemented using the likes of WebdriverIO and executed across multiple browsers via services such as Sauce Labs. Alternatively, the test could be implemented at the integration level, for example, as an unmocked Redux test. Regardless, the frontend and BFF component should be owned by the same team, and thus coordinating the first leg should not be an obstacle.

For this example, the first leg is implemented as a Mocha test using the Supertest client library. The developer has both the frontend project and BFF project cloned locally. The BFF component is running locally using the serverless-offline plugin to simulate the execution environment. The frontend test initializes the Replay VCR library to record the interaction. Once the recording is captured on the frontend side, it is ultimately checked in, and from that point on, the test will execute against the recording without the BFF component running locally.

```
import 'mocha';
import * as supertest from 'supertest';

const endpoint = 'http://0.0.0.0:3000';
const client = supertest(endpoint);
const replay = require('replay'); // start vcr

describe('submit-order', () => {
  it('should submit the order', () => {
    const ID = '00000000-0000-0000-0000-000000000000';
    return client.put(`/orders/${ID}/submit`)
      .send({ id: ID })
      .expect(200);
```

```
  });
});
```

The following is the plugin fragment from the `serverless.yml` file of the BFF component. The serverless-offline plugin is used to simulate the execution environment locally. The plugin processes the metadata in the `serverless.yml` to create a local server that simulates the API gateway and execute the functions. The `baton-vcr-serverless-plugin` is responsible for initializing the Replay VCR in the context of the local server so that calls to resources, such as DynamoDB and S3, are recorded.

```
plugins:
  - baton-vcr-serverless-plugin
  - serverless-offline
```

Next, the recording of the request payload is copied from the frontend project to the BFF project. Again, the test is implemented using Mocha and Supertest. However, this time, the baton-request-relay library is used to read the recorded request payload so that the recording can drive the Supertest call to the BFF component and assert that the response matches the recorded response. The serverless-offline plugin and the baton-vcr-serverless-plugin are used on this side as well; however, the offline server is automatically started as part of the npm test script.

```
import 'mocha';
import * as supertest from 'supertest';
import * as relay from 'baton-request-relay';

const endpoint = 'http://localhost:3000';
const client = supertest(endpoint);

describe('submit-order-relay', () => {
  it('should relay the submit-order request', () => {
    // read recording
    const rec = relay(`./fixtures/frontend/submit-order`);

    // make the recorded request
    return client[rec.request.method](rec.request.path)
      .set(rec.request.headers)
      .send(rec.request.body)

      // assert status code and body match recorded response
      .expect(rec.response.statusCode)
      .expect(rec.response.body);
  });
});
```

In this first leg of the end-to-end scenario, we have recorded a request/response payload that the frontend expects the BFF component to support. The frontend project will execute this test as part of its test suite to assert that its expectations of the BFF contract have not changed. We have copied the recording to the BFF component and created a test that will assert that the component upholds its contract with the frontend. The test also records its interactions with the component's resources. If this test fails, then it is an indication that the component has been changed in a backward-incompatible manner.

Order submitted leg

The next leg of the end-to-end scenario asserts the order-submitted contract between the BFF component and the EO component. The order-submitted event is emitted using the database-first variant of the event sourcing pattern. To drive this test case, we need to capture the event payload produced by the DynamoDB stream of the orders table. There is no fancy way to capture this payload. We simply copy the JSON string from the CloudWatch log of the `trigger` function and store it as a file in the BFF project. This string should be present in the log shortly after recording the submit-order leg.

This test directly invokes the `trigger` function handler with the captured DynamoDB stream event. We initialize the Replay VCR so that we can record the order-submitted event that is published to the Kinesis stream. The assertion of this test is the proper matching of the recorded order-submitted event. We must stub the UUID generator to produce a deterministic value, otherwise, the Kinesis recording would never match and the test will always fail.

```
import 'mocha';
...
import { handle } from '../../../src/trigger';

// the captured DynamoDB event
const EVENT = require('../../../fixtures/downstream/order-submitted.json');

describe('trigger', () => {
  before(() => {
    const replay = require('replay'); // start vcr
  });

  it('should publish order-submitted', (done) => {
    sandbox.stub(uuid, 'v1').callsFake(() => {
      // hold the event id constant
      return '00000000-0000-0000-0000-000000000001';
    });
```

```
    // invoke the function handler
    handle(EVENT, ctx, done);
  });
});
```

Next, the recording of the order-submitted event payload is copied from the upstream BFF project to the downstream EO project. The baton-event-relay library is used to read the recorded order-submitted event so that it can be passed as input to the `listener` function handler. We initialize the Replay VCR to record the event emitted by the EO component. This iteration of the EO component will immediately produce the order-received event because the ESG component has not yet been implemented. Again, we hold the UUID generator constant, as well as the generation of the event timestamp. On the upstream side, we do not need to override the timestamp generation because the timestamp is pulled from the recorded DynamoDB stream event.

```
import 'mocha';
...
import { handle } from '../../../src/listener';

import * as relay from 'baton-event-relay';

describe('order-submitted-relay', () => {
  before(() => {
    const replay = require('replay'); // start vcr
  });

  it('should process the order-submitted event', (done) => {
    const rec = relay(`./fixtures/upstream/order-submitted`);

    sandbox.stub(uuid, 'v1').callsFake(() => {
      // hold the event id constant
      return '00000000-0000-0000-0000-000000000002';
    });

    sandbox.stub(utils, 'now').callsFake(() => {
      // hold the timestamp constant
      return 1512975699218;
    });

    // invoke the function handler
    handle(rec.event, ctx, done);
  });
});
```

In this second leg of the end-to-end scenario, we have recorded the order-submitted event payload that the downstream EO component expects the upstream BFF component to support. As mentioned previously, asynchronous contract tests work in the opposite direction of synchronous contract tests. The EO team creates the test in the upstream BFF project that produces the order-submitted event that the EO component expects. If the BFF component logic produces an event that fails to match the recording, then it has made a potentially backward-incompatible change. The recording is copied to the downstream EO component and the team creates a test to ensure that the order-submitted event payload contains the data expected by the orchestration logic.

The remaining legs of the end-to-end scenario all follow the asynchronous contract test pattern. The BFF team will create upstream tests in the EO project to record the order-received and order-fulfilled events and assert that they have not changed. The payloads are copied to the BFF component and downstream tests are created to assert that the events contain the expected data. When the ESG team starts development, it will create upstream and downstream contract tests for the fulfill-order event and the EO team will create upstream and downstream tests for the fulfill-order-received and fulfill-order-complete events. If needed, the teams can perform manual exploratory testing to increase their level of confidence.

Summary

In this chapter, we discussed how we must realign our testing strategies to provide the necessary confidence within the context of cloud-native systems. We looked at how we need to shift testing to the left and make it an integral part of the deployment pipeline. Each task branch workflow implements just enough code to accomplish the task and all that code is completely tested. All automated testing is performed within the pipeline to ensure that we fail fast, and with a tight feedback loop. This necessitates testing components in isolation to account for the complexities of testing distributed systems. We leverage transitive testing techniques to accomplish end-to-end testing as an aggregation of multiple isolated tests. Test automation has transformed the traditional tester role into a test-engineering discipline. However, we still need to perform manual exploratory testing to help ensure that we are building the correct system.

8
Monitoring

In the previous chapter, we continued our deep dive into the human factors of cloud-native. We discussed the need to realign our testing strategies within the context of cloud-native systems. We shifted testing all the way to the left and made it an integral part of the deployment pipeline by employing isolated and transitive testing techniques to overcome the complexities of testing distributed systems. We also discussed the emergence of the Test Engineering discipline.

In this chapter, we will continue to discuss the human factors of cloud-native. We will shift some aspects of testing all the way to the right into production to assert the success of continuous deployments and increase team confidence. We cover the following topics:

- Shifting testing to the right
- Key performance indicators
- TestOps
- Real and synthetic traffic
- Observability
- Alerting
- Focusing on mean time to recovery
- Performance tuning

Shifting testing to the right

Confidence, confidence, and more confidence: the promise of cloud-native is to enable companies to rapidly and continuously deliver innovation to their customers with confidence. Throughout this book, the speed of innovation and the stability of the system are the primary motivations driving the architecture of cloud-native systems and the methods we employ to deliver these systems. Confidence is so important that a crisis of confidence will stifle innovation. Cloud-native drives cultural change precisely because we build upstream trust by increasing the business's confidence in our cloud-native architecture and practices.

Disposable infrastructure increases confidence because our automated deployments become repeatable and routine. Bounded isolated components increase our confidence because they provide proper bulks to limit the blast radius when a component fails. Value-added cloud services increase our confidence because we delegate the management of complex capabilities to the cloud provider. The global scalability of cloud-native systems increases our confidence that the system will meet the needs of an expanding user base.

We are confident that we are building the right product because we deliver features as a series of controlled experiments to test the value proposition with real users. Disposable architecture increases our confidence that we can turn on a dime when those experiments show that the value proposition lies in a different direction. We increase our confidence by decoupling deployment from release to minimize the risk of any given deployment and by controlling the batch size of the change. We further increase our confidence in deployments by realigning our testing strategies, such that testing is an integral part of the deployment pipeline and improved by isolated and transitive testing techniques.

However, try as we might, we cannot eliminate the honest human error. It is inevitable that there will be system failures. As a cloud-native system grows, so does the probability of a failure. It becomes unrealistic to strive to maximize the mean time between failures. Instead we must focus on the mean time to recovery. Distributed infrastructure, bounded isolated components, and value-added cloud services empower self-sufficient, full-stack teams to respond quickly in the face of failure, once the failure and the resolution are identified. Therefore, identifying failures proactively and having the necessary information available for root cause analysis are the key drivers for minimizing the mean time to recovery.

To be proactive, we must shift some testing all the way to the right into production. We must identify the system's key performance indicators and actively monitor and alert on these values when they deviate from the norm. We cannot rely solely on real user activity. We need to synthesize traffic such that the system continuously emits a signal to monitor. Our bounded isolated components must be observable. They must emit sufficient information to support the key performance indicators and facilitate root cause analysis. We must avoid alert fatigue so that teams can trust the alerts and jump into action.

Key performance indicators

A focus on the mean time to recovery is critical to achieving the promise of cloud-native. The traditional focus on maximizing the mean time between failures is too conservative a posture for companies to thrive in this day and age. Companies must be lean, move fast, experiment, and pivot quickly. We must be willing to make mistakes and rapidly adapt. Fortunately, the cloud-native concepts that empower teams to rapidly deliver innovation also empower them to rapidly repair and roll-forward. Yet, in order to make a repair, we must first identify the need for a repair.

We are already confident in our ability to move fast. We have spent the vast majority of this book on the topic. However, to be truly confident in the pace of cloud-native, we must be confident that we will detect problems in our cloud-native systems before our users do. When our customers do find the need to report a problem, we want the support team to be able to inform the customer that the solution is already being deployed. To achieve this, the mean time to recovery is predicated on the mean time to detection.

We will be discussing the observability of our cloud-native systems, proven alerting techniques, and methods for root cause analysis. We will learn to alert on symptoms instead of causes. However, our cloud-native systems will produce many observable signals and many of these signals will reflect symptoms. We will monitor and record all these symptoms, but we cannot focus on all this information simultaneously. How do we optimize the signal to noise ratio to turn this data into useful information? We will absolutely automate all this monitoring, but some signals are more important and more valuable than others. These are the system's key performance indicators.

Netflix provides a classic example. They have identified a single indicator that provides a critical window into the health of their system, **Starts Per Second** (**SPS**). This is literally the rate at which their customers press the play button. To this one metric, they apply a double exponential smoothing algorithm to produce a clear signal that can be monitored for anomalies. When this signal deviates from an acceptable range then it is time to start sending out pages; it is time to start waking people up in the middle of the night. All the rest of the data that is collected is supporting material to discover the root cause of the identified symptom.

Every system has key performance indicators. Monitoring and reacting to these signals is a new testing paradigm that is performed in production. In pre-production, we execute test scripts and assert their results. In production, we observe critical signals and assert their normality. Teams will incrementally uncover the key performance indicators of their components. This is a major part of the modern test engineering practice, as we discussed in Chapter 7, *Testing*. Test engineers will apply their deep functional knowledge and testing expertise to help devise these crucial tests.

Monitoring production systems is traditionally an operations role. These skills and techniques are a necessity for asserting the health of our cloud-native systems. The skills of test engineering and operations are blending into a modern TestOps practice (https://dojo.ministryoftesting.com/lessons/the-future-of-software-testing-part-two). This is a high-value practice that facilitates our ability to rapidly deliver innovation with confidence. Identifying the key performance indicators of a system is the objective and art of the TestOps practice. We will now turn our attention to the mechanisms of continuously testing these key performance indicators in production.

Real and synthetic traffic

Key performance indicators and a focus on the mean time to recovery are all well and good, but they are also largely academic unless there is traffic running through your cloud-native system. International companies will likely have traffic around the clock, but many systems do not have an international user base. Furthermore, even though the system as a whole may be receiving continuous traffic, individual regions will receive different levels of traffic throughout the day.

We are continuously deploying changes into production and we need to proactively assert the health of the system immediately after each deployment to be confident in the success of the deployment. However, without traffic in the system, there is no information available to assert the health of the system. This is particularly true when we are performing a canary deployment in an off-peak region, as we discussed in Chapter 6, *Deployment*.

We certainly want to monitor real user traffic and fully understand the quality of their user experience. We also need to continuously synthesize predictable traffic to sufficiently fill the gaps in real traffic to support asserting the health of the system. We will use real-user monitoring and synthetic transaction monitoring in combination to help ensure we have proper test coverage in production to build our level of confidence.

Real-user monitoring

First impressions are critical to the success of modern systems. Users have many choices and expect extremely fast response times. A poor user experience has a significant impact on bounce rate. To minimize this risk, we need to monitor the user experience so that we are aware of performance issues and make any necessary improvements. However, it is no longer possible to solely rely on server-side monitoring to gauge the performance of the user experience. In cloud-native systems, a significant amount of the end-user experience executes on the client side. Therefore we need full-stack monitoring to assert the quality of the user experience.

More than likely, your team has used tools, such as Pingdom Website Speed Test (`https://tools.pingdom.com/`) or Google PageSpeed Insights (`https://developers.google.com/speed/pagespeed/insights/`), to perform some one-off testing to understand the performance characteristics of your web pages. This is certainly better than nothing; however, it would be much better to have the user applications sample this performance data in real time and periodically submit this information to track the performance experienced by real users. This technique is called **real-user monitoring** (**RUM**). RUM is considered passive monitoring because it is initiated by actual users. Getting started can simply involve initializing a third-party library in an application and registering with the SaaS provider.

RUM provides us with both technical and functional insights. On the technical side, we get detailed page performance and error information, which can drive continuous performance improvement and highlight performance regressions. We can also see the system performance when accessed from around the globe, which can identify the need for additional regional deployments and which regions to consider.

On the functional side, we can monitor how users actually use the system. For example, what combination of functionality is used within a typical user session and which features are used more than others or not at all. This information plays a large role in evaluating the outcome of our individual experiments, which help drive the product direction. For example, individual page statistics could inform the results of an experiment, which performed A/B testing on multiple variations of a feature.

Real-user monitoring is an important technique, which helps drive a product's direction by collecting quantitative information around individual experiments. This information is then analyzed in conjunction with the qualitative feedback from the real users to help make well-informed decisions. RUM can play a role in smoke testing deployments; however, its passive nature is generally not deterministic enough. Therefore, we need to generate synthetic traffic as well.

Synthetic transaction monitoring

Synthetic transaction monitoring (**STM**) is continuous testing in production. We use this technique to generate a regular, consistent, and deterministic flow of traffic through the system. STM is considered proactive monitoring because the teams generate the traffic. Instead of waiting for users to produce traffic and instead of relying on intermittent manual smoke testing, the teams define a sufficient set of scripts that provide just enough test coverage to give the teams confidence that their components are healthy.

Synthetic transactions include more than simple pings to check for uptime. A significant amount of information and confidence can be derived from simple uptime checks. They are so easy to implement with a third-party service that your test suite should include these at an absolute minimum. They are a perfect starting point, but page pings are not enough to fully gauge the health of dynamic systems.

All the crucial user flows of the system should have a synthetic transaction test. Following the 80-20 rule of thumb, we should aim to cover the 20% of the system that is used 80% of the time. These are the flows that the end user cannot live without. Put another way, they are the flows that will cause users to bounce to another system when they are not working properly.

Synthetic transactions execute continuously at a prescribed interval and fulfill the role of smoke tests. As part of story planning and the creation of the deployment roadmap, a team should identify which synthetic transactions cover the components that will be changed in each deployment so that the team knows how to assert the success of the deployment. If no smoke tests exist, then the team must prioritize creating them as part of the task plan. Like all cloud-native testing, these scripts should start simple and evolve alongside the components to provide just enough cover to give the team the necessary confidence.

We can also think of synthetic transactions as the modern equivalent of traditional end-to-end tests, which execute in a full-blown environment. Our transitive end-to-end testing technique, as we discussed in `Chapter 7`, *Testing*, solves the pitfalls of traditional end-to-end testing, resulting in a stable testing suite that the teams can rely on at the pace of cloud-native development. Synthetics also fill the role of smoke tests, but smoke tests are usually a fairly small set of absolutely essential tests. Following the guidance of the testing automation pyramid, synthetic transactions are at the tip of the pyramid. We should only implement just enough of these tests to provide a proper balance between team confidence and the maintenance effort. However, if you are not yet confident with these modern techniques, you can leverage synthetic transactions to fill any perceived gap between transitive testing and essential smoke tests.

It is important to point out that we need to distinguish synthetic transactions from real transactions. When executed in production, synthetic transactions will be aggregated into business metrics and reports, unless care is taken to segregate them. It is preferable to use the natural grouping of your data to accomplish this segregation. For example, if your system supports multiple tenants, then a fake tenant would perform all the synthetic transactions. In an e-commerce system, a fake customer, tagged as fake, could purchase fake products, which are also tagged as fake. All reports and metrics would filter out data tagged as fake. If there is no natural segregation in the system's data, then a more invasive approach can be employed. A special URL parameter can be added throughout the scripts, that is propagated throughout the code paths to short-circuit functionality as necessary.

There is one more way in which synthetic transactions differ from traditional test scripts. Traditional testing asserts the results of each test as they are performed. The scripts of synthetic transactions certainly allow for conditional logic and can report their success or failure, but the intent is to simulate the traffic of actual users. This traffic then produces the signals that we monitor for our key performance indicators. All the data we collect from real users is collected from synthetic transactions as well. Real traffic has ebbs and tides, whereas synthetic traffic provides the continuous signal we need to continuously assert the health of the system. Now we turn our attention to the observability of the system and how we consume the signal produced by the steady flow of traffic.

Observability

The classic statement, "it works great in my environment", represents a lack of observability. Traditionally, operations and development teams have used different tools to observe the behavior of their systems. Operations have historically been largely limited to black-box monitoring. Ops could monitor the operating system, processes, memory, CPU, disk I/O, network I/O, some log files, and the database, but they had little visibility into the inner workings of the applications. When a system underperformed, the Ops team could confirm the fact that is was underperforming, but could not necessarily state why it was underperforming.

Eventually, the development team was brought in to investigate the problem in a lower environment, where they can use profilers and debuggers to perform white-box testing and potentially diagnose the problem and propose a solution. However, lower environments are out of context and often cannot reliably reproduce the problem. Regardless, the traditional mean time to a resolution is much too long.

Under today's standards of always-on, zero downtime systems, with users who can choose to go elsewhere, and with features that are continuously evolving in an effort to increase user stickiness, we must be able to observe the inner workings of our systems at any time and in any environment. We cannot afford to try to reproduce a condition at a more convenient time. We must observe the system in real time and retain the data for both immediate and historical analysis. During an event, we need full situational awareness so that we can respond promptly and prudently. After an event, we need information, much like a flight recorder, to perform a post-mortem that drives continuous improvement.

Here is an apt quote by Alexis Lê-Quôc (`https://www.datadoghq.com/blog/monitoring-101-collecting-data/`), co-founder and CTO of Datadog:

> *"Collecting data is cheap, but not having it when you need it can be expensive, so you should instrument everything, and collect all the useful data you reasonably can."*

Monitoring is absolutely critical to fully deliver on the promise of cloud-native. We will identify the key performance indicators for our systems that enable teams to respond to incidents well before our customers notice the problem. To accomplish this, we need to maximize the observability of our cloud-native systems. We need data from our system that can be turned into actionable information. Collecting data may be cheap, but we need guidelines to help us turn this mountain of data into valuable information. We will discuss how to measure the system, the categories of information we are collecting, and alternate approaches to collecting the measurements.

Measurements

The first step to increasing the observability of a component is to take measurements of the important aspects of the component. We refer to measurements as metrics. A metric is a time series of data points that we can monitor, aggregate, slice, and dice to observe the inner workings of the component. Each measurement consists of a name, a timestamp, a value, and a set of tags. The name denotes **what** is being measured, the timestamp indicates **when** it was measured, the value specifies **how much** was measured, and the tags qualify **where** the measurement was taken. The following is a measurement of the latency of a function:

aws.lambda.duration 2017-12-20 01:30:00 1ms region:us-east-1,functionname:helloworld

It is important to distinguish between the name and the tags of a measurement. Cloud-native systems are extremely dynamic. What we measure is relatively stable; however, where we measure it will be dynamic. In the preceding example, we measure the latency of a function. We want to take this measurement for all functions. In this example, we also know that this measurement was taken for the `helloworld` function in the east region. Tags allow us to aggregate measurements across many different dimensions so that we can slice and dice the data to glean information.

Typical tags will include the cloud account, the region, the component name, the function, and the stage. If you have a context flag denoting synthetic transactions, then this could be a useful tag as well. Tags must have a low or reasonable cardinality over a period of time. For example, dates and identifiers have a high cardinality and thus are not good tag values. Suffice to say that high cardinality tags will cause your storage costs to balloon and reporting performance to suffer. This is indicative of time series databases in general. SaaS monitoring tools will not necessarily restrict you from using high cardinality values, but your cost will skyrocket and if enough values are collected in a short time period then the support team will likely contact you so the bill does not surprise you. Keep in mind that these are monitoring tools, not business intelligence tools.

We can also give the values we measure more meaning by specifying a metric type of gauge, count, or histogram. A **gauge** is the most basic type of metric. A gauge measures the value of a specific thing over time, such as free system memory. A **count** represents a long-running counter that can be incremented or decremented over time, such as page hits on a website or the length of a queue. A **histogram** produces several aggregate measurements (avg, count, max, min, p95, median) to describe the statistical distribution of a set of values, such as the latency of a function. With these basic building blocks, we can begin to measure work and resource metrics.

Work metrics

Now that we know how to take measurements of our cloud-native components, we need to categorize the measures so that we can turn this data into actionable information and to help understand what measurements should be taken. The first category is work metrics. Work metrics represent the user-visible output of the system. They tell us what the system is doing from the external perspective. When we discuss alerting, we will see that a degradation of work metrics represents symptoms of an underlying cause. Work metrics include the rate of *throughput* for a unit of time, the rate of *errors*, and the performance or *duration/latency* of the unit of work. Collecting work metrics is also commonly referred to as the RED Method (`https://dzone.com/articles/red-method-for-prometheus-3-key-metrics-for-micros`) for rate, errors, and duration.

With regard to our cloud-native components, we certainly want to collect work metrics for our boundary components. Throughput, errors, and latency are metrics that are readily available for value-added cloud services such as API gateways and function-as-a-service. For reactive systems, we also need to collect metrics for domain events. We need to understand the rate at which domain events are produced and the rate at which they are consumed. A single component can consume all events and feed domain event metrics into the monitoring system to track the rate at which events are produced. To track the rate of consumption, each stream processor needs to measure the count of domain events by type that it successfully consumes. The objective is to assert that the rate of domain event consumption is in line with the rate of domain event production. In the performance section, we discuss tuning stream processors.

Resource metrics

The second category of measurements is resource metrics. Resource metrics represent the internal workings of the system. They tell us at a lower level what the system is doing to produce the user-visible output. When we see a degradation of work metrics, our resource metrics help us determine the underlying cause of the user-visible symptoms. Resource metrics include the percentage of capacity that is *utilized*, the extent to which the resource is *saturated* with queued, waiting, or throttled work, and the rate of *errors* produced by the resource. Collecting resource metrics is also commonly referred to as the USE Method (`http://www.brendangregg.com/usemethod.html`) for utilization, saturation, and errors.

Value-added cloud services, such as cloud-native databases and event streams, are the resources that are consumed by our cloud-native components. These resources are provisioned with a specific capacity allocated. When we exceed that capacity then additional requests will be throttled. It is important to track saturation as well as utilization because utilization is tracked as an average over a period of time. These averages typically smooth out short periods of overutilization. Saturation metrics represent this overutilization. We design our components to be resilient in the face of short periods of saturation, such that they retry with an exponential back-off. Autoscaling can resolve the short-term capacity limits, but the resource metrics will help us fine-tune our capacity allocations.

Events

Our third category of measurements is events, both system events and external events. These are distinct from our domain events. Events are discrete, infrequent occurrences, such as a recent deployment, the autoscaling of a cloud-native database, a fault in a stream processor, or recorded alerts that show a resource metric or work metric that is not behaving normally. Events provide crucial context to the behavior of the system. When we are investigating a problem via a dashboard, events that correlate with metric fluctuations often lead to the root cause.

Most monitoring tools integrate with the webhooks of Git repositories, such as GitHub and BitBucket. When performing many deployments per day, these integrations are very important to maintaining situational awareness. The event consumer that monitors the rate of domain events in production should also record faults as system events in the monitoring system. When investigating the root cause of a fault event, the presence of a deployment event for an upstream component would suggest that the upstream component just deployed a backward incompatible change that is the cause of the faults.

It is also interesting to point out that alerts, which are recorded as events, are themselves a form of observability. We can think of these alert events as higher-order observations because they build on the lower-level measurements that in and of themselves are just data. It is the higher-order observations that cause us to jump into action to resolve a problem. Now that we know what to measure, let's discuss how we transmit the measurements so that they can be monitored and drive these alerts.

Telemetry

Once we have made our measurements, we need to transmit the observations to the monitoring system for processing. In other words, our components will be taking measures and storing them locally. These measurements need to be collected from all the different locations and consolidated in the monitoring system for reporting and alerting. This process of collection is referred to as telemetry. There are several telemetry approaches for collecting the metrics. We can classify these approaches as cloud provided, agents, and logs.

All cloud providers collect metrics about the performance of their services and retain these values for a limited amount of time. These metrics are made available in the cloud console of each service. The ability to create custom dashboards across services is also provided to varying degrees. Third-party SaaS monitoring tools arguably provide higher-value offerings for custom metrics, custom dashboards, monitoring, and alerting and metrics integration with many different tools. Some of these tools, such as Datadog, integrate with the cloud providers and continuously consume the cloud-provided metrics and retain them for an extended period.

Our cloud-native components fully leverage value-added cloud services. The presence of the cloud provider metrics means that our cloud-native components have reasonably high observability with little extra effort. With the addition of a third-party SaaS monitoring tool, teams can quickly put monitoring and alerting in place, with just the cloud-provided metrics, and start deploying with greater confidence. These tools can monitor the entire pipeline when the integrations for Git, CI/CD, and issue tracking are configured.

Agents are currently the most typical approach for collecting custom metrics. StatsD is an open source agent created by Etsy. Many, if not most, monitoring tools use StatsD or an enhanced version to collect metrics. An agent runs as a separate process on the instances of a container cluster. The component code is instrumented to make calls to the agent API to record counters, gauges, and histograms, as discussed earlier. The agent aggregates the measures and periodically sends the aggregated measurements to the monitoring system, typically every 30 or 60 seconds.

As a result of this architecture, little to no overhead is placed on the component to record the metrics with the local agent. The agent is then able to perform calculations, such as calculating the statistical distribution of histograms, and efficiently send the aggregated metrics in bulk to the monitoring system. This approach assumes that the code can be instrumented and that the agent can be installed on the cluster instances.

Logging is both an old and a new approach to collecting metrics. Traditional tools, such as Apache HTTP Server, record their metrics in a log file. AWS CloudFront has cloud-provided metrics but records more detailed metrics in log files. Applications, in general, have always written errors and exceptions to log files. As a form of back-box monitoring, these logs can be tailed and parsed to extract metrics and events that can be sent to the monitoring system. There are many tools that specialize in processing logs.

However, logging is a sticking point with regard to cloud migration, because of the ephemeral nature of cloud infrastructure. For example, if a traditional system is configured for autoscaling in the cloud, when an instance is autoscaled up and logs are recorded on the instance and when the instance crashes or is autoscaled down, then the logs are destroyed with the instance. Cloud-native systems are designed to continuously send log statements to a central location, such as AWS CloudWatch Logs. Third-party monitoring systems integrate with these logging services to extract the raw log data and process it into actionable information. The use of structured logging makes this process easier.

Function-as-a-service presents an interesting challenge for collecting custom metrics. First, it is not possible to install an agent because the function owner is not in control of the machine instance. Next, even if access to the instance were available, each invocation could be on a different instance, because stickiness is not guaranteed. One alternative is to batch metrics in the function call and send them to the monitoring system via a direct API call. However, this adds significant latency to each function invocation. Furthermore, since metrics are sent for each invocation, there is no opportunity to batch measurements across invocations and create histogram distributions.

Structured logging is a natural approach to recording custom metrics when using function-as-a-service. This is a case of what's old is new again with cloud-native. Functions are instrumented by recording structured log statements for counters, gauges, and histograms. The monitoring system continuously processes the centralized logs and extracts the structured statements. This processing is able to calculate the statistical distributions for the histograms from the individual statements. Now that we have collected the measurements in the monitoring system, we can turn our attention to alerting.

Alerting

Alerting is a double-edged sword that we have to learn to use productively. The teams have created synthetic transactions to exercise their components on a regular basis to help assert the success of their deployments and the health of their components. Each component has been instrumented to sufficiently increase the observability of its internal operation. As a result, the teams are now awash in a sea of metrics. Categorizing this data into work metrics, resource metrics, and events helps to make sense of the different signals emitted by the components. Some teams have honed in on their key performance indicators, while others are still waiting for the dust to settle. Regardless, there is too much information to consume manually. Monitors need to be defined to watch the data and alert the team accordingly.

The classic problem with monitoring is alert fatigue. Teams will receive far too many alerts when monitors are not well crafted. Receiving too many alerts is not much better than manually crunching the metrics. It is still information overload. We eventually stop paying attention to the alerts. Or worse, we set up scripts to automatically stuff them into a folder that may never be reviewed. Instead, we want timely alerts. Our objective is to focus on the mean time to recovery. If we inadvertently ignore important alerts then we are no better off than no monitoring at all. The general guidelines (`https://docs.google.com/document/d/199PqyG3UsyXlwieHaqbGiWVa8eMWi8zzAnOYfcApr8Q/edit`) are to alert liberally, but page judiciously on symptoms rather than causes.

Many, if not most, alerts will be strictly informational. These low severity alerts need no immediate action. They are just recorded for future reference, which in and of itself is a form of observability. For example, when an autoscaling policy is triggered or when the latency of a service increases above a threshold, then we want to record these facts. These observations need no intervention. The autoscaling policy is performing as intended and the latency may be temporary. However, these higher-order observations may be useful in later analysis. When performing the root cause analysis of a real problem, these observations may help highlight an important pattern when correlated with other seemingly unrelated observations.

Moderate severity alerts should also result in notifications via email, chat room, and/or the creation of a prioritized ticket in the issue tracking system. These alerts need timely but not immediate attention. No one needs to be woken in the middle of the night for these observations. For example, when the iterator age on an event stream processor starts to increase then this is probably worthy of a notification. This may be a temporary condition that goes away or if it continues to age then action will be necessary before unprocessed events start to expire from the stream. This early warning gives the team ample time to investigate and act accordingly.

The user-visible symptoms are usually our key performance indicators or at least candidates. For example, the change in throughput of pressing the play button is a symptom of a root cause, such as some resource being over-utilized or not available. Paging on both the cause and the symptom increases alert fatigue, as does prematurely paging on just the cause. Paging on the symptom also decouples the monitor from the implementation details, which may change over time. There are exceptions, such as when a stream processor's iterator age is approaching expiration. In all likelihood, a high severity alert would have already been generated because useful work is clearly not progressing through the stream. Yet another alert is warranted to increase the urgency for a resolution.

Moderate-level alerts enable teams to react before a recovery is necessary. High-level alerts trigger teams into immediate action. Low-level alerts collect potentially valuable observations that come to light when diagnosing a problem. Now we turn our attention to the process of leveraging the metrics and observations for diagnoses.

Focus on recovery

We have accepted the reality that to err is human and that our bounded isolated components will inevitably experience failures. We will instead focus our energies on the mean time to recovery. We have instrumented our components to be highly observable and we have strategically created synthetic transactions that continuously generate traffic through the system so that we can observe the behavior of key performance indicators. We have created alerts that monitor the key performance indicators, so that we can jump into action as soon as a problem is detected. From here we need a method for investigating the problem and diagnosing the root cause that allows us to focus our attention and recover as quickly as possible.

Teams should create a dashboard for each component in advance. A dashboard should display all the work metrics for a component and the metrics for the resources it consumes. All events should be overlaid on the dashboard as well. Note that it is the grouping of different metrics on a dashboard and where they are placed on the dashboard that implicitly correlates the metrics. Define filters for the appropriate tags, such as account, region, stage, and so forth. All the metrics on the dashboard should filter by these tags and for the selected date and time range.

Once we have been alerted to a symptom we can investigate the root cause in a methodical manner. Start with the top-level work metric that identified the symptom. Investigate the metrics of the resources that the work component depends on, such as is the database capacity saturated. Determine if there are any events related to the component or its resources, such as a code deployment. If the root cause is not identified at this level, then dig deeper and repeat. For example, investigate the next upstream or downstream component for issues. The data lake can also be a useful source of information. For example, the search engine can reveal the details of the domain event payloads to help diagnose data-related issues.

For stream processors, it is often useful to observe the problem in action. If the processor is in an infinite loop or producing fault events, it is sometimes necessary to let the processor continue to fail to collect more measurements and help identify the pattern of the problem. The processing is asynchronous and isolated, therefore the end user is less directly impacted, which affords the team a little more time with a little less pressure to diagnose the problem without jumping to conclusions and making snap judgments that can cause more issues. This can be a powerful tool if the stream processor is sufficiently instrumented and it leverages the Stream Circuit Breaker pattern. The fault events can be resubmitted after a resolution is put in place.

Once a solution is identified, the team will roll-forward by creating a task to implement, test, and review the fix and then perform the automated deployment. It may be necessary or potentially convenient to roll-back the previous deployment while working on the fix. However, with sufficiently small batch sizes, it is usually easier and just as fast or faster to roll-forward.

In the case of a regional failure, it will be necessary to failover to the next closest region. Our cloud-native components leverage value-added cloud services that handle availability zones failover for us. However, when one or more of these services experiences a failure, regardless of how infrequent, they will impact the entire region. To account for this, we create regional health checks to monitor the crucial services for a significant increase in their error rate. An alert would trigger the DNS service to route the region's traffic to the next best region until service is restored.

We can also leverage the observability of our cloud-native components and our diagnostics methodology to proactively tune our components based on quantitative information from production usage. We will discuss performance testing and tuning next.

Performance

Performance testing is another topic that cloud-native tends to turn on its head. Systems built on traditional architectures often forgo performance testing, because it can be a long and tedious process, but ultimately pay the price when major bottlenecks are eventually discovered in production. On the flip side, performance testing often yields little valuable information, because traditional architectures typically have a fairly low level of observability. These performance tests largely treat the system as a black box with little or cumbersome white-box monitoring.

Cloud-native systems are composed of bounded isolated components and leverage value-add cloud services. The performance surface area of these characteristics is extremely different from traditional systems. Bounded isolated components share no resources other than event streaming. They perform no inter-component synchronous communication. All synchronous communication is performed within the component against value-added cloud services that are specifically provisioned for and owned by the bounded isolated component. Therefore, each component is entirely in control of its own performance tuning.

Most value-added cloud services are very explicit about how capacity is allocated and billed. Traditional resources are cluster-based. You allocate a cluster size and you eventually determine, through testing or production usage, how much throughput can be sustained on the chosen cluster size. Value-added cloud services are typically provisioned based on the desired throughput. If you know and/or can predict the required throughput then you can provision more accurately. Built-in autoscaling accommodates for any variation, without the need to define complicated policies.

Some value-added cloud services, such as an API Gateway or a function-as-a-service, implicitly scale to meet demand but do so within an upper throttling limit. These are soft limits that can be raised with a simple support request. These limits can come into play during peak usage scenarios, so teams do need to be aware of these limits. However, because of the high degree of isolation and the built-in autoscaling, it is entirely reasonable for teams to forgo upfront performance testing and tune resources as the usage patterns solidify.

As always, teams need to implement all synchronous calls to handle throttling with retry and exponential back-off logic. Most SDKs provide this out of the box. In stream processors, back-pressure should be added to accommodate for the current capacity allocations, to try to avoid the need for retries as much as possible. With these protections in place, a team can leverage the observability of their components to monitor current activity and quantitatively forecast future needs. This works well in combination with incremental experiments, as each slice is exposed to a controlled set of users.

It is important not to over-optimize too early in the development life cycle, as this often results in wasting valuable development resources for little improved value in performance. It is better to tune performance component by component as the metrics highlight valuable opportunities for improvement. It is interesting to note that performance has two benefactors in cloud-native. For example, the latency of an interaction with a BFF component may be more than sufficient from the end user's point of view. However, if the invocation rate of that interaction is extremely high, then a reduction in latency could have a significant impact on cost and also improve the user experience.

A typical example is a high traffic read operation. Such an operation would pass through an API gateway and invoke a function that reads from the database over and over again. Adding a short cache-control header to the response would cause the request to be frequently handled by the CDN, thus removing the latency and cost of the API gateway and function invocations and the increased database read capacity. Alternatively, if the response changes very infrequently, then storing the JSON in blob storage and serving it directly out of the CDN results in a significant reduction in cost and delivers consistently low latency, not just when there is a cache hit.

High volume stream processors will likely be candidates for performance tuning. The iterator age of the function will be the leading indicator. We have discussed how an increase in an iterator age can be an indication that a stream processor is experiencing an error and is caught in the retry loop. The *Stream Circuit Breaker* pattern discussed in `Chapter 3`, *Foundation Patterns*, provides the mechanism to avoid the retry loop. However, the iterator age is also an indication that the stream process simply cannot keep pace with demand. If the high rate events persist for too long then the processor could start to drop events.

Improving the performance of a stream processor can take many dimensions. First, increasing the shard count could spread the load across multiple instances of the processor, so long as the partition key is well distributed. Next, an increase in the batch size and/or the memory allocation could allow the processor to more efficiently process the load. For function-as-a-service, it is important to understand that increasing the allocated memory does not necessarily equate with higher costs. For typical pricing algorithms, if doubling the allocated memory cuts the execution time in half then the cost is the same. Alternatively, increasing the batch size along with increasing the memory, may allow more throughput with fewer invocations and less execution time.

The bottleneck could also be related to the utilization or saturation of the target resources. When invoking a cloud-native database, we want to maximize utilization by optimizing the request batch size to minimize the number of network requests while also optimizing the number of parallel requests to maximize the use of asynchronous non-blocking IO. The optimal combination of batch size and parallel requests should not saturate the allocated capacity, which would result in throttling and inefficient retries. Back-pressure can be added to rate limit the flow within the allocated capacity.

To identify the optimal tuning for a specific stream processor, it may be necessary to undergo some more traditional performance testing for the specific isolated component. Keep in mind that when such tests are performed, they should not be performed in the production account, as the increased activity will count against the soft limits of the account and negatively impact the production workload.

Summary

In this chapter, we discussed the need to shift some testing to the right into production where we continuously monitor key performance indicators and focus on the mean time to recovery in an effort to increase our confidence in the stability of our cloud-native systems. We leverage both real and synthetic traffic and fully instrument our cloud-native components to maximize the observability of the system. We discussed the need to alert liberally, but page judiciously on user-visible symptoms rather than causes. Once a problem is identified, we investigate the system's work metrics, resource metrics, and events to diagnose the root cause and determine the appropriate actions that must be taken to recover quickly. We also discussed how the observability of a cloud-native system enables teams to continuously tune and improve the performance of the system.

9
Security

In the previous chapter, we continued our deep dive into the human factors of cloud-native. We discussed the need to maximize the observability of our cloud-native systems. We shifted some testing all the way into production, where we continuously monitor key performance indicators and focus on the mean time to recovery in an effort to increase our confidence in the stability of our cloud-native systems. We also discussed how observability enables continuous performance tuning and improvement.

In this chapter, we will continue to discuss the human factors of cloud-native. We leverage the shared responsibility model of cloud-native security and adopt the practice of security-by-design to implement secure systems. We cover the following topics:

- Shared responsibility model
- Security by design
- Accounts as code
- Defense in depth
- Encryption
- Disaster recovery
- Application security
- Regulatory compliance

Shared responsibility model

Security is arguably the biggest hurdle to cloud adoption. It takes a lot of confidence for a company to delegate its security responsibilities to a cloud provider. There is that word confidence again. This lack of confidence is certainly understandable to some degree because security is a complicated topic with many layers. However, how can any company rapidly and continuously deliver innovation to market with the confidence that they have met all their security obligations? One of my customers put it best when he said, *"There is no way I can build a system as secure as I can in the cloud, because I simply do not have the resources to do so."*

Every company has a value proposition and its core competencies are focused on that mission. When push comes to shove, because the time to market is of the essence, it is not unusual for security to get shortchanged. If you need an example, ask yourself if your system relies solely on disk level encryption to secure your data at rest. This practice has become so common, because the alternative requires some extra elbow grease, that we as an industry are largely ignoring the fact that this practice is wholly insufficient. We will discuss this in detail in the *Encryption* section. We will take a recent and notorious breach as an example. We must learn from these mistakes.

Cloud providers, by contrast, understand that security is of the utmost importance precisely because of market pressure. A lapse in security by a cloud provider could cause a large swing in market share. Specific security requirements certainly drive customers towards one cloud provider or another. However, cloud providers do not take on sole responsibility for the security of their customer's systems. Security in the cloud is based on a *shared responsibility model*, whereby the cloud provider and the customer work together to provide system security. Generally speaking, below a certain line in the architecture is the responsibility of the cloud provider and above that line is the responsibility of the customer.

If we draw the shared responsibility line at the lowest level with infrastructure-as-a-service then the cloud provider is responsible for the security of the facilities, the network infrastructure, the virtualization infrastructure, and the physical security of hardware. Above this line, the customer is responsible for the security of everything else from the operating system on up. As we leverage value-added cloud services more and more, the shared responsibility line moves higher and higher. In our cloud-native systems, we are aiming to fully leverage these value-added cloud services. Ultimately, the aim is to draw the line high enough such that our responsibility is focused on protecting the confidentiality, integrity, and availability of the data and not the infrastructure itself.

By leveraging value-added cloud services and optimizing the shared responsibility model, companies can focus on securing their data, which they know best, and let the cloud provider focus on the non-differentiating aspects of securing the cloud services, which they know best. This is similar to how value-added cloud services let us focus on multi-regional deployments because the services already provide multi-availability-zone support. This is how companies rapidly and continuously deliver innovation to market with confidence that they have met all their security obligations within the limits of their scarce resources.

The shared responsibility model and value-added cloud services empower self-sufficient, full-stack teams to build secure components. Within this context, teams must employ the practices of security-by-design and defense-in-depth to fully leverage the security tools provided in the cloud. We will see that these practices simply become an integral part of the cloud-native development methodology.

Security by design

Security-by-design, security-as-code, and security-first are all themes regarding how we as an industry can improve our ability to deliver secure systems. Security-first is certainly a good theme because we simply cannot graft security onto our systems after the fact. However, we need more than security-first. We need a continuous focus on security.

Security-as-code is extremely important. Human error is the root cause of the vast majority of system breaches. This human error can be the inevitable result of configuration drift, as systems are manually configured, patched, and tuned to the point that there is no conformity or traceability and quality suffers. Or human error can result when the sheer effort required to manually patch a system with a known security fix leads to an inertia that leaves value information exposed. Our cloud-native systems are powered by the automation of disposable infrastructure, which leads to high quality, conformity, and traceability. To be fully automated we must treat security requirements the same as any other requirement and work them through our cloud-native development pipeline.

Yet, security-as-code is not enough, because there is a step needed before we should start coding. This is why I prefer the term security-by-design. It is more deliberate and it is continuous. The cloud provides us many tools to carry out our security responsibilities. However, we need to understand these tools and know when to apply them. When we design a story, during story planning sessions and working out the task deployment roadmap, we need to incorporate these security features into the design of the cloud-native component. We will discuss many of these features in the *Defense in depth* section.

Security-by-design should actually start well before the story level. As we architect the feature roadmap we need to classify the sensitivity level of each feature and its individual stories. When we include the sensitivity level as a prominent part of the development process, it puts security front and center. Then during a story planning session, the sensitivity level is a signal to the team that there are additional security concerns that must be addressed, such as specific data elements that must be encrypted or tokenized, as we will discuss in the *Encryption* section.

Each security requirement is ultimately implemented, tested, reviewed, and deployed as a task following the task branch workflow approach discussed in `Chapter 6`, *Deployment*, and `Chapter 7`, *Testing*. As such, the security requirements are continuously and incrementally designed and fully automated. This level of traceability and conformity is also crucial for regulatory compliance, as we will discuss.

Accounts as code

Before we can build and deploy our cloud-native components we need to build and deploy the cloud accounts that they will run in. Far too often insufficient attention is paid to the architecture of cloud accounts. As we discussed in `Chapter 2`, *The Anatomy of Cloud Native Systems*, there is a great deal of thought that needs to put into the design of cloud accounts to ensure proper bulkheads. We certainly need to have separate accounts for production and development. In production, components could be spread across multiple accounts, such as separate accounts for front-office and back-office components. To support regulatory compliance, while also minimizing the scope of compliance, we may isolate certain components with higher sensitivity to their own accounts with additional access restrictions and procedures. A master account for consolidated billing is always recommended, as is a separate recovery account, as we will discuss later in the *Disaster recovery* section.

Once we have designed the architecture of our account hierarchy and topology, we need to codify the implementation of each account. This is no different from how we implement our cloud-native components. Each account is managed in its own project and versioned in its own source code repository. We create a CI/CD pipeline for each and follow the same task branch workflow approach that we discussed in `Chapter 6`, *Deployment*. Each task will deploy new account scoped resources or enhance existing resources. These resources are defined in a `serverless.yml` file just like we do for any component. By treating accounts as the code, we benefit from all the quality, conformity, and traceability of disposable infrastructure.

The first task in the creation of each account after an empty account has been created is to enable auditing. For AWS, this includes enabling CloudTrail for all regions and recording the audit logs in an S3 bucket. From this point on, all administrative actions taken in an account are audited. Therefore, it is important to enable auditing as early as possible to have complete traceability. The next task should create the necessary access policy to grant a third-party monitoring service permission to retrieve metrics from the account, as we discussed in `Chapter 8`, *Monitoring*. The first monitor I create is always on the audit trail to alert on any and every change to the identity and access management system.

These initial tasks, although automated, are not triggered by the pipeline because we have not granted the pipeline access to the account. Thus, the next task is to define the roles, policies, and a user account for the pipeline. Once the access has been granted for the CI/CD pipelines, then all further tasks will be executed via the pipeline when a pull request is accepted. This includes the pipeline for the account project and any other pipeline jobs that target the specific account. The details of these access permissions will depend on your needs, but the point is that the creation of the access permissions is automated.

Thus far we have only granted the root user, the monitoring system, and the CI/CD pipeline access to the account. Next, we need to grant user privileges. Least privileged access and separation of duties are the fundamental principles that should guide the definition of access policies. Assigning individual users to groups to grant access to an account is typically a manual process. However, the definitions of the groups and policies are treated as code. A change to the policies is initiated as a change request, the changes are declared in code and follow our task branch workflow. Once the pull request is accepted then the policy changes are applied to the account. Note that the team requesting a change in policy could implement the declarations and submit the pull request that is then reviewed and accepted by the security team.

In addition to least privilege and separation of duties, an account should enforce the use of strong authentication. Both strong passwords and **multi-factor authentication** (**MFA**) should be required. Use of access keys should be limited to just the CI/CD pipeline, which must store the keys securely. Developers should only need an access key to the Dev account. All access keys should be rotated frequently. The previous first steps needed an access key to bootstrap the account, but that access key should be destroyed once the pipeline is configured.

The maintenance of any other account-scoped resources should be automated as well, such as DNS and certificates. How these resources are allocated to stacks should follow the cloud-native principles of being bounded and cohesive, such as we discussed in `Chapter 2`, *The Anatomy of Cloud Native Systems*. We will also be automating security at every layer of the system, as we will discuss next.

Defense in depth

Security and redundancy go hand in hand. Each layer of the system architecture has its own fortification. This redundancy ensures that if an outer layer is breached, then the next layer can potentially thwart the attack or at least slow it down long enough for the initial breach to be repaired. The number of layers in our cloud-native components is purposefully shallow. All inter-component communication is performed asynchronously via event streaming and all synchronous intra-component communication is with highly available, value-added cloud services, such as cloud-native databases. Our boundary components, such as a BFF component, have the most layers with an edge layer, a component layer, and a data layer; whereas fully asynchronous components will not have an edge layer, because they are entirely internal. The following diagram summarizes the topics we will discuss at the different layers:

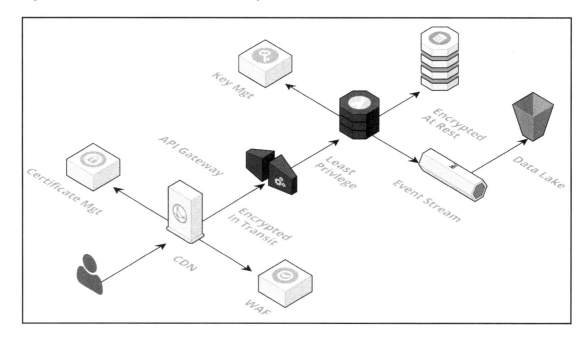

Edge layer

We touched on the importance of leveraging the edge of the cloud in the *API Gateway* pattern, in `Chapter 4`, *Boundary Patterns*. Cloud providers have vast and expansive edge capabilities spread around the globe. These edge capabilities obviously have enormous performance benefits, but their security benefits are on par or more so. It is recommended to route all traffic, `PUT`, `POST`, `DELETE`, `GET`, and so forth, through the CDN, to minimize the attack surface of a cloud-native system. By walling off all other avenues to the system, all traffic must pass through the CDN, which provides managed network level DDOS attack protection. Cloud providers have advanced DDOS offerings, but simply leveraging the CDN provides significant default protection. As a result, an attack is handled at the edge, which reduces the impact of triggering autoscaling policies on internal components. The CDN is also responsible for encryption of data in transit at the edge, as discussed in the *Encryption* section.

A WAF is another important edge capability for providing application layer threat protection. All traffic flowing through the CDN is filtered against the rule set of the WAF. These rules protect against typical **Open Web Application Security Project** (**OWASP**) threats such as SQL injection and cross-site scripting as well as dynamic threats such as blocking specific IP addresses. A specific self-sufficient, full-stack team will usually own the WAF rule set that is plugged into the CDN for each boundary component.

This security team will build the components that react to traffic patterns and dynamically update the WAF rule set. One such component would periodically synchronize the rule set with the publicly available IP reputation list of bad actors, such as spammers, malware distributors, and botnets. Another component would process the CDN access logs and block IP addresses that exceed request limits to stop HTTP floods. While another component would process the CDN access logs and block IP addresses that are submitting bad requests to search for vulnerabilities. It may also be possible to create rules that implement virtual patches for known vulnerabilities, such as the notorious Struts vulnerability. Such rules would give teams additional time to implement and deploy proper patches to their components.

Component layer

The component layer has many different security responsibilities. A BFF component will deploy its own CDN that is connected to the WAF, as discussed earlier. The BFF component will play a role in DDoS protection as well, by employing an API gateway that will handle throttling and by providing sufficient autoscaling to absorb traffic that reaches its internals. Each component will also monitor for and alert on deviations from normal request rates, as discussed in `Chapter 8`, *Monitoring*.

Least privileged access is another important responsibility of each component. Following security-by-design practices, teams will define strict permissions for each component to grant it access to its required resources. For example, an API gateway will be granted specific permissions to the functions that it accesses and those functions will be granted specific permissions to the resources they access, such as cloud-native databases and event streams. All cloud services and resources originate with no access privileges, which helps guarantee least privileged access, so long as teams are specific in the access they grant to their components.

Each component is responsible for encryption of data in transit and at rest, as we will discuss in the *Encryption* section. Each BFF component is responsible for processing JWT tokens, as we will discuss in the *Application security* section.

Data layer

Many of the security requirements at the edge and in component layers are very mechanical and in many cases boilerplate. This is a definite benefit of leveraging value-added cloud services. This, in turn, frees teams to focus on the much more specialized security requirements of securing the data layer. Securing the data layer is more difficult because the requirements are domain specific and thus require input from domain experts. For example, we need domain knowledge to classify the sensitivity level of the different domain entities and their individual data elements. This is why security-by-design is so very important. The shared responsibility model in combination with value-added cloud services allows us to focus on the most important aspect of securing our data, but we must put the practices in place to do so.

We discussed granting access to data resources earlier, in the *Component layer* section. We will discuss encrypting data at rest in depth in the next section on encryption. In the *Encryption* section, we will also discuss some nuances of securing domain events. We will discuss backup and recovery in the *Disaster recovery* section.

Encryption

Security in depth is a critical component of cloud-native security. Multiple levels of least privileged access help ensure that access is controlled at each layer of the technology stack. Value-added cloud services, such as CDN, WAF, API gateway, function-as-a-service, and cloud-native databases, take responsibility for many of the non-differentiated aspects of securing cloud-native systems. Drawing the line of the shared responsibility model as high as possible enables teams to focus their core competency on the security of the data layer.

Following our security-by-design practices, teams need to classify the sensitivity level of their domain data. Based on these classifications, teams then design the proper levels of obfuscation into their components. For each request/response payload, for each database table, for each event type, a team must design how data will be obfuscated at the field level.

Data in transit

Coarse-grained encryption of data in transit is necessary when one side of the communication channel is not able to encrypt the individual elements of the request or response. For example, user interfaces are not able to encrypt data elements because they cannot secure the private key. Therefore, clients will send the data as-is through an encrypted channel, such as HTTPS, and the server-side will decrypt the data for the client before sending it on the encrypted channel.

Fortunately, value-added cloud services make it very easy for cloud-native systems to enforce the encryption of data in transit. For example, API gateways, function-as-a-service, event streams, and cloud-native databases typically only support HTTPS, therefore there is no option but to encrypt the data in transit. These fully managed services handle the certificates so we do not have to.

When using a CDN, we have the choice to use HTTPS or not. For example, a public static website would not necessarily require the use of HTTPS. However, when we use the CDN in front of an API gateway we need to require HTTPS. The CDN is typically used to customize the domain name of an API. In this case, we need to provide a custom SSL certificate to the customer. To make this easy, cloud providers offer a certificate management service. These services integrate with the CDN, take the headache out of creating a certificate, and will automatically renew and deploy the certificate when it expires.

Data at rest

Encrypting data at rest is a fundamental security requirement. However, encrypting data at rest is a much more complicated problem space than encrypting data in transit. For data in transit, we can reasonably take a coarse-grained approach and require that all traffic over all communication channels use SSL. We can do this because communication is a transient event between two parties, where the consumer has been authenticated and its client software is trusted. Encryption at rest is a more complex problem space because once data is stored, there will be many more interactions with many more parties over the life of the data.

Unfortunately, a coarse-grained approach to encrypting data at rest is insufficient. I think it is fair to say that the data in many data breaches that have been publicly reported were likely encrypted at rest. However, they were encrypted at rest using disk-based encryption. Disk-based encryption is a false sense of security. Far too often, disk-based encryption is used to check the box on a security requirement when it doesn't actually satisfy the requirement or at least the spirit of the requirement.

The problem with disk-based encryption is that it is only effective when the disk is disconnected from the system, in other words, when the disk is being used as a paperweight. So long as the disk is connected to the system and the key that was used to encrypt the data, then the data is automatically decrypted when it is read from the disk. This is fine, so long as the party and/or software doing the reading can be trusted. However, when the data has a long life and there are many interactions with many different parties, then the likelihood increases that human error will accidentally make the data accessible.

For example, let's say that a user has legitimate permission to access all the data in a database. Once a query is executed and the data is returned then the data has been decrypted at this point and the user can read all the data in its entirety. This may be perfectly reasonable at this point. But what if the data is exported? Was the disk that the data was exported to encrypted? Maybe the data is then uploaded to an S3 bucket for some ad-hoc analysis. Is access to the bucket restricted and was server-side encryption enabled? Was the data thoroughly deleted from the disk after it was uploaded to S3? Are we certain that someone won't innocently make the S3 bucket public at some later date? Even with server-side encryption, the data of a public bucket will be decrypted when it is read. This type of human error happens so frequently that AWS has instituted a program to notify accounts regarding public buckets.

As another example, a bug in the software at a higher layer in the technology stack could open up a vulnerability that allows malicious access to lower layers of infrastructure, such that rogue applications can be installed. At that point, the rogue applications could likely access that database with the permissions available on the infected machines. Even if the permissions were restricted to read access, the data would still be decrypted as it is read from the database. This is a plausible description of what might have happened in a recent and notorious public breach.

The point of both these examples is to emphasize that disk-based encryption, although easy to implement, is a woefully inadequate solution to encrypting data at rest. It solves only one piece of the puzzle. To truly solve this problem we need to encrypt data at rest using application-side encryption. Unfortunately, application-side encryption has been generally avoided because it is subject to the human error of omission. In other words, it is not as easy to implement, therefore teams may neglect to implement it properly or at all. Fortunately, value-added cloud services and security-by-design address this problem directly.

Application level encryption is the superior approach to securing data at rest because it effectively allows us to redact sensitive data. In all our preceding examples, the sensitive data will remain encrypted until someone or something, with permission to access the encryption keys and knowledge of which fields are encrypted, decrypts the data. An added bonus is that it also improves performance for all cases where the data does not need to be decrypted. The perceived downsides of this approach are easily addressed, as we will discuss next, plus they are outweighed by the serious downsides of disk-based encryption.

Envelope encryption

First and foremost, effective application level encryption is predicated on strong security-by-design practices. As teams architect the feature roadmap, the sensitivity level of the features must be classified. This starts to drive the design of the domain model, such that sensitive data is properly isolated. At the story level, a team will identify the exact data elements that must be encrypted, evaluate alternatives such as tokenization, determining if the data needs to be queried and filtered by encrypted fields, and whether or not the sensitive data should be included in domain events.

Teams will use the cloud provider's key management service to encrypt sensitive fields using an approach called **envelope encryption**, which is the process of encrypting one key with another key. A master key is created at deployment time, whereas data keys are created at runtime. Each time a domain entity is saved, a new data key is generated to minimize the need for rotation. The sensitive information is then encrypted with the data key. The data key is encrypted with the master key and saved along with the domain entity. Later, when the domain entity is retrieved the data key is decrypted and then used to decrypt the sensitive information.

Performing queries and filters on sensitive data require additional work because it is not possible to filter on an application level encrypted field. Instead, an additional field must be created that will contain a one-way hash of the sensitive data. The user entered search value is hashed as well to perform the comparison. This means that wildcard searches on these values are not possible. In the case of **Personally identifiable information** (**PII**), such as zip codes or states, this is not a problem, but it does make searching based on street address more cumbersome.

Tokenization

Tokenization is an interesting alternative to encryption that works for some types of data. A token is a generated value that replaces and references the real value. It cannot be used in place of real value. It can only be used to look up the real value. A tokenized value has the advantage that it resembles a real value. An example of a tokenized credit card number is 4111-XXXX-YYYY-1111. The tokenized value can be securely used throughout the system because it is not the real number. For example, this value could be securely presented to a user in a user interface and recognized as representing a credit card number. The user would recognize the last four digits of their card and the first four digits would indicate the type of card. Yet the token is useless until securely exchanged for the real value, which requires proper permissions.

Tokenization is used in conjunction with isolation. A dedicated component often called a vault, is responsible for generating the tokens and storing the tokenized values. This component is isolated in its own cloud account with strict rules regarding who is allowed access to operate the account. Background checks and clearances are often required. This capability is usually purchased as-a-service from a third-party.

Domain events

The domain events that we exchange in our reactive cloud-native systems have interesting nuances with regard to data at rest because of their durability and immutability. In many cases, an event is produced and discarded after it is consumed. However, some consumers store events for a period of time or indefinitely, as is the case with the data lake. This means that we must retain the keys for all domain events with encrypted values if we need to be able to read those values. Regulations, such as the upcoming EU **General Data Protection Regulation** (**GDPR**), add another wrinkle for immutable events because of the requirement to forget a user's PII data upon request.

There are many possible solutions and combinations of solutions to these nuances. The first and most common option is to de-identify the data in domain events. In this case, the sensitive data is only ever accessible in the context of the owning component. Tokenization is an alternative for some data elements because there are no keys to retain and the data can be forgotten by removing the data from the vault, which effectively de-references the tokens. A third alternative is crypto shredding, in which the encryption key is purposefully deleted rendering the data useless. Security-by-design is critical for teams faced with these kinds of requirements.

Disaster recovery

In `Chapter 2`, *The Anatomy of Cloud Native Systems*, we discussed a disaster that befell a company named Code Spaces, which they were not able to recover from. Code Spaces was the victim of a malicious ransomware attack. Their account was compromised, they fought back and the contents of their entire account was ultimately deleted. They had no way to recover. This sounds frightening, and it certainly is, but it is an entirely avoidable problem. They perished so that we could learn from their mistakes.

Malicious attacks are not the only type of disaster. Honest human errors can result in a disaster. This ought to be a much more bounded disaster, assuming proper bulkheads are in order. Nevertheless, we must make provisions for such an occurrence. And of course, there are natural disasters that must be accounted for. All these scenarios have significant overlap in their appropriate response, which we will cover here.

In the case of a malicious attack, we, of course, want to endeavor to prevent such an event in the first place. We have already discussed the necessary provisions in this chapter. We need strong passwords and multi-factor authentication. All cloud providers worth their salt support MFA for account access. A software token application, such as Google Authenticator, can be easily installed on smartphones and linked to a user in an account. Use of access keys for automation should be severely limited to just the CI/CD pipelines and only as needed for super users in production accounts. These keys should be rotated frequently. Where possible, mechanisms for generating temporary keys should be employed. In some cases, it may be worth the additional effort to tunnel access through a bastion account.

Once a user is authenticated, least privileged access should be granted. Permissions to delete resources should be significantly curtailed, particularly in production accounts. Permissions to assign permissions must be restricted to a limited set of users. As the saying goes, with great power comes great responsibility. All users, but particularly super users, must take great care not to expose their access keys. For example, never check access keys into source control. Certainly not in hosted providers, such as GitHub, even if the project is private.

I have personally witnessed a scenario where an access key was stored in a private GitHub account and the account was inadvertently made public in the wee hours of the night. Within hours, that key was found by bots and used to create EC2 instances in our account in all regions up to the account limits to mine bitcoins. By morning, our monitors had alerted us to the fact, just prior to being alerted by cloud support as well. As I recall, they were able to tell us which GitHub account exposed the access keys, which means this kind of problem warranted the creation of their own bots. Fortunately, this was just our development account and the attack was not necessarily malicious. Had this been a production account it would have limited our ability to scale out additional instances, but there was no attempt to otherwise harm the account. This event made for a very exciting morning and a grand tale, but most importantly it highlights the need to be vigilant with your access keys.

Natural disasters, such as severe weather, are typically restricted to a single region. Honest human errors ought to be restricted to a single region as well. Multi-regional deployment is the frontline solution to these disasters. Value-added cloud services make multi-regional deployment extremely practical. This does not mean that every component warrants multi-regional deployment. However, critical components with high **service level agreements (SLA)** are worthy candidates.

Start with one component in an active-passive configuration. Deploy the API gateway, functions, and cloud-native databases in multiple regions. Enable regional replication for the cloud-native databases. Configure DNS to route traffic to the secondary/passive region only when there is a failure in the primary/active region. Use the secondary region for canary deployments, as we discussed in `Chapter 6`, *Deployment*. Do not create scripts that automatically deploy to all regions, otherwise, an honest human error may impact all your regions. Once you are comfortable with this first step into multi-regional deployment, then update the DNS routing to allow for active-active to the nearest region and repeat for other components.

Multi-regional deployments, however, do not ward off a malicious attack or a catastrophic human error with automation across regions. In these cases, backups are necessary for recovery. Yet, to be effective, backups themselves must be replicated to a separate region and a separate account. In the case of Code Spaces, they did have backups. However, those backups were only stored in the same account alongside the original data and thus were deleted along with everything else. Assuming that strong authentication and least privilege are employed, then in the unlikely event that an account is compromised, then it is even more unlikely that a second recovery account is simultaneously compromised as well.

Start by adding an additional recovery account with strong authentication in an unused region. This account will only store backups in blob storage. Configure the data lake to replicate to this new account. A data lake is the audit trail of all events produced by the system. From the data lake, we can replay events to repair components. Therefore, so long as the data lake is securely replicated to the recovery account, then it is possible to use the data lake to recover from a disaster. However, using the data lake to replay all the system's events, from essentially the beginning of time, will be a time-consuming process. Yet, it is good to have this as an option, it is comprehensive and it can be put in place quickly. Restoring backups, in general, is time-consuming, therefore multi-regional deployments are the preferred first order of recovery for the cases discussed previously.

From here, each team is responsible for putting proper backups in place for their data stores. This typically involves leveraging native backup features to back up data to local blob storage that is then replicated to the recovery account. If a data store does not support backups, then reverse the process by first putting the data in blob storage, which triggers an event to put the data in the target data store. Backup the data in each region. We are already replicating across regions, so this does mean that backups will be redundant for each region, but it also means that data will continue to be backed up even when a region is down and traffic has failed over. Put another way, storage is cheap compared to the complexity of trying to optimize the backup mechanism. Since the data is already replicated many times, teams can reduce cost by reducing the redundancy in the blob storage itself and using the infrequently accessed options. Add lifecycle rules to age the backups as well.

Incident response is crucial for disaster recovery. As we discussed in `Chapter 8`, *Monitoring*, we want to focus on the mean time to recovery, which is predicated on the mean time to detection. Health checks will monitor the health of each region so that traffic is only routed to healthy regions. As mentioned in the *Accounts as code* section, we need to monitor the cloud audit trail for unexpected activity that could indicate an intrusion, such as changes in access rights or deletion of the audit trail itself. Sudden increases in resource utilization warrant investigation, as do moderate but consistent increases in off-peak periods.

In any case, we work the methodology, as discussed in `Chapter 8`, *Monitoring*, to diagnose the situation and take appropriate action. An incident response plan should be put in place for when the diagnosis is a security breach or a disaster in general. Teams should perform periodic drills and chaos testing, such as testing the backups or purposefully shutting down a region, respectively.

Application security

Up to this point, our focus has been on cloud-native security from the system perspective. The seams between all the layers are sealed and access to the system is tightly guarded. Now we turn our attention to securing the application of the system. We can loosely think of this as securing the users of the applications versus the owners of the system. If you are just a developer at heart, then this is where you may have traditionally started. However, as self-sufficient, full-stack teams, this is only part of our overall responsibility for security. We can say that we are no longer application engineers or system engineers; instead, we are now all cloud-native engineers.

As application engineers, we have all likely built a user management system of some sort or another. Fortunately, in cloud-native, this un-differentiated activity is now delegated to value-added cloud services that provide federated identity management capabilities and support standards, such as OAuth 2.0, OpenID Connect, and **JSON Web Tokens (JWT)**. Our application and business logic are decoupled from the actual security mechanisms more so than ever before. As summarized in the following diagram, we will discuss how to integrate with federated identity management at the application, API Gateway, and business logic levels:

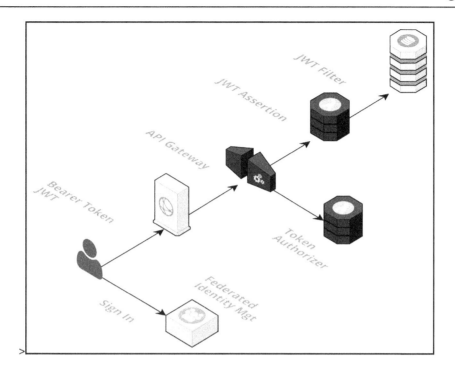

Federated identity management

Following our security-by-design practice, we first need to think about the users of our applications and how they will prefer to sign into our applications. Do we have customers who will want to sign in using their social media credentials? Will employees be using the applications with their corporate credentials? What about multiple third-parties who will want to sign in using their corporate credentials? We also need to decouple all these details from our frontend applications and our BFF components.

To satisfy these requirements, we can leverage a federated identity management service, such as AWS Cognito, Auth0, or Azure Active Directory B2C. With these services, we can integrate many different identity providers, such as social media, SAML 2.0, and OpenID Connect compliant providers, into a unified development experience for our frontend applications and BFF components based on OAuth 2.0, OpenID Connect, and JWT.

Frontend applications will integrate with the sign up, sign in, and sign out user interfaces provided by these services. If you find yourself writing a custom login screen then you are more than likely on the wrong track. Instead, your frontend code should redirect to the third-party sign-in page when it does not have a validate JWT token. Once authenticated, the user is redirected back to your application with a JWT token that you securely save in local storage so that it can be passed along on requests to BFF components. The identity token will also contain user information, such as the user's name, that can be leveraged for display purposes and claims that can be used for role-based screen rendering. If you find yourself making additional calls to retrieve permissions then you are likely on the wrong track again.

Federated identity management is an external service, so we will want to implement an External Service Gateway component to encapsulate backend integration with the chosen service, as we discussed in `Chapter 4`, *Boundary Patterns*. The example for the External Service Gateway pattern implemented a bridge to translate AWS Cognito events into domain events on the internal event stream. This allows other components to react to events in the external service, such as user sign-up and sign-in. These services do provide CRUD APIs to interact with users; however, they generally have low throttling thresholds and our objective is to eliminate inter-component synchronous communication. Therefore, BFF components will want to leverage the CQRS pattern to cache needed user information in a materialized view. If your application needs a user management BFF component to list users, invite users, and assign permissions, then the external service gateway component would react to domain events from the BFF component to synchronize with the federated identity management service.

API gateway

When the frontend applications interact with their BFF component they will do so through an API gateway and pass along the JWT token from their local storage in the authorization header. This is a bearer token, which means that it is critical to communicate over HTTPS so that the token cannot be intercepted. This will not be a problem since API gateways typically require the use of HTTPS.

The API gateway acts as a barrier at the edge of the system and is responsible for verifying the signature of the bearer token. If you are using the federated identity management service of your cloud provider then the turnkey integration with the API gateway will likely be all that you need to secure your API at this layer. This turnkey integration was demonstrated in the *API Gateway* pattern in `Chapter 4`, *Boundary Patterns*. For more complex scenarios you can write a custom token authorizer. This typically just involves downloading the public **JSON Web Key** (**JWK**) for the token issuer and using it to verify the token with your JWT library of choice. Once verified, the decoded token is passed along as contextual information to the business logic layer.

JWT assertion and filter patterns

At the business logic layer, security processing should be extremely lightweight. The federated identity management service abstracts away any difference between the various identity providers. The JWT token has already been verified and decoded by the API gateway, so no extra library is needed to handle the token. The identity token should usually include all the necessary user information and claims needed, such that no additional data needs to be retrieved from the database. The business logic simply uses the contents of the token to support its requirements.

The UUID or username of the authenticated user should be used to stamp any database update or event for auditing purposes. The claims/entitlements in the token can be used for conditional control flow or to assert business level validations. A more interesting scenario has to do with database filters. A RESTful resource will typically include URL and/or query parameters, such as `/tenants/{tenantId}?param1=123`. To enforce data privacy we would need to assert that the user making the request is a member of the specified tenant. This information should be available as a claim in the token. The business logic would need to assert that the tenantId URL parameter is equal to the tenantId claim in the token. Furthermore, we should always use the values from the token in database filters instead of the values in the parameters in the request, because the token has been more strongly asserted as valid based on the signature. This helps avoid a bug in the business logic assertion that could allow a different tenant's data to be exposed.

Regulatory compliance

Compliance with the many security certifications, regulations, and frameworks, such as SOC, PCI, and HIPAA, is of extreme importance to cloud providers because it is important to cloud consumers. This is evident by the extent to which a cloud provider's value-added services have been approved under these different assurance programs. Simply put, as cloud customers, we are subject to these assurance programs, therefore we must choose a cloud provider that has been approved as well. Failing to support a specific program can be a competitive disadvantage for a cloud provider.

This is another benefit of the shared responsibility model. As we draw the line higher and higher with the use of value-added cloud services, we also inherit more and more security controls from the cloud provider. This, in turn, allows us to focus our attention on the security controls that are in line with our core competencies. To live up to our responsibilities as cloud customers, it is important to recognize that compliance in many ways has more to do with human factors than it does with technical factors. In many cases, to be compliant, we must demonstrate that security practices are followed on a daily basis. This is where cloud-native, disposable infrastructure and security-by-design play significant roles. By making security an integral part of the daily methodology and fully automating all deployments, we can achieve a level of quality, conformity, and traceability that is very demonstrable.

As an example, for any given requirement an auditor will ask a team to demonstrate compliance. The team would present the auditor with the history of task branch workflows. They would show the requirement in the issue tracking system that is linked to the code changes in source control. Those changes would be linked to the pull request that shows that the change was reviewed, passed all tests, and was approved. The pull request, in turn, is linked to the specific immutable deployment by the CI/CD pipeline, which is also corroborated by the cloud audit trail. The cloud audit trail would also show any manual changes that have taken place, which would have triggered an alert in the monitoring system. This level of conformity and traceability on each successive requirement makes for a very smooth audit because it makes an auditor's job easy due to how straightforward it is for the auditor to attest to the security and compliance of the system.

From here, the test engineering practices take over because continuous testing is another aspect of compliance and governance. For example, the team that owns the WAF and the OWASP rules would work with the various teams that own BFF components to automate penetration testing on a continuous basis. Cloud providers and third-party vendors offer a growing number of governance tools that continuously monitor the configuration of value-added cloud services. Test engineers would configure these tools to alert teams to deviations from expected practices. In essence, the same API-driven nature of cloud resources, which make immutable disposable infrastructure possible, also facilitates governance.

From a practical standpoint, it is also important to limit your system's exposure to any specific compliance requirements. For example, PCI compliance is only required for any part of the system that actually handles a credit card number. With traditional monolithic systems, this inevitably drew the entire system into the scope of compliance. However, with cloud-native systems, we can limit the scope to a specific component or a small set of components and isolate those components in a dedicated account that is operated by a team of employees with the necessary clearance. The rest of the system would only handle tokenized representations of the credit card numbers. This does not relinquish other teams from practicing security-by-design, but it does significantly reduce the burden to demonstrate compliance.

Regional requirements are an important part of security-by-design. We need to be aware of data that must be restricted to certain geographical regions. For example, PII needs to be restricted to the country of origin and cannot be replicated to regions in other countries. Data requirements like this should be owned by specific, bounded, isolated components. The multi-regional deployment and replication of these components would be carefully designed. The data in events emitted by these components would be carefully encrypted, tokenized, and/or de-identified, such that the events can travel safely downstream.

Summary

In this chapter, we discussed how the shared responsibility model of cloud security, when combined with value-added cloud services, enables teams to focus their energies on the security of their data. We leverage the practices of security-by-design and security-as-code to increase confidence in the security of cloud-native systems by eliminating the human factors of implementing defense-in-depth policies, such as least privilege and encryption, through automation. Nevertheless, we discussed safeguards to ensure continuity of service in the event that we need to recover from a disaster. In addition to overall system security, we discussed application level security topics, such as OAuth, OpenID Connect, and JWT. We also discussed how the increased quality, conformity, and traceability of cloud-native systems facilitate regulatory compliance.

10
Cloud Native Application Design

In this chapter, we will dive deep into the development of cloud native architectures, using microservices and serverless computing as a mature CNMM state. Starting with the evolution of computer systems from monolithic and moving through much more mature architectures, this chapter will cover containers, orchestration, and serverless, how they fit together, and why they are considered mature on the application-centric design axis.

From monolithic to microservices and everything in between

Client-server applications have always been popular. However, as networking technology and design patterns have evolved, the need to have less tightly coupled applications intercommunicating has given way to **service-oriented architectures** (**SOAs**). An SOA is the concept of breaking down the components that make up a monolith or server into more discrete business services. SOA components are still self-contained. However, they are significantly smaller in scope than the traditional monolithic application and enable faster maintenance and decoupled interactions. The traditional client could still be considered a component of an SOA application, but, instead of communicating directly with a monolithic server, there would be an intermediation layer, or server bus, that accepts the call and distributes to other services for processing. These other services could offer data persistence or collect additional information to make a business decision. The SOA approach has opened up the ability to distribute systems and allow a massive change in interaction among other systems, even those outside a company's internal systems.

Cloud computing continues to evolve these patterns because of increasingly lower costs for these services, as well as the rising availability of resources to create services. Microservices, which are similar to SOAs, are an evolution that allows for a specific service to be broken down into even more discrete components. A service in an SOA is a black box that performs a full business function. Microservices are made up of that function, which is broken down to perform subsets of the larger business function. This will further increase system maintenance and speed to make functionality updates and also reduce the blast radius of code or hardware faults. A cloud native architecture will have various maturity levels on the cloud native maturity model, including using cloud native services, application-centric design and automation, and application design principles. Microservices offer a way to achieve all of those principles so as to enable scale and fault tolerance that is hard to achieve with any of the other traditional ways of system design.

System design patterns

The evolution of systems design is one where various pressures impacted the way systems were built and deployed to solve ever more complex business problems. This section will cover these patterns in more detail and provide additional insights into how they work and the challenges they faced, forcing evolution. To understand how solution architecture has progressed, it is important to define a few key concepts, namely primitives, subsystems, and systems.

Regardless of the design pattern, primitives are the base level of the overall solution, often referred to as functions, tasks, or microservices, depending on the style. By design, a primitive is supposed to be the most basic unit that is capable of performing an action. Primitives are often so specialized that, by themselves, they are not capable of having a direct impact on the subsystem they belong to. Instead, they perform one task quickly and efficiently. Subsystems are logical groupings of primitives that form a discrete business function. Subsystems do not have to be a single component, although they can be depending on the design architecture. They do, however, need to have a logical flow that results in a business function being achieved. The primitives that make up the subsystem could be function calls within the same code block or a completely separate microservice, as long as the results end in a completed outcome for the system. Systems are the top level of the solution, and are often made up of many subsystems that intercommunicate with each other, or other systems, to complete an entire process from beginning to end.

Cloud native architectures are the product of this evolution. It's important to understand the makeup of an architecture and the originations of the patterns so further evolution can continue and the best design for a specific business requirement can be used and evolved over time. There are three main design patterns, namely monolithic, client server, and services. Each uses the concept of systems, subsystems, and primitives. However, the implementation of each is the key differentiators that allow for them to be more robust and cloud native.

Monolithic

From the early days of information technology and the advent of computing power to speed up computational tasks, the preferred design pattern for an application was monolithic. Simply put, a monolithic design pattern is one in which all aspects of the system are self-contained and independent from other systems or processes. This pattern worked great with the large mainframe monoliths that existed and allowed for the code logic, storage devices, and printing to all be done in the same location. Networking, as we know it today, was not possible and what little connectivity was available was significantly slower, preventing additional systems from being interconnected. As new business requirements were identified, they were designed directly in the existing monolith, making them critical and very tightly coupled. Ultimately, monolithic design patterns enabled all tasks to be executed to complete a desirable outcome.

As technology advanced and the needs of computational power were evolving, system designers found that adding new functionality into a monolith was cumbersome and potentially introduced hard-to-identify bugs. They also realized that reusing components and tasks was a great way to save time, money, and reduce code change bugs. This modular approach to systems design, which was still mostly monolithic, enabled reuse and allowed for more targeted maintenance updates to take place without impacting the entire application or system. This philosophy continued to evolve as technology advanced and allowed for the splitting apart of some of the largest monoliths into separate discrete subsystems, which could then be updated independently. This concept of decoupling components is a key driving factor into the evolution of system designs and will continue to get more and more discrete as technology advances.

Client server

Eventually, as technology costs lowered and design patterns continued to advance to more sophisticated levels, a new style of architecture became popular: client server applications. The monolith still existed to provide the backend processing power and data storage required. However, because of advances in networking and database concepts, a frontend application, or client, was used to provide a user experience and transmit data to the server. The client application is still tightly coupled with the server application. However, it allows for potentially many clients connecting into the server and therefore distributing the application to a field workforce or public users on the internet. This evolution of the modular approach also changed the way IT departments deployed and maintained systems, with different groups responsible for the client and server components, and skill sets started to specialize and focus on how to further drive efficiencies.

Services

Client server applications worked very well, but the coupling of components caused slow and risky deployments for mission-critical applications. System designers continued to find ways to separate components from each other to reduce the blast radius of failure, increase the speed of deployments, and reduce risk during the process. A services design pattern is where business functions are broken down into specific objectives to complete in a self-contained manner that doesn't require knowledge of or dependencies on the state of another service. This self-contained independent state of the service is in itself the definition of decoupling and marks a major evolutionary change from monolithic architectures. The change to services design is directly related to the reduction in the price of compute and storage and the increase in network sophistication and security practices for intercommunication. Lowering costs allows for many computing instances of services to be created across wider geographical regions and with a more diverse set of business functional requirements.

Services are not just custom code designed to solve a business problem. In fact, as cloud vendors mature their services, often a managed offering is created to help remove the undifferentiated heavy lifting of some piece of a system. These individual services fit into the services category and often make up specific functions in a large distributed and decoupled solution, for example, using a queueing service or storage service as a function of the design. In a monolithic system architecture, all of these components would need to be developed and would exist in a single application stack with tightly coupled interconnectivity and significant risk of failures, slowdowns, or faulty code. Mature cloud native architectures are specifically designed to take advantage of these vendor services in addition to custom functions, all working as one to react to different events, and ultimately driving business outcomes with as little complexity as possible.

While services-based architectures are very popular with cloud native architectures, the evolution of services design has taken time. From the first iteration of SOAs, to microservices, to functions, each pattern breaks up the functionality even more to decouple their interactions as much as possible.

Service-oriented architectures (SOAs)

A services design pattern that has been around since before the cloud is the SOA. This is the first major evolution of breaking down a monolithic application into separate parts to reduce the blast radius and help make application development and deployment processes faster to support business velocity. SOA design patterns are often still a large application split into subsystems that interact with each other just as they would in a monolithic system. However, they often have an intermediation layer in between (for example, an **Enterprise Service Bus** (**ESB**)).

The use of an ESB to mediate service requests allows for heterogeneous communication protocols and further service decoupling, often through the exchange of messaging. The ESB allows for message translation, routing, and other forms of mediation to ensure that the consumer service is receiving the messages in the right form at the right time. Because SOA design patterns are often combined to make a large and complex enterprise system, individual services often contain a full set of business logic for a specific subsystem. This design allows for the service to be partially self-contained and send messages, through the EBS, to provide or request data from other subsystems.

This SOA design approach drastically increased the ability for systems to be more distributed, serve business needs faster, and take advantage of cheaper compute resources. However, there are some drawbacks that are associated with SOAs as well. Because services interact with other components through an ESB, it can quickly become a bottleneck or single point of failure. Message flow becomes very complicated and any disruption to the ESB could cause significant slowdowns or queueing of messages, clogging up the entire system. In addition, because each service requires a specific message type formatted with its requirements, testing of the full composite application becomes very complicated and not isolated, slowing down business velocity. For example, when two services have significant business logic updates, each with new and enhanced message formats, the deployment will require an update to both subsystems and the ESB, potentially disrupting the entire composite application.

Microservices

The evolution of SOAs has led to continued breakdown of business functionality into even smaller components, often referred to as microservices. These are still services, as defined earlier. However, the scope of the services and the way they intercommunicate has evolved to take advantage of technology and pricing. Microservices are often used to help reduce some of the challenges faced with SOAs, while continuing to mature the services model. There are two key differentiators for microservices designs when compared to SOA: the scope of service and communication methods.

Microservices are designed the further specialize the scope of the service. With SOAs, a service will act as a full subsystem that has a large block of business functionality where a microservices architecture will break down that subsystem into components closer to primitives that perform a subset of the main service. The microservice might have business logic or it might just perform a workflow task, such as a database transaction, auditing, or logging. If it contains business logic, the scope will be much smaller than an SOA service and will usually not be a standalone component able to complete a full business task. This breakdown of the functionality allows for the service to scale independently from other components and often execute based on an event to reduce the time the cloud resources are being used and paid for.

The other key differentiator of a microservice is the communication method. SOAs will often communicate with heterogeneous protocols through an ESB, where microservices expose an API that can be called from any consumer service. This exposure of an API allows for the service to be developed in any language that will have no impact from other services and their development language or approach. Because of the decoupled nature of the API layer, changes to the service logic often require no coordination between consumer services, and even when the API itself is modified only the consumer services need to be notified, which can often be done via dynamic API endpoint identification and navigation.

Why services matter

A key differentiator of the cloud is the way applications are designed and deployed, with services-based architecture being the most popular. Services matter because they allow for applications to be designed into ever smaller components that have faster deployment velocity allowing business ideas to come to market quicker. In addition, the smaller a service or function, the smaller the blast radius, meaning that a fault or bad code only impacts a relatively small amount of connected services. This reduced blast radius has a significant improvement on the risk profile of code deployments and the time required to roll back if something bad was introduced:

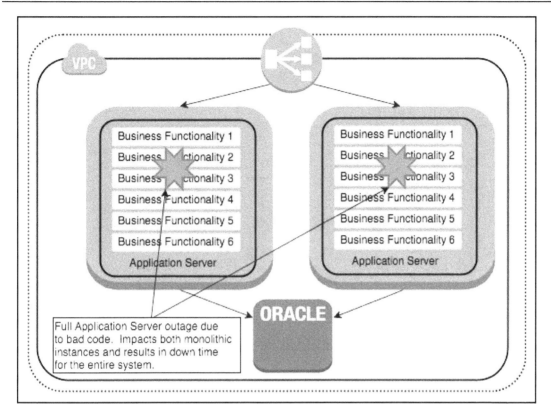

A monolithic system deployed for high availability

The preceding diagram shows a monolithic system, deployed to multiple instances for high availability, but using a design pattern to deploy the full application functionality into an application server on each instance. In this case, the business functionality boxes are an example of a subsystem that would have many different functions, or primitives that are included to complete the required functionally. In this example, the deployment of new code must be done at the system level and will likely require scheduled downtime and a full redeploy of the entire application artifact. If any of the newly deployed code has an unintended bug in a subsystem or primitive, the entire application will be impacted since it's all deployed together. This unscheduled outage will roll back the entire application artifact, even subsystems that were working as intended in other parts of the system. This design is not very flexible and causes long and stressful **big bang** deployments that need to be planned for weeks or months in advance.

By decoupling systems and the business functionality into separate subsystems, the interaction points between these subsystems is significantly lowered and often they will never communicate at all. Using subsystems and primitives in the form of services allows for the changes being made to be vastly less impactful to the wider organization, causing the risk associated with those changes to go down because the blast radius is reduced to only those services directly related to it. Depending on the requirements, a subsystem might still be an isolated coupled component or broken into many primitives:

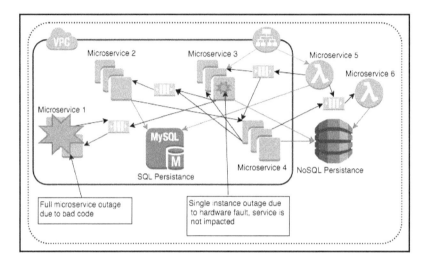

The original monolithic application

In the preceding diagram, the original monolithic application was redesigned and deployed into separate subsystems and primitives, using a mix of instances, containers, functions, and cloud vendor services. Not all services interact with each other or persist data, so if there are problems in the environment most are still usable. Subsystem 1 shows as having an outage due to bad code being deployed, which will be discovered and resolved by the appropriate services team. Meanwhile, all other services are still operating with no impact, unless they were to interact with subsystem 1. The diagram also shows the impact of a single instance outage due to hardware fault, a common occurrence that should not impact the entire system or any individual service. Subsystem 3 would detect that it lost an instance in its fleet and automatically deploy a new instance or container to keep up with incoming requests. Primitive Microservices 5 and 6 are executed as event-based code blocks that interact with other primitives to persist data, interact with message queues, or perform a business function.

Services matter since they allow for separation of functionality, reduce blast radius, increase business velocity and, if done correctly, reduce the cost to run the full system.

Containers and serverless

Cloud native architectures have matured over the years as the patterns evolve to take advantage of the newest advances in cloud technologies. Microservices are currently the hot topic for architecture trends since they allow for massive decoupling of components while utilizing cloud native services in ways that would be impossible with on-premises software. However, microservices are just a pattern. There are multiple ways to construct a microservice with various technologies and approaches, and containers and serverless approaches are the most common. This is not to say that microservice systems cannot be designed with more traditional virtual instances; in the right use case, that is still very applicable. What it means is that containers and serverless technologies allow for systems to be designed and deployed at scale and with agility that typically comes with microservices. They are more aligned with the goals of microservices. This section will explore containers and serverless, explaining what that means, and how they can be used to design cloud native architectures.

Containers and orchestration

Containers are a natural progression of additional isolation and virtualization of hardware. Where a virtual instance allows for a bare metal server to have multiple hosts, hence gaining more efficiencies and usage of that specific server's resources, containers behave similarly but are much more lightweight, portable, and scalable. Typically, containers run a Linux, or, in some cases, Windows operating system. However, a lot of the bloat and unused components are removed, and they handle the traditional startup, shutdown, and task management, and not much else. Developers are then able to include specific libraries or languages and deploy the code and configurations directly to the container file. This is then treated as the deployment artifact and published to a registry to be deployed or updated across the fleet of containers already running in the cluster via the orchestration service.

Because of the lightweight nature of containers, they make for an ideal technology to run in a cloud environment and for extreme decoupling of an application into microservices. The scaling aspect of containers can take place across nodes to maximize the resources on that instance and by using many hosts to form a cluster that are all maintained and scheduled by the orchestration service. For file storage, the service can use local ephemeral filesystem locations, or if the data needs to persist, the files can be stored in a persistent volume which is mounted and accessible by all containers in the node. To make the container placement and scaling easier, some orchestration tools use pods, or containers coupled together to act as a single unit that are instantiated together and scale together.

Registries

A container registry is simply a public or private area for the storage, and serving, of pre-built containers. There are many options for a registry that can be used, and all the major cloud vendors have a hosted version of registries that can be made private for a specific organization. In addition, there are many public hosted registries, such as the Docker Hub registry, that holds publicly available pre-built container files that have lots of common configurations ready to use. Depending on the needs of an organization, any of these would work. However, once the learning phase is completed, it's recommended that hosted private registries are always used. In addition to being much more secure for private container images, if hosted in the cloud environment, this also provides close proximity to the orchestration service for a faster deployment pipeline.

Registries play a critical role in the CI/CD pipelines that will be used for deployment of applications. We have a simple pipeline where the developer checks code into the repository of choice (in this case, a GIT repository). That push triggers a build using Jenkins, which will build the container, test the newly formed container using predefined scripts, and push that container to the registry service. Once in the registry, the orchestration tool will trigger a pull from the registry that will take the new container and perform an update or deploy. There are a few ways to achieve the final deployment: either a rolling update for zero downtime or a new deployment following the configuration requirements.

Orchestration

The orchestration of containers is where the hard part comes in. If an application was designed to use containers as a large monolithic stack that performs all the tasks required for the subsystem to execute, then deploying those containers becomes a pretty easy task. However, this also defeats the purpose of using containers and microservices, which is to decouple the components into small services that interact with each other or other services. As a subsystem is broken down into many separate primitive microservices, the ability to coordinate those services, made up of one or many containers, becomes very difficult. Some services will be relatively small and will only be used sparingly, while others will be very high volume and require strict scaling and high availability configurations In addition, the deployment of new containers to the cluster is critical and usually needs to be done with little or no downtime, making a service that performs those updates very valuable.

There are many types of container orchestration tools on the market, and each cloud vendor will have one or more managed versions, or an organization can choose to set up and maintain their own orchestration tools, depending on their requirements. One of the most popular orchestration services is Kubernetes, which can run on any cloud platform, on-premises, or a hybrid of both. There are reasons to use a cloud vendor's container orchestration service over a third-party tool, most notably the native interaction of the containers and other cloud services provided by the vendor. However, even now cloud vendors are deploying their own managed Kubernetes services as well. Here are some of the key concepts from a Kubernetes deployment:

- **Kubernetes master**: This is responsible for maintaining the desired state for your cluster.
- **Kubernetes node**: Nodes are the machines (VMs, physical servers, and so on) that run your applications and cloud workflows. The Kubernetes Master controls each node; you'll rarely interact with nodes directly.
- **Pod**: This is the basic building block of Kubernetes; the smallest and simplest unit in the Kubernetes object model that you create or deploy. A pod represents a running process on your cluster.
- **Service**: An abstraction that defines a logical set of pods and a policy by which to access them, sometimes called a microservice.
- **Replica controllers and ReplicaSets**: These ensure that a specified number of pod replicas are running at any one time. In other words, they make sure that a pod or a homogeneous set of pods is always up and available.
- **Deployment**: Provides declarative updates for pods and ReplicaSets.
- **DaemonSet**: Ensures that all (or some) nodes run a copy of a pod. As nodes are added to the cluster, pods are added to them. As nodes are removed from the cluster, those pods are garbage collected. Deleting a DaemonSet will clean up the pods it created.

Container usage patterns

Containers are a great tool for designing and implementing cloud native architectures. Containers fit well in the cloud native maturity model. Specifically, they are a native cloud service from the vendor, they allow for extreme automation through CICD, and they are great for microservices due to their lightweight and scalable attributes. There are a few key patterns used where containers are a central component, namely microservices, hybrid and migration of application deployment, and business innovation through agility.

Microservices with containers

Containers are often synonymous with microservices. This is due to their lightweight properties, containing only a minimal operating system and the exact libraries and components needed to execute a specific piece of business functionality. Therefore, applications, whether designed as new or a broken down monolithically, will be designed to contain exactly what is needed, with no additional overhead to slow down the processing. Microservices are made to be small and perform specific business functionalities, which are often designed by different teams, but deployed at the same time. Therefore, a small team could develop a specific service using containers, with their desired programming language, libraries, API implementation style, and scaling techniques. They are free to deploy their business function, via a container push to the registry and a CICD deployment without impacting any other service in the mesh of interacting services. Alternatively, other small teams could develop their own services, using their own style, and not have to worry about anything about the API of the other services.

The use of containers for microservices works well for keeping small groups agile and moving fast. It also allows for the architecture standards board to implement guidelines that all services must follow without impacting the agility of the design team. For example, a logging framework, security approach for secrets, orchestration layer, and the CICD technology could be mandated but the programming languages would be open to what the team wants to use. This would allow the composite system to be managed centrally and each service to be designed individually.

Hybrid and migration of application deployment

Containers are a great way to run a hybrid architecture or to support the migration of a workload to the cloud faster and easier than with most other methods. Since a container is a discrete unit, whether it's deployed on-premises (such as a private cloud) or in the public cloud (for example, AWS), it will be the same. This pattern then allows for the architecture team to deploy the full composite application (multiple microservices, containerized applications, and so on) to on-premises and use the cloud environment to be the **disaster recovery** (**DR**) or failover site, or vice versa. It also allows for a low risk migration of a containerized application from on-premises to the cloud, making this a favorite way to perform large-scale migrations after the applications have been containerized. Unfortunately, it's not quite that simple; there are changes that are needed to support the surrounding components that make up the system depending on which cloud and orchestration solution is being used. For example, if using Kubernetes both on-premises and in the cloud, there could be changes needed to the Kubernetes manifest file to support different ingress methods, persistence volumes, load balancers, or other components.

More complex use cases are also possible, including running active workloads across on-premises and the chosen cloud vendor or moving containers from various clouds (often called multi-clouds). The purpose of implementing this architecture would be to take advantage of pricing constructs or moving away from problematic clouds (for example, those with latency issues, downed data centers, and so on) without having to go into a full business continuity scenario. However, the complexity of this type of workload distribution across clouds is very high, and would not be possible for many applications. Only those workloads that were specifically designed to ensure that data persistence and **online transaction processing** (**OLTP**) was properly handled would be successful. At this stage of the maturity of cloud broker tooling, distributed databases, and networking latency, it is recommended to use only a single cloud platform for cloud native applications.

Container anti patterns

In the world of cloud computing, containers are not only a popular way to achieve cloud native architectures, but they are quickly becoming the standard with which to design microservices. However, there are some use cases where containers are not always suited, specifically using containers for multiple concerns. The concept of concerns, or focus areas of a component, is that each module or class should have responsibility over a single part of the functionality. In the case of containers, multiple concerns would mean having a web server and database running in the same container. Following the services approach, breaking down monoliths into discrete components will ensure the applications have a lower blast radius and are easier to deploy and scale independently. This is not to say that a container should only have a single thread, but that it should have only a single role. There are ways for containers to share persistent disks and intercommunicate, but putting multiple components or concerns on the same container is not the right way. Simply put, containers are not virtual machines.

Treating containers as virtual machines is not limited to deploying multiple concerns into a single container. Allowing SSH daemons (or other types of console access) on a container defeats the purpose of the container in the first place. Since containers are a discrete component, they should be set up, configured, and have their code deployed as part of the initial development phase. That in turn becomes the deployment artifact which is pushed to the repository and deployed via the orchestration tooling used. Allowing direct console access to the container means that modifications can be made, the container is no longer an immutable component, and the consistency of the contents can no longer be trusted. Instead, if the container needs an update due to a bug or enhancement, that should be done to the base container, tested through proper channels, and pushed to the repository for deployment.

If the application requires multiple concerns or SSH access, consider using cloud-instance virtual machines instead of containers. Alternatively, to become more cloud native, work on the application to decouple it or enhance the CICD pipeline to allow for faster and more consistent deployment processes.

Serverless

Serverless does not mean the absence of servers; however, it does mean that resources can be used without having to consider server capacity. Serverless applications do not require the design or operations team to provision, scale, or maintain servers. All of that is handled by the cloud provider. This approach is probably the first time ever where the developers can focus on exactly what they are best at: writing code. In addition to the flexibility and focus this allows, the cost implications to serverless applications is a huge advantage over more traditional approaches, even containers. Serverless pricing is typically done by the runtime of the service, priced at the 100 millisecond duration. Designing services that execute a piece of code at such short intervals meets the definition of a microservice and takes maximum advantage of serverless technology.

In most cases when serverless is discussed, the first thing thought of is Function as a Service. The big three cloud providers each have their version of this: AWS Lambda, Azure Functions, and Google Cloud Functions. Each behaves roughly the same and allows for the deployment of code and execution as an event. For the most part, this type of serverless service is where the place of code execution is considered a core component for all serverless design patterns. However, there are other cloud vendor services that fall into the serverless category, and in most cases these primitives are used together to form subsystems in the cloud environment. According to AWS, there are eight high level areas that have serverless services. These are compute, API proxy, storage, data stores, inter process messaging, orchestration, analytics, and developer tools. With one or more services in each of these categories, complex system designs can be achieved that are cheaper, more scalable, and have significantly less management overhead than traditional services to achieve the same business outcome.

Scaling

Serverless applications are able to scale by design, without the requirement of having to understanding individual server capacity units. Instead, consumption units are the important factor for these services, typically throughput or memory, which can be automatically updated to have more or less capability as the application requires. In addition, for functions (such as AWS Lambda), since they are short lived (less than five minutes), they do not auto scale like an application deployed to a cloud server instance when the CPU is heavily used. Functions are designed to execute as an event so every time that event happens they trigger the function, which executes exactly once and dies off. Hence, the scaling capabilities of functions happen by the nature of the events triggering them, not by adding additional instances via an auto scaling group. Functions are designed to be triggered often by the event source, such as every time a message is put in a queue or a stream, which could be thousands of times a second.

For example, take a typical web server cluster running Apache for serving a web application's front page. Every time a user makes a request to the site, a worker thread is created to serve the page to the user and wait for additional interactions. As the users increase, more threads are created and eventually the instance is working at full capacity and additional instances are required, which are instantiated via an auto scaling group, providing more threads to serve users. This design works fine; however, it doesn't maximize the resources required, instead creating a full instance for use when required, charging the company by the minute as it's running. This same design using an API proxy and function will still be able to dynamically serve the user, but the thread or function will only execute when called and then go away, charging the company per execution at a 100 millisecond amount.

Serverless usage patterns

The ways to utilize serverless technology is limited to only the imagination of the design team involved in the system creation. Every day new techniques are developed that further expand the designs of what can be achieved with serverless, and due to the fast pace of innovation by the cloud providers, the new features and services in this area are increasing all the time. However, with multiple years of maturity at this point, a few core serverless design patterns have emerged, namely web and backend app processing, data and batch processing, and system automation.

Web and backend application processing

The easiest way to describe this design pattern is to compare it with a traditional three-tier application architecture. For many years, the dominant approach to a scalable web app was to set up a load balancer, web servers, app servers, and databases. There are many types of third-party tools and techniques to support this design and, if done properly, a fault tolerant architecture can be achieved that will scale up and down to support the spike in traffic that the application will experience. The challenge with this approach is that it does not fully take advantage of the cloud native services and still relies on capacity planning, people to manage the environment, and lots of configuration to ensure proper cluster setup and failover. This exact same three-tier application can be designed using fully serverless technologies that will enable the administration, execution, fault tolerance, and other administration to be handled by the service, at a fraction of the cost.

We have a fully serverless implementation of a three-tier application. The static frontend page is hosted in an object storage, Amazon S3, where it is served to users who call it from their browsers. Since this service allows for pages to be served, it will handle all of the requirements of load distribution and processing power automatically and not require a web server to be set up to host the web application. Once the user interacts with the page in a way that requires dynamic processing, an API call is made to Amazon API Gateway, which acts as a scalable entry point to execute the code to dynamically execute the user's request via an AWS Lambda function, which is called on an event per API call. The Lambda function has virtually unlimited abilities perform other actions. In this use case, the function will update an Amazon DynamoDB table for data persistence. Other backend functionalities can be performed by forked functions, such as putting messages in queues, updating a topic for further messaging, or executing an entirely new subsystem backend that performed whatever requirement the system has.

Data and batch processing

One of the biggest advantages of using the cloud is the ability to process large amounts of data quickly and efficiently. The two most common high-level approaches are real-time and batch data processing. Similar to the previous example, each of these patterns has been around for a while and there are ways to achieve them using more traditional tools and approaches. However, adding serverless will increase velocity and reduce pricing.

We have the real-time processing and analysis of a social media data stream, and it could just as easily be a click stream analysis of all web properties to support ad analytics. The stream or click stream comes in via a streaming data service, Amazon Kinesis, which executes a Lambda function on each micro batch of data that is processed and analyzed, based on the requirement. The Lambda function then stores the important information in a DynamoDB table, which could be sentiment analysis (if the social media stream is used) or popular ad clicks (if the click stream is used). Once the metadata is stored in the table, additional reporting, analysis, or dashboards can be designed and implemented as another subsystem using additional serverless services.

To show how data processing can be achieved for batch data processing, consider the case where batch files are placed in an object storage, Amazon S3. These files could be anything, images, CSV files, or other blobs that need to be processed or modified in some way before the data processing is completed. Once the file is placed in the object store, an AWS Lambda function executes and modifies the file for the purposes required. This batch process could be to execute other subsystems that use the data, modify the image to change its size, or to update various data stores with parts of the data required. In this example, a DynamoDB table is updated, a message is put in a queue, and a notification is sent to the user.

System automation

Another popular serverless design pattern is to perform common environment maintenance and operations. Following the CNMM requirement to have full automation, functions are a great way to execute the tasks of the system demands. As cloud landscapes grow, automation will ensure that the critical tasks to support that growth stay consistent and do not require the organization to linearly scale up the operations team supporting the environment. The possibilities for how to implement services that perform these administration tasks is limitless, bound only by the requirements and creative thinking of the operations team.

Some common administration use cases are to set up functions that execute on a schedule and check every instance across all accounts for proper tagging, correctly sized instance resources, stopping unused instances, and cleaning up unattached storage devices. In addition to routine administration tasks, serverless application designs can also be used for security administration. Examples include using functions to execute and verify the encryption of objects put in storage or disks, verifying account user policies are correctly applied, and performing checks against custom compliance policies on instances or other system components.

Serverless anti patterns and concerns

Serverless is a growing and critical way to achieve success with cloud native architectures. Innovation is happening all the time in this space, and will continue for many years. However, there are some patterns that do not directly apply to serverless architectures. For example, long-running requests are often not valid given the short-lived time for a function (less than 5 minutes). In cases where a request will take longer than the duration of the function service being used, containers are a possible alternative, since they do not have a time to live duration like functions.

Another example of an area of concern for serverless is when an event source executes in a manner that is not consistent with expectations, hence triggering the function more than expected. In a traditional server instance application, this scenario would saturate the CPU quickly and bog down the instance until it crashed, stopping the scenario. In a serverless environment, since each function is a discrete unit, they will never stop executing, even if that is not the desired intention. At best this will cause an increase in the cost of that function, at worst this could cause data corruption or loss depending on the nature of the function. To prevent this, testing should be done to ensure that triggers are appropriate for that function. In addition, as a failsafe, setting up alerts on total invocations for that function is a good idea, which will notify operations if the function is firing out of control and allow for human intervention to stop the processing.

Finally, knowing the cloud vendor's services and which ones work in conjunction with each other is important. For example, some AWS services are trigger sources for Lambda and others are not. The Amazon Simple Notification Service can trigger a Lambda function every time a message is put on the topic; however, the Amazon Simple Queue Service cannot. Therefore, knowing how the services fit together and when to invoke a function and when a custom solution (for example, listeners on an instance instead of a function) is required will ensure that the subsystems fit together using the best methods.

Development frameworks and approaches

There are many frameworks and approaches taken to design horizontal scalable applications in the cloud. Due to the nature of each of the cloud providers, each has their own specific services and frameworks that work best. In Chapter 14, *Amazon Web Services*, a comprehensive outline of doing this with AWS can be found. In Chapter 15, *Microsoft Azure*, Microsoft Azure's approach is detailed. Chapter 16, *Google Cloud Platform*, breaks down the patterns and frameworks that work best for that cloud. Each of these are similar, yet different, and will be implemented differently by each customer design teams.

Summary

In this chapter, we dived deep into the development of cloud native architectures, using microservices and serverless computing as a design principle. We were able to learn the difference between SOAs and microservices, what serverless computing is and how it fits into a cloud native architecture. We learned that each of the mature cloud vendors has a unique set of frameworks and approaches that can be used to design scalable architectures on those platforms.

11
How to Choose Technology Stacks

The world of cloud computing is vast, and while there are a few dominant players in the cloud vendor space, there are other parts of the ecosystem that are critical to success. How to decide which cloud vendor to use? What types of partners should be considered and what do they bring to the table? How will procurement change or stay the same in the cloud? How much do you want to rely on the cloud vendor to manage services? These are all important and valid questions that will be answered in this chapter.

Cloud technology ecosystems

Consideration of the cloud ecosystem and how to leverage it is a critical step in the cloud native journey. There are three main areas to focus on when thinking about partners on this journey: cloud providers, ISV partners, and system integrators. Together, along with the company people going on the journey, they will make up the foundation of the people, processes, and technology used to transform the business with cloud computing.

Public cloud providers

This book is focused on public cloud providers, which, in the fullness of time, will most likely be the dominant way companies consume IT resources. The cloud, as it is today, began in 2006 when **Amazon Web Services** (**AWS**) launched its first public services (Amazon Simple Queueing Service and Amazon Simple Storage Service). From there, they raced to add features at a very fast pace of innovation, with virtual server instances, virtual networking, block storage, and other foundational infrastructure services. In 2010, Microsoft released Azure, similar to AWS, with features designed to mimic what AWS had started and compete for customers in this space. Also during this time, Google began releasing more platform services, which ultimately became Google Cloud Platform, where it stands today.

While there are other clouds out there, with different niche focus areas and approaches to addressing customer requirements, these three comprise the dominant global market share for cloud services. Making the decision on a cloud vendor can appear complex when originally researching the vendors, mainly because less dominant players in the space try to position themselves as better situated than they are by showing cloud revenues or market share on services that are really not cloud at all. Since there is no one definition of a cloud and how to report revenues for it, and each company can say whatever they want about their services, it's important to understand the richness and scale that a cloud vendor has before making decisions. Each of the three major cloud vendors have very compelling foundational services (often referred to as Infrastructure as a Service) and have moved into higher-value managed cloud offerings (sometimes referred to as Platform as a Service), which offer everything from databases, to application services and Devops tools, to artificial intelligence and machine learning services.

There are many criteria that customers consider when choosing a cloud vendor, some of which have to do with the technology they have used in the past and are comfortable with. Some additional areas to consider are as follows:

- Scale: The cloud vendor business is one of scale and ability to deliver anywhere at any time. Even if a customer doesn't currently need cloud resources on a global scale, or to do a massive scale out in a single geography, using a cloud vendor that can do this is critical to ensure they have the experience, funding, and desire to continue to grow and innovate.
- Security/compliance: The priority of all cloud vendors should be security. If a cloud vendor doesn't focus on this and already has the majority of compliance certifications, it is best to stay clear and choose a vendor that makes this a priority.

- Feature richness: The pace of innovation is ever increasing and cloud vendors are moving into areas that were not even considered a few years ago. Whether it be machine learning, blockchain, serverless, or some other new technology, the cloud vendors that are constantly innovating are the ones to focus on.

- Price: While never the sole a reason to choose a vendor, price should always be considered. Contrary to popular belief, the cloud vendor market is not a race to the bottom in terms of pricing. Scale and innovation allow vendors to lower prices by passing along savings to customers (another reason why scale matters). The three major cloud vendors are all cost competitive at this point, but it's important to continuously monitor the price of services.

Gartner has for many years done deep analysis on the cloud vendor market. The most recent version of the Gartner magic quadrant for cloud infrastructure services can be found here: `https://www.gartner.com/doc/3875999/magic-quadrant-cloud-infrastructure-service`.

Independent software vendor (ISV) and technology partners

Cloud vendors are the base of any cloud native strategy, while ISV and technology partners will form a core component in this journey. In a lot of cases, the cloud vendors have tools that are native to their platforms and will fill the exact needs of customers. However, there are many reasons why they cannot meet all the requirements, and that is where ISV and technology partners come in. Even in cases where the cloud vendor has a specific service to solve a problem, customers often prefer to use third-party tools for various reasons. For one, third-party tools are often more mature or feature-rich, since they have often been around a long time and have adopted the cloud for their products. In other cases, a company may have extensive relationships or skill sets using specific ISV products, making it an easy decision to make them a part of their cloud journey. And finally, there are many cases where the cloud vendor doesn't have a comparable service, so using these third-party vendors will allow companies to solve problems without having to develop the capability from scratch.

At this point in the maturity curve of cloud computing, the vast majority of traditional ISVs have made the decision to adopt a cloud strategy. Similar to other companies, these ISVs spent a lot of time and effort evaluating cloud service vendors and standardized on one (or multiple, depending on the type of product). Common usage models for ISV products include customer managed product deployment or Software as a Service. Typically, the ISV or technology partner will have decided on their chosen pricing model, which directly relates to the consumption model offered to the customer.

Customer managed products

In the case of customer managed products, the ISV has chosen to either create or migrate their existing product to a cloud-based model. Often, this means the vendor has taken significant steps to adopt cloud native architectures themselves and then sell their product to the end customer. In its simplest form, the product has been tested with one or more cloud vendors to ensure it works as intended, ensuring that the customer can install and configure it in a similar manner as doing so on-premises. Examples of this approach would be SAP or various Oracle products. In more complex scenarios, the ISV re-architects the product to take advantage of the cloud vendor's native services and microservices to achieve a level of scale, security, or availability that would be difficult to achieve if using the same product on-premises. Regardless of the approach the ISV has taken, choosing the right product requires careful evaluation of the features and pricing models, and comparisons with similar cloud vendor services if applicable, to ensure the product has the scalability and security needed for a cloud native architecture.

Software as a Service

ISVs and technology partners have often chosen to completely redesign their offerings to be service usage-based, making consumption easier for the customer. To achieve this, the vendors will almost always choose a specific cloud vendor and develop their offering on top of the cloud vendor, making their software available to customers but not giving access to the underlying cloud vendor infrastructure or services. In the case of some very large vendors, they actually prefer to run their own private cloud or on-premises environments that integrate with the customer's chosen cloud services, given their core competency in hyper-scale cloud management.

Software as a Service (SaaS), which is very much cloud computing, is not a core component of the large cloud vendors and should not be considered when evaluating a cloud vendor for the majority of workloads being designed. Some large cloud vendors also have SaaS applications that run on their cloud, similar to what ISVs would do, and could be considered for integration purposes, for example, Microsoft and Office 365 or LinkedIn. That said, SaaS vendors absolutely have a critical role in the cloud native journey for many customers, since they offer their services directly to customers regardless of the customer-chosen cloud. The integration of SaaS offerings with customer workloads and data stores is one of the most common ways these services are used in conjunction with custom-designed cloud native workloads. Examples of large SaaS offerings are Salesforce and WorkDay, which offer very sophisticated business logic that integrates well with company systems.

There are also many cases where the ISV or technology partner has offerings where the customer can procure a self-managed version and deploy it in their chosen cloud, or leverage a SaaS version of the same offering. There are many reasons why a vendor might decide to make their offerings available this way. Often, a customer might want to keep the data and control of the product in their environment, or they already have existing licenses they use. Other times, the customer wants to move fast and since they don't already have the software in use, they go directly to the SaaS version so all they need to do is integrate it with their existing systems. Ultimately, ISV and technology partners want to do what their customers ask for, and this should be an important area to consider when choosing a vendor.

Consulting partners

Consulting partners, or **system integrators** (**SIs**), have been around since almost the beginning of IT itself. The concept is that companies don't have the time, resources, or desire to skill up on new technology or scale out their workforce to handle the demands of their business requirements. Therefore, these SI partners are used to fill gaps and help the company move faster with people who can quickly make an impact and deliver projects and business results. These types of partners come in many shapes and sizes, and the relationship they have with the company can be very transactional, or strategic and long term, depending on how the individual company decides to handle their business. Typically, SI partners can be viewed as either niche players, regionally focused, or global/large scale, each having a key place in a company's journey.

Niche SI partners

Niche partners are those companies that offer very specific services on a type of technology, cloud, or area of focus. Often, these partners will be relatively small in size, but have some of the most experienced experts in their respective areas. They are used as subject matter experts on large projects or to own the delivery of a specific project in their area of expertise. At the stage of cloud computing today, there are niche SI partners that have a core competency in specific cloud vendors, and even specific services at one or all of the cloud vendors. The scale of this partner is not the driving force behind being selected for a customer requirement; their technical depth in the chosen area is the area to focus on. When evaluating niche SI partners, customers should consider the certifications of individual resources on the respective technologies, delivery time frames, and customer references where similar work has been done. Niche SI partners are often used to consult on cloud native design and architecture, big data architecture and data structure requirements, or security and compliance for specific industries or requirements.

An anti-pattern for using a niche SI partner is their ability to scale their people beyond their core competency.

Regional SI partners

Regional SI partners are popular with companies that operate in a specific geography or region, since the partner will usually have all the resources located in that area. Often considered strategic partners with senior executive relationships, these partners will help the customer define their strategy and execute specific projects with customer resources. They will usually have a mix of deep technical experts and enough scale to be able to execute large and complex projects for the customer, which would include project management, technical architecture, development, and testing. As with all partners, regional SI partners are often focused on specific verticals, technologies/clouds, or other areas that enable them to differentiate themselves. They are also very responsive to customer needs and can make the difference between success and failure with a cloud native journey. An example of a regional SI partner helping customers on their cloud native journey is Slalom.

An anti-pattern for using a regional SI partner is their ability to support global initiatives that require potentially thousands of people or having a super-long-term strategic view of the company.

Global SI partners

Global SI partners are popular for their scale and ability to support the largest, longest, and most complex projects customers have. As the name implies, they are global in nature, operating in most countries in the world, with a significant presence in all geographies. From the beginning, global SI partners have played a role in helping outsource IT operations, design, strategy, and delivery for big and small companies alike, allowing them to focus on their core business. Global SI partners often have board room-level relationships and will have been involved in the long-term strategic focus of the company for decades, providing resources and technology that align to the customer's requirements. They will execute complex global deployments across multiple cloud providers, geographies, or technologies. An example of a global SI partner helping customers on their cloud native journey is Accenture.

An anti-pattern for using a global SI partner is that quality can sometimes be sacrificed for scale, allowing for a global reach with more junior resources. In addition, given their global nature, the delivery of critical projects is often done in a region where the customer doesn't have operations, making coordination complicated.

Procurement in the cloud

One of the reasons that the cloud is so popular, and that cloud native architectures are becoming the normal method of designing workloads, is due to the procurement and consumption model used. The easy way to think about this is the ability to procure using **operational expenditure (OpEx)** instead of the traditional **capital expenditure (CapEx)**, which can have a large impact on the way a company handles revenues, taxes, and long-term depreciation of assets. However, that is just the surface of the impact that the cloud has on the way organizations procure their IT resources.

The shift to pay per use consumption by cloud vendors has enabled ISVs to also align their business model, making their products easier to consume alongside the chosen cloud vendor services. This change can have a significant impact on the way that organizations negotiate contracts with ISVs, often lowering their overall bill by only paying for what they used instead of long-term contracts based on the number of CPUs the software sits on. In addition to third-party ISVs modifying their procurement model, cloud vendors often offer a cloud marketplace, allowing ISVs to have a digital catalog to list their wares, making it easier for customers to find, test, buy, and deploy software.

All of these changes are designed to allow customers to fundamentally change their purchasing behaviors to be user-friendly, with faster alignment to business requirements and easier identification of offerings that can solve their business problems.

Cloud marketplaces

Using a cloud vendor marketplace as a location to find and procure software required for their business to operate in the cloud is one way companies are able to have the tools needed at any moment. Fundamentally, customers are looking to either develop new workloads or move existing workloads to the cloud, modernize the workload if it was migrated, and then manage their landscape at scale with a streamlined workforce. The bigger the company, the more complex their business requirements can become due to the range of different stakeholders, business units, and customer segments. Procurement of ISV products can take teams of people and months of time to get the right legal terms and conditions, sizing requirements, billing model, and so on. Cloud vendor marketplaces are one way to help companies minimize these blockers to using the software they need, when they need it.

Depending on the maturity of these marketplaces, there could be thousands of different software packages, across just about every category, available for the company to choose from. With the push of a button, or an API call, purchasing and deployment of the ISV product into the customer cloud landing zone, this software can be deployed in minutes, tested, and integrated to the environment when required. Procurement of software using a cloud marketplace has the additional benefit of ensuring that the software is configured and hardened to the specifications of the vendor. There is usually little or no additional configuration required to get the software working. The cloud services being used are still paid for separately (for example, the cost of the instances, storage, network usage, and so on) and in most cases the software is just an additional pay per use line item on the cloud vendor bill.

Marketplace and service catalogs

Cloud vendors often have a service catalog feature that allows for pre-created application stacks or complex solutions to be stored and deployed when required by users with the right permissions. This approach, when combined with the marketplace, offers a powerful way to allow the service design teams to choose the right software, stage it in the catalog location, and either deploy it or have the operations team deploy it following company guidelines. The following diagram shows where the marketplace and a service catalog offering might fit into an organization's procurement strategy:

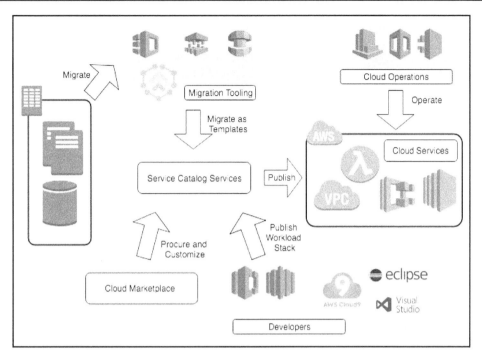

Marketplace and service catalog offering

In this example, the service catalog is acting as an intermediary location for the company to publish customer development patterns, procure cloud marketplace software, or migrate on-premises workloads before being pushed to the target cloud landing zone.

Cloud marketplace anti-patterns

The cloud marketplace can be a powerful tool to allow companies to acquire software with little or no long-term negotiating. It also allows companies to test new software to determine whether it will solve a business problem with ease and little in the way of upfront costs. However, there are cases where using the marketplace is not a fit. For example, if a company already has a long-term strategic relationship with an ISV vendor, with custom patches, or other specific product offerings, then deploying the software themselves is usually preferred. Alternatively, if a company feels they have an especially complicated use case (large scale, additional security, and so on) and the core competency to manage the deployment themselves, it would usually chose to forgo the marketplace and design and deploy the software solution themselves.

Licensing considerations

The previous section identified some areas of consideration with regards to procurement and discussed the common pay-as-you-go model of consumption. Typically, the cost of cloud vendor services would not be considered licenses, but consumption; however, there are often additional license costs associated with it, depending on what software is being used. Traditionally, licenses for software followed a model of paying based how many CPUs or cores the software would be installed on, giving a way for the vendor to understand how much of the software was being used. That worked fine while customers were making large upfront CapEx investments in hardware and knew exactly which servers would run which software. The cloud breaks that model due to its elastic nature. So, how then should customers pay for the licenses of the software being used? ISVs still want to get paid for the amount of use, so they need to identify other ways, typically their key metric of usage. Some common cloud-based approaches are:

- Network throughput, storage amount, or other physical component. They meter and bill by how much network traffic is used, how many Gigabytes (GB) of storage are used, or other hardware metrics that are not CPU-based.
- Per host. Server instances are still very popular in the cloud, and will be for a long time. Depending on the software, charging a per host fee will be enough to get an accurate accounting of how much of the software is used. This would usually be charged on a unit of time basis (for example, hours) to account for elasticity and would not be tied to the CPUs.
- Percentage of cloud vendor spend. For software that is used across the entire cloud landscape, such as monitoring or endpoint security, vendors might charge a small percentage of the overall customer cloud spend. This would allow for elastic growth and shrinkage to be accounted for in the payment to the ISV.
- By transaction. Some ISVs have very high transactional rates, but very low sizes of transaction. By metering the amount of transactions and charging a small amount per transaction, the ISV can account for elasticity and still give a pay-per-use model to the customer.

Cloud vendor pricing models

It's important for customers to fully understand the pricing metric for each piece of technology being purchased. This is true especially with cloud vendors, who can have complex pricing models for services that are very new and otherwise hard to price. Since a lot of the technology services offered by cloud vendors are new or offered in a way that is new, the pricing mechanisms can be very different and require a thorough understanding of how much of the service will be used, so there are no surprises in the cost of usage. For base infrastructure services, such as virtual instances or blob storage, the metric for pricing is usually per hour or per month, with the rate going up as the size goes up. However, for managed cloud services, the price can be more complicated. The following are some examples from popular AWS services used in cloud native microservice architectures: AWS Lambda and Amazon DynamoDB.

Given the complexity and options for pricing, it's critical for the design team to understand how these services will be used in the architecture. Even small changes to the size of transactions, runtime of functions, or other aspects can cause a significant increase in the bill if the system scales high enough.

Example - AWS Lambda pricing

This example of AWS Lambda pricing is taken directly from the AWS service pricing page, and additional details can be found on that page.

Lambda counts, as a request, each time it starts executing in response to an event notification or invocations call, including test invocations from the console. You are charged for the total number of requests across all your functions.

Duration is calculated from the time your code begins executing until it returns or otherwise terminates, rounded up to the nearest 100 ms. The price depends on the amount of memory you allocate to your function.

The following table shows the free tier seconds and the approximate price per 100 ms associated for different memory sizes:

Memory (MB)	Free tier seconds per month	Price per 100 ms ($)
128	3,200,000	0.000000208
192	2,133,333	0.000000313
256	1,600,000	0.000000417
320	1,280,000	0.000000521
2,816	145,455	0.000004584
2,880	142,222	0.000004688

2,944	139,130	0.000004793
3,008	136,170	0.000004897

Pricing example 1:

If you allocated 512 MB of memory to your function, executed it 3 million times in one month, and it ran for 1 second each time, your charges would be calculated as follows:

- Monthly compute charges
- The monthly compute price is $0.00001667 per GB and the free tier provides 400,000 GB
- Total compute (seconds) = 3 million * (1s) = 3,000,000 seconds
- Total compute (GB) = 3,000,000 * 512 MB/1024 = 1,500,000 GB
- Total compute - free tier compute = Monthly billable compute GB
- 1,500,000 GB - 400,000 free tier GB = 1,100,000 GB
- Monthly compute charges = 1,100,000 * $0.00001667 = $18.34
- Monthly request charges
- The monthly request price is $0.20 per 1 million requests and the free tier provides 1M requests per month
- Total requests - free tier requests = monthly billable requests
- 3M requests - 1 million free tier requests = 2 million monthly billable requests
- Monthly request charges = 2 million * $0.2/M = $0.40
- Total monthly charges
- Total charges = compute charges + request charges = $18.34 + $0.40 = $18.74 per month

Example - Amazon DynamoDB pricing

This example of Amazon DynamoDB pricing is taken directly from the AWS pricing page, and additional details can be found on that page.

Unlike traditional NoSQL deployments that ask you to think about memory, CPU, and other system resources that could affect your throughput, DynamoDB simply asks you to specify the target utilization rate and minimum to maximum capacity that you want for your table. DynamoDB handles the provisioning of resources to achieve your target utilization of read and write capacity, and then auto-scales your capacity based on usage. Optionally, you can directly specify read and write capacity if you prefer to manually manage table throughput.

The following table summarizes key DynamoDB pricing concepts:

Resource type	Details	Monthly price
Provisioned throughput (write)	One **write capacity unit** (**WCU**) provides up to one write per second, enough for 2.5 million writes per month	As low as $0.47 per WCU
Provisioned throughput (read)	One **read capacity unit** (**RCU**) provides up to two reads per second, enough for 5.2 million reads per month	As low as $0.09 per RCU
Indexed data storage	DynamoDB charges an hourly rate per GB of disk space that your table consumes	As low as $0.25 per GB

Manual provisioning example: Assume that your application running in the US East (N. Virginia) region needs to perform 5 million writes and 5 million eventually consistent reads per day on a DynamoDB table, while storing 8 GB of data. For simplicity, assume that your workload is relatively constant throughout the day and your table items are no larger than 1 KB in size.

- **Write capacity units** (**WCUs**): 5 million writes per day equals 57.9 writes per second. One WCU can handle one write per second, so you need 58 WCUs. At $0.47 per WCU per month, 58 WCUs costs $27.26 per month.
- **Read capacity units** (**RCUs**): 5 million reads per day equals 57.9 reads per second. One RCU can handle two eventually consistent reads per second, so you need 29 RCUs. At $0.09 per RCU per month, 29 RCUs costs $2.61 per month.
- Data storage: Your table occupies 8 GB of storage. At $0.25 per GB per month, your table costs $2.00.

The total cost is $31.86 per month ($27.14 of write provisioned throughput, $2.71 of read provisioned throughput, and $2.00 of indexed data storage).

Open source

Similar to traditional on-premises environments, customers will have a large range of software options to choose from when starting on their cloud native journey. As pointed out already, licensing considerations are critical to understand before making any decision. Open source software can be very effective in the cloud, and often the preferred method for companies to fill important gaps in their technology landscape. Whether it's using some of the fantastic projects found at the Apache Foundation or from other locations, customers should consider these options when making decisions.

For example, a very popular security information and event management (SIEM) solution is the ISV Splunk, which will do large-sale log aggregations and event management. While often considered best of breed for these types of solutions, there are some alternative open source projects that are similar, specifically the **ELK** stack (short for **ElasticSearch**, **Logstash**, **Kibaba**). Both achieve similar results, each with different pricing models that can be attractive to different types of customers. Often the open source alternative will come with strong community support but a less polished configuration model, causing the customer to need skills in the technology to set it up and make it run effectively.

It's also important to remember that with open source software, the physical resources (for example, virtual instances, storage, networking, and so on) are still going to have costs associated while in use; only the software will be free.

Cloud services

Cloud providers have a lot of services, and innovation is accelerating; therefore, understanding how to choose the right service to solve business problems can be a tough prospect. The large cloud providers have designed their services to be like building blocks that can be used together to solve problems that may never have been considered for that specific service. This approach allows customer design teams to be creative and think outside the box with experimentation and fail fast projects. The key is to have a good understanding of what services are actually available. Foundational infrastructure services, once the growth drivers of the cloud, have matured to a state where they are often decided on by default. Setting up landing zones with specific networking addresses, subnets, security groups, and routes is done with Infrastructure as Code, using a consistent and approved model. However, there are still some important foundational considerations, specifically regarding operating systems.

Moving up the service stack is where the large public cloud vendors start to differentiate from their peers. The offerings vary by provider and can include anything from managed database platforms to fully trained machine learning facial recognition. Understanding how these services fit into a cloud native strategy, how to price them for at-scale usage, and if there are alternatives that have a more niche feature to meet architecture needs is critical along the journey.

Cloud services – vendor versus self-managed

In the early days of the cloud, the foundational infrastructure services were reason enough to develop new workloads there. However, as those services matured and the cloud vendors quickened their pace of innovation, they began to develop other services that were managed versions of existing software customers had been using. The reason for this is simple: the goal of the large cloud providers is to innovate on behalf of the customer so that the undifferentiated heavy lifting of managing environments is reduced, freeing up time and resources for business requirements. One of the early areas where this approach was used successfully was with databases. The large cloud vendors will have managed versions of popular database platforms for customers to use. But should a customer use the cloud managed version or deploy and manage them on their own? The answer to that question really comes down to whether an organization has the core competency in that technology and believes they can do it cheaper and faster than the cloud vendor can. Even then, companies that decide to manage their own software should be prepared to have a fast rate of iteration so that they keep up with the latest software for that service; otherwise, they will be passed as the cloud vendor innovates on the service.

Self-managed approach

Setting up databases, sometimes with clusters or other high availability approaches, and including the correct disk type and networking requirements, can be challenging. For years, this skill set, often referred to as a database administrator (DBA), was one that required very skilled and experienced professionals to do correctly. The cloud does not change this, and those same DBAs are needed to install, configure, and manage database platforms. In the early days of the cloud, this was the approach taken as companies moved or developed workloads in the cloud, self-managing their software. Using virtual instances, ISV vendor software, and experienced professionals, most workloads can be run just the same in the cloud as they did on-premises.

Using open source packages and having access to the latest technology is one reason that companies can still manage their own software. While cloud vendors innovate fast, they still take some time to get a production-ready version of a hot new technology, so to shorten the time to market with that technology, companies will choose to do this themselves. Other reasons for companies to do this is that they feel they have a strong competency in a specific package or pattern, and prefer to own the setup and management of that software. The more complex or mission critical a software package, the more difficult and expensive the resources will be to manage it.

Managed cloud services

Vendor-managed cloud services are a way for customers to use the technology they need without having to deal with the undifferentiated lifting of managing the operations of the technology. Cloud vendors spend a lot of time and resources to design services that mimic or exceed the way that companies manage similar technology on-premises. For example, cloud vendors have database services that offer the same popular database platforms, but are automatically configured to span data centers, take incremental backups, tune themselves, and even failover or self-heal when there is a fault. This type of service typically uses automation to allow for huge numbers of these to be running at any time for their customers, and they are responsible for all aspects of the operations (operating system, software patching, backups, and so on).

As cloud vendors grow in maturity, more and more services are being offered that are managed by the vendor, and customers should consider these as they become available. Mature cloud native organizations will attempt to leverage as many of these vendor managed or serverless offerings as possible, to allow the focus of their resources to be on developing business value.

Vender lock-in

Throughout the history of IT, there has been a common theme of vendors making their products sticky and hard to migrate away from. While this trend is seemingly done to support customer requirements, if often makes it difficult, if not impossible, to switch to a newer technology, leaving customers locked into the vendor they originally chose. The best example of this behavior is the old guard database vendors that use proprietary code and stored procedures, which for large databases can represent a significant amount of investment and be critical to the application. This type of innovation is great while it's still going strong, allowing for customers to use new features as soon as they are released by that vendor. But what happens if that vendor slows down or pivots from that platform, and the innovation isn't keeping pace with customer needs? All that investment in stored procedures and code written to the database specification will prevent that customer from switching to a faster moving, more innovative platform.

The cloud is different in this regard. The old way, of IT being the cost center, and setting up and managing software packages using company servers and hardware, is over. Cloud native companies have learned that using the old model will only commoditize their offerings and allow for no way to differentiate them in the market. The only way to prevent this is to offload that undifferentiated heavy lifting of IT service management and focus resources on the business requirements. Cloud vendors innovate across a number of areas, constantly, and show no signs of slowing down. They devote significant effort and resources to security and cutting-edge services, which have proven to be impossible for individual companies to keep up with. Cloud native organizations embrace these managed cloud services and while some people might consider that cloud lock-in, mature companies understand this is the new way of doing business.

Even with this new way of thinking, there are some considerations that organizations should take into account to be able to leverage other cloud vendors if the event should arise:

- Have an exit plan. Every decision that is mission-critical requires a plan of how to exit or migrate if the need arises. Know which applications are capable of moving quickly, what data goes with them, and how it's done.
- Design loosely coupled and containerized applications. Following the 12-factor app and other cloud native design principles, designing loosely coupled applications will enable easier movement with less risk of blast radius issues.
- Organize and manage critical data closely. Know exactly what data you have, where it resides, and its classification and encryption requirements. This will ensure that if the decision is made to move to a different cloud, the order of operations for the data is already known.
- Automate everything. Using Infrastructure as Code and other DevOps philosophies will allow for minimal changes to the automation to support another cloud. Automation is key to a cloud native company.

Operating systems

Foundational infrastructure services typically include cloud virtual instances. These instances require an operating system to run, and for the cloud, that often comes down to choosing between a flavor of Linux or a version of Windows. In addition to virtual instances, containers also require a flavor of operating system to run, albeit a slimmed down version, to deploy code and the frameworks that make them execute. Even with mature cloud native architectures, there will most likely be some instances still being used to handle various tasks and edge cases that cannot use serverless or a similar technology. Therefore, operating systems in the cloud are going to be around for a while and are an important choice to make.

Windows versus Linux

The old question of Windows versus Linux is one that most customers have to agree on at some point. However, for any cloud deployment of size, most likely there will be a mixture of both Windows and Linux, with different versions and flavors of each. Therefore, it's important to know which versions are needed and which are offered by the cloud vendor. Typically, the cloud vendor will have many different flavors of each operating system; some will have an associated licensing cost, others will be free to use. The price of the operating system can add up to be a significant portion of the bill, so trying to minimize their use, or using those that are free to use, is recommended for customers who are going fully cloud native.

Do operating systems really matter any longer?

The real question is do operating systems really matter any longer? The answer is yes and no. Yes, because containers are still a common technology for developing microservices and therefore an operating system is required. No, because as the architecture matures, more and more managed cloud services will be leveraged with serverless as a core component of cloud native architecture. Because managing the operations and licensing of operating systems can add up fast, mature cloud native companies limit their use to only legacy workloads and areas that still require specific libraries to be installed.

Since the cloud is an API-driven environment, the definition of operating systems is changing somewhat. Of course, virtual instances and containers still require operating systems. However, the full-scale cloud environment itself is turning into an operating system of sorts. Microservices, events, containers, and vendor managed services are now intercommunicating via API service calls, object storage, and other decoupled methods. This trend to think of the cloud, and the cloud native workloads that are deployed there, as a large scale operating system is going to continue to grow in popularity.

Summary

In this chapter, we learned the answers to the questions you may ask while deciding on which technology stack to choose. The next chapter talks about scalability and availability in cloud architectures.

12
Optimizing Cost

In this chapter, we are going to learn how to frame and communicate the inherent cost advantages of cloud platforms. You will finish this chapter with a firm understanding of the cloud pricing models available today and how to optimize them. These models are viewed differently by businesses, so we will cover which aspects of the model are appealing to certain business leaders.

Once we have a firm understanding of the pricing model, we'll dive into building economic business cases for adopting cloud. We'll demonstrate this through several examples to show you the inherent cost benefits and flexibility that cloud can afford. Finally, we'll cover common toolsets and services available to ensure that we are monitoring, controlling, and optimizing costs in a cloud native way.

Before we begin, let's define **cost** as *the expense that a business incurs in bringing a product or service to the market*. **Price** is defined as *the amount an entity (consumer or business) pays for a product or service*. Finally, **opportunity cost** is defined as *the benefit that an entity (consumer or business) could have received, but gave up, to take another course of action*. Stated differently, an opportunity cost represents an alternative that's given when a decision is made.

Before the cloud

Before we can discuss the cost of building cloud native applications, we need to turn back the clock to examine infrastructure before the cloud, namely on-premises systems. When an enterprise deems it necessary to establish or expand its IT infrastructure, a number of actions have to be taken regarding:

- **Physical space**: Finding space in the existing data center or buying/renting new space for the data center buildout.
- **Electric power**: This can be easily overlooked. Deploying a large scale array of servers requires large power conduits that may not exist in a new location or be available in the current space. In addition, redundancy and backup power generators are often required to continue critical operations in case of a power outage or disaster.
- **Physical Security**: Paramount in enterprise deployments, establishing physical security to the hardware supporting a data center requires key/badged access points, security personnel, cameras, and security equipment.
- **Network connectivity**: Depending on the site chosen, broadband connectivity may not exist or be of insufficient bandwidth to support steady state data center functionality. In most cases, data centers require a physically redundant network connection to support network failover scenarios. This may require digging, burying, and trenching another line on the part of the **internet service provider (ISP)**, which may take months (in the worst case scenario, permits are required from the local and regional governing authorities to bury a single network strand).
- **Cooling**: Computing equipment generates lots of heat, and they need to operate within certain temperature ranges to maintain optimal performance. The newest data centers have passive cooling systems (if built in cold climates), but the vast majority require large air conduits that are built-in to move the waste heat from the computers and pull in cool air.

- **Physical hardware**: After all of the preceding points have been addressed, the actual compute, storage, and network equipment that gives the data center its business value needs to be ordered, shipped, received, racked, stacked, connected, tested, and brought online. This takes teems of data center operations resources to accomplish and dozens of man hours per rack.
- **Staff**: While all of the preceding points are being dealt with, the company in question needs to hire, train, and compensate a large number of staff to design, order, install, test, and operate all the items noted previously.

It's no surprise that data center buildouts are planned out months and years in advance. Large capital investments are needed to bring together the necessary teams and resources so that they can complete the build and become production ready.

Cloud cost view

The advent of cloud has all but eliminated the limitations provided by each of the preceding points. Cloud providers now completely manage the *undifferentiated heavy lifting* for their customers. They've bought the physical space to house the data centers; deployed network, electric, and cooling systems to support millions of machines; managed security of the physical infrastructure, performed background checks, and segregated duties to ensure that no staff has both physical and logical access to systems; designed and deployed state-of-the-art cooling systems; and have a staff of focused operations engineers to maintain their massive fleets of data centers. For a further discussion on the cloud providers' scale, please refer to `Chapter 13`, *Scalable and Available.*

In every one of these points, the CSPs aggregate and reduce costs through economies of scale. A company such as AWS or Azure can spend more time designing more secure systems than other enterprises because they have more resources, money, and commitment for ensuring security. In the case of cooling, CSPs can apply greater engineering know-how to developing greener, more efficient cooling systems than any other enterprise in the market. For example, Google is using seawater to cool its data centers in Finland, which reduces stress on local freshwater sources and local electric generation, and increases efficiency. You can refer to `https://www.wired.com/2012/01/google-finland/` to read more about this.

Apart from the tangible benefits of adopting cloud, there are several intangible cost benefits (opportunity costs), which are enumerated as follows:

- **Reduced complexity**: Adopting the cloud eliminates the *undifferentiated heavy lifting* to manage your business's IT infrastructure. Lengthy license pricing negotiations are eliminated because the cloud provider has pre-negotiated bulk licensing agreements with vendors. In other cases, the CSP provides a marketplace of third-party software that's available on the platform with rates baked into the cost of the compute resource. Finally, the cloud gives your business the ability to devote the human capital previously concerned with managing that complexity to more business critical tasks. This reduction in complexity saves the business dollars, directly and indirectly.

- **Elastic capacity**: Adopting the cloud gives the enterprise the unprecedented ability to expand or contract their IT infrastructure on the fly. This elasticity allows businesses to expand on successes and contract quickly after a failed experiment, or to follow seasonal business needs or daily user fluctuations. Enterprises no longer need to forecast demand years in advance and plan accordingly—they can manage and expand their business today, with cloud consumption mirroring their own business trends.

- **Increased speed to the market**: Enterprises competing for market dominance need *agility* to be successful. The ability to design, develop, test, and launch products supported by IT projects more quickly is a dominant factor in whether a company succeeds or fails. Adopting cloud native architectures is a key factor in increasing the speed with which a company can iterate product development.

- **Global reach**: The hyperscale cloud providers have a global network of data centers that are available to all customers. Any size of customer can leverage the global network to expand its products or services globally within minutes. This greatly reduces time to the market and allows companies to reach new markets with ease.

- **Increased operational efficiency**: Each of the major CSPs provides tools to decrease time spent on basic operational controls and checks, which helps automate many of these functions. Resources (people, capital, and time) are freed up so that they can be spent on building the company's differentiating product. In a similar vein, people within the organization can now spend time solving valuable and difficult problems, leading to higher job satisfaction.

- **Enhanced security**: The CSPs manage their portion of the shared security model, which frees up customer resources to focus on their portion of the security model. By providing native security tools on the platform, CSPs amplify and automate security functions on the customer side of the shared responsibility model. These have large effects on how an organization is modeled and operated, enhancing security and freeing up resources to focus on greater *application* security.

These tangible and intangible cost benefits are enormously beneficial to every single organization with an IT department. This is explained well by the upswing in cloud adoption that started in 2013 by large enterprises. The collective realization dawned on these entities that the cloud has many upsides and almost no downsides to adoption—the sole valid exception being the unrealized return on capital investments made recently in the IT infrastructure (for example, Company X just invested $50 million in a new data center that came online last month). Unless Company X can find a way to relinquish their new data center and recuperate commensurate sunk costs, the math is likely not in favor of cloud adoption until the next refresh cycle (this term is used to describe the time in-between the replacement of computers and associated computer hardware).

Cloud economics

In many companies, a central IT organization manages infrastructure and charges back the price of IT services vended to the **lines of business** (**LOB**) plus their own administrative costs (known as a *chargeback model*). It is important to realize that the chargeback price rarely equals the price of cloud (for an equivalent stack). In these pricing exercises, rarely do central IT organizations take into account facility costs, security, cooling, water, and electric in their prices.

The price of a cloud stack must be compared to the chargeback price **plus** capital expenditures (building and equipment), operational expenditures (electricity, cooling, water), staffing, licensing (costs for virtualization software, ISV/third-party tools, and so on), facilities, overhead, and opportunity costs. This is referred to as **Total Cost of Ownership**, or **TCO**. Azure (`https://www.tco.microsoft.com/`) and AWS (`https://awstcocalculator.com/`) have TCO calculators that allow users to make reasonable numerical assertions for TCO based on a few assumptions (labor, electric, storage, facility, and so on).

These TCO analysis tools help you compare tangible costs between the current on-premises deployment and their equivalent environment on the CSP platform. These do not account for intangibles (read: opportunity costs) that are to be gained by adopting a cloud platform.

To find out the pure price of cloud services, we need to shift the discussion to another set of tools. There are pricing calculators available with the major CSPs that allow you to price out a given architecture on the CSP's platform with great accuracy (given your assumptions around data usage, code execution, GB storage, and so on are accurate). The AWS Simple Monthly Calculator (`https://calculator.s3.amazonaws.com/index.html`), Microsoft Azure Pricing Calculator (`https://azure.microsoft.com/en-us/pricing/calculator/`), and the Google Cloud Pricing Calculator (`https://cloud.google.com/products/calculator/`) are all available online and are free to use.

CapEx versus OpEx

When building the business case for cloud, one of the most compelling arguments to senior leadership (read: C-suite) is the ability to shift IT spending from **Capital Expenditures (CapEx)** to **Operational Expenditures (OpEx)**. A capital expense is defined as money spent by a business on acquiring or maintaining fixed assets, such as land, buildings, and equipment. An operating expense is defined as the ongoing cost for running a business/system or providing a service/product.

There are several advantages that make up a compelling business case for leaders to transition to an OpEx model, which are enumerated as follows:

- **Lower, recurring costs versus large, upfront investments**: As mentioned earlier in this chapter, building out a data center requires large amounts of time and resources to bring the compute power online. The cost associated with the time and resource allocation to building a data center is large. In an OpEx model, the business can achieve the same end result without a large, upfront investment.
- **Tax benefits**: Operating expenses are treated differently than capital expenses. In general, business are allowed to write off operating expenses the year they are incurred—or said another way, these outlays can be deducted in their entirety from a business's taxable revenue. However, in general, capital expenses must be deducted more slowly over a schedule defined by the government tax office (for example, IRS in the US). These schedules typically range from 3-5 years, over which the cost of the capital expense can be deducted from a business's tax outlay.
- **Greater transparency**: The cloud enables a great degree of cost transparency, which allows business leaders to justify and draw conclusions from investment decisions. With a native cloud environment, conclusive market tests can be conducted to increase or decrease IT spending (for example, we paid X dollars for Y amount of storage and compute time, leading to a Z% increase in online revenue).

- **Capital depreciation**: Similar to the tax benefits noted previously, businesses can avoid capital depreciation on their upfront expenses by adopting a cloud-based OpEx model. Capital depreciation is the gradual decrease in value of an asset owned by a company. In the IT industry, this is unavoidable as there are always better performing servers, storage devices, and network components coming to market, driving down the value of older equipment.
- **Easier growth**: Tied to the natural elasticity of cloud resources, OpEx models allow for spending that matches natural business growth and contractions, whereas fixed capital investments can lie idle or provide a ceiling to business capacity.
- **No commitment or lock-in**: A concern that business leaders have when purchasing any technology service or product is lock-in—an arrangement according to which a company is obliged to deal only with a specific product or service. This lock-in can be in the form of an exclusive service contract or technology portability limitations (where the barrier to changing systems to work with another product is too costly). This is largely eliminated by cloud as there is no upfront payment or term-based contract necessary to consume cloud services (that being said, term-based discount contracts are available from CSPs. If you are willing to commit to a minimum amount of spend on the platform, CSPs will give incremental discounts over the life of the contract (typically 3-5 years). However, this is in no way mandatory). Companies can choose to increase or decrease their consumption on the platform (or eliminate it altogether) without any limitations.

Cost monitoring

CSP platforms are inherently built to be cost transparent. There are no hidden fees or service charges that a customer can't see until they begin building on the platform. All pricing is posted and kept updated on the sites of the big three and is readily available to anyone interested in pricing out an architecture. As mentioned earlier, pricing calculators are available from the CSPs to help prospective customers price out an environment before building. This trend was first established by AWS when they released their initial cloud services and have remained true to this day.

In a similar vein, once systems have been built on the cloud, each CSP has native services to help monitor, drill down, and explore service consumption and their related costs. AWS's **Billing & Cost Management Dashboard** is a perfect example of these cloud native capabilities. Features such as AWS Cost Explorer allow users to drill down into monthly bills, look at historical spends, and anticipate future spending. Budgets allow users to set custom budgets that can trigger alerts or alarms when the cost or usage of something has exceeded the set limits. These tools allow cloud admins to confidently set guardrails around the usage and costs incurred through cloud services:

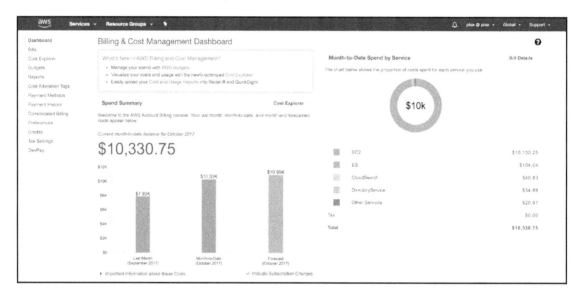

The **Billing & Cost Management Dashboard** of the author's AWS account.

We can very easily ascertain the last, current, and next month's costs in one simple view. On the right, we can see which services we are incurring costs for.

Cloud Native Architecture Best Practice: Every cloud administrators' second task (after establishing MFA and securing root credentials) should be to familiarize themselves with the cost explorer dashboard and services for their chosen cloud platform.

Central to being able to navigate the thousands or millions of resources that an enterprise will provision in a cloud environment is tagging. Tagging is the fundamental method with which resources can be assigned to cost centers, programs, users, lines of businesses, and purposes. Without tagging, a cloud environment would be almost impossible to properly maintain across a large organization. We will cover best practices for tagging as it relates to cost management in the next section.

Historically, IT budgets have been exposed to capital investment models that are expended upfront. With the cloud, this was shifted to OpEx models where consumers had more control over operational costs. The next step in this evolution is the ability to set hard or soft limits for spending within portions or across the entire IT landscape of an enterprise. These budgets are enforced natively in the platform through APIs or notification services that alert admins when consumption is exceeding these thresholds.

AWS Budgets (`https://aws.amazon.com/aws-cost-management/aws-budgets/`), Azure Spending Budgets (`https://docs.microsoft.com/en-us/partner-center/set-an-azure-spending-budget-for-your-customers`), and GCP Budgets (`https://cloud.google.com/billing/docs/how-to/budgets`) are examples of cloud native methods to control and limit spending. This is a critical feature for large organizations where the activities and spending of certain groups may not immediately be visible to leadership or budget owners.

Cloud Native Architecture Best Practice: Set budgets for each cloud account tied to different groups across your organization. These budgets can be revisited and modified in the future. Perhaps more importantly, the budgets set a soft limit in order to enforce certain behaviors. Giving carte blanche to teams, allowing them to rack up a limitless bill, is not a best practice. Giving teams a budget limit will instill better operational practices and force them to think outside the box, leading to more inventive thinking when it comes to designing systems.

Budget thresholds can be set to alert administrators when costs exceed limits, when the use of certain services/features exceed set limits, or when consumption of pre-paid resources (such as Reserved Instances on AWS EC2) exceed set limits. These budgets can be aligned on different periods (monthly, quarterly, or annually), giving admins flexibility in how they choose to enforce constraints across the organization. Optionally, notifications can be set to alert you when you're approaching certain percentages of the budget:

Setting budgets is an effective way of monitoring cloud costs. Systems will automatically notify you when you are approaching or exceed set spend amounts. The following shows you this setting:

Billing alarms can be configured to trigger email notifications. This allows you to minimize overspending and keep your cloud environment cost optimized. The following screenshot shows the notification setup:

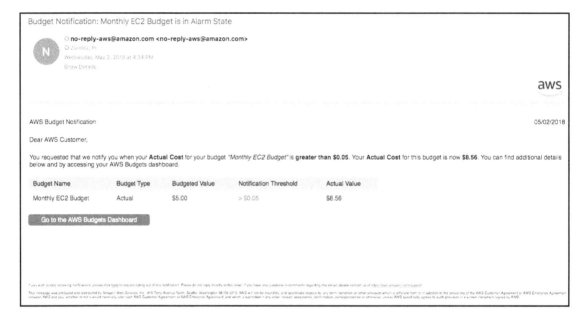

The notification setup information

There are also third-party tools that work across different cloud platforms to aggregate, display, and predict costs—these will be introduced in the Cloud Native Toolkit at the end of the chapter.

When taking into account best practices for deployment and management discussed in the previous chapters, immutable architectures require a unique approach. Since each deployment replicates the entire stack or a modular component of it, we can price it out before deployment. Using AWS Cloudformation, on the final confirmation page before deployment, you can confirm the stack's monthly cost using the **Cost** link beside **Estimate Cost**. This navigates the user to a prepopulated Simple Monthly Calculator:

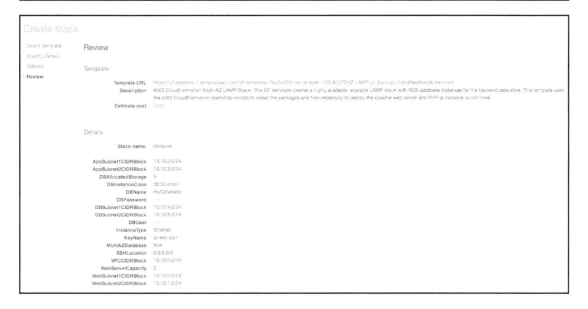

When managing deployments as stacks expressed as code, each stack can be priced out before deployment (as in the preceding case of the CloudFormation stack being deployed on AWS).

The following screenshot shows an example simple monthly calculator estimate, which was generated from a sample CloudFormation template deployment (shown in the previous screenshot):

An example of the generated monthly calculator estimate

Tagging best practices

For large enterprises or small startups alike, tagging is the most critical daily activity to be performed in order to enable cost transparency. CSPs can report and display billing transparently, but those charges will mean little to the business or end users if they can't allocate or track costs to key business functions.

Tagging is a native function supported by all leading CSPs and supports customization. Since each business, organization, and consumer has unique internal processes and terminology, it is important to develop a tagging strategy that works for you.

Cloud Native Architecture Best Practice: Tagging will very quickly become burdensome and impossible to maintain if tags are not designated at launch time. Within a couple of weeks, the entire environment can be untagged (and thus impossible to manage) if development life cycles are short enough. A cloud native cost optimized environment automatically detects (and even deletes) resources that aren't tagged. This very quickly forces teams to treat tagging as a critical activity.

Automatic enforcement of tags can be done in a number of ways. Using the command-line interface, a list of untagged resources can be generated for each service (for example, AWS EC2, EBS, and so on). Native CSP tools such as AWS Tag Editor can be used to manually find untagged resources. The optimal cloud native route would be to build a rule requiring tags on native cloud services that do this automatically, such as AWS Config Rules. Config Rules checks the environment constantly for tags that you specify as required. If they are not, manually or automatic intervention can be performed once detected:

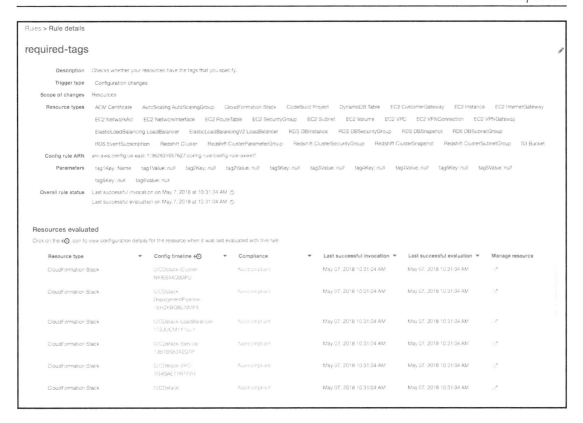

The previous screenshot shows how AWS Config Rules allow automatic detection and reporting of resources that are not tagged.

The following screenshot shows how AWS Tag Editor can be used to manually search for resources without tags, though this is more cumbersome than automatic detection (especially in large enterprise environments where thousands of resources are being used and consumed):

AWS Tag Editor

In a fully mature environment, every deployment is managed as code using deployment pipelines. In this pipeline, a gate should be used to enforce proper tagging of the template. Upon deployment, the tags should flow down to all resources in the template, if written properly. The key to tagging is automation, and by designating tags at the top-level construct (a stack template), we are minimizing the manual intervention needed and increasing the accuracy of our tags.

Cost optimization

Now that we have an approach for collecting, tracking, and viewing costs in a cloud environment, how do we optimize these costs? There are two distinct camps on what is meant by *optimizing costs*. One camp hears *minimize* (to reduce to the smallest possible amount) while the other hears *maximize* (to make the best use of). Both camps are technically correct, since no IT organization has a bottomless budget (hence you minimize to constrain costs within your budget). However, today's leading organizations have changed the way they look at IT outlays. They seek to maximize business benefits and link technology investments to business outcomes. This is what is meant by *maximizing/optimizing* our technology costs. The first question requires technology decisions. The second requires technical experimentation, patience, and business acumen.

Compute optimization

Typically, the largest savings in a cloud environment are realized during a *right sizing* exercise for the compute resources. Since compute typically dominates costs, it is reasonable to expect that the biggest cost savings can be found here. **Right sizing** refers to the act of selecting the most adequately sized virtual machine for the given application (size here refers to the amount of CPU and memory allocated to the machine).

This problem is acutely present in environments that were just migrated from on-premises to a cloud environment. The resource sizing process for on-premises typically goes through many approvals and requisite teams, each layer adding extra cushion to CYA. This results in overpowered machines that are then migrated to comparable VMs in the cloud.

 Cloud Native Architecture Best Practice: After a successful migration, or after the successful deployment of a cloud native application, collect baseline resource utilization for each of your compute resources. Use this data to properly size your VMs to the necessary performance levels.

If your application can run in clusters and is stateless, it is advantageous to use more numerous, smaller instances. This optimizes for better cost (and performance), since you will be able to scale the cluster to better match demand. AWS and Azure have a rich set of VM sizes to choose from that can match any use case. GCP offers Custom Machine types where the user can set the sizing that's available. This offers even more control over matching machine resources to application demand.

Storage optimization

After compute, storage costs typically dominate cloud bills. Some of these costs include the virtual disks/volumes attached to each VM; the object storage services hosting application artifacts, pictures/videos, and documents; archival data service usage; and the backup of this data to backup services.

For all forms of data storage, it is important to establish a life cycle that is as automated as possible. Data and backups should naturally flow down this life cycle until they are put into archives for compliance purposes or deleted. Tags should be used to designate which data stores or objects are needed long-term for compliance purposes. Scripts should be used to manage these, though cloud native services exist to aid users in this effort.

The AWS **Simple Storage Service (S3)** is a highly durable service for storing objects. S3 supports life cycle policies, which allow users to designate a transition from S3-standard to cheaper and lower performant services that Standard-IA (infrequent access), One Zone-IA, and Glacier (long-term archival cold storage). All three of these target transition services are cheaper than the standard S3 service. Objects can also be set to permanently delete after X days of being created. This can be set at the bucket level, which cascades down to all folders and objects.

The data life cycle manager for AWS EBS also provides a native solution to managing hundreds or thousands of volume level backups. For large enterprises, this task would prove cumbersome as automated tools would have to be built to query, collect information, and delete old or expired snapshots. This service from AWS allows users to natively build these life cycles.

Serverless implications

Serverless architectures are a unique costing challenge. Most of the effective cost optimization efforts fall in writing effective code in order to reduce the code's execution time or the number of executions required. This is evident from the pricing model of serverless code execution services such as AWS Lambda, which charges based on the number of executions, execution time, and allocated memory to the container that runs the code (`https://s3.amazonaws.com/lambda-tools/pricing-calculator.html`). Memory size can be optimized by tracking the amount of memory used per execution (this can be tracked in AWS CloudWatch).

Other *serverless* cloud services, such as AWS Kinesis and Athena, follow a similar data-based pricing model (per shard hour and payload units for Kinesis, per TB of data scanned for Athena). These services are almost always cheaper than their comparable services (such as Apache Kafka and Presto), which are hosted on self-managed compute nodes.

Cloud native toolkit

Many of the cloud native tools for cost optimization are natively available on their respective platforms. However, two drivers may (rightly so) drive businesses to use non-native services to optimize costs:

- The independence of a third party to deduce cost optimization areas
- The ability to work across two or more cloud environments (multi-cloud architectures)

This space is getting squeezed as CSPs replicate many of the features provided by these companies natively on the platforms. Many of the tools that provided cost optimization have been forced to pivot to management and operational automation.

Cloudability

One of the last remaining independent tools focused on cost transparency is Cloudability, which gives users a detailed budget and daily reports based on detailed metrics it collects from your cloud environments. It is currently available and integrates with the major CSPs.

AWS Trusted Advisor

This service from AWS could make an appearance in several chapters of this book due to the amount of value it gives cloud users of AWS. Trusted Advisor provides automated cost optimization, security risk, performance optimization, and fault tolerance recommendations. Trusted Advisor will notify users if instances are not properly sized, if resources are idle or unused, among many other checks to minimize cost.

Azure Cost Management

Powered by their acquisition of Cloudyn, Azure Cost Management is an effective way to track use and expenditures for your Azure landscape. It provides recommendations on instance right sizing and identifies idle resources.

Summary

In this chapter, we learned and defined the cost structure of current enterprises managing their own data centers. We established a common set of terminology to help us understand and measure the cost benefit of cloud adoption.

We learned how cloud economics drives huge advantages and savings for customers, as well as how the model for pricing has shifted from capital expenditures to operational expenditures, a key difference between legacy systems and cloud native.

Finally, we established strategies for tagging which helped enable detailed cost analysis and traceback. These strategies help optimize architectures.

In the next chapter, we will talk about operational excellence.

13
Scalable and Available

In the previous chapters of this book, we defined what a cloud-native architecture is and the impact these architectures have on people, processes, and technology. The journey to building cloud-native systems is neither straightforward nor short. It can take years to fully realize the potential of going cloud-native as your organization and culture matures. Skill sets and problem solving approaches need to change over time. Mistakes are made, lessons are learned, and systems evolve. We introduced a framework for defining the journey to cloud-native. The journey impacts your business, people, governance, platform security, and operations. Each application and each company can have varying levels of maturity depending on where they are in their journey. In order to better understand this journey, we established a Cloud Native Maturity Model. This is a useful model to understand where your organization, application stack, or system currently is on the journey, and what features it may need to become more cloud-native. Furthermore, we introduced the **software development life cycle** (**SDLC**) of cloud-native applications and learned how to choose the best technology stack that works for our use case.

In the next chapters of this book, we seek to define the core pillars of cloud native design. These design pillars are core features that make a system cloud-native. These features on their own are not exclusive to cloud applications or systems. However, when taken together, they are a set of features that no other platform but cloud can bring to the table. We will introduce these pillars one by one in the following chapters. For each pillar, we will state core design tenets to guide your architecture and deployment. We will examine particular use cases on how these tenets can be applied to different layers of an application stack. We will discuss tools, open source projects, cloud-native services, and third-party software solutions that can help support these objectives.

In this chapter, the reader will first gain an understanding of the scale at which modern cloud providers operate. There has been a clear departure from ordinary scale (the scale of data centers with which most seasoned IT practitioners are familiar with) to *hyper-scale*. This hyper-scale cloud infrastructure inherently forms many of the constructs and approaches discussed in this chapter. We will also introduce the core tenets of a scalable and available cloud system, which will help the reader make informed architecture decisions. Finally, we will discuss the current tools available to users to help build self-healing infrastructures which form the basis of resilient, cloud-native architectures.

The following topics will be covered in this chapter:

- Global Cloud infrastructure and common terminology
- Cloud infrastructure concepts (regions and AZs)
- Autoscaling groups and load balancers
- VM sizing strategies
- Always-on architectures
- Designing network redundancy and core services
- Monitoring
- Infrastructure as Code
- Immutable deployments
- Self-healing infrastructure
- Core tenets of scalable and available architectures
- Service oriented architectures
- Cloud Native Toolkit for scalable and available architectures

Introduction to the hyper-scale cloud infrastructure

When deploying systems or stacks to the cloud, it is important to understand the scale at which leading cloud providers operate. The three largest cloud providers have created a footprint of data centers, spanning almost every geography. They have circled the globe with large bandwidth fiber network trunks to provide low latency, high throughput connectivity to systems running across their global data center deployment. The scale at which these three top-tier cloud providers operate are so much larger than the other players that it's necessitated the industry to adopt a new designation, hypercloud. The following diagram depicts the global footprint of AWS, the largest cloud provider by total compute power (estimated by Gartner):

In this image, each orange dot represents an autonomous *region*. The number within each orange dot represents the number of AZs. Green circles represent regions that have been announced but are not yet generally available.

In addition to the fleet of data centers that have been built and are managed, hypercloud providers have deployed high bandwidth trans-oceanic/continental fiber networks to effectively manage traffic between each of their data center clusters. This allows customers of the respective platforms to create distributed applications across multiple geographies with very low latency and cost.

Now let's have a look at the image that captures AWS global data center and network trunk infrastructure (AWS shared their global schematics publicly for the first time at their annual developer conference re:Invent in November 2016, which was presented by AWS VP and the distinguished engineer James Hamilton). The image is as follows:

Google Cloud Platform (**GCP**) and Microsoft Azure provide similar geographic coverage. All three hypercloud platforms provide core cloud services from an infrastructure abstraction called a **region**. A region is a collection of data centers that operate together under strict latency and performance requirements. This in turn allows consumers of the cloud platform to disperse their workloads across the multiple data centers comprising the region. AWS calls this **availability zones** (**AZs**) and GCP calls it **zones**.

Cloud Native Architecture Best Practice: Disperse workloads across multiple zones within a region to make the stack highly available and more durable against hardware or application component failure. This often costs nothing extra to implement, but gives stacks a distinct operational advantage by dispersing compute nodes across multiple isolated data centers.

The following diagram shows three different AZs within one region:

As shown in the previous diagram, dispersing compute workloads across multiple AZs within a region reduces the *blast radius* in the event of a service interruption (whether it's an application or machine failure). This usually costs nothing extra from a cost perspective, as the AZs are purposefully built to be highly performant and extensible with each other within a region.

A key concept to understand and minimize when designing cloud-native systems is the *blast radius*. We define the blast radius as *the applications or ancillary systems that can be affected by the failure of a core design component*. This concept can be applied to a data center or a single microservice. The purpose is to understand the dependencies within your own architecture, evaluate your appetite for risk, quantify the cost implications of minimizing your blast radius, and design your stack within these parameters.

Central to minimizing your blast radius in the cloud is effectively utilizing the distributed quality of the regions and zones. There is a series of services that are offered by major providers that help architects do this effectively: load balancers and auto-scaling groups.

Load balancers are not a unique development to cloud, but the major platforms all have native services that provide this functionality. These native services provide much higher levels of availability, as they are running on many machines instead of a virtual load balancer running on a VM operated by the cloud consumer.

Cloud Native Architecture Best Practice: Use the native, cloud-offered load balancers whenever possible. These relinquish operational maintenance from the cloud consumer to the cloud provider. The cloud user no longer has to worry about maintaining the uptime and health of the load balancer, as that will be managed by the CSP. The load balancer runs across a series of containers or fleet of VMs, meaning that hardware or machine failures are dealt with seamlessly in the background without impact to the user.

The concept of load balancers should be familiar to all who work in the IT industry. Flowing from and adding to the concept of LBs are cloud services, which allow users to provide DNS services coupled with load balancing. This combination allows users to build globally available applications that extend seamlessly to geographies of your choosing. Services such as Amazon Route53 on the AWS platform allow users to engineer latency-based routing rules and geo-restriction to connect end consumers to the most performant stack (or to preclude availability of these services based on the end users' location). An example of this would be restricting access to your application to users based in Iran, Russia, or North Korea for the purposes of following the current sanctions laws.

Cloud Native Architecture Best Practice: Use cloud-native **Domain Name System** (**DNS**) services (AWS Route53, Azure DNS, or GCP Cloud DNS). These services integrate natively with load balancing services on each platform. Use routing policies such as **latency-based routing** (**LTR**) to build globally available performant applications that run across multiple regions. Use features such as Geo DNS to route requests from specific geographies (or countries) to specific endpoints.

Another important tool in the cloud-native toolbox is the deployment of **auto scaling groups** (**ASG**) – a novel service abstraction that allows users to replicate and expand application VMs dynamically based on various alarms or flags. In order to deploy an ASG, a standardized image of the application must first be pre-configured and stored. ASGs must almost always be coupled with load balancers in order to be used effectively, since traffic from the application consumer must be intelligently routed to an available and performant compute node in the ASG fleet. This can be done in several different ways, including round robin balancing or deploying a queueing system. A basic auto-scaling configuration across two AZs is shown in the following diagram:

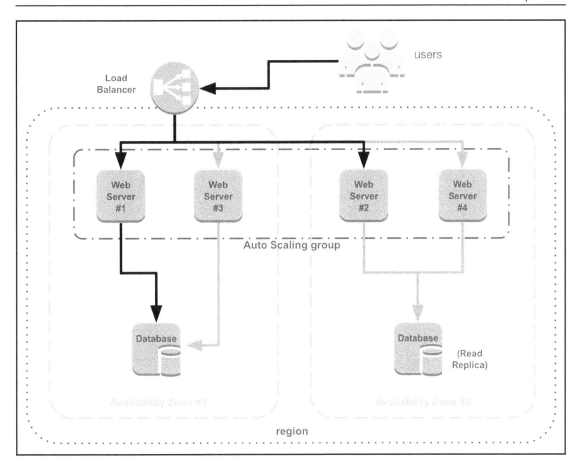

The ASG in the previous diagram is set to a minimum of two VMs, one in each availability zone (**Web Servers #1** and **Web Servers #2**). Traffic to these nodes is depicted in black. As more users access the application, the ASG reacts by deploying more servers to the ASG across the multiple AZs (**Web Servers #3** and **Web Servers #4**), with the additional traffic depicted in gray.

Now we have introduced the critical elements in a resilient cloud system: load balancing, auto-scaling, multi-AZ/ region deployments, and global DNS. The auto-scaling feature of this stack can be replicated using elastically expanding/contracting fleets of containers as well.

 Cloud Native Architecture Best Practice: When architecting a stack, it is more cost-effective to use smaller, more numerous VMs behind a load balancer. This gives you greater cost granularity and increases redundancy in the overall system. Creating a stateless architecture is also recommended, as it removes dependencies on a single application VM, making session recovery in the event of a failure far simpler.

Let's have a look at the comparison between auto-scaling groups with different VM sizes:

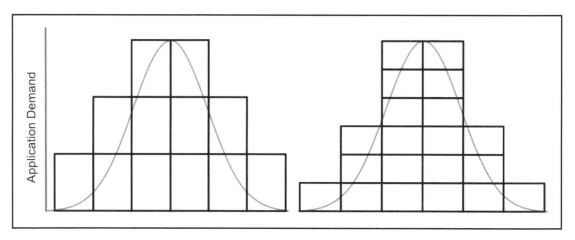

There is an advantage to creating auto-scaling groups with smaller VMs. The blue line in the preceding graph represents the demand or traffic for a given application. The blocks each represent one virtual machine. The VMs in the auto-scaling group deployment on the left contain more memory, computing power, and a higher hourly cost; the VMs in the right deployment have less memory, computing power, and hourly cost.

In the preceding graph, we have demonstrated the advantage of using smaller compute nodes in an ASG fleet. Any spaces within a block that appear above the blue line are wasted resources that are paid for. This means that the performance of the system is not ideally tuned to the application's demand, leading to *idle* resources. By minimizing the VM specs, significant cost savings can be achieved. Furthermore, by reducing the size of the VMs, the application stack becomes more distributed in nature. The failure of one VM or container will not jeopardize the entire health of the stack since there are more VMs in the group to fail over to.

Utilizing load balancers services with auto scaling groups; dynamic routing; stateless architectures utilizing highly available and performant DB services, dispersed among multiple zones (or groups of data centers); represents a mature, cloud-native architecture.

Always-on architectures

For many years, architects have always had two primary concerns: the *availability* of a given system and the *recoverability* of the system (often referred to as **disaster recovery**). These two concepts exist to address inherent qualities of a system deployed on a limited, on-premise infrastructure. In this on-premise infrastructure, there are a finite number of physical or virtual resources performing very specific functions or supporting a specific application. These applications are built in such a way that it negates the ability to run in a distributed manner across multiple machines. This paradigm means that the overall system has many single points of failure, whether it be a single network interface, a virtual machine or physical server, a virtual disk or volume, and so on.

Given these inherent fault points, architects developed two principle assessments to gauge the efficacy of a system. The systems' ability to remain running and perform its function is known as availability. If a system does fail, the recoverability of a system is gauged by two measurements:

- **Recovery time objective** (**RTO**): The time needed to bring the system into an acceptable functional state after a failure
- **Recovery point objective** (**RPO**): The acceptable length of time the system can lose data during an outage

When considering a completely cloud-native architecture, several important factors affect these old paradigms and allow us to evolve them:

- **The cloud provides architects (for all practical purposes) an infinite amount of compute and storage.** The *hyper-scale* nature of the leading cloud providers that we discussed earlier in this chapter demonstrates the size and scope of modern systems.

- **Services provided by cloud platforms are inherently fault tolerant and resilient in nature.** Consumption or integration of these services into a stack provides a level of availability that can rarely be matched when trying to construct a highly available stack utilizing home grown tools. For example, AWS **Simple Storage Service** (S3) is a fault tolerant and highly available object storage service that maintains 99.999999999% durability (meaning the chance of an object becoming permanently lost is miniscule). **Service Level Agreement** (SLA) availability for the S3 standard is 99.99%. Objects you upload to S3 are automatically replicated across two other AZs in the region for redundancy at no additional cost to the user. The user simply creates a logical storage vehicle called a **bucket** and uploads their objects there for later retrieval. The physical and virtual machine maintenance and oversight is handled by AWS. To try and approach the level of availability and durability provided by AWS with your own system would require an immense amount of engineering, time, and investment.

- **Native services and features are available that aid architects and developers in monitoring, flagging, and performing actions to maintain the health of a system.** For example, the Cloudwatch monitoring service from AWS gives metrics on performance and health of virtual machines in a stack. You can combine Cloudwatch metrics with auto-scaling groups or instance recovery, which automate system responses to certain performance levels. Combining these monitoring services with serverless function execution, architects can create an environment where the system can respond to metrics in an automated fashion.

Given these cloud features, we believe the new paradigm for cloud architectures allows us to achieve an **always-on** paradigm. This paradigm helps us plan for outages and architect in such a manner that the system can self-heal and course-correct without any user intervention. This level of automation represents a high level of maturity for a given system, and is the furthest along the Cloud Native Maturity Model.

It is important to note that every human endeavor will eventually fail, stumble, or become interrupted, and the cloud is no exception. Since we lack precognition and are constantly evolving our capabilities in IT, it is *inevitable* that something will break at some given point. Understanding and accepting this fact is at the heart of the always-on paradigm—planning for these failures is the only guaranteed way to mitigate or avoid them.

Always-on – key architectural elements

There are defining features of cloud-native architectures that allow for an always-on, technically resilient architecture. This is not an all or nothing proposition, and many deployments will feature a mix of the features we are going to be talking about. Do not overwhelm yourself or your architects by believing all these features can be incorporated into a deployment overnight. An iterative, evolutionary approach is needed to adopt the key design elements we will be discussing. As Werner Vogels (CTO Amazon) says, "Everything always fails." If we plan for inevitable failure, we can design systems to avoid it.

Network redundancy

Connectivity into the cloud and across all your environments should be provided in a highly available, redundant manner. There are two main implications for this in a cloud-native world. The first implication is the physical connectivity from an on-premise environment or customer into the cloud. All hypercloud providers provide a private express network connection alongside ISP partners (for example, AWS Direct Connect, Azure ExpressRoute, and GCP Cloud Interconnect). It is a best practice to back up the primary, high bandwidth connection with a failover option (another private connection or a VPN tunnel over the internet) by utilizing separate physical links.

Cloud Native Architecture Best Practice: Utilize redundant network connections into your cloud environment by using two physically different and isolated network fibers. This is especially important for enterprises that are relying on their cloud environments for business critical applications. In the case of smaller or less critical deployments, either a combination of private fiber and VPN, or two VPN links may be considered for lightweight environments.

The second implication is the redundancy of physical and virtual endpoints (both in the cloud and on-premise environment). This is largely a moot point for cloud endpoints since each of them are provided in an *as-a-service* gateway configuration. These virtual gateways are running on the cloud providers' hypervisor across multiple physical machines across multiple data centers. What is often overlooked is that the cloud-native mentality must extend down from the cloud to the customer endpoint as well. This is necessary in order to ensure no single point of failure exists to hobble a system's performance or availability to end customers. Thus, a cloud-native approach extends to a consumer's on-premise network connectivity. This means utilizing multiple, redundant appliances with parallel network links, mirroring the way cloud providers build out their physical data centers' connectivity.

Cloud Native Architecture Best Practice: For enterprises and business critical environments, utilize two separate physical devices on the customer side (on-premises) as the termination point of your cloud connection. Architecting for always-on in the cloud is a null point if your connection to the environment is hobbled by a hardware-based, single point of failure on the customer side.

Let's have a look at the following diagram showing connection between cloud provider and corporate data center:

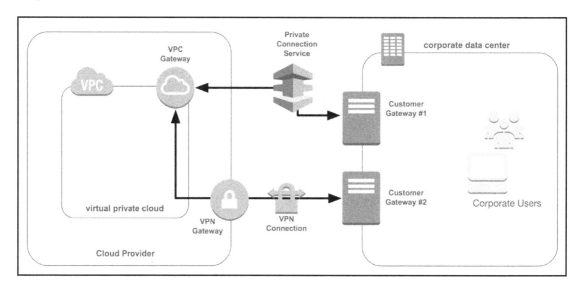

When connecting from a corporate data center, office location, or customer site into a cloud environment, use redundant connectivity pathways to maintain cloud environment availability. In the event of an appliance failure, physical fiber outage, or service interruption, a redundant pathway should always be available. This can be a combination of a high cost, high performance primary line and a low cost, low performance secondary line (that is, VPN over the internet).

Redundant core services

Making key services and applications that are consumed by the rest of the IT stack redundant is another important design facet of cloud-native architectures. The enterprise has a lot of legacy services that are only just beginning to adapt to the cloud native model. When migrating to the cloud, it is critical to re-architect or refactor these applications to dependably run in the new environment.

An example of this is the **Active Directory** (**AD**), a critical component for enabling productivity for almost every enterprise. AD maintains and grants access to people, machines, and services by authenticating and authorizing their actions.

There are varying levels of cloud native maturity for standing up AD services. At one end of the spectrum, companies simply extend their network to the cloud and utilize the same AD infrastructure that exists on-premise. This represents the least performant pattern and minimizes the benefits of what the cloud has to offer. In a more advanced pattern, architects extend the forest to the cloud by deploying **domain controllers** (**DC**) or **read-only domain controllers** (**RODCs**) in the cloud network environment. This provides higher levels of redundancy and performance. For a truly cloud-native AD deployment, leading cloud platforms now provide native services that stand up fully managed AD deployments that run at scale and cost fractions of maintaining your own physical or virtual infrastructure. AWS provides several variants (AWS Directory Service, Managed Microsoft AD, and AD Connector), while Microsoft provides Azure AD and Google Cloud has Directory Sync. The following diagram shows three different active identity options, ranging from least (Option #1) to most performant (Option #3), based on where the domain controllers are hosted.

A range of AD deployments are demonstrated in the following diagram:

The first option is to rely on connectivity to the on-premise AD server for AD authentication and authorization. The second option is to deploy a DC or RODC in the cloud environment. The most cloud-native method is to offload this *undifferentiated heavy lifting* to a native cloud service. The cloud service deploys and manages the AD infrastructure, relinquishing the cloud consumer of these menial tasks. This option results in substantially better performance and availability. It is deployed across multiple AZs automatically, provides scale-out options with a few clicks to increase the number of Domain Controllers, and supports the advanced features needed from an on-premise AD deployment (such as single sign-on, group-based policies, and backups).

In addition to this, the cloud AD services natively integrate with other cloud services, easing the burden during the VM deployment process. VMs can be very easily added to domains, and access to the cloud platform itself can be federated based on identities and users in the AD. It should also be mentioned that these cloud services are generally (if not fully) supportive of **Lightweight Directory Access Protocol** (**LDAP**), meaning alternatives to Microsoft AD such as OpenLDAP, Samba, and Apache Directory can be used.

Domain Name System (**DNS**) follows a similar pattern to AD, with varying levels of cloud nativity based on the deployment model. For the highest level of availability and scalability, utilize leading cloud services such as AWS Route53, Azure DNS, and Google Cloud DNS (which are discussed later on in this book). Hosted zones (public and private) supported by these internal services give the best performance per unit cost. Aside from AD and DNS, other centralized services include AV, IPS, IDS, and logging.

Apart from the core services an enterprise may consume, most large-scale application stacks require middleware or queues to help manage the large and complex traffic flows through the stack. As you might suspect, there are two major patterns an architect can use for a deployment. The first is to manage their own queueing system that's deployed on the cloud's virtual machines. The cloud users will have to manage the operational aspect of the queue deployment (examples such as products from Dell Boomi or Mulesoft), including configuring multi-AZ deployments to ensure high availability.

The second option is to use a queue or message bus service offered by the cloud platforms. The undifferentiated heavy lifting is managed by the CSP—all that remains to the architect or user is to configure and consume the service. The leading services one may consider are AWS **Simple Queue Service** (**SQS**), AmazonMQ, Amazon **Simple Notification Service** (**SNS**), Azure Storage Queues and Service Bus Queues, and GCP Task Queue.

Cloud-based queue services reside on redundant infrastructures, guaranteeing at-least-once delivery, while some support **First In First Out** (**FIFO**). The ability of the service to scale allows the message queue to provide highly concurrent access to many producers and consumers. This makes it an ideal candidate to sit at the center of a decoupled Services Oriented Architecture (SOA).

Monitoring

To cloud-native applications, monitoring is the equivalent of the body's nervous system. Without it, signals to expand and contract auto-scaling groups, optimize infrastructure performance, and the end user experience would be impossible. Monitoring needs to be applied at all levels of the stack to maximize feedback, help guide intelligent automation, and inform IT owners on where to focus efforts and dollars. An adage that should serve as a mantra for all architects and engineers is: *If you can't measure it, you can't manage it.*

Monitoring in a cloud-native environment must principally cover four areas:

- **Infrastructure Monitoring**: Collects and reports on the performance of hosts, network, databases, and any other core cloud services that are consumed within your stack (remember, even cloud services can fail or be interrupted, thus they must be monitored for health and performance).
- **Application Monitoring**: Collects and reports on the use of local resources supporting application runtime, as well as application performance that's unique to your cloud-native app (for example, Query return time).
- **Real Time User Monitoring**: Collects and reports all user interactions with your website or client. This will often be the "canary in the coalmine" when the system begins to show faults or experience service degradation.
- **Log Monitoring**: Collects and reports logs that are generated from all hosts, applications, and security devices into a centrally managed and extensible repository.

 Cloud Native Architecture Best Practice: Across all monitoring use cases, it is advised to keep a historical trail of data whenever possible. Interesting and novel usage patterns emerge from these historical datasets that can help inform when to pre-emptively scale or identify problematic or underperforming service components.

Across all four of the previously stated use cases, cloud natively supports the creation, ingestion, and storage of logs. AWS Cloudwatch and CloudTrail, Azure Monitor, Google Cloud Stackdriver Monitoring, and IBM Monitoring and Analytics are all examples of the native services provided on these platforms.

The following diagram depicts the different sources of logs encountered in a hybrid environment (cloud and on-premise):

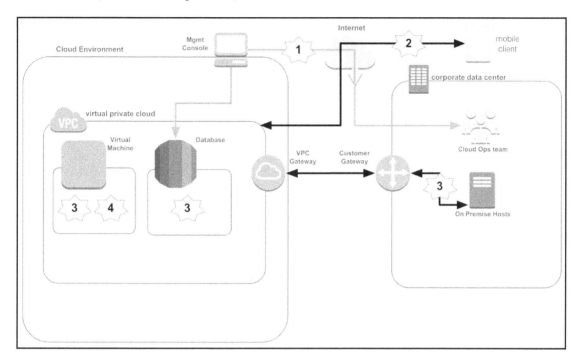

The sources can be:

- **Source 1:** Logging of API calls made to change settings and configurations of the environment by IT teams and machines
- **Source 2:** End user logs generated by the mobile and desktop of web clients
- **Source 3:** Infrastructure performance logs generated by resources in the cloud and on-premise
- **Source 4:** Custom logs generated by your application that are specific and deemed pertinent to the overall health of the stack

In most cases, there are several solution variants to choose from, ranging from native cloud services, third-party products deployed and managed on the cloud compute resources, and a combination of both. For the enterprise, popular (albeit sometimes expensive) options include Splunk, Sumo Logic, Loggly, and Dynatrace. These third-party solutions provide extensive capabilities that collect, store, and analyze high volumes of data that's generated across all four use cases. Standard APIs are available to build and feed data sources natively into the products.

Encroaching on this space and constantly providing more features and capabilities, CSPs have launched their own logging and monitoring services which integrate natively with other services on the platform. An example of this is AWS CloudTrail and Cloudwatch. These services help provide a mature, turnkey service that provides logging capabilities natively on the platform. They both integrate easily with other services offered by AWS, thus increasing their value to the user.

AWS CloudTrail helps enable governance, compliance, operational, and risk auditing of the AWS environment by logging each unique account interaction. CloudTrail leverages the fact that underlying every account event (a user or machine initiated configuration change) is done through APIs. These API requests are captured, stored, and monitored through CloudTrail. This provides operations and security teams a full 360° view into **who** changed **what** and **when**. AWS CloudWatch is a complementary service that allows users to collect and track metrics from the platform or from custom generated sources at the application level. CloudWatch also allows users to build custom dashboards, thus making aggregation of relevant metrics for operations teams and reporting much more simple. Finally, CloudWatch allows users to set alarms that can automatically trigger events (such as sending an SMS or email notification) when certain resource conditions are met (such as having a large CPU utilization or under-provisioned DB read capacity).

The following screenshot is an example of a custom dashboard built with AWS CloudWatch:

Each graph in the preceding screen is a customizable widget that can represent myriad metrics collected from other services on the platform. Custom metrics can also be ingested into and monitored by the service.

CSPs other than AWS offer similar services with a constantly expanding set of features and rich capabilities. It is worth noting that this is a noticeable theme within the industry — third-party partners' (3PP) offerings are constantly encroached upon by the CSPs as they expand their services and features. This push and pull is a boon to cloud consumers as the whole industry is propelled forward more quickly in this highly competitive environment:

Cloud Native Architecture Best Practice: Build several dashboards, each giving you insight into one application stack or relevant operational group. This one-to-one relationship will allow you to quickly and easily view all relevant data for one autonomous stack, making troubleshooting and performance tuning much simpler. This can also be used to simplify reporting.

Building upon *Figure 5.8*, we can now flesh out services to specific use cases, which is shown in the following diagram:

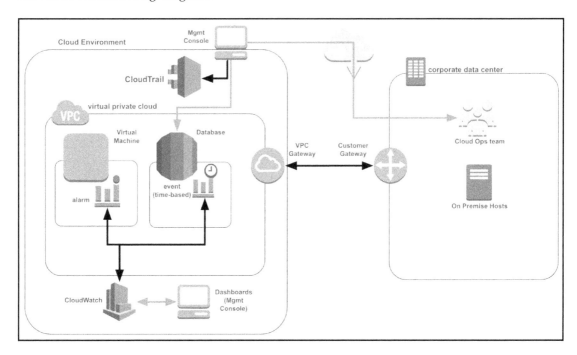

AWS CloudTrail serves as an audit trail for every API call made to the cloud environment. This allows owners to maintain complete visibility into who is performing what actions with which resources. Amazon CloudWatch provides native metric gathering and reporting capabilities. These custom dashboards can even collect and report logs from on-premise hosts and systems.

Instantiating services such as CloudWatch and CloudTrail, then creating a customized dashboard based on the usage environment and application you are supporting, are critical first steps to setting up a cloud-native environment and application.

Infrastructure as Code

The very nature of the cloud materially separates the cloud user and the resources they are provisioning and consuming. This eliminates the possibility of being able to physically troubleshoot non-performant or failed devices. This necessitates the digitization of all functionality that was done by walking to resources and interacting with them. This is certainly not the sole reason, but it was a leading design imperative in the nascent days of the cloud. CSPs have built their platforms from the ground up with APIs. Each service and feature can be utilized, configured, consumed, or otherwise interacted with programmatically through a set of defined APIs. The syntax, descriptions, **command-line interfaces** (**CLIs**), and usage examples are published and maintained by each CSP and are available for free for all to scrutinize and utilize.

Once software defined configuration had taken root, it became possible to express the whole IT environment or stack through code. The concept of **Infrastructure as Code** (**IaC**) was born. Many of the same concepts, approaches, and tools that developers used to collaborate, test, and deploy their applications could now be applied to infrastructure (compute resources, databases, networks, and so on). Suffice to say this development has been one of the largest contributions to the rapid advancement of IT systems in general, as it allowed infrastructure architects to iteratively evolve their systems as quickly as developers.

In order to set up a highly available, scalable, and resilient application, it is important for cloud architects to adopt many of the principles at the heart of software development today. The evolutionary approach afforded by treating your IaC is the enabling factor to reach a high stack maturity (that exhibits high levels of availability, scalability, and resiliency). Do not assume that your cloud-native application will be mature and resilient from day one. With each day, new efficiencies and failovers must be built into it. This evolutionary approach is core to achieving success (often called the "cloud journey" in industry parlance).

Cloud Native Architecture Best Practice: Manage a series of IaC stacks instead of building one large monolith IaC stack. Common approaches are to separate core network configurations and resources into one stack (this is typically a one time configuration that sees very little change over time and is a common resource used across all applications, thus necessitating its own dedicated stack). Segregate applications into their own stacks or multiple stacks. Shared resources between applications should rarely be included in the stack of a single application — manage it in a separate stack to avoid missteps between two teams.

Building upon *Figure 5.6*, we can now define our entire cloud network infrastructure as a code template (we will call this the network stack), as shown in the following diagram:

Everything within the gray dotted line is defined as code within the network stack template. Any changes that need to be made to the network stack can be managed by making changes to the code contained therein.

Building upon *Figure 5.4*, we can see one approach to managing an application with IaC. The web server configuration, auto-scaling group, and elastic load balancer are defined and managed in the Web Stack Template. The database configuration and resources are managed in the Database Stack Template, as shown in the following diagram:

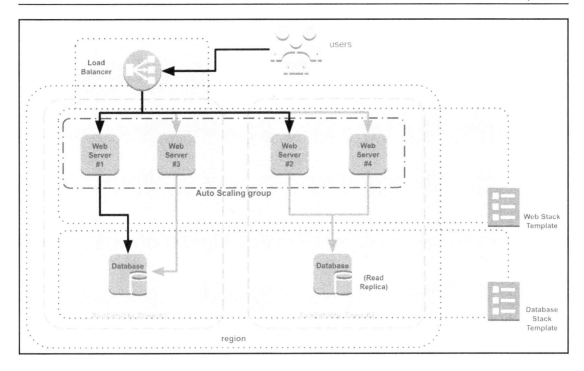

There are native cloud services and third-party options to use here. AWS CloudFormation, **Azure Resource Manager** (**ARM**), and GCP Deployment Manager are examples of native CSP services. Code can often be written in **JavaScript Object Notation** (**JSON**) or **Yaml Ain't Markup Language** (**YAML**), previously known as **Yet Another Markup Language**.

A popular third-party tool is Terraform by HashiCorp. Terraform works across all major clouds and on-premise, allowing users to create a unified IaC landscape across a hybrid infrastructure environment. Terraform supports its own format for configurations (otherwise known as templates), creatively named terraform format, but JSON is also supported. While not strictly IaC, there are many tools that perform configuration management, such as Vagrant, Ansible, Chef, and Puppet.

A mature deployment in AWS, for example, would utilize both CloudFormation with a configuration management tool such as Chef to automate and reduce deployment errors.

Immutable deployments

Immutable means something does not change over time or is unable to be changed. An immutable deployment is the approach that once an application stack is deployed and configured, its state is fixed. If there are any necessary modifications, the entire application stack or stack element is redeployed.

Cloud VMs are inherently no more reliable or durable than on-premise machines. Their primary advantage is that they are *standardized* and *easy to replace*. Imagine you are building a complex Lego building set. If you break one yellow 4 x 2 brick, you wouldn't wait to repair that brick, so you can continue building your structure. You would reach into the bucket and find the next identical brick and continue building. Treating cloud resources in a similar fashion is appropriate. More succinctly and ruthlessly put, a common adage is "Treat your resources like cattle, not pets." Be ready to cull the underperforming cattle in order to free your pastures for healthy ones.

If we continue with the Lego analogy, we can gain several advantages by treating the whole completed structure (a castle, for example) as immutable. Any changes that we want to make to the castle (adding a drawbridge, for example) would be built and tested in a second castle that we would build. The first functions normally until we have completed testing and are ready to promote the new castle with its updated drawbridge.

Treating application stacks in this manner, by replacing the entire system at the lowest level possible each time, triggers several benefits:

- Replacing a system at the lowest level encourages you to automate every deployment step.
- Failing back to a previous version is easy and straightforward since the healthy, old stack remains running until the new stack is tested and ready, as opposed to rolling updates, where the live stack is updated with the changes you want to make. If something goes wrong, one has to roll back the updates, hoping that they can reverse all changes made. Each phase of a rolling update and rollback bring the system down. This is unnecessary with immutable deployments.
- By encouraging automation, every change will need to exist as a script. There will be tough lessons for teams who continue to make manual changes, as no server is special and may be de/re-commissioned at any time.
- Scripting everything means you can build production-like systems for development and testing very easily by changing a few lines of code.
- Most importantly, new infrastructures can be tested in isolation, without risking the production stack. For business critical applications, this is paramount to ensure revenue generating systems are unaffected.

Treating your deployments as immutable isn't a configuration change, but a mindset and cultural shift that needs to occur in the organization. It's become an option because of the new capabilities that cloud offers, specifically IaC (whether it be AWS CloudFormation, Azure ARM, or Terraform).

There are other cloud tools available as well that help provide yet more automation and ease the deployment burden. Cloud services such as AWS Elastic Beanstalk manage the operational burden of a deployment, leaving the user to focus on building and owning the code development of the application. The user simply uploads their code to the service and Elastic Beanstalk handles the rest (with a few configuration parameters given by the user). Services such as Elastic Beanstalk have immutability at the heart of the deployments, allowing you to provision a new 2.0 stack alongside your original 1.0 stack. You can perform testing and slowly accept more user traffic in the 2.0 version. When you are sure the 2.0 stack is ready for production, you can complete the cutover. If the new stack is faulting, you can fail back quickly to the original environment. This is done simply by changing the load balancing settings to direct traffic from the old to the new stack (or vice versa).

Furthermore, there are now cloud services that enforce configuration rigidity and help you maintain immutability. Services such as AWS Config and Config Rules help track configuration changes over time, allowing users to monitor changes of resources and view states. These metrics can be consumed through the API to feed your own notification/remediation system, or you can use Config Rules to automatically enforce certain actions based on how the resources have changed.

Immutability is a key design paradigm to adopt in the journey to cloud native maturity. By managing deployment changes at the lowest resource level, you are encouraging automation and increasing the availability of the application.

Self-healing infrastructures

Another important paradigm to adopt for cloud-native applications as it relates to scalability and availability are self-healing infrastructures. A self-healing infrastructure is an inherently smart deployment that is automated to respond to known and common failures. Depending on the failure, the architecture is inherently resilient and takes appropriate measures to remediate the error.

The self-healing aspect can apply at the application, system, and hardware levels. The cloud has completely taken responsibility for "hardware self-healing". No such thing *technically* exists, as we have yet to figure out a way to repair broken hard disks, torched CPUs, or to replace burned-out RAM without human interaction. As cloud consumers, however, the current state of affairs mimics an idealistic future. CSPs deploy people behind the scenes to repair and replace failing hardware resources quickly and furtively. By our strict definition, we have yet to approach self-healing physical infrastructures since human intervention is still needed. However, as cloud consumers, we do not need worry about this, as we are completely divorced from the physical layer.

At the system and application level, we have many methods at our disposal to help build self-healing infrastructures and cloud-native applications. A few examples are given as follows, and we will cover tools to use later in this chapter:

- **Auto-scaling groups** are a perfect example of self healing systems. While we typically associate ASGs with scalability, ASGs can be tuned to discard and reprovision unhealthy VMs with new ones. Sending custom health metrics or heartbeats to your monitoring system is key to utilizing this capability. It's important to architect apps as stateless, since this will allow sessions to be handed across one VM to another within an ASG.
- **DNS Health Checks** available on the cloud platforms allow users to monitor and act upon the health of a specific resource, the status of native monitoring services, and the states of other health checks. You can then intelligently and automatically reroute traffic based on the health of the stack.
- **Instance (VM) Autorecovery** is a feature that CSPs such as AWS provide to automatically recover an unhealthy instance when there is an underlying hardware failure. If there is a loss of network connectivity, loss of system power, software issues on the physical host, or hardware issues on the physical host that impact network reachability, AWS will replicate the instance and notify the user.
- **Database failover or cluster** features are available through managed DB services on the major CSPs. Services such as AWS RDS (Relational Database Service) give users the ability to provision multi-AZ deployments. By using SQL Server Mirroring for SQL; Multi-AZ deployments for Oracle, PostgreSQL, MySQL and MariaDB; and clustering for Amazon's proprietary DB engine called Aurora, these services support highly available DB stack components. In the event of a failure, the DB service automatically fails over to a synchronized standby replica.

Core tenets

Cloud-native applications must be scalable and available. In order to achieve this bar, resilient systems in the cloud must make use of the concepts introduced in this chapter. We've summarized the core tenets that one should abide by to build cloud-native applications as follows:

- Compute is distributed and the application is stateless:
  - Distribute across multiple zones and geographies. Take full advantage of the scale of hyper-cloud providers and build your own systems to be multi-zonal or multi-regional.
  - A stateful application keeps data about each session on the machine and uses that data while the session is active. A stateless application, however, does not keep any session state data on the server/host. Instead, the session data is stored on the client and passed to the server as needed. This allows compute resources to be used interchangeably as needed (for example, when an ASG expands or contracts the number of compute resources in a group).

- Storage is non-local and distributed:
  - Utilize cloud storage services which provide redundancy to your data by design. Services from AWS such as **Simple Storage Service (S3)** and **Elastic Block Store (EBS)** automatically replicate your data across multiple AZs and multiple hard disks.
  - Utilizing distributed caching solutions such as Redis and Memcache helps support stateless application architectures. This offloads common data and objects from the elastic web and app layers into a common data store.
  - Use database solutions that distribute data and tolerate hardware or node failures. Multi-AZ database deployments or fully managed NoSQL DB services like AWS DynamoDB provide inherent redundancy and resiliency.

- Create physically redundant network connections:
    - Even the most advanced applications can fail if network connections are severed and there is no failover plan. Architect redundant network connectivity to the cloud from your existing data center or network exchange. This is a foundational architecture decision that will pay dividends in an extreme failure event. This mentality also applies to network hardware on-premise. Do not terminate a private link and its redundant VPN connection on the same network gear. Have at least two physically separate resources to rely on.

- Monitor extensively and exhaustively:
    - Without intelligent, thorough, and continuous monitoring, you cannot build a scalable and highly available system. By monitoring at all levels of the stack, you can build automation to enable self-healing infrastructures and find common failure modes. Furthermore, as you build a historical record of how the system behaves over time, patterns emerge for you to intelligently scale ahead of anticipated traffic increases and address system performance bottlenecks.

- Use IaC:
    - By expressing stacks as code, you can apply all the benefits of agile software development methodologies to the deployment and management of IT systems. This is a crucial point in order to build cloud-native applications, since without it, several of the concepts introduced in this chapter would not be possible.

- Every deployment is immutable:
    - Enforce a policy of adopting changes to a system at the lowest level possible. If you need to apply an update or patch an application, deploy a new updated VM based on a new image or launch a new container with your updated application. This is as much a cultural shift for the organization as it is a technological one.

- Design and implement the self-healing infrastructure whenever possible:
    - Reduce your operational overhead by deploying resources and building systems that repair themselves. Expect and anticipate failures, even in the cloud. CSPs services and virtual machines are not immune to hardware or network failures, nor should you expect 100% uptime. Take this into account and deploy across multiple geographic zones and distribute.

- Deployment anti-patterns are automatically reported and prevented:
  - By treating IaC and adopting immutable deployments, every change to a stack can be monitored and inspected. Build in configuration checks and rules into the environment to prevent changes. Build code checks into your pipeline to flag non-compliant systems before they are deployed.
- Create and maintain an Operational Control Pane:
  - Create custom dashboards tailored to your application and system. Use a combination of built-in cloud logging services and custom metrics to aggregate critical data into one view. Furthermore, create rules to flag or notify admins when metrics exceed normal behavior.
- Scalability versus Elasticity—know the difference and architect appropriately:
  - The scalability afforded by cloud gives users almost infinite capacity to grow their application. Scalability requirements for your application will depend on where your users are based, your global ambitions, and which specific resource type is needed. Elasticity is an architectural feature which you must design and build into your system. This means that your system can expand and contract to match a user's demand. This leads to performance and cost optimization.

Service-oriented architectures and microservices

The origin of cloud development for the leading CSPs stems from the pain of managing monolithic systems. As each company (Amazon.com retail site, Google.com's indexing of the web) was experiencing tremendous growth, the traditional IT systems were incapable of keeping up with the rate of expansion and evolving at a necessary pace to enable the innovation that was needed. This story is true and well-documented in the public sphere for both AWS and GCP. As their internal systems matured around these services (provided initially as internal only to product development teams), Amazon took the step to provide these services to external customers on a utility-based billing system.

Many businesses and architects now see the virtue in this decoupling process, calling the fully decoupled environment a **service-oriented architecture (SOA)**. We define SOAs as *digital environments where each constituent system providing the lowest level of application functionality is run independently and interacts with other systems solely through APIs*. In practice, this means each service is deployed and managed independently (ideally as a stack managed by IaC). Services can be dependent upon other services; however, this exchange of data is accomplished through APIs.

SOAs and microservices are at the mature end of the CNMM for scalability and availability. Decoupling your application or IT environment requires years of work and technical discipline.

Cloud-native toolkit

Now that we have a firm understanding of the and strategies around architecting scalable and available systems, in this section, we will introduce tools, products, and open source projects to help implement these strategies. These tools will help you design more mature systems along the Automation and Application Centric Design axes of the CNMM.

Simian Army

The Simian Army is a suite of tools made available by Netflix on GitHub as an open source project. The *army* consists of monkeys (different tools) ranging from Chaos Monkey and Janitor Monkey to Conformity Monkey. Each monkey specializes in a certain objective, such as bringing down a subsystem, removing underutilized resources, or resources that do not conform to predefined rules (such as tagging). Using the Simian Army tool is a great way to test your systems in a *gameday-like* situation, where your engineers and admins are on the alert and are ready to remedy the system if it fails to deal with the outcome of the Simian Army's attack. Netflix has these tools running consistently during the work day, allowing engineers to constantly test the effectiveness of their design. As subsystems are taken down by the army, the self-healing aspects of the applications are subjected to punishing tests.

The Simian Army is on GitHub at `https://github.com/Netflix/SimianArmy`.

Docker

Docker is a software container platform that allows you to package up an application with all its dependencies and requisite libraries into a self-reliant module. It moves the architecture design center of gravity from host/VM to containerized applications. Containers help eliminate the risk of incompatibilities or version conflicts between the application and the underlying OS. Furthermore, they can easily be migrated across any machine running Docker.

As it relates to cloud-native applications, containers are an effective way to package applications for runtime, great for version management, and efficient in operating deployments. Docker is a leading solution in this space, and its **Community Edition (CE)** is free to use.

In addition to Docker, there are several noteworthy open source projects that can help maximize the use of Docker and help create cloud-native systems:

- **Infrakit** is a toolkit for infrastructure orchestration. It emphasizes the immutable architecture approach, and breaks down automation and management processes into small components. Infrakit provides infrastructure support for higher-level container orchestration systems and makes your infrastructure self-healing. It has many plugins to other popular tools and projects, such as Swarm, Kubernetes, Terraform, and Vagrant, and supports AWS, Google, and VMWare environments (`https://github.com/docker/infrakit`).

- **Docker Swarm(kit)** is a cluster management and orchestration tool for Docker Engine 1.12 and later. It allows your Docker container deployment to support service reconciliation, load balancing, service discovery, and built-in certification rotation. **Docker Swarm** standalone is also available, but has seen its active development cease as Swarmkit has surged in popularity (`https://github.com/docker/swarmkit`).

- **Portainer** is a lightweight management UI for Docker environments. It's simple to use and runs on a single container that can run on any Docker engine. When building an operational control pane, UIs such as Portainer are indispensable in pulling together a master view of the environment and systems. (Go to `https://github.com/portainer/portainer` and `https://portainer.io/` to learn more).

Kubernetes

With the popularity and success of Docker expanding in the mid 2010s, Google recognized the trend of containerization and contributed significantly to its adoption. Google designed Kubernetes from scratch to orchestrate Docker containers, basing it off of their internal system infrastructure orchestration system called Borg. Kubernetes is a powerful, open-source tool that helps mount storage systems, check application health, replicate application instances, autoscale, roll out updates, load balance, monitor resources, and debug applications, among many other capabilities. In 2016, Kubernetes was donated to the Cloud Native Compute Foundation, ensuring it would remain free to use and supported by an active community (`https://kubernetes.io/`).

Terraform

Terraform by Hashicorp is a popular tool for building, changing, and versioning **IaC** (**IaC**). As opposed to native cloud platform services such as AWS CloudFormation or Azure ARM, Terraform works across CSPs and on-premise data centers. This gives a distinct advantage when handling infrastructure resources across a hybrid environment (`https://github.com/hashicorp/terraform`).

OpenFaaS (Function as a Service)

Combining a few of the tools mentioned previously (Docker, Docker Swarm, and Kubernetes), OpenFaaS is an open source project that allows you to easily build serverless functions. The framework helps automate the deployment of an API gateway to support your function and collected metrics. The gateway scales according to demand, and a UI is made available for monitoring purposes (`https://github.com/openfaas/faas`).

Envoy

Originally developed at Lyft, Envoy is an open source edge and service proxy designed for cloud-native applications. Proxy services are key to adopting service oriented architectures—of which mature designs provide the best scalability and availability (`https://www.envoyproxy.io/`).

Linkerd

Another open source project supported by the Cloud Native Compute Foundation, Linkerd is a popular service mesh project. It's designed to make SOA architectures scalable by transparently adding service discovery, load balancing, failure handling, and smart routing to all inter-service communication (`https://linkerd.io/`).

Zipkin

Based on the Google Research paper titled *Dapper, a large-scale distributed systems tracing infrastructure*, Zipkin is an open source project that operationalizes what was conceived in the paper. Zipkin helps architects troubleshoot and optimize latency within their microservice architectures by asynchronously collecting span data, and rationalizing this data through a UI (`https://zipkin.io/`).

Ansible

A popular open source configuration management and orchestration platform, Ansible is part of RedHat's software offering. It relies on agentless communication between nodes and control nodes. It supports playbooks to automate and deploy application infrastructure stacks (`https://www.ansible.com/`).

Apache Mesos

Mesos is, in essence, a cluster manager that provides your applications the ability to scale beyond a single VM or physical machine. Mesos allows you to easily build a distributed system across a pool of shared resources. By providing common functionality that any distributed system needs (for example, failure detection, task distribution, task starting, task monitoring, task killing, and task cleanup), Mesos has become a popular choice the supporting big data Hadoop deployments. Mesos was created at the University of California at Berkeley's AMPLab and became an Apache Foundation top-level project in 2013 (`http://mesos.apache.org/`).

Saltstack

Another open source configuration management and orchestration project, the Saltstack project is an option for managing cloud-native deployments at scale. Consider using salt if your deployment is heavily skewed towards the use of Linux-based OS distributions. Salt was written by Thomas S Hatch and was first released in 2011 (`https://github.com/saltstack/salt`).

Vagrant

An open source project owned by Hashicorp, Vagrant gives users a consistent method of configuring virtual environments. When used in conjunction with automation software, Vagrant ensures scalability and portability across all virtual environments. The first release of Vagrant was written in 2010 by Mitchell Hashimoto and John Bender (`https://www.vagrantup.com/`).

OpenStack projects

OpenStack is an open source project umbrella for building smaller, open source projects, mimicking all the services found in today's leading CSPs. OpenStack projects range from compute, storage, and networking to data and analytics, security, and application services.

Compute:

- Nova – Compute Service: `https://wiki.openstack.org/wiki/Nova`
- Glance – Image Service: `https://wiki.openstack.org/wiki/Glance`
- Ironic – Bare Metal Provisioning Service: `https://wiki.openstack.org/wiki/Ironic`
- Magnum – Container Orchestration Engine Provisioning: `https://wiki.openstack.org/wiki/Magnum`
- Storlets – Computable Object Store: `https://wiki.openstack.org/wiki/Storlets`
- Zun – Containers Service: `https://wiki.openstack.org/wiki/Zun`

Storage, backup, and recovery:

- Swift – Object Store: `https://wiki.openstack.org/wiki/Swift`
- Cinder – Block Storage: `https://wiki.openstack.org/wiki/Cinder`
- Manila – Shared Filesystems: `https://wiki.openstack.org/wiki/Manila`
- Karbor – Application Data Projection as a Service: `https://wiki.openstack.org/wiki/Karbor`
- Freezer Backup, Restore and Disaster Recovery: `https://wiki.openstack.org/wiki/Freezer`

Networking and content delivery:

- Neutron – Networking: `https://docs.openstack.org/neutron/latest/`
- Designate – DNS Service: `https://wiki.openstack.org/wiki/Designate`
- DragonFlow – Neutron Plugin: `https://wiki.openstack.org/wiki/Dragonflow`
- Kuryr – Container Plugin: `https://wiki.openstack.org/wiki/Kuryr`
- Octavia – Load Balancer: `https://wiki.openstack.org/wiki/Octavia`
- Tacker – NFV Orchestration: `https://wiki.openstack.org/wiki/Tacker`
- Tricircle – Networking Automation for Multi-Region Deployments: `https://wiki.openstack.org/wiki/Tricircle`

Data and analytics:

- Trove – Database as a Service: `https://wiki.openstack.org/wiki/Trove`
- Sahara – Big Data Processing Framework Provisioning: `https://wiki.openstack.org/wiki/Sahara`
- Searchlight – Indexing and Search: `https://wiki.openstack.org/wiki/Searchlight`

Security, identity, and compliance:

- Keystone – Identity Service: `https://wiki.openstack.org/wiki/Keystone`
- Barbican – Key Management: `https://wiki.openstack.org/wiki/Barbican`
- Congress – Governance: `https://wiki.openstack.org/wiki/Congress`
- Mistral – Workflow Service: `https://wiki.openstack.org/wiki/Mistral`

Management tools:

- Horizon – Dashboard: `https://wiki.openstack.org/wiki/Horizon`
- Openstack Client – Command-line Client: `https://www.openstack.org/software/releases/ocata/components/openstack-client-(cli)`
- Rally – Benchmark Service: `https://rally.readthedocs.io/en/latest/`
- Senlin – Clustering Service: `https://wiki.openstack.org/wiki/Senlin`
- Vitrage – Root Cause Analysis Service: `https://wiki.openstack.org/wiki/Vitrage`
- Watcher – Optimization Service: `https://wiki.openstack.org/wiki/Watcher`

Deployment tools:

- Chef Openstack – Chef Cookbooks for OpenStack: `https://wiki.openstack.org/wiki/Chef`
- Kolla – Container Deployment: `https://wiki.openstack.org/wiki/Kolla`
- OpenStack Charms – Juju Charms for OpenStack: `https://docs.openstack.org/charm-guide/latest/`
- OpenStack-Ansible – Ansible Playbooks for OpenStack: `https://wiki.openstack.org/wiki/OpenStackAnsible`
- Puppet OpenStack – Puppet Modules for OpenStack: `https://docs.openstack.org/puppet-openstack-guide/latest/`
- Tripleo – Deployment Service: `https://wiki.openstack.org/wiki/TripleO`

Application services:

- Heat – Orchestration: `https://wiki.openstack.org/wiki/Heat`
- Zaqar – Messaging service: `https://wiki.openstack.org/wiki/Zaqar`
- Murano – Application catalog: `https://wiki.openstack.org/wiki/Murano`
- Solum – Software development life cycle automation: `https://wiki.openstack.org/wiki/Solum`

Monitoring and metering:

- Ceilometer – Metering and data collection service: `https://wiki.openstack.org/wiki/Telemetry`
- Cloudkitty – Billing and chargebacks: `https://wiki.openstack.org/wiki/CloudKitty`

- Monasca – Monitoring: `https://wiki.openstack.org/wiki/Monasca`
- AODH – Alarming service: `https://docs.openstack.org/aodh/latest/`
- Panko – Event, metadata indexing service: `https://docs.openstack.org/panko/latest/`

There are many more tools (open source and not) that are available, with many up and coming projects that are under incubation now. This list should not be seen as the be-all and end-all list of definitive tools, but simply a shortlist of some of the most popular tools being used at the time of writing this book. The important takeaway here is that automation and freedom is key.

Summary

In this chapter, we introduced you to hyper-cloud scale and all the implications this aggregation of organized compute means to IT consumers. The global scale, consistency, and reach of these cloud platforms has changed the way we need to think about scalable and available systems.

We introduced the concept of always-on architectures, and the key architectural elements that comprise these systems. Network redundancy, redundant core services, extensive monitoring, IaC, and immutable deployments are all important elements to architect into any cloud-native system.

Building on this always-on approach, we introduced the concept of self-healing infrastructures. For large-scale, cloud-native deployments, automating the recovery and healing of a system is a key feature. This allows systems to recover on their own, but more importantly frees up critically important human resource time to work on improving the system, allowing evolutionary architectures.

We wrapped up this chapter by introducing some of the most popular tools available to architects and IT professionals today. These tools cover all matter of use cases, from configuration managements, automation, monitoring, testing, and microservice mesh management.

14
Amazon Web Services

Amazon Web Services (**AWS**) is the pioneer in the cloud computing space. It started offering IT infrastructure services in 2006, when the term cloud computing hadn't even been coined! The first few services that AWS launched were Amazon **Simple Queue Service** (**SQS**), Amazon **Simple Storage Service** (**S3**), and Amazon **Elastic Compute Cloud** (**EC2**), and ever since there's been no stopping. Today, AWS is probably one of the most advanced and mature public cloud providers, with presence across 18 geographic regions, 130+ services, and has already announced plans to launch many more in the days ahead. Over a period of time, AWS has also diversified into various new technology and solutions spaces, that has even blurred the typical definitions of IaaS, PaaS, and SaaS. In this chapter, we will discuss some of these differentiators and new architectural patterns which can help you with a mature cloud-native experience by leveraging multiple AWS services. The following are some of the specific topics that you will learn about in this chapter:

- AWS' cloud-native services, strengths, and differentiators around CI/CD, serverless, containers, and microservices concepts, and covering the following services:
    - AWS CodeCommit
    - AWS CodePipeline
    - AWS CodeBuild
    - AWS CodeDeploy
    - Amazon EC2 Container Service
    - AWS Lambda
    - Amazon API Gateway

- Management and monitoring capabilities for AWS cloud-native application architectures
- Patterns for moving off monolithic application architectures to AWS native architectures
- Sample reference architectures and code snippets for CI/CD, serverless, and microservices application architectures

To keep yourself updated on the latest AWS announcements and service launches news, subscribe to the following resources:

- What's new page (`https://aws.amazon.com/new`)
- AWS blog (`https://aws.amazon.com/blogs/aws`)

AWS' cloud native services (CNMM Axis-1)

As a start, let's look at the core services that AWS has to offer, which will be relevant to creating your applications in a cloud-native way.

Introduction

AWS offers a very rich portfolio of services that includes core components around infrastructure capabilities, such as Amazon EC2 (virtual servers in the cloud), Amazon EBS (block storage for EC2), Amazon S3 (cloud-based object storage), and Amazon VPC (isolated cloud resources using virtualized networks). These services have existed for multiple years now and are pretty mature for an enterprise-scale deployment level as well. Apart from scale, these services have very deep feature sets that provide ample options to the end customers to pick and choose configurations as per their specific business requirements. As an example, Amazon EC2 offers more than 50 different types of instances to cater to various possible workloads and use cases. So, if a customer to host a **high-performance computing** (HPC) workload, then there's an option to use *compute optimized* instances, whereas if you have a NoSQL database that is hungry for high IOPS with low storage latency, then *storage optimized* instances come in handy.

In fact, AWS has been adding newer instances types as well as updating to newer, faster processors with larger memory footprints every year, which makes it easier for the customers to leverage the latest and greatest compute configurations without having to worry about typical data center procurement and upgrade cycles. Likewise, on the storage and networking front, Amazon EBS, Amazon S3, and Amazon VPC provide multiple configuration options that can provide flexibility when required.

Couple of the biggest benefits that cloud provides are Elasticity and Agility, which basically means that you can spin up and down your infrastructure in lines with your application's needs. This is very different from the traditional data center approach, where everything had to provisioned for peaks, because of which the infrastructure resources were either way too underutilized or were not scalable for some unpredictable peaks. This has radically changed with the cloud, where providers such as AWS have come up with innovative services such as Auto Scaling, wherein you can automatically change your compute fleet size based on certain application behaviors, such as increased CPU utilization or even custom application monitoring metrics. Apart from triggers based on scaling, you can also autoscale the compute capacity based on time-based usage patterns, for example, hourly, daily, or weekly variability in usage. Very similar to compute autoscaling, AWS also offers Elastic EBS volumes, wherein you can increase volume size, adjust performance, or change the volume type while the volume is in use. These types of services and capabilities are definitely differentiators for the cloud and have in fact become the new normal to build web-scale applications. However, in order to use some of these autoscaling features, applications also need to be ready from an architecture standpoint. As an example, if you want to use autoscaling capabilities for your web server fleet to accommodate increased load on your website, then one of the core changes needed from an application standpoint is that you should not have session state information stored locally on any web server. The same should be externalized in a cache (such as Amazon ElastiCache) or even a database (such as Amazon DynamoDB), so that you can seamlessly scale up or down your webservers fleet without having to worry about a users' session disruption because of that.

The following is a sample architecture that AWS publishes for auto-scalable web applications using various core services:

Now, over and above the core building blocks, such as the ones mentioned in the preceding diagram, AWS offers various higher-level managed services that make it easier for the end user to quickly start deploying their applications without having to worry too much about the underlying infrastructure. As an example, there's Amazon RDS, which is a managed relational database service for MySQL, PostgreSQL, Oracle, SQL Server, and MariaDB. Amazon RDS provides flexibility to set up and operate a relational database while automating time-consuming administration tasks, such as hardware provisioning, database setup, patching, and backups. So, by using this service, you can quickly get started with your database deployments without requiring any specific database administrator level skills. Apart from this, AWS also offers many other services, such as AWS Elastic Beanstalk (to run and manage web apps) and Amazon OpsWorks (to automate operations with Chef), which are like higher-level services in the category of PaaS.

Using these services, you can quickly get your applications running on AWS without getting into the nitty-gritty of the underlying infrastructure. With Amazon OpsWorks, you get an extra set of controls as well, wherein if you want to automate a specific application setup/launch procedure, then you have the capabilities to do that using your own custom Chef recipes.

Other than the preceding points, AWS also offers PaaS services in the big data / analytics and AI space, such as Amazon EMR (hosted Hadoop framework), Amazon Kinesis (works with real-time streaming data), Amazon Lex (builds voice and text chatbots), Amazon Rekognition (searches and analyzes images), and Amazon Polly (turns text into lifelike speech). Using these types of service, developers and data architects can easily create their applications by focusing more on the business logic than the underlying infrastructure management aspects.

Over the last few years, AWS has aggressively moved much further in terms of offering totally newer types of services, which are closer to SaaS. These are mainly the services as part of its business productivity category, such as Amazon Chime (a managed service for video calls and chat), Amazon WorkDocs (enterprise storage and sharing service), and Amazon Connect (managed contact center service). This is a fairly new area for AWS as well, but as these services along with the ecosystem matures, it will create new possibilities for end users to look at the cloud, not just from an infrastructure or platform perspective, but to also utilize productivity software in a pay-as-you-go model.

AWS platform – differentiators

CNMM is a maturity model wherein if you are using only core building blocks from the cloud (such as, infrastructure components), then you are also cloud-native, but might be less mature than someone else who might be using services higher up the stack to actually get the full benefits of Cloud. So, based on this concept, if you have to truly leverage the power of AWS cloud, then you should focus on a few of the areas that are talked about in the following sections.

KRADL services

As mentioned in the previous section, AWS has many innovative services that can help architect a multitude of use cases and business problems. However, there are few services that are like AWS differentiators, and so AWS highly recommends that you utilize those instead of trying to build your own comparative capabilities, which may not be as scalable, feature rich, or robust such as AWS offerings.

These services together are known as **KRADL**, and what each letter represents is as follows:

- **K**: Amazon Kinesis
- **R**: Amazon Redshift
- **A**: Amazon Aurora
- **D**: Amazon DynamoDB
- **L**: AWS Lambda

Let's analyze the preceding points in a little detail, based on AWS' definition of these services.

Amazon Kinesis: Amazon Kinesis makes it easy to collect, process, and analyze real-time streaming data so that you can get timely insights and react quickly to new information. With Amazon Kinesis, you can ingest real-time data such as application logs, website clickstreams, IoT telemetry data, and more into your databases, data lakes, and data warehouses, or build your own real-time applications using this data. Amazon Kinesis enables you to process and analyze data as it arrives and respond in real-time instead of having to wait until all of your data is collected before the processing can begin. More details are available at https://aws.amazon.com/kinesis/.

Amazon Redshift: Amazon Redshift is a fast, fully managed data warehouse that makes it simple and cost-effective to analyze all your data using standard SQL and your existing **business intelligence** (**BI**) tools. It allows you to run complex analytic queries against petabytes of structured data, using sophisticated query optimization, columnar storage on high-performance local disks, and massively parallel query execution. More details are available at https://aws.amazon.com/redshift/.

Amazon Aurora: Amazon Aurora is a MySQL and PostgreSQL-compatible relational database engine that combines the speed and availability of high-end commercial databases with the simplicity and cost-effectiveness of open source databases. It provides up to five times better performance than MySQL with the security, availability, and reliability of a commercial database at one tenth of the cost. Amazon Aurora is a managed database service, built on a fully distributed and self-healing storage system that keeps your data safe. More details are available at https://aws.amazon.com/rds/aurora/.

Amazon DynamoDB: Amazon DynamoDB is a fast and flexible NoSQL database service for all applications that need consistent, single-digit millisecond latency at any scale. It is a fully managed cloud database and supports both document and key-value store models. Its flexible data model, reliable performance, and automatic scaling of throughput capacity, makes it a great fit for mobile, web, gaming, ad tech, IoT, and many other applications. More details are available at https://aws.amazon.com/dynamodb/.

AWS Lambda: AWS Lambda lets you run code without provisioning or managing servers. You only pay for the compute time you consume – there is no charge when your code is not running. With Lambda, you can run code for virtually any type of application or backend service – all with zero administration. Just upload your code and Lambda takes care of everything required to run and scale your code with high availability. You can set up your code to automatically trigger from other AWS services or call it directly from any web or mobile app. More details are available at `https://aws.amazon.com/lambda/`.

Most of the preceding services are Amazon proprietary, so sometimes, end users become conscious about the fear of lock-in. However, the reality is that even in an on-premises world, customers make use of so many different packaged applications (such as databases and ERPs), which themselves are hard to get away with. So, it's more of a perception of lock-in than reality when the same logic is applied to these cloud-native services. In fact, if we take a deeper look, services such as Amazon Aurora and Amazon Redshift offer the same PostgreSQL/SQL interface, so that creates an easily portable mechanism for the applications to be rewired to another platform, if need be. Another perspective to it is that if the customer wants to create similar services on their own, then it will probably take quite a bit of time and effort to not just create but to operate as well as iterate on new features, like AWS does. So, at the end of the day, it's always beneficial to focus on your core business and rather consume these higher-level services from AWS.

Another angle to look at here is that the KRADL services are very unique to AWS platform compared to other cloud providers. For some of these, other cloud providers have come up with comparative offerings, but as AWS was first in the space with many of these and has been iterating regularly on new features ever since, they have the most mature offerings.

 Take a look at this interesting infographic from 2ndWatch, an AWS Consulting Partner, around their analysis of AWS' cloud-native services: `http://2ndwatch.com/wp-content/uploads/2017/05/Cloud-Native-Services.pdf`.

AWS native security services

One of the aspects that's key for any customer in a public cloud is to have the right security posture as per workloads and corporate governance policies. At times, it can be hard to map the controls from an on-premise environment to cloud, as it's not an apple to apple type of comparison. However, in recent times, AWS has innovated on many new services specifically in the security space, which aims to bring down this gap between on-premise controls to native AWS capabilities.

AWS has had the Amazon **identity and access management** (**IAM**) service for multiple years, using which you can manage your cloud-based users and groups and their access permissions on various AWS resources. With this service, you can enable fine-grained access controls (like, say, apply restrictions to specific API calls in your environment being allowed from specific IP address ranges), integrate with corporate directory to grant federated access, and even enable only **multi-factor authentication** (**MFA**) based actions on any service.

Now, IAM is a must-have service in order to operate in the AWS environment. However, a couple of other cloud-native services that are often missed but are highly useful for any type of environment are as follows:

- **AWS Key Management Service**: AWS **Key Management Service** (**KMS**) is a managed service that makes it easy for you to create and control the encryption keys used to encrypt your data, and uses **hardware security modules** (**HSMs**) to protect the security of your keys. AWS Key Management Service is integrated with several other AWS services to help you protect the data you store with these services. More details are available at `https://aws.amazon.com/kms/`.
- **AWS CloudTrail**: AWS CloudTrail is a service that enables governance, compliance, operational auditing, and risk auditing of your AWS account. With CloudTrail, you can log, continuously monitor, and retain events related to API calls across your AWS infrastructure. CloudTrail provides a history of AWS API calls for your account, including API calls made through the AWS Management Console, AWS SDKs, command-line tools, and other AWS services. More details are available at `https://aws.amazon.com/Cloudtrail/`.

Both of the preceding services are fully managed, integrated with various other AWS services, and super easy to use. In fact, with these type of easy to use and configurable services, the level of controls that any startup customer gets is the same as any enterprise customer using the AWS platform. This is the true power of democratization that cloud previous, wherein all the services or features are available to everyone, thereby making it a level playing field for innovation and new application models.

As a result of these cloud-native services, customers don't need to procure expensive key management appliances, buy, or build custom software packages to perform these must-enable functionalities for your deployments. Having said that, some of these services are only limited to cloud-based environments, so if you have a hybrid environment that includes on-premise infrastructure components, then having a single pane of glass to manage or monitor everything using these services becomes a little challenging.

Apart from the core capabilities that these services provide in terms of functionality, using advanced architectural patterns, one can also create self-learning or self-adapting security models as well. As an example, if you have enabled CloudTrail logging for your account, then based on the API activity logs that the service delivers in your Amazon S3 buckets, you may select to perform some specific actions dynamically if you find any unexpected activity or malicious usage of your AWS account resources. To orchestrate this entire use case, AWS Lambda can be pretty handy, wherein you can define your custom logic to not just detect but even react based on certain conditions. This can be further clubbed with advanced techniques such as machine learning or deep learning wherein instead of just reacting to specific conditions, you can actually build a model to train itself and pre-empt any conditions, even before they occur. Of course, this requires additional effort and greater expertise to create these types of self-adapting security systems, but with the type of service and building block that the cloud now provides, it's definitely possible to move in that direction.

Apart from AWS KMS and AWS CloudTrail, AWS has many other new security services that further help address specific use-cases:

- **Amazon Inspector**: Amazon Inspector is an automated security assessment service that helps improve the security and compliance of applications deployed on AWS. Amazon Inspector automatically assesses applications for vulnerabilities or deviations from best practices. After performing an assessment, Amazon Inspector produces a detailed list of security findings prioritized by level of severity. These findings can be reviewed directly or as part of detailed assessment reports that are available via the Amazon Inspector console or API. More details are available at `https://aws.amazon.com/inspector/`.
- **AWS Certificate Manager**: AWS Certificate Manager is a service that lets you easily provision, manage, and deploy **Secure Sockets Layer (SSL)** / **Transport Layer Security** (**TLS**) certificates for use with AWS services. SSL/TLS certificates are used to secure network communications and establish the identity of websites over the internet. AWS Certificate Manager removes the time-consuming manual process of purchasing, uploading, and renewing SSL/TLS certificates.
- **AWS WAF**: AWS WAF is a web application firewall that helps protect your web applications from common web exploits that could affect application availability, compromise security, or consume excessive resources. AWS WAF gives you control over which traffic to allow or block your web applications by defining customizable web security rules. You can use AWS WAF to create custom rules that block common attack patterns, such as SQL injection or cross-site scripting, and rules that are designed for your specific application. More details are available at `https://aws.amazon.com/waf/`.

- **AWS Shield**: AWS Shield is a managed **distributed denial of service** (DDoS) protection service that safeguards web applications running on AWS. AWS Shield provides always-on detection and automatic inline mitigations that minimize application downtime and latency, so there is no need to engage AWS Support to benefit from DDoS protection. More details are available at `https://aws.amazon.com/shield/`.

- **Amazon GuardDuty**: Amazon GuardDuty is a managed threat detection service that provides you with a more accurate and easy way to continuously monitor and protect your AWS accounts and workloads. More details are available at `https://aws.amazon.com/guardduty/`.

- **Amazon Macie**: Amazon Macie is a machine learning-powered security service to discover, classify, and protect sensitive data. More details are available at `https://aws.amazon.com/macie/`.

The biggest benefit of all of the previously mentioned cloud-native services is that you can start to utilize them at any point in time, without having to worry about license procurement, complex configuration, and so on. However, as these services are still new as compared to some of the enterprise ISV software packages with comparable functionalities, for more complex use cases or deeper feature/functionalities, they may not fully meet the needs. For those kind of scenarios, AWS also offers an AWS Marketplace, where multiple ISV partners have cloud-optimized software packages available, which are quick and easy to deploy in the AWS environment. So, depending on the use cases as well as feature set requirements, it's always advised to first evaluate these AWS cloud-native services and then, if need be, look at other ISV solutions.

Machine Learning/Artificial Intelligence

In the last couple of years, AWS has shown a serious commitment to take their offerings in machine-learning/artificial intelligence space to a completely different levels. During its annual developer conference (AWS re:Invent) in 2017, AWS made some big announcements on its ML/AI offerings, which have also gained immense popularity since then. The following are some of the services, which are key from AWS' ML/AI portfolio perspective:

- **Amazon SageMaker**: This enables data scientists and developers to quickly and easily build, train, and deploy machine learning models with high-performance machine learning algorithms, broad framework support, and one-click training, tuning, and inference. Amazon SageMaker has a modular architecture so that you can use any or all of its capabilities in your existing machine learning workflows. For more information, you can refer to `https://aws.amazon.com/sagemaker/`.

- **Amazon Rekognition**: This is a service that makes it easy to add powerful visual analysis to your applications. Rekognition Image lets you easily build powerful applications to search, verify, and organize millions of images. Rekognition Video lets you extract motion-based context from stored or live stream videos and helps you analyze them. For more information, you can refer to `https://aws.amazon.com/rekognition`.
- **Amazon Lex**: This is a service for building conversational interfaces using voice and text. Powered by the same conversational engine as Alexa, Amazon Lex provides high quality speech recognition and language understanding capabilities, enabling an addition of sophisticated, natural language chatbots to new and existing applications. For more information, you can refer to `https://aws.amazon.com/lex`.
- **Amazon Polly**: This is a service that turns text into life-like speech. It enables existing applications to speak as a first-class feature and creates the opportunity for entirely new categories of speech-enabled products, from mobile apps and cars, to devices and appliances. For more information, you can refer to `https://aws.amazon.com/polly`.

Other than the preceding services, AWS also supports many of the popular machine learning frameworks and libraries, which are used by data scientists and developers on a regular basis, including Apache MXNet, TensorFlow, PyTorch, the Microsoft **Cognitive Toolkit** (**CNTK**), Caffe, Caffe2, Theano, Torch, Gluon, and Keras. These are offered as an **Amazon Machine Image** (**AMI**), so it is pretty easy to get started with just a few clicks. This clubbed with the GPU compute instances and instances with **field programmable gate arrays** (**FPGAs**) make the processing of complex algorithms and models much faster and easier, thereby ensuring that the overall platform is comprehensive to address any kind of ML/AI use cases.

Object storage (S3, Glacier, ecosystem)

AWS offers multiple different types of storage services, such as for block storage, file storage, object storage, and archive storage. Although all of these services are independent of each other and can be used individually, for various use cases, customers make use of multiples of these services together to also provide various storage tiering options. As an example, Amazon EBS is the block storage that's attached to the Amazon EC2 instances for local data persistence as well as processing. Whenever data needed to be shared between multiple EC2 instances as file shares, Amazon EFS comes in handy as the same EFS share can be attached to EC2 instances using the NFS v4.1 interface.

Now, when data needs to be backed up, a long-term, more durable storage, then Amazon S3 comes into the picture, where not just raw data but even EBS volume snapshots are stored redundantly across various Availability Zones. For long term archival, data can be moved from Amazon S3 to Amazon Glacier. So, using this mechanism, a complete life cycle of data management can be created using multiple storage services.

Other than Amazon EBS, **Amazon Machine Images** (**AMI**) using which Amazon EC2 instances can be spun up, are also by default stored in Amazon S3. Likewise, all the logs, such as Amazon CloudTrail logs or Amazon CloudWatch logs, are also persisted in Amazon S3. Even AWS migration services such as AWS Snowball, AWS Database Migration Service, and AWS Server Migration Service all have integrations with Amazon S3. Likewise, for any big data architecture involving Amazon EMR, Amazon Redshift, or even Amazon Athena, Amazon S3 is a key component in the overall system. It acts either as a source or/and a target during the life cycle of data being sliced and diced for various analytical problems. Similarly, many other AWS services behind the scenes make use of Amazon S3 for object storage or even backup purposes.

As a result of all these different scenarios, Amazon S3 is one of the key AWS services that should be part of any cloud-native deployment on AWS. In fact, apart from integrations with various other AWS services, Amazon S3 also has deep feature set, which provides flexibility for various application needs. For example, within Amazon S3 there are multiple different storage classes, so depending on your object access patterns, durability, and availability requirements, any of these options can be utilized:

Storage Class	Durability (designed for)	Availability (designed for)	Use case
STANDARD	99.999999999%	99.99%	Ideal for performance-sensitive use cases and frequently accessed data
STANDARD_IA	99.999999999%	99.9%	Optimized for long-lived and less frequently accessed data, for example, backups and older data where frequency of access has diminished, but the use case still demands high performance
Reduced Redundancy Storage (RRS)	99.99%	99.99%	Meant for non-critical, reproducible data that's stored at lower levels of redundancy than the STANDARD storage class

Amazon S3 also has multiple security-related functionalities, like encryption options (server side or client side encryption), versioning of objects to retain history, and MFA protection on object deletion.

Amazon S3 also has a rich ecosystem of ISV partners that either integrate directly with Amazon S3 APIs or use it as a source or a target for multiple storage related use cases. You should look at Amazon's Storage partner solutions at `https://aws.amazon.com/backup-recovery/partner-solutions/` to understand the current ISVs that support Amazon S3 (and other storage services) as part of their solutions.

Based on the preceding points, Amazon S3 is clearly a service that is central to many architectures and is definitely a service that cannot and should not be ignored for any cloud-native deployments. Some sample cloud-native use cases that might be applicable for multiple users are as follows:

- **Web applications**: Amazon S3 can be used as a storage for static content, such as videos, images, HTML pages, CSS and other client-side scripts. So, if you have a totally static website, then there's no need of any web server; just use Amazon S3! If you have global user base and want to cache frequently accessed content in locations closer to your users, then Amazon S3 along with Amazon CloudFront can be a great combination.

- **Logs storage**: For an end-to-end system, there are multiple logs that are generated by various applications and even infrastructure components. These can be persisted locally on disks and analyzed by solutions such as **Elasticsearch, Logstash, and Kibana (ELK)**. However, at scale, lots of customers use Amazon S3 as a sink for all the logs wherein log data from various sources can be streamed to S3 using either open source options such as Fluentd (`https://www.fluentd.org/`), AWS Services (such as CloudWatch Logs or Amazon Kinesis), or commercial ISV offerings (such as Sumologic) that are there in the AWS Marketplace as well. Irrespective of the solution to stream the data or analyze it, Amazon S3 is good candidate for any type of log. In fact, as logs get older, they can be either purged or even transitioned to a less expensive storage (Amazon S3-IA or Amazon Glacier) by using life cycle policies.

- **Data lakes** - Amazon S3 is a great service that can be used to create very highly scalable data lakes, where pre-processed, processed, or even intermediate data can be stored throughout the data processing pipeline. AWS has a reference architecture and an automated deployment module, which further showcases the use of Amazon S3 as a central service in this scenario. You can read about it at `http://docs.aws.amazon.com/solutions/latest/data-lake-solution/welcome.html`.

- **Event-driven architectures** - APIs and loosely coupled architectures are a common pattern these days. Along with APIs comes in a paradigm of having event driven architectures, wherein with a simple API invocation, you can trigger a series of workflows of backend processing. Now, although there are multiple components involved in this type of architectural pattern, from a storage perspective, Amazon S3 can be a pivotal component for a couple of use cases:
    - Suppose you have an API/event-driven architecture to kick-start a media processing pipeline, so for that all the raw media mezzanine objects can be stored in Amazon S3. Likewise, post processing the final video/audio/image output can be put in S3 to be delivered using Amazon CloudFront.
    - Coordination between various services can happen using Amazon S3 as a storage and trigger mechanism. As an example, let's consider there's a Service-A, which starts processing objects in Bucket-A. After it's done, it writes the object in Bucket-B, which then sends an event notification for, say, an `s3:ObjectCreated:*` event, which can be handled by Amazon Lambda functions to trigger on the next step in the workflow. So, this can continue to create a loosely coupled pipeline that is based off S3 as a coordination mechanism.
- **Batch processing** - AWS launched a service for batch computing use cases, called AWS Batch. Although this service can be used for multiple use cases, however, big data/analytics types of use cases are the most common. As a result, Amazon S3 becomes a key service here with its ability to store and process objects at scale. As an example, the following diagram from the AWS website demonstrates batch computing use case from a Financial Services industry wherein data from various sources is collected at the end of the day to run reports and view market performance. So, as is evident, Amazon S3 becomes a sort of master storage for various processing layers down the line:

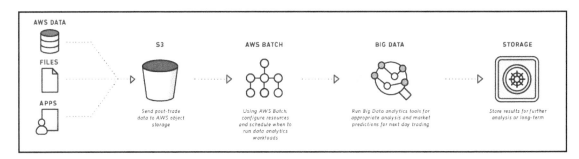

Application centric design (CNMM Axis-2)

In the previous section, we saw some of the key cloud-native services that AWS has to offer. Now, in this section, we will look at the second axis of CNMM on how to create AWS native architectures. Although there are multiple different architectures and approaches, we will focus on two key patterns – serverless and microservices. In fact, these two patterns are related as well since the services that help us create a serverless pattern are also applicable to creating smaller, single functionality, fine-grained services in a system. So, let's explore more about how to create a microservice that is also serverless in nature in the next section.

Serverless microservice

The core concept around a serverless microservice is a three-step pipeline, such as the one shown in the following diagram:

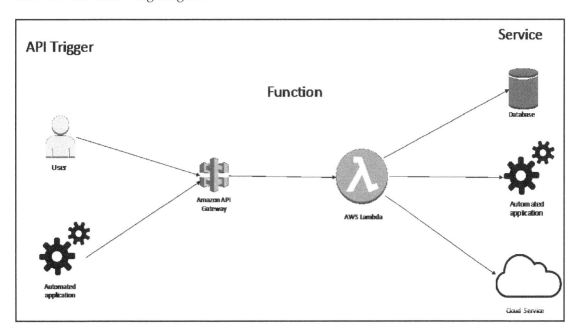

Let's discuss these steps in detail.

API trigger

The microservice can be invoked in two ways as follows:

- An end user who's directly interacting with a web-based portal (or even CLI commands)
- An automated application or another microservice that invokes this service in the chain of an orchestrated workflow

The APIs can also be invoked with some system events, which can then be used to trigger an API with a scripted mechanism.

Function

Once the API is invoked by the *Trigger* layer, it's received by the Amazon API Gateway, which can perform traffic management, authorization and access control, validation, transformation, and monitoring followed by invoking the backend, which in this case would be hosted in AWS Lambda.

AWS Lambda is a serverless compute environment, wherein you simply upload your code (Node.js, Python, Java, or C#), define the trigger, and the rest is handled by the service. So, as in the preceding sample architecture, API Gateway will invoke the Lambda function to execute the business logic there. Within that business logic, you can perform any type of action, which is also detailed in the following section.

Service

Within the AWS Lambda function, although you can perform any backend action, the following are the most common ones that most customers perform:

- Do the entire processing within the AWS Lambda function, which may involve data processing to transformation, local scripts execution, and so on, and finally the result is stored in a data store for long-term persistence. A perfect choice for lots of customers in this scenario is Amazon DynamoDB, which again extends the serverless architecture with no host to manage and is easy to integrate with AWS Lambda with API/SDKs.
- For interacting with another third-party external service or even another microservice within the same environment, many customers use AWS Lambda to invoke those other services. These invocations can be synchronous or asynchronous, depending on the use case.

- Another possibility here is to integrate with other cloud services to perform some other actions. As an example, suppose you want to trigger a LAMP stack creation using an API, so in this case you could invoke CloudFormation from your Lambda code to bring up a new LAMP stack environment.

These are just examples on how to create serverless microservices in AWS, but generally the possibilities are infinite.

Serverless microservice – sample walkthrough

Now that we have covered the basics of a serverless microservice in AWS, let's do some hands-on exercises with a sample application using multiple AWS services.

So, let's create an actual microservice to retrieve weather information for any location. For this, we will use the following architectural components:

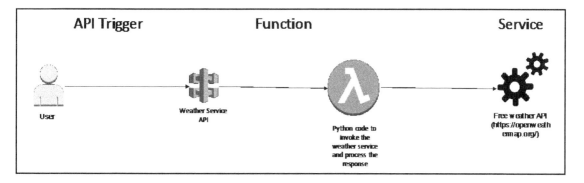

AWS Lambda function creation and configuration

Sign in to the AWS console and select the **Lambda** from the under the **Compute** services. Then, follow these instructions to create a Lambda function:

1. Click on the **Create a function** button.
2. Select the **Blueprint** option, and choose the **microservice-http-endpoint-python3** blueprint.

3. Click on the **Configure** option, and then specify the following values. The following values will be used to configure the Amazon API Gateway endpoint for this microservice:

    1. Set **API Name** to `Serverless Weather Service`.

    2. Set **Deployment Stage** to `prod`.

    3. For **Security**, set it to **Open**. Using this as the option, we will be able to access our API without any credentials (for production workloads, it's always recommended to enable API security with either the **AWS IAM** or **Open with** access key options).

4. In **Create function**, specify the following values:

    1. Basic information section:

        1. Enter a function name (for example, `WeatherServiceFunction`).

        2. Select **Python 3.6** from the **Runtime** list.

        3. For **Description**, use **cloud-native - Serverless Weather Service**.

    2. Lambda function code:

        1. In the **Code Entry Type** field, select the **Upload a .zip file** option. Get the sample Python code ZIP file, `Cloudnative-weather-service.zip`, from the `https://github.com/PacktPublishing/Cloud-Native-Architectures` GitHub location and upload it.

    3. Lambda function handler and role:

        1. For the handler, specify the value as `lambda_function.lambda_handler`.

        2. For the **Role**, select the option **Create new role from template(s)**.

        3. For the **Role Name**, specify **WeatherServiceLambdaRole**.

        4. In the **Policy Templates** option, select the dropdown with the value **Simple Microservice Permissions**.

    4. Tags:

        1. Specify **Key** as `Name` and **Value** as `Serverless Weather Microservice`.

2. Advanced settings:
    1. Set the **Memory** selection to **128 MB**.
    2. Set **Timeout** value as 0 minutes and 30 seconds.
    3. Leave the rest of the settings with the default value.

5. After the preceding configurations are done, review the settings on the final screen and hit **Create function**. In a matter of a few minutes, your Lambda function will be created and you should be able to view it on the **Functions** list, as follows:

As for the logic, within the Lambda code, it's a simple code that does three things:

- Retrieves the `zip` and `appid` parameters from the received request.
- Invokes the `GET` operation on OpenWeatherMap's API with the `zip` and `appid` parameters as inputs.
- Receives the response and sends it back to the API Gateway to be returned to the end user.

The code is as follows:

```
import boto3
import json
from urllib.request import Request, urlopen
from urllib.error import URLError, HTTPError

print('Loading function')

def respond(err, res=None):
    return {
        'statusCode': '400' if err else '200',
        'body': err if err else res,
        'headers': {
            'Content-Type': 'application/json',
        },
```

```
    }

def lambda_handler(event, context):
    '''Demonstrates a simple HTTP endpoint using API Gateway. You have full
access to the request and response payload, including headers andstatus
code.'''
    print("Received event: " + json.dumps(event, indent=2))

    zip = event['queryStringParameters']['zip']
    print('ZIP -->' + zip)
    appid = event['queryStringParameters']['appid']
    print('Appid -->>' + appid)
    baseUrl = 'http://api.openweathermap.org/data/2.5/weather'
    completeUrl = baseUrl + '?zip=' + zip + '&appid=' + appid
    print('Request URL--> ' + completeUrl)

    req = Request(completeUrl)
    try:
        apiresponse = urlopen(completeUrl)
    except HTTPError as e:
        print('The server couldn\'t fulfill the request.')
        print('Error code: ', e.code)
        errorResponse = '{Error:The server couldn\'t fulfill the request: '
+ e.reason +'}'
        return respond(errorResponse, e.code)
    except URLError as e:
        print('We failed to reach a server.')
        print('Reason: ', e.reason)
        errorResponse = '{Error:We failed to reach a server: ' + e.reason
+'}'
        return respond(e, e.code)
    else:
        headers = apiresponse.info()
        print('DATE    :', headers['date'])
        print('HEADERS :')
        print('---------')
        print(headers)
        print('DATA :')
        print('---------')
        decodedresponse = apiresponse.read().decode('utf-8')
        print(decodedresponse)
        return respond(None, decodedresponse)
```

Configuring the Amazon API Gateway

After performing the preceding steps, go to the **Amazon API Gateway** service in the **AWS Console** and you should see an API like the following already created:

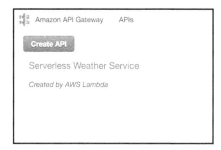

Now, let's configure this API to match our needs:

1. Click on the API's name, **Serverless Weather Service**, to drill down into its configuration.
2. Select the **Resources** option on the left-hand side and then on the right-hand side, expand the resources to show /WeatherServiceFunction/ANY and you should see its details as follows:

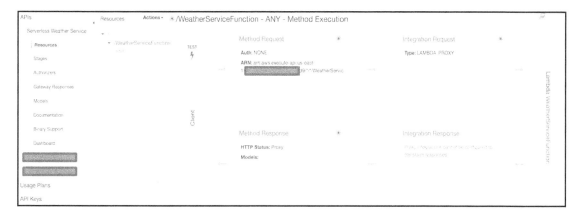

3. Click on **Method Request** and expand the **URL Query String Parameters** option. Under that, use the **Add query string** button to add the following parameters:
   1. Set the name to zip and check the **Required** checkbox.
   2. Add another parameter, set the name to appid, and check the **Required** checkbox.

4. In the preceding pane, select the **Request Validator** option and set its value to **Validate body, query string parameters, and headers**.

5. After completing the preceding settings, your **Method Execution** screen should look as follows:

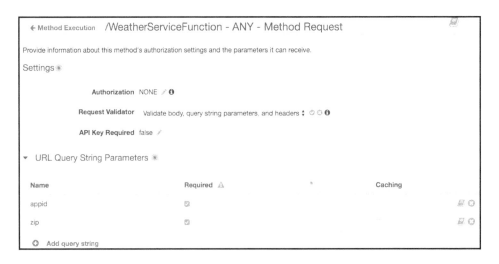

Setting up a Weather Service Account

In order to get the latest weather information, our microservice will invoke APIs from a third-party weather service, OpenWeatherMap (`https://openweathermap.org`). So, go to the URL and create a new, free account. Once you have created an account, go to your account settings and note down the API key from the following option:

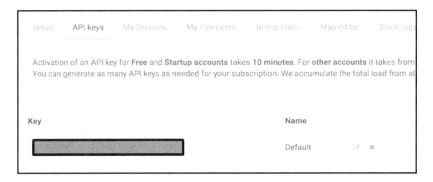

This key will be used to authenticate our API calls to the OpenWeatherMap service.

Testing the service

Now that we have all the necessary pieces set up, let's go back to the Amazon API Console and try testing the service. For that, follow these steps:

1. Open the `/WeatherServiceFunction/ANY` file under the Resources option, and hit the **Test** option.
2. Under the method, select **Get** as the option.
3. For the query string, we need two inputs: the ZIP code of the city for which you want to query the current weather and the OpenWeatherMap's API key. To do this, create a query string such as `zip=<<zip-value>>&appid=<<app-id>>`. In this, replace the italicized values with actual inputs and form a string such as `zip=10001&appid=abcdefgh9876543qwerty`.
4. Hit the **Test** button at the bottom of the screen to invoke the API and the Lambda function.
5. If the test is successful, you will see a response with **Status: 200**, and in the response body, you will get the weather information in a JSON format, as follows:

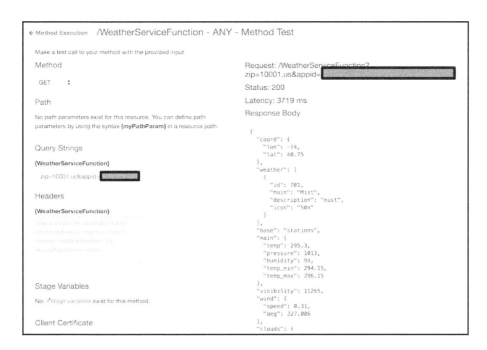

If there's an error in test execution, check the logs in the bottom half of the screen to debug the issue.

Deploying the API

After successfully testing the API, we have to deploy the API as well so that it can be active in the **prod** environment. For that, select the **Deploy API** option from the **Actions** drop-down menu within the API configuration screen, as follows:

Once the API is deployed, you can go to the **Stages** option on the left-hand side, select the **prod** stage, and under that, **GET** the HTTP method, as follows:

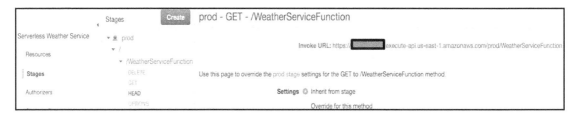

You can copy the deployed API's URL and try accessing it by providing the `zip` and the `appid` parameters as part of the URL as follows:

```
https://asdfgh.execute-api.us-east-1.amazonaws.com/prod/WeatherServiceFunct
ion?zip=10001,us&appid=qwertyasdfg98765zxcv
```

 Note: Please replace the highlighted text with your environment's specific values.

To make the testing process of the deployed API easier, you can also use the sample HTML page, which is available at the `https://github.com/PacktPublishing/Cloud-Native-Architectures` GitHub link, as follows:

1. Download the HTML page, edit the source to update your API endpoint on *line 28*, and save it:

```
<form method="get" action="https://<<updated-
endpoint>>>/Prod/weatherservice">
```

2. Open the web page in a browser, supply the required field values, and hit the **Get Weather** button to retrieve the weather for that location:

Cloud Native - Serverless Microservice Example

Retrieve Current weather for a location:

Zip Code: 10001

OpenWeatherMap App Id (API Key):   jhvhbvhkbkjvhvhvh

Get Weather

Serverless microservice automation using AWS SAM

As we learned in the previous section, it's very easy to build a simple serverless microservice from the AWS console. However, if you have to do the same using an automated and scripted way, then there are other mechanisms to achieve it. One of the most popular ways in the AWS environment is to use AWS CloudFormation, wherein you can create your own templates to describe the AWS resources, and any associated dependencies or runtime parameters, required to run your application. You can also visualize your templates as diagrams and edit them using a drag-and-drop interface, or even use the AWS command-line interface or APIs to manage the infrastructure components. Since everything you do in CloudFormation is using JSON or YAML formatted text files, as a result you are effectively managing your infrastructure as code.

Using AWS CloudFormation, you can create and update AWS Lambda, API Gateway, and various other services, which might compose your serverless microservice. Now, although this is easy to do, sometimes you have a simple application and rather than writing a pretty long and elaborate CloudFormation, it's better to use some other mechanisms. For the same reason, Amazon created the AWS **Serverless Application Model** (**SAM**), which is natively supported by AWS CloudFormation and provides a simplified way of defining the Amazon API Gateway APIs, AWS Lambda functions, and Amazon DynamoDB tables needed by your serverless application.

AWS SAM is a powerful way to create your serverless applications quickly as it requires significantly less code and configurations as compared to CloudFormation. To use SAM to create your applications, you primarily need three things:

- A SAM YAML template with configurations of your resources (Lambda function, API Gateway, and DynamoDB tables)
- An AWS Lambda function code `.zip` file
- An API Gateway's API definition in a Swagger format

 You can find more information on AWS SAM at the following GitHub repository: `https://github.com/awslabs/serverless-application-model/`.

Now, in order to create the same weather serverless microservice example using AWS SAM, let's look at the steps and code snippets.

SAM YAML template

The following is the SAM YAML template for the Weather Service example. It broadly consists of three components:

- An API Gateway definition that points to the Swagger file for detailed configuration.
- An AWS Lambda function configuration with a link to code the `.zip` file, handler name, and runtime environment. In order to link this Lambda function with the API gateway instance, it also has details on the REST API methods and the URI paths, which will be used as triggers to the Lambda function.
- The final section is around output, which is basically the URI of the API endpoint once the entire stack has been created by SAM:

```
AWSTemplateFormatVersion: '2010-09-09'
Transform: AWS::Serverless-2016-10-31
Description: A simple cloud-native Microservice sample, including
an AWS SAM template with API defined in an external Swagger file
along with Lambda integrations and CORS configurations

Resources:
  ApiGatewayApi:
    Type: AWS::Serverless::Api
    Properties:
      DefinitionUri: ./cloud-native-api-swagger.yaml
      StageName: Prod

Variables:
      # NOTE: Before using this template, replace the <<region>>
and <<account>> fields
      # in Lambda integration URI in the swagger file to region
and accountId
      # you are deploying to
      LambdaFunctionName: !Ref LambdaFunction

  LambdaFunction:
    Type: AWS::Serverless::Function
    Properties:
      CodeUri: ./Cloudnative-weather-service.zip
      Handler: lambda_function.lambda_handler
      Runtime: python3.6
      Events:
        ProxyApiRoot:
          Type: Api
          Properties:
            RestApiId: !Ref ApiGatewayApi
```

```
          Path: /weatherservice
          Method: get
     ProxyApiGreedy:
       Type: Api
       Properties:
         RestApiId: !Ref ApiGatewayApi
         Path: /weatherservice
         Method: options
```

The output from the preceding code is as follows:

```
ApiUrl:
  Description: URL of your API endpoint
  Value: !Join
    - ''
    - - https://
      - !Ref ApiGatewayApi
      - '.execute-api.'
      - !Ref 'AWS::Region'
      - '.amazonaws.com/Prod'
      - '/weatherservice'
```

API definition Swagger file

APIs are everywhere these days, including in packaged applications, cloud services, custom applications, and devices. However, it can be a nightmare for different applications to integrate with each other if everyone used their own standards and mechanisms to define and declare their API interfaces. So, to help with the standardization process and bring some structure to the world of REST APIs, the OpenAPI initiative was created. More details can be found at `https://www.openapis.org/`.

In order to create APIs that are compliant with **OpenAPI Specification** (**OAS**), Swagger (`https://swagger.io/`) provides various tools that help enable development across the entire API life cycle, from design and documentation to test and deployment.

The AWS API Gateway supports importing or exporting API definitions from the Swagger API format, which is YAML based. To better integrate with the AWS API Gateway, there are additional elements that can be added to the Swagger definition, and the following is a sample YAML for the serverless weather microservice, which has both standard Swagger elements with AWS API Gateway-specific configuration parameters.

In order to use this sample in your environment, please update the region and AWS account number parameters as per your AWS account settings in the following template:

```
swagger: "2.0"
info:
  title: "Weather Service API"
basePath: "/prod"
schemes:
- "https"
paths:
  /weatherservice:
    get:
      produces:
      - "application/json"
      parameters:
      - name: "appid"
        in: "query"
        required: true
        type: "string"
      - name: "zip"
        in: "query"
        required: true
        type: "string"
      responses:
        200:
          description: "200 response"
          schema:
            $ref: "#/definitions/Empty"
      x-amazon-apigateway-request-validator: "Validate body, query string
parameters,\
        \ and headers"
      x-amazon-apigateway-integration:
        responses:
          default:
            statusCode: "200"
        uri: arn:aws:apigateway:us-
east-1:lambda:path/2015-03-31/functions/arn:aws:lambda:region:account-
number:function:${stageVariables.LambdaFunctionName}/invocations
        passthroughBehavior: "when_no_match"
        httpMethod: "POST"
        contentHandling: "CONVERT_TO_TEXT"
        type: "aws_proxy"
    options:
      consumes:
      - "application/json"
      produces:
      - "application/json"
      responses:
```

```
      200:
        description: "200 response"
        schema:
          $ref: "#/definitions/Empty"
        headers:
          Access-Control-Allow-Origin:
            type: "string"
          Access-Control-Allow-Methods:
            type: "string"
          Access-Control-Allow-Headers:
            type: "string"
    x-amazon-apigateway-integration:
      responses:
        default:
          statusCode: "200"
          responseParameters:
            method.response.header.Access-Control-Allow-Methods:
  "'DELETE,GET,HEAD,OPTIONS,PATCH,POST,PUT'"
            method.response.header.Access-Control-Allow-Headers:
  "'Content-Type,Authorization,X-Amz-Date,X-Api-Key,X-Amz-Security-Token'"
            method.response.header.Access-Control-Allow-Origin: "'*'"
        requestTemplates:
          application/json: "{\"statusCode\": 200}"
        passthroughBehavior: "when_no_match"
        type: "mock"
definitions:
  Empty:
    type: "object"
    title: "Empty Schema"
x-amazon-apigateway-request-validators:
  Validate body, query string parameters, and headers:
    validateRequestParameters: true
    validateRequestBody: true
```

AWS Lambda code

The Python-based Lambda code for this application is the same as it was in an earlier section. You can download the ZIP file from the `https://github.com/PacktPublishing/Cloud-Native-Architectures` GitHub location.

AWS SAM usage

Behind the scenes, AWS SAM uses AWS CloudFormation's change sets functionality
(http://docs.aws.amazon.com/AWSCloudFormation/latest/UserGuide/using-cfn-
updating-stacks-changesets.html). In order to create our serverless weather
microservice example using SAM, follow these steps:

1. Download the SAM YAML template, API Gateway Swagger file, and AWS
   Lambda code .zip file in a single directory.

2. Create an Amazon S3 bucket (from the AWS console or the API) with any
   available name, such as CloudNative-WeatherService.

3. Now, it's time to upload the Lambda code and Swagger API file definition to the
   S3 bucket you created in the previous step and then update the SAM YAML file
   with their S3 locations. To do this, you can use the following AWS CLI
   command, which automatically handles all of this and creates a resultant SAM
   YAML file, which can be used in successive steps:

```
aws Cloudformation package \
--template-file ./Cloudnative-weather-microservice.yaml\
--s3-bucket CloudNative-WeatherService \
--output-template-file Cloudnative-weather-microservice-
packaged.yaml
```

 If you don't have AWS CLI already installed and configured, then please
refer the AWS documentation at http://docs.aws.amazon.com/cli/
latest/userguide/installing.html.

4. Once the packaging command is completed successfully, the next step is to start
   with the actual deployment. For this, use the following command, specifying the
   packaged YAML file from the previous step and the name of the stack that you
   are about to create:

```
aws Cloudformation deploy \
--template-file ./Cloudnative-weather-microservice=-packaged.yaml\
--stack-name weather-service-stack \
--capabilities CAPABILITY_IAM
```

5. Once the preceding command completes successfully, you can go to the AWS
   CloudFormation console to see the stack status there. From the Outputs tab of the
   completed CloudFormation stack, you will see a parameter called **ApiURL** with
   a value of your API Gateway's Weather Service API endpoint. With that, your
   API is all set and you can test the same using the procedure which was explained
   in previous sections.

Automation in AWS (CNMM Axis-3)

Amazon has had a long-time culture of having smaller teams that are self-contained, fully responsible for an end-to-end execution from planning to operations. These teams are nimble, have different roles (product management, developer, QA engineer, infra/tooling engineers, and so on) to manage all aspects of the software delivery cycle, but the team is big enough to be fed by two pizzas!

The whole concept around the two-pizza team is to keep them independent, fast moving, and better collaborating to avoid any overheads in terms of communication and processes. This is also an ideal setup from a DevOps perspective, where the team is responsible for a complete release life cycle, which also includes deploying to production environments and infrastructure management.

The other benefit that this setup provides is that each team is responsible for a specific piece of business functionality that often integrates with other components in the system using simple APIs that are REST/HTTP-based. This is essentially the core concept around a microservice, which further brings in agility and loosely connected components to bring in greater resilience and scalability to the overall system.

Amazon has multiple different businesses and teams internally that follow these principles and provide everyone with a common scalable software deployment platform, called **Apollo**. This deployment service has been used by thousands of developers across Amazon over multiple years, so it has been iterated upon and made robust for enterprise grade standards.

If you are interested in learning more about the story of Apollo, then refer this blog post by Werner Vogels, the Amazon CTO: http://www. allthingsdistributed.com/2014/11/apollo-amazon-deployment-engine.html.

Based on this internal experience, Amazon has created many of the AWS capabilities as well. They range from simple APIs, SDKs, and CLI support, to fully-fledged services to enable source code management, continuous integration, and continuous delivery/deployment to software pipeline management. We will explore more of these in the next section.

Infrastructure as code

One of the core benefits of the cloud is the capabilities it provides for infrastructure automation and treating everything like code. Though AWS has REST APIs for all the services offers and also supports various Software development kits for various popular programming languages (such as Java, .NET, Python, Android, and iOS), over and above these is one of the most powerful services it has: AWS CloudFormation.

AWS CloudFormation gives developers and systems administrators an easy way to create and manage a collection of related AWS resources, provisioning and updating them in an orderly and predictable fashion. The following is a sample CloudFormation Designer depiction of a simple deployment, which has an EC2 instance with one EBS volume and an Elastic IP address:

Now, when this simple deployment is turned into a YAML CloudFormation template, it looks like the following:

```
AWSTemplateFormatVersion: 2010-09-09
Resources:
  MyEC2Instance:
    Type: 'AWS::EC2::Instance'
    Properties:
      ImageId: ami-2f712546
      InstanceType: t2.micro
      Volumes:
        - VolumeId: !Ref EC2V7IM1
  MyPublicIP:
    Type: 'AWS::EC2::EIP'
    Properties:
      InstanceId: !Ref MyEC2Instance
  EIPAssociation:
    Type: 'AWS::EC2::EIPAssociation'
    Properties:
      AllocationId: !Ref EC2EIP567DU
      InstanceId: !Ref EC2I41BQT
  MyEBSVolume:
    Type: 'AWS::EC2::Volume'
    Properties:
      VolumeType: io1
      Iops: '200'
      DeleteOnTermination: 'false'
      VolumeSize: '20'
  EC2VA2D4YR:
    Type: 'AWS::EC2::VolumeAttachment'
    Properties:
      VolumeId: !Ref EC2V7IM1
      InstanceId: !Ref EC2I41BQT
  EC2VA20786:
    Type: 'AWS::EC2::VolumeAttachment'
    Properties:
      InstanceId: !Ref MyEC2Instance
      VolumeId: !Ref MyEBSVolume
```

Now that your core infrastructure components have been turned into a scripted fashion, it's very easy to manage them like any other application code, which can be checked in to a code repository, changes can be tracked at the time of committing, and can be reviewed before deployment to the production environment. This whole concept is known as **Infrastructure-as-Code**, and helps not just with routine automation but also enables deeper DevOps practices in any environment.

Apart from AWS' services, there are many popular third-party tools such as Chef, Puppet, Ansible, and Terraform, which further help operating infrastructure components in a scripted, code-like manner.

CI/CD for applications on Amazon EC2, Amazon Elastic Beanstalk

AWS provides a bunch of services to create your application's Continuous Integration and Continuous Deployment pipelines natively on AWS. There are also many popular tools, such as Jenkins, Bamboo, TeamCity, and Git, that can either be independently set up on AWS or even integrated with the CI/CD services that AWS offers. As a whole, there are plenty of options and users can pick and choose the right ones as per their needs:

Capability	AWS Service	Other tools
Source code repository, version control, branching, tagging, and so on	AWS CodeCommit	Git, **Apache Subversion** (**SVN**), Mercurial
Compiles source code and produces software packages that are ready to deploy	AWS CodeBuild	Jenkins, CloudBees, Solano CI, TeamCity
Tests automation covering functionality, security, performance, or compliance	No direct AWS services, but AWS CodeBuild can integrate with various testing tools	Apica, Blazemeter, Runscope, Ghost Inspector
Automated code deployments to any instance	AWS CodeDeploy	XebiaLabs

Apart from the preceding services, AWS also offers two other services that help in DevOps-related implementations:

AWS CodePipeline: This helps you fully model and automate your software release processes in the form of pipelines. A pipeline defines your release process workflow, and describes how a new code change progresses through your release process. A pipeline comprises a series of stages (for example, build, test, and deploy), which act as logical divisions in your workflow.

The following is a sample CodePipeline based CI/CD pipeline and uses various other services like AWS CodeCommit, AWS CodeBuild, AWS Lambda, Amazon SNS, and AWS CodeDeploy to orchestrate the entire process. As CodePipeline integrates with AWS Lambda, it also gives you additional options to customize actions and workflows in line with your CI/CD process requirements:

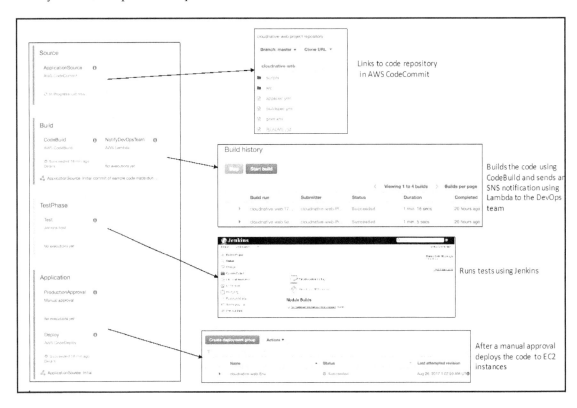

Using the previously mentioned CI/CD process, you can either have in-place updates, which is code being deployed to the same EC2 instances, or have a new fleet of instances to perform Blue/Green deployment, in which Blue is the current environment and Green is the new environment with the latest code changes. The concept of Blue/Green deployments is also based on the cloud best practices of *immutable infrastructure*, wherein your instances and environment are totally replaced rather than being updated in case of any new configuration or code release. This is analogous to the immutable variables in many programming constructs where you instantiate them once and they can never be updated, which makes the process of any changes easy and consistent, avoiding any conflicts, as it's always a new variable or instance.

The main benefits of performing **Blue/Green** deployments are as follows:

- You don't touch an existing environment, thereby making the application updates less risky
- You can gradually roll over to the new (**Green**) environment and can easily roll back over to the previous (**Blue**) deployment if there are any issues
- You treat the infrastructure as code, baking the entire process of creating **Blue/Green** deployments within your application deployment scripts and processes

The following is a sample **Blue/Green** deployment using AWS CodeDeploy, where you replace an autoscaled set of EC2 instances behind an ELB (**Blue** environment), to a new set of autoscaled instances (**Green** environment). You can find more details on the process in the AWS documentation at `http://docs.aws.amazon.com/codedeploy/latest/userguide/welcome.html#welcome-deployment-overview-blue-green`:

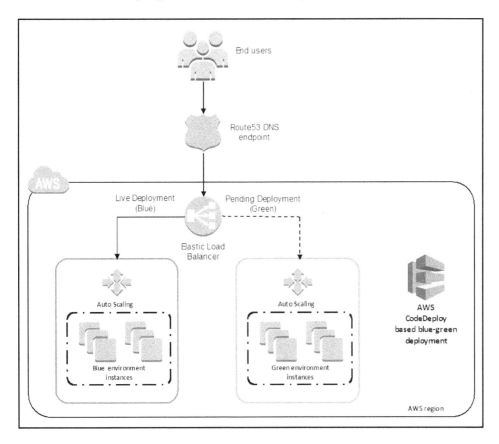

In order to quickly use and integrate the various AWS DevOps oriented services, AWS has another service called AWS CodeStar. This service provides a unified user interface and a project management dashboard, including an integrated issue tracking capability, enabling you to easily manage your software development activities in one place. This service also offers various templates of sample applications that can deployed to Amazon EC2, AWS Elastic Beanstalk, and AWS Lambda, and managed using various DevOps services. The following is a screenshot of the AWS CodeStar dashboard for one of the provided sample applications:

CI/CD for serverless applications

The process to manage the CI/CD pipelines is very similar to the process described in the previous section around managing application environments in Amazon EC2. The main steps involved for automating this process for a serverless application are as follows:

CI/CD for Amazon ECS (Docker containers)

Containers have revolutionized the software packaging aspects, by enabling the creation of lightweight, standalone, and executable packages of a piece of software that includes everything needed to run it: code, runtime, system tools, system libraries, and settings that can be deployed on various computing environments. Although there are multiple different types of container platforms, one of the most popular ones is Docker containers. Amazon offers the Amazon **EC2 Container Service** (**ECS**) and Amazon **Elastic Container Service for Kubernetes** (**EKS**) to deploy and manage Docker containers at scale and in a reliable fashion. Amazon ECS and Amazon EKS also integrate with various other AWS services such as Elastic Load Balancing, EBS volumes, and IAM roles to make the process of deploying various container-based applications even easier. Along with Amazon ECS and Amazon EKS, AWS also offers an Amazon **EC2 Container Registry** (**ECR**) to store, manage, and deploy Docker container images to an Amazon ECS-based environment.

In order to build a CI/CD workflow to deploy various application versions on to Amazon ECS, the following is a high-level workflow using services such as AWS CodePipeline, AWS CodeBuild, AWS CloudFormation, and Amazon ECR:

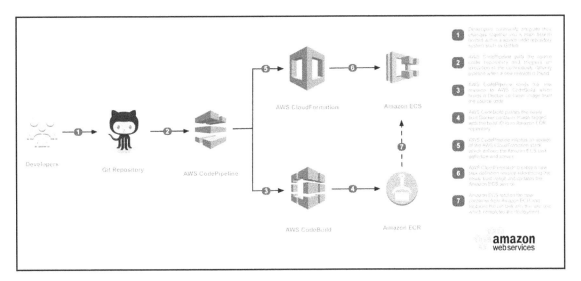

CI/CD for security services – DevSecOps

As discussed in the previous section, AWS has multiple cloud-native AWS services and most of them have SDKs, APIs that make it easier to integrate them with other applications and processes. Another key theme we just discussed is DevOps, which is basically a combination of cultural philosophies, practices, and tools that increase an organization's ability to deliver applications and services at high velocity. Now, if applications are being rapidly delivered at a high velocity to various environments and security organization's policy-related checks that are not integrated in those processes, then it can create a nightmare for the organization, wherein some controls might be left unattended for being exploited. As a result, having security woven into DevOps is a must and it's also called DevSecOps (or SecDevOps).

The core way to achieve this is to treat the security components and services in an infrastructure-as-code fashion and integrate them with the existing DevOps practices. As an example, if the Corporate Security team of an organization has defined standards around how VPCs should be set up for any environment, which NACL rules should be applied and how IAM users and their policies should be created, then those should be documented in CloudFormation templates, which the application teams just refer to and reuse by applying the capability of nested CloudFormation stacks. This way, the security team focuses on creating and updating the security and networking components that lie in their area of responsibility and the application team focuses on the code, the testing process, and deployment across the fleet of servers as per the environment.

Other than infrastructure provisioning aspects, this practice can be taken to the next level by also involving security checks along the entire software development pipeline, by including tests for areas such as the following:

- Ensuring that code analysis tools are integrated and security-related findings are addressed before pushing to production
- Enabling audit logs, including services such as AWS CloudTrail logging, apart from standard application logging

- Running various security tests, including virus/malware scans and penetration testing, which might be required for compliance-sensitive workloads
- Checking databases and various other static configuration and binary files, and that PHI/PII data (such as credit card numbers, social security numbers, and health records) is either encrypted or obfuscated and not available in plain text for any possible exploits

Many customers also make use of custom logic and applications to automate various stages of the preceding pipeline using AWS Lambda. These functions can not just be executed proactively, but also can be triggered by various reactive means such as event triggers from sources such as CloudWatch monitoring, CloudWatch Events, and SNS alerts.

A couple of other services that help in an effective DevSecOps implementation are AWS Config and Amazon Inspector. AWS Config can help assess, audit, and evaluate the configurations of your AWS resources, whereas using Amazon Inspector you can automatically assesses applications for vulnerabilities or deviations from best practices, thereby providing the base rules and frameworks out of the box, which can be augmented with your custom policies and checks using Amazon Lambda-based definitions.

Patterns for moving off monolithic application architectures to AWS native architectures

In the earlier sections, we discussed multiple options to create greenfield cloud-native applications using various AWS services. That part is a little easy, as you are starting fresh and so you can use various cloud services as you architect your solutions. However, if you have a huge technical debt in an on-premise environment and want to reduce that by moving over to a cloud platform such as AWS, then it takes more effort and planning.

In recent years, AWS has matured its migration services, methodology, and messaging to make it easier for organizations to not just think of greenfield but even plan for brownfield implementations in AWS. They have a methodology of the **6Rs**, which possibly covers every scenario for any workload migration to AWS. The 6Rs that AWS has are Rehosting, Replatforming, Repurchasing, Refactoring/Re-Architecting, Retire, and Retain.

The following is a snapshot of this methodology:

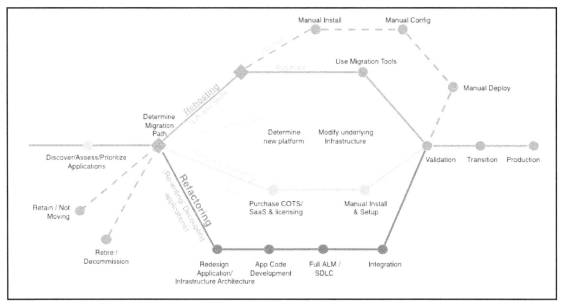

In order to develop the partner ecosystem with the 6Rs aligned methodology, AWS has a **Migration Acceleration Program** (**MAP**), which is now the backbone of its entire enterprise segment migration strategy. More details on the program is available at `https://aws.amazon.com/migration-acceleration-program/`.

Apart from the this, AWS has a more holistic framework for any organization that's planning to start their cloud journey, and it's called AWS **Cloud Adoption Framework** (**CAF**). This is a detailed framework covering six different perspectives oriented towards Business and Technology stakeholders in any organization:

- Business
- People
- Governance
- Platform
- Security
- Operations

More details on AWS CAF are available at the following link: `https://aws.amazon.com/professional-services/CAF/`.

Summary

In this chapter, we focused on AWS and its capabilities based on the CNMM described earlier. So, in line with that, we focused on understanding the core AWS capabilities around building cloud-native architectures and effectively operating in your applications in that environment. We then dived deep into a sample serverless microservice application, leveraging various key AWS services and frameworks. Finally, we understood the principles around DevOps and DevSecOps and how those translated to various different application architectures ranging from deploying on Amazon EC2, Amazon Elastic Beanstalk, AWS Lambda, and the Amazon EC2 Container Service. Finally, we looked at migration patterns to move your applications to AWS and the concept of the 6Rs and the AWS CAF.

15
Microsoft Azure

Microsoft Azure had a very different start compared to AWS. It was originally launched in 2009 as the Windows Azure platform, where the focus was on developers and **Platform-as-a-Service (PaaS)** components. The initial set of services that were launched were Windows Server AppFabric and ASP.NET MVC2 to help developers build applications using the frameworks and services in the cloud. The only infrastructure components at that time were Windows Server virtual machines to enable hybrid use cases, but the overall strategy was still geared towards developer community, which was radically different from AWS, who had more infrastructure components around that time being offered apart from some basic application-centric services. With this foray into the cloud, Azure continued the push towards application aspects until 2014, when it changed the whole strategy to go into the IaaS space as well and also rebranded the platform to Microsoft Azure.

 Refer to this first blog post, announcing the launch of Windows Azure:
`https://news.microsoft.com/2009/11/17/microsoft-cloud-services-vision-becomes-reality-with-launch-of-windows-azure-platform/`.

Since the time Microsoft entered the cloud IaaS market with the launch of Azure Virtual Machines in June 2012 (with general availability in April 2013), Azure has grown dramatically in terms of its global presence as well as the services it has to offer. At the time of writing this book, Microsoft Azure has 36 regions globally, with plans for six additional regions to come online in the near future. One point to consider here is that there's a subtle difference in the way AWS describes its regions versus Microsoft Azure. For AWS, it's a cluster of **Availability Zones (AZs)** that make up a region, and an AZ can comprise one or more data centers in itself, whereas for Microsoft Azure, a region is a geographic location where it has a data center. Microsoft recently announced that it will also now offer AZs like AWS, however that feature is still in beta and will take some time to roll out globally. So, for users who are looking for high availability deployments in Microsoft Azure in the interim, there's another option called Availability Sets (details are available at `https://docs.microsoft.com/en-us/azure/virtual-machines/windows/manage-availability?toc=%2Fazure%2Fvirtual-machines%2Fwindows%2Ftoc.json#configure-multiple-virtual-machines-in-an-availability-set-for-redundancy`).

Another important aspect of Microsoft's cloud business is that apart from Microsoft Azure, it also has services around Microsoft Office 365 and Microsoft Dynamics 365 CRM, which are included in there.

To keep yourself updated on the latest Microsoft Azure announcements and service launches news, subscribe to the following resources:

- Azure Updates page: `https://azure.microsoft.com/en-us/updates/`
- Microsoft Azure Blog: `https://azure.microsoft.com/en-us/blog/`

In this chapter, we will cover the following topics:

- Microsoft Azure's cloud native services, strengths, and differentiators around CI/CD, serverless, containers, and microservices concepts, covering the following services:
    - Azure functions
    - Visual Studio team services
    - Azure container service
    - Azure IoT
    - Azure machine learning studio
    - Office 365
- Understanding cloud native database capabilities:
    - Azure Cosmos DB
- Management and monitoring capabilities for Microsoft Azure native application architectures
- Patterns for moving off monolithic application architectures to Microsoft Azure native architectures
- Sample reference architectures and code snippets for CI/CD, serverless, containers, and microservices application architectures

Azure's Cloud Native Services (CNMM Axis-1)

The first and foremost aspect in being cloud native is to understand and utilize the cloud provider's services, which can help differentiate beyond the core infrastructure layer.

As per various independent analyst reports and analysis, Azure is the only cloud provider that's close to AWS in terms of its cloud services and ability to execute. So, in lines with that, Azure has multiple offerings that not just cover the core aspects such as compute, storage, networking, and databases, but multiple higher services in the space of data/analytics, AI/cognitive, IoT, web/mobile, and enterprise integration. In the next subsection, we will focus on some of these higher-level applications and managed services that can help anyone be more cloud native and harness the full power of the platform, so let's dive right into it.

Microsoft Azure platform – differentiators

In a very similar vein as the previous chapter on AWS, where we discussed some of the differentiating services from Amazon, let's look at some of the Azure services that are its core differentiators and are recommended to build effective cloud native application architectures. These services also greatly improve the productivity of the teams developing the applications as they can now focus on the core business logic rather than having to worry about stitching together basic capabilities on their own, which often is not as scalable and fault-tolerant compared to what the cloud providers can offer with their years of experience operating those components across global and multi-customer environments. So, let's dive into a few key Azure services that can further accelerate your cloud native journey.

Azure IoT

Microsoft Azure has a set of services that help us build connected platforms and solutions, which help us ingest massive amounts of data from devices (or things), applying rules on the fly to filter data, analyzing in real-time, and persisting to various data stores for creating different types of views and solutions on top of it. One of the main services that Azure has in this space is Microsoft Azure IoT Hub, which has multiple features that you can use to connect, manage, and operate a connected device's environment. Although it has multiple features, some of the specific ones are as follows:

- **Device registration, authentication, and authorization**: One of most important aspects in an IoT scenario is ensuring that devices are properly provisioned and securely connecting to the backend. To enable this, Azure IoT provides options through the portal and the API to create individual devices, which provides an individual device endpoint within the cloud. This method of individually adding the devices using the portal is viable only when you have limited devices and so you can add them one by one. However, if you have thousands of devices that you would like to register, then Azure IoT Hub provides a separate `ImportDevicesAsync` method that you can use to bulk upload, delete, or even apply status changes to thousands of devices in one API call. Likewise, if you want to bulk export registered devices information, then the `ExportDevicesAsync` method can help. Once the devices have been created, apart from the endpoint, a symmetric X.509 key is also created, which helps with device authentication. This, clubbed with policy-based access controls and a secure communication channel (TLS-based encryption), make it secure for the devices to connect and exchange information with the IoT Hub. The following is a high-level breakdown of these controls:

- **Communication protocols**: Different devices have different types of protocol and integration support. However, in most IoT scenarios, MQTT, AMQP, and HTTPS are the protocols that most of the devices support. Azure IoT Hub also supports all of these protocols, making it thereby easier to connect the majority of the devices out of the box, without any major configuration requirements. However, sometimes, some devices have different types of protocols and communication mechanisms that do not fall under this supported protocols set. So, for such scenarios, there's a Microsoft Azure IoT Protocol Gateway (`https://github.com/Azure/azure-iot-protocol-gateway/blob/master/README.md`), which the customers can fork from GitHub, make any changes as per translation requirements, and deploy it on Azure VM instances. This makes it easier to cater to a variety of devices so that they can be connected and be managed using the Azure IoT Hub service:

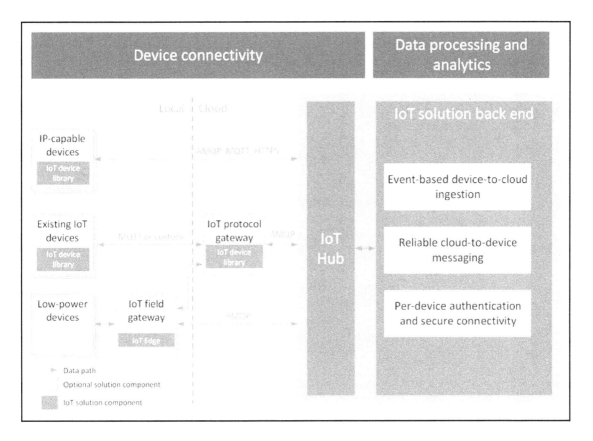

- **Device Twins**: Devices are not always connected to the backend IoT Hub, but your backend application often needs to query the last known status of the device or even wants to set a particular status as soon as the device connects to the backend using IoT Hub, so for such device state synchronization-related operations, Azure IoT Hub provides device twins functionality. These device twins are JSON documents that have tags (device metadata), and properties (desired and reported), using which you can create your desired application logic to communicate and update the devices:

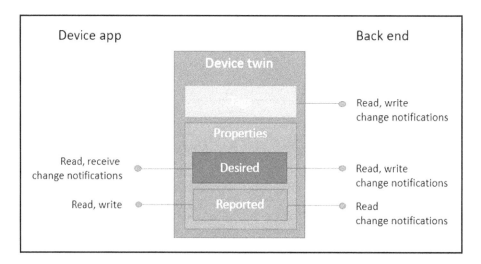

- **Azure IoT Edge**: Sometimes, instead of sending over the data from devices to the cloud, it's easier to perform analytics or a simple computation at the edge itself. A typical scenario of this would be a use case, wherein the devices are in a remote location and the network connection might be flaky or expensive, so for those scenarios, edge analytics makes sense. To enable this aspect, Azure has a capability called IoT Edge, where you can run your code and logic closer to the devices itself using multiple SDKs (C, Node.js, Java, Microsoft .NET, and Python) that Azure offers. This enables a seamless hybrid cloud architecture, where some logic is executable at the edge, and more complex processing data is transmitted to the cloud, with various services helping with the scalable processing there.

Apart from Azure IoT Hub, Azure also offers out of the box industry and use case-specific solution offerings that customers can directly deploy with a click and scale to production grade architecture as per their specific requirements. Behind the scenes, these solutions make use of multiple Azure services, such as Azure IoT Hub, Azure Events Hub, Azure Stream Analytics, Azure Machine Learning, and Azure Storage. This is a differentiator for the Azure IoT service, as other cloud providers only offer core building blocks for the connected devices and IoT use cases, whereas Azure also offers out-of-the-box, ready-to-use solutions.

Here is a snapshot of the solutions that the Azure IoT Suite offers currently:

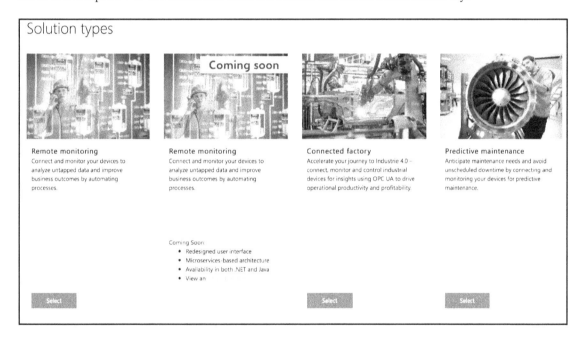

Azure Cosmos DB

Azure Cosmos DB is Microsoft's globally distributed, multi-model database. Azure Cosmos DB enables you to elastically and independently scale throughput and storage across any number of Azure's geographic regions. Azure Cosmos DB guarantees single-digit-millisecond latencies at the 99th percentile anywhere in the world, offers multiple well-defined consistency models to fine-tune performance, and guarantees high availability with multi-homing capabilities (more details are available here: `https://azure.microsoft.com/en-us/services/cosmos-db/`).

Azure Cosmos DB was launched in May 2017, however it's not really a brand-new offering per se. It actually inherited lots of functionality from its predecessor, Azure DocumentDB, which was launched a couple of years prior to it, and was more focused on the NoSQL-based architectural pattern. However, Azure CosmosDB is just not a simple reincarnation of Azure DocumentDB with a new name; it actually introduced multiple new functionalities and capabilities which were not there before. The three important differentiators that new Cosmos DB brings in are:

- **Globally distributed deployment model**: Azure has multiple regions, and if you want to deploy an application that spans many of those regions with a shared database, then CosmosDB allows that with a global deployment model. You can select the regions where your DB instance is replicated either during the time of creation of your database, or you can do that later too when the database is active. You can also define which region is *read* or *write*, or *read/write*, as per your requirements. Along with that, you can also define the failover priorities for each of the regions to handle any large scale regional events and issues.

For some use cases, you may want to restrict the data to a specific location or region (like for data sovereignty, privacy, or in-country data residency regulations), and then to meet those needs you can control this using policies that are controlled using the metadata of your Azure subscription:

- **Multi-model APIs**: This is one of the biggest differences from the earlier version of Azure DocumentDB, as now it supports various other models:
  - **Graph database** - This is the model in which data has multiple vertices and edges. Each vertex defines a unique object in the data (such as a person or device) and it can be connected to n-number of other vertices using edges, which define a relationship between them. To query Azure Cosmos DB, you can use the Apache TinkerPop graph traversal language, Gremlin, or other TinkerPop-compatible graph systems, such as Apache Spark GraphX.
  - **Table** - This is based on the Azure table storage, which is basically a NoSQL key-value approach to storing massive amounts of semi-structured datasets. Cosmos DB adds the global distribution capabilities here on top of Azure Table Storage APIs.
  - **JSON documents** - Cosmos DB also provides the option to store JSON documents in your database, which can either be accessed using existing DocumentDB APIs or newer MongoDB APIs.
  - **SQL** - Cosmos DB also supports some basic SQL functions using the existing DocumentDB API. However, this is not as full-fledged as the Azure SQL database, so if advanced SQL operations are required, then Cosmos DB might not be a fit for that.
- **Consistency models**: Normally, other cloud databases provided limited options in terms of how the data is replicated across different partitioned nodes and geographies. The most common options in distributed computing are as follows:
  - **Strong Consistency**, where the response is only returned after the commit is successful across different replicas and so read after write would ensure that you have the latest value
  - **Eventual Consistency**, where the response after a commit is immediately returned and various nodes synchronize the data eventually, thereby leading to a scenario wherein immediate read after write may give a stale value

However, Cosmos DB has taken it to the next level. It has introduced various other consistency models (bounded staleness, session, and consistent prefix) that lie between strong and eventual consistency models, as follows:

The following is a screenshot from the Azure CosmosDB portal, which shows these consistency model settings:

As a result of all of these differentiating capabilities, Azure Cosmos DB is a great choice for multiple cloud native scenarios such as shared databases for globally distributed application architectures, telemetry, and the state information store for connected platforms/IoT and backend persistence for serverless applications.

Azure machine learning studio

Microsoft initially launched the service under the name of Azure Machine Learning; however, they later changed it to Azure Machine Learning Studio in line with its core capabilities of being able to manage the entire process using the Studio itself (Visual Workbench). It's a managed service that you can use to create, test, operate, and manage predictive analytic solutions in the cloud. The core value proposition of this service is that you do not necessarily need to be a data scientist in order to build machine learning models as it provides multiple sample datasets and analysis modules, which can be used together to create your machine learning experiment. Once you have tried, tested, and trained your experiment, you can use it to start generating predictive analysis for your actual data and expose them as web services as well. The following diagram summarizes these core concepts in a concise manner:

One of the biggest benefits of Azure Machine Learning Studio is that there are multiple algorithms that are available out of the box as follows:

- **Anomaly Detection**: Identifies and predicts rare or unusual data points, such as predicting a credit risk or detecting a fraudulent activity.
- **Classification**: Identifies what category new information belongs to. It could be a simple yes/no or true/false categorization, or a complex one such as the sentiment analysis of a social media post.
- **Clustering**: Separates similar data points into intuitive groups, such as predicting customer taste or the level of interest in a particular item.
- **Recommendation**: Predicts the likelihood that a user would prefer an item based on a previous user interaction. This is typical in online shopping portals, where additional product options are provided based on your past browsing history.
- **Regression**: Forecasts the future by estimating the relationship between variables, such as predicting car sales figures for the next few months.
- **Statistical Functions**: Mathematical computations on column values, calculating correlations, z scores, probability scores, and so on.
- **Text Analytics**: Works with both structured and unstructured text to detect the language of input text, creates n-gram dictionaries, and extracts the names of people, places, and organizations from unstructured text.
- **Computer Vision**: Image processing and image recognition tasks to detect faces, image tagging, color analysis, and so on.

To learn more about Azure Machine Learning algorithms, refer to the cheat sheet at the following link: `https://docs.microsoft.com/en-us/azure/machine-learning/studio/algorithm-cheat-sheets`.

As you can see, there are multiple algorithms already available; however, developers/data scientists often need to extend or modify some of the functionalities, so also possible to use R or Python script modules and Jupyter notebooks.

In terms of execution, as we mentioned previously, you can expose your machine learning workflow to external applications using REST web services. In this, there are two broader options based on the type of execution models as follows:

- **Request Response Service** (**RRS**): For stateless, synchronous execution
- **Batch Execution Service** (**BES**): Batch processing in an asynchronous way

Visual Studio Team Services

As we discussed in the previous chapter, AWS offers multiple services that enable successful DevOps practices in any organization. Likewise, Azure has a set of services/features DevOps that help developers build applications leveraging CI/CD principles and processes. In fact, even before Microsoft had cloud-based services in this space, it had an on-premises platform called Team Foundation Services (TFS), which developers and teams could make use of to deliver quality products. With an increased emphasis and focus on the cloud, Microsoft launched a cloud-based service called Visual Studio Team Services (VSTS), which is like a *cloudified* version of the pre-existing TFS. The biggest benefit for VSTS is, of course, that it is a managed platform. Azure does lots of heavy lifting on behalf of the customer so that they can focus on their core business of developing applications with proper collaboration and practices. Also, since TFS has been in existence for quite some time, VSTS is also a rich platform with multiple inbuilt capabilities and third-party integrations.

 To understand the differences between VSTS and TFS, refer to the following link:
https://docs.microsoft.com/en-us/vsts/user-guide/about-vsts-tfs

Since our focus here is on cloud native capabilities, let's dive deeper into VSTS and discuss a few of the main functionalities that it provides:

- The first and the foremost is the ability to manage code, various versions, and branches. For the same, VSTS provides a couple of options, including Git (distributed) or Team Foundation Version Control (TFVC), and a centralized, client-server system. For using Git-based repositories, developers can make use of variety of IDEs, including Visual Studio, Eclipse, Xcode, and IntelliJ. Likewise, for TFVC, you may use Visual Studio, Eclipse, and Xcode. The VSTS cloud-based UI also provides various options to explore the code files in the project, and look at push/pull and commits-related details from there itself.

- The other important aspect is the ability to have continuous integration and continuous deployment, which is central to any successful DevOps practice. So, again, VSTS enables this by using various functionalities that includes being able to create build and release definitions, creating libraries of build variables that may vary as per environment, as well as the definition of deployment groups where you can define target instances that are Windows, Ubuntu, or RHEL.

- In order to implement DevOps, many teams also make use of Scrum, which are Kanban software development methodologies. So, it's important to integrate these processes with the code development practices, and that's what VSTS also helps with by providing project dashboards, sprint backlogs, task dashboards, and related visualizations to enable closer planning and collaboration. It not only helps project managers to evaluate the overall status, but even product managers to write stories, developers to link their tasks/bug fixes/checkins to respective stories, and QA teams to write their test cases and record results, thereby providing an end to end platform.

- Apart from core service capabilities, another key aspect is to have ecosystem partner integrations available in an out-of-the-box or easy to use manner. That's exactly what Visual Studio Marketplace offers. You can select multiple plugins, including for work item visualization, code searching, slack integration, and more. Refer to the following link for more details of the available software and integrations: `https://marketplace.visualstudio.com/vsts`

Interestingly, VSTS Marketplace also has a plugin to manage and integrate with AWS services such as Amazon S3, AWS Elastic Beanstalk, AWS CodeDeploy, AWS Lambda, and AWS CloudFormation: `https://marketplace.visualstudio.com/items?itemName=AmazonWebServices.aws-vsts-tools`.

Office 365

One of the most popular products that Microsoft has had for multiple years is Microsoft Office. With the advent of cloud, Microsoft started a SaaS offering of the same set of applications under the umbrella of Office 365. So, with that, anyone (home, business, or education users) could go online, get a subscription of the Office 365 suite, and start using it directly from the browser of their choice. Now, although this is a cloud-based offering from Microsoft, it technically doesn't fall under the Azure umbrella as Azure is more infrastructure and platform services oriented. However, we still wanted to cover it here, as Office 365 is an important piece to Microsoft's overall cloud business and many enterprises while making a move to cloud also factor in Office 365 as one of the core applications to migrate to in that transformation journey. The following are the applications that Microsoft offers as part of Office 365:

As we discussed previously, there's a close link between Azure and Office 365, and one of the main areas of integrations is authentication. What this means is that behind the scenes, Office 365 uses Azure AD to manage user identities. The other benefit of this linkage is that if a customer is using Active Directory on-premises for their user identities, then they can sync the passwords from there to Azure AD and set up single sign-on as well. This makes it easier for the end users as they don't have to remember additional credentials other than their corporate identities, and the experience of logging into Office 365 is also seamless.

One another reason that Office 365 is important is because of competitive reasons with other cloud providers. So, although AWS offers a set of business applications (such as Amazon Workdocs and Amazon Chime), and likewise Google has G Suite, from an enterprise adoption perspective, Microsoft has had the lead for multiple years. Office has been the de facto collaboration and productivity platform. So, for this reason as well, it makes it easier for customers to migrate and adopt Office 365 with minimal disruption to their business.

Application Centric Design (CNMM Axis-2)

As discussed in the previous chapter, creating serverless and microservice-based applications is a key cloud native way to differentiate as compared to pre-cloud era design patterns. So, let's look at how can we design such applications in Microsoft Azure cloud using multiple key services.

Serverless microservice

In this section, we are going to create a serverless microservice application on Microsoft Azure. In order for you to easily compare and learn capabilities across cloud providers, we will use the same example of creating a Weather Services application, which we discussed in the previous chapter on AWS. So, as a refresher, the overall application will have three main parts:

- An API trigger to invoke the application.
- A function that is written in Azure Functions.
- An external weather service to which we will pass some parameters and get results:

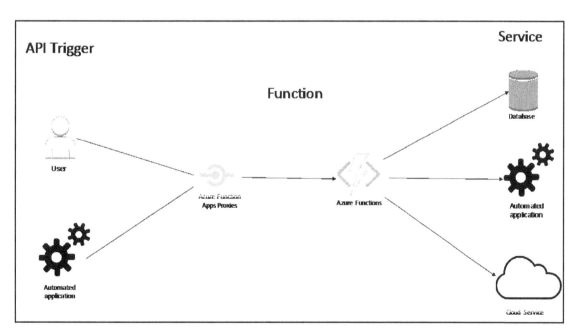

Serverless microservice – walkthrough

In order to create the previously mentioned service, follow these steps in Azure portal:

1. Click the Create a resource button found on the upper left-hand corner of the Azure portal, and then select **Compute** | **Function App.**
2. Create the **Function App**, as per the settings in the following screenshot (some settings might vary as per your account and existing resources):

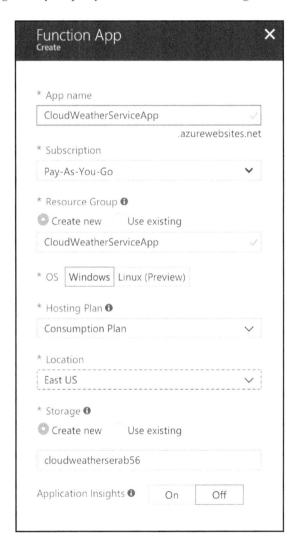

3. Once the **Functions App** is created, it's time to create our core business logic in the form of an Azure function. So, for that, expand your new function app, then click the + button next to **Functions**, and create a new **HTTP trigger** function as follows:

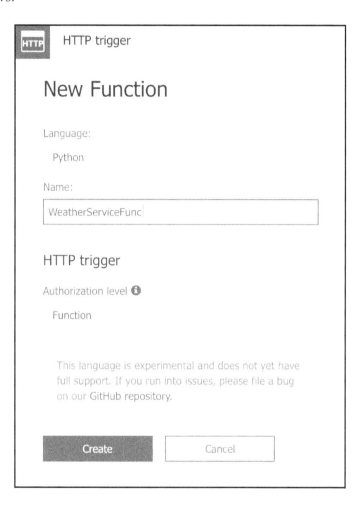

4. Once the function is created, edit the inline code and use the following Python-based logic:

```
## importing required libraries
import os
import sys
import json
import argparse
import urllib
from urllib2 import HTTPError, URLError
```

```
## response construction and return
def write_http_response(status, body_dict):
    return_dict = {
        "status": status,
        "body": body_dict,
        "headers": {
            "Content-Type": "application/json"
        }
    }
    output = open(os.environ['res'], 'w')
    output.write(json.dumps(return_dict))

## extract input parameter values
zip = os.environ['req_query_zip']
countrycode = os.environ['req_query_countrycode']
apikey = os.environ['req_query_apikey']

print ("zip code value::" + zip + ", countrycode:" + countrycode + ",
apikey::" + apikey)

## construct full URL to invoke OpenWeatherMap service with proper inputs
baseUrl = 'http://api.openweathermap.org/data/2.5/weather'
completeUrl = baseUrl + '?zip=' + zip + ',' + countrycode + '&appid=' +
apikey
print('Request URL--> ' + completeUrl)

## Invoke OpenWeatherMap API and parse response with proper exception
handling
try:
    apiresponse = urllib.urlopen(completeUrl)
except IOError as e:
    error = "IOError - The server couldn't fulfill the request."
    print(error)
    print("I/O error: {0}".format(e))
    errorcode = format(e[1])
    errorreason = format(e[2])
    write_http_response(errorcode, errorreason)
except HTTPError as e:
    error = "The server couldn't fulfill the request."
    print(error)
    print('Error code: ', e.code)
    write_http_response(e.code, error)
except URLError as e:
    error = "We failed to reach a server."
    print(error)
    print('Reason: ', e.reason)
    write_http_response(e.code, error)
```

```
else:
    headers = apiresponse.info()
    print('DATE :', headers['date'])
    print('HEADERS :')
    print('---------')
    print(headers)
    print('DATA :')
    print('---------')
    response = apiresponse.read().decode('utf-8')
    print(response)
    write_http_response(200, response)
```

5. Save the function, add sample query parameters (as shown in the preceding screenshot), and test your function. To look at all the function execution logs and results, you can go to the **Monitor** option under your function name and see the details as follows:

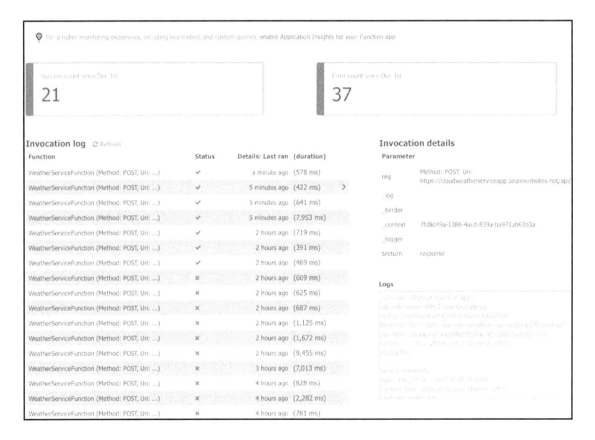

6. Once you have unit tested the Azure Function from the portal, go to the **Integrate** option under your function and ensure that the HTTP GET method is enabled, apart from the other settings, as follows:

7. Now, it's time to create an external facing API interface using proxies. To do that, you must first retrieve your Azure function URL from the top-right corner of your function definition, as follows:

8. To expose this Azure function using an API, create a new proxy by pressing the + sign against the **Proxies** option. Ensure that it has the settings, like in the following screenshot. In the backend URL field, put the URL of your Azure function that you copied in the previous screenshot:

With this, your serverless microservice is now ready and you can test it using a web browser or CLI, which is detailed in the following subsection.

Browser-based testing

You can copy the deployed API's URL from the Proxy URL field and then try accessing it by providing the `zip`, `countrycode`, and the `appid` parameters as part of the URL, as follows:

```
https://asdfqwert.azurewebsites.net/?zip=10001&countrycode=us&apikey=qwerty
asdfg98765zxcv
```

Note: Please replace the highlighted text with your environment's specific values.

Command-line-based testing

For this, you need to run the following commands:

```
$ curl -X GET
'https://asdfqwert.azurewebsites.net/?zip=10001&countrycode=us&apikey=qwert
yasdfg98765zxcv
"{"coord":{"lon":-74,"lat":40.75},"weather":[{"id":802,"main":"Clouds","des
cription":"scattered
clouds","icon":"03d"}],"base":"stations","main":{"temp":266.73,"pressure":1
024,"humidity":44,"temp_min":266.15,"temp_max":267.15},"visibility":16093,"
wind":{"speed":3.1,"deg":320},"clouds":{"all":40},"dt":1514582100,"sys":{"t
ype":1,"id":1969,"message":0.004,"country":"US","sunrise":1514549991,"sunse
t":1514583454},"id":0,"name":"New York","cod":200}"
```

Automation in Azure (CNMM Axis-3)

The entire concept of the public cloud is based on the premise that you can easily utilize and integrate the cloud services using APIs, SDKs, and REST web services. Another layer to this paradigm is the higher-level automation and orchestration services that cloud providers have created, which make it even easier to leverage the true power of cloud with less human intervention and thereby enable self-healing, autoscalable applications. Apart from this, developers can now assume greater responsibility to manage the full stack of their application environment on their own rather than have a separate ops team that they had to rely on earlier. This enables rapid releases, faster time to market, and increased agility in the application development lifecycle. As we discussed in the previous chapter, AWS offers services such as Amazon CloudFormation, AWS CodePipeline, AWS CodeBuild, and AWS CodeDeploy to enable these practices and culture, so in a very similar way, Azure has a whole bunch of services that can be used to enable DevOps, automation, and more cloud native application development practices. So, let's explore more around these concepts in the following sections.

Infrastructure as code

As discussed in the previous chapter as well, one of the key cloud automation techniques is to manage infrastructure-as-code, so that effective DevOps practices can be implemented. Like AWS offers Amazon CloudFormation, in a very similar manner, Azure has a service called **Azure Resource Manager** (**ARM**) Templates. Using this service, users can create standardized, repeatable JSON-based templates, which can be used to provision entire application stacks as a single entity to a resource group. The Azure portal provides an interface to directly author/edit the template there, or if users prefer an IDE-based development, then Visual Studio Code also offers extensions using which makes it easy to author ARM templates. The visual editor in the Azure portal also helps detect any JSON syntactical errors (such as missing commas curly braces, and so on), but semantic validations are not supported. Once you have finalized the template, you can deploy it either directly using the Azure portal, or even use CLI, PowerShell, SDKs, and so on to create your application environments. If there's any error during the template deployment phase, ARM provides debugging as well as output details, which comes in handy for evaluating progress and correcting any issues. Unlike AWS CloudFormation, ARM templates don't support YAML, which is more human-readable and generally more concise than JSON.

In order to effectively use Visual Studio Code to develop ARM templates, refer to the following blog post: `https://blogs.msdn.microsoft.com/azuredev/2017/04/08/iac-on-azure-developing-arm-template-using-vscode-efficiently/`.

One differentiating feature for Azure Resource Manager is around subscription governance, wherein the account owner can register for a resource provider to be configured with your subscription. Some resource providers are registered by default, whereas for the majority, the user has to opt for them using a PowerShell command such as the following:

```
Register-AzureRmResourceProvider -ProviderNamespace Microsoft.Batch
```

Azure team has a GitHub repository where it hosts hundreds of sample templates for ARM. So, taking a basic example of a LAMP stack from there, it can be easily used to create a new template in ARM from the Azure portal, as follows:

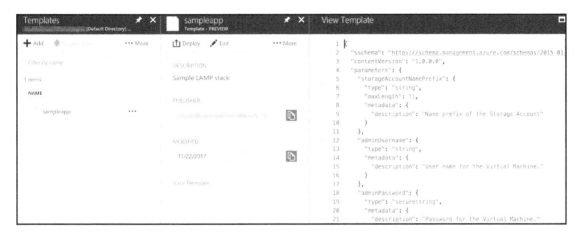

A snippet of that same LAMP stack template is as follows, and the complete template is available at: `https://github.com/Azure/azure-quickstart-templates/tree/master/lamp-app`:

```
{
    "$schema":
"https://schema.management.azure.com/schemas/2015-01-01/deploymentTemplate.
json#",
    "contentVersion": "1.0.0.0",
    "parameters": {
      "storageAccountNamePrefix": {
        "type": "string",
        "maxLength": 11,
        "metadata": {
          "description": "Name prefix of the Storage Account"
        }
      },
```

```
      "adminUsername": {
        "type": "string",
        "metadata": {
          "description": "User name for the Virtual Machine."
        }
      },
      ......
      ......
      ......
      ......

      {
        "type": "Microsoft.Compute/virtualMachines/extensions",
        "name": "[concat(variables('vmName'),'/newuserscript')]",
        "apiVersion": "2015-06-15",
        "location": "[resourceGroup().location]",
        "dependsOn": [
          "[concat('Microsoft.Compute/virtualMachines/',
variables('vmName'))]"
        ],
        "properties": {
          "publisher": "Microsoft.Azure.Extensions",
          "type": "CustomScript",
          "typeHandlerVersion": "2.0",
          "autoUpgradeMinorVersion": true,
          "settings": {
            "fileUris": [
"https://raw.githubusercontent.com/Azure/azure-quickstart-templates/master/
lamp-app/install_lamp.sh"
            ]
          },
          "protectedSettings": {
            "commandToExecute": "[concat('sh install_lamp.sh ',
parameters('mySqlPassword'))]"
          }
        }
      }
    ]
}
```

Unlike Amazon CloudFormation, ARM doesn't provide a visualization option natively, but there are tools available online that can help. The following is one such visualization of the LAMP stack template that's generated using `http://armviz.io/editor/4`:

Now, as described previously, you can easily define an entire stack in an ARM template, but you often need more elaborate, step-by-step (sequential or parallel) orchestration across different systems and services. Sometimes, you also want to trigger that workflow, based on some events, such as code changes in GitHub. So, for those comprehensive types of orchestration tasks, Azure has a service called Azure Automation. Using this service, you can create either a textual runbook where you directly write a PowerShell or Python script/module that defines your business logic, or if you don't want to directly interact with the code that much, then there's a graphical runbook mode as well. In the latter, you have a canvas in the Azure Automation portal, where you can create various individual activities from a broad variety of library items, define configuration for all the activities, and link them together to run a complete workflow. Before actually deploying that workflow, you can also test it there itself and debug or modify it based on results and logging output.

The following is a sample graphical runbook that's available in the Azure Automation Gallery, which connects to Azure using an Automation Run As account and starts all V2 VMs in an Azure subscription, in a resource group, or a single named V2 VM. As you can see in the following screenshot, on the left-hand side are PowerShell cmdlets, other runbooks, and assets (credentials, variables, connections, and certificates), which can be added to the canvas in the center to modify the workflow. On the right-hand side is the configuration screen, where settings for each of the activities can be updated and their behavior defined as per the required business logic:

CI/CD for serverless applications

As discussed in the earlier section of this chapter, you can easily create serverless applications using Azure functions. It's easy to develop and deploy your Azure functions directly from the portal itself, however that's neither efficient from a team collaboration perspective and nor does it offer the possibility to automate the processes in-line with DevOps methodologies. So, to address that, Microsoft has a set of tools, specifically around VSTS integration with Azure functions, which makes it easy to orchestrate the entire CI/CD pipeline. There are more options as well from a deployment sources standpoint, such as Bitbucket, Dropbox, OneDrive and so on, but in this section we will focus more on VSTS, which is one of the most common methods.

 Go to the following link for more details on Visual Studio tools for Azure Functions: `https://blogs.msdn.microsoft.com/webdev/2016/12/01/visual-studio-tools-for-azure-functions/`

Now, in order to effectively deploy the same Azure function to different types of environments, it's of utmost importance to separate out the core logic from the environment-specific configuration details. In order to do that, you can create an Azure functions type of a project from Visual Studio which has your core business logic in one or more functions. To manage environment-specific configuration aspects, these can be woven together in ARM templates. This also helps deploy stage-specific Azure functions in their own resource groups, which again brings a clear separation that's needed to meaningfully implement CI/CD processes.

The following is a high-level architecture diagram explaining the overall process:

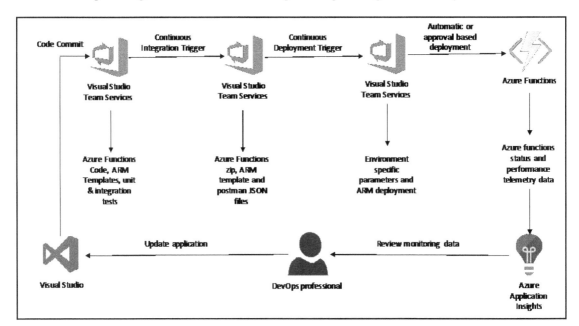

As shown in the preceding diagram, in terms of the continuous integration process, there are three main steps such as are common for most projects, though these can be custom tailored as per individual requirements:

1. Build the code.
2. Run unit tests and ensure that everything looks good.
3. Create the solution package that can be deployed to the respective environments.

Once the CI process is complete, it's time to move to the continuous deployment phase. Usually, most customers have different phases in the pipeline, Dev, Test, UAT, and finally Production. All of these can be orchestrated using Visual Studio Team Services, where you can define the deployment process, which includes environment-specific configurations as well as the approval process. For lower-level environments, such as Dev and Test, most customers usually follow an automatic deployment process based on unit testing results, but for higher-level environments such as UAT and Production, it's a common practice to include a manual approval process to control gating procedures based on lower environments test results. To complete the DevOps loop, the final deployments are monitored using Azure Application Insights, which help with further refinement and application updates to improve application functionality across environments.

CI/CD for Azure container service (Docker containers)

Microsoft offers a managed Docker container service, **Azure Container Service** (**AKS**), using which customers can easily deploy scalable, open source APIs-based container deployed applications. The most important aspect that AKS provides is the orchestration and placement-related aspects for the containers, so that the end users can focus on their core applications rather than having to worry about launching and scaling applications manually. For the orchestration aspects, AKS offers a few options, such as Docker, Swarm, Kubernetes, and Mesosphere DC/OS, which are shown in the following screenshot:

Another important aspect for any managed container platform is the functionality of a container registry where you can store master copies of different container images based on application stacks and configuration. For this, Azure offers **Azure Container Registry** (**ACR**), which is private registry for you to tag and upload images there.

Container-based applications often need to access and persist data in an external data volume. Azure files can be used as this external data store. Refer to the following link for more details: `https://docs.microsoft.com/en-us/azure/aks/azure-files`.

Now, in order to enable CI/CD practices with the Azure Container Service, the steps are very similar to the ones described in the previous section around enabling CI/CD for Azure functions. At a high level, the following are the key steps and the flow to enable these practices:

1. Store your application code in a code repository such as the Visual Studio Team Services Git repository. Apart from the core application code, this may also include Docker files and compose and deployment files, which will be needed to create Docker images and enable deployment as per various environment-specific requirements.

2. Any time a code change is committed to the code repository, it triggers a continuous integration build process in VSTS and creates new Docker images, which are then stored in the Azure Container Registry.

3. Once the new Docker images are released to the registry, it triggers a new release using VSTS, which can be gradually promoted from Dev, Test, UAT, and then Production.

4. This release process is integrated with different orchestrators supported by AKS, which pull the latest Docker image from the container registry and push it out the running instances to bring up the latest version of the application.

As part of the preceding process, multiple customizations can be performed, like being able to run particular types of tests or integration with other systems, which can be again easily managed using VSTS-based CI/CD pipelines.

The Kubernetes extension for VSTS is available on the Visual Studio Marketplace: `https://marketplace.visualstudio.com/items?itemName=tsuyoshiushio.k8s-endpoint`.

Patterns for moving from monolithic application architectures to Azure native architectures

Although cloud migrations have common patterns and methodologies, every cloud provider brings in a different flavor to it with their services and overall messaging. So, like we discussed earlier, AWS has a 6Rs migration methodology, but when it comes to Azure's methodology, it's pretty simplistic. As per `https://azure.microsoft.com/en-us/migration/`, it mainly categorizes migration into three parts:

- **Discover**: In this phase, you assess the current state of virtual machines, databases, and applications in an on-premises environment and evaluate their migration path and priority.
- **Migrate**: This is the actual process of moving your applications, databases, and VMs to the Azure cloud by using cloud native or third-party tools, which help you transfer the bits by means of replication.
- **Optimize**: Once your applications and data is in the Azure cloud, you can further fine-tune for costs, performance, security, and management by leveraging better architectures and more cloud native services. Also, this phase is more like an iterative one, as optimization has to be done regularly and repeatedly based on changing applications needs and newer cloud services.

For the preceding three phases, Azure has a set of cloud native services along with a few key partners that it recommends as alternatives. The following is a table that summarizes a few of those options. For the latest information, it's recommended to check out `https://azure.microsoft.com/en-us/migrate/partners/`:

Phase	Azure Native Tools/Services	Partner Tools/Services
Discover	Azure Migrate (VM assessment), Data Migration Assistant (database assessment)	Cloudamize, Movere, TSO Logic, CloudPhysics
Migrate	Azure Site Recovery (VM migration), Azure Database Migration Service (Database migrations)	Cloudendure, Velostrata
Optimize	Cloudyn (now part of Microsoft)	N/A

Apart from the preceding tools, Azure also offers a different messaging service compared to AWS when it comes to hybrid cloud computing aspects. AWS focuses more on its cloud native services and how they can be leveraged or extended to manage resources, even in private on-premises environments, thereby bridging the gap between the private and public cloud to enable hybrid computing environments. When it comes to Azure, it takes it a step further with the notion of enabling a hybrid cloud with a key service in that space called Azure Stack. The way Azure defines this service is as follows:

"Azure Stack is an extension of Azure, bringing the agility and fast-paced innovation of cloud computing to on-premises environments. Only Azure Stack lets you deliver Azure services from your organization's datacenter, while balancing the right amount of flexibility and control-for truly-consistent hybrid cloud deployments."

-Source - https://azure.microsoft.com/en-us/overview/azure-stack/

The key use cases that Azure Stack tries to address are as follows:

- Edge and disconnected
- Cloud applications to meet varied regulations
- Cloud application model on-premises

Now, even though the preceding points may seem compelling to enable a hybrid cloud environment with a singular set of management tools and DevOps processes across the Azure public cloud and Azure Stack, there are some key cons as well, which the users have to be aware of in this approach. One of the main challenges here is that Azure Stack takes the user back to the days of managing servers and data centers, where you again have to do the heavy lifting around racking, stacking the Azure Stack boxes, and then of course manage the cooling, power-related operational aspects to keep it up and running. So, net-net, although Azure Stack enables deploying containers, microservices, and PaaS environments locally, since you still have to manage the underlying infrastructure, it is not a truly *cloud native* type of architectural pattern.

Summary

In this chapter, we focused on the Microsoft Azure cloud platform in line with the CNMM model we described earlier. We started with the basics of Microsoft Azure, its brief history, and then deep into a few of its differentiating services and offerings. We then looked at the same sample serverless microservice application that we used in Chapter 14, *Amazon Web Services*, as well, and deployed it on Azure using Azure functions and proxies. After that, we focused on DevOps and CI/CD patterns and how those relate to both serverless and Docker container-based application models. Finally, we looked at Azure's cloud migration guidance, how it differentiates from AWS' messaging, followed by Azure Stack-related hybrid cloud aspects.

16
Google Cloud Platform

As per various analyst reports, the third most significant public cloud provider is Google with their **Google Cloud Platform** (**GCP**). The origins of GCP can be tracked back to 2008 when Google launched the Google App engine to focus on the developer community with its foray into **platform as a service** (**PaaS**) types of offerings. Slowly and gradually, Google has expanded the set of services that it offers and it was really around 2012 that Google started to step up the focus around the pace of releases and geo expansion, which gradually made it one of the dominant players in this space. Since then, GCP has expanded into multiple different spaces ranging from core services like compute, storage, networking, and databases to many higher-level application services in the space of big data, IoT, **artificial intelligence** (**AI**), and API platforms and ecosystems.

To keep yourself updated on the latest GCP announcements and service launches news, subscribe to the following GCP blog: `https://cloud.` `google.com/blog/`.

In this chapter, we will focus on the following:

- Google Cloud Platform's cloud-native services, strengths, and differentiators around CI/CD, serverless, containers, and microservices concepts, covering the following services:
    - Google Kubernetes Engine
    - Google Cloud Functions
    - Cloud AI
- Management and monitoring capabilities for GCP native application architectures
- Patterns for moving off monolithic application architectures to Google Cloud Platform native architectures

- APIs, SDKs, open source frameworks, and partner ecosystem support to build cloud-native applications
- Sample reference architectures and code snippets for CI/CD, serverless microservices application architectures

GCP's cloud-native services (CNMM Axis-1)

As discussed in earlier chapters, let's first understand what type of cloud-native services Google Cloud offers that can help the end users and benefit businesses from the true power of various services and platforms.

Introduction

Google was a little bit of a late entrant to the public cloud space, but in the last few years it has really picked up pace in terms of its services coverage as well as customer adoption. As per various analyst reports, it ranks third as a cloud provider (after AWS and MS Azure) based on overall vision and its ability to execute, making it a promising candidate for any kind of cloud-native application's development and deployment. So, let's look at some of the services that it offers in that space and how it can potentially help you adopt them effectively.

Google Cloud Platform – differentiators

Google has many interesting services in the space of **machine learning** (**ML**) / **artificial intelligence** (**AI**), application containerization, and collaboration, which we will focus on in this section. In fact, many of these services are a result of Google creating them for their internal usage or even for the consumer business, which are now being productized and available under the Google Cloud umbrella. So, let's dive in a bit and understand a few key concepts, which are very popular with customers.

Cloud AI

Google was one of the first cloud providers to offer services in the Artificial Intelligence and machine learning space, with a multitude of services in this domain catering to different types of users from developers to data scientists. Also, most of these services/APIs have originated from Google's internal usage and existing product offerings, which have now been exposed as APIs/services under the Google cloud umbrella. These services cover a variety of AI/ML use cases, like the following:

- **Image and Video Analysis**: One of the common requirements for most of the organizations starting with their AI/ML journey is to classify and understand the context and metadata around their images and video streams. In the image analysis space, Google offers a Cloud Vision API (`https://cloud.google.com/vision/`), which can help classify images into thousands of categories, detect individual objects and faces within images, and find and read printed words contained within images. You can also detect any explicit content, identify logos, landmarks, or even search the web for similar images. Similarly, for video analysis, Google offers Cloud Video Intelligence (`https://cloud.google.com/video-intelligence/`), which can search every moment of every video file in your catalog, quickly annotates videos stored in Google Cloud Storage, and helps identify key entities within your video and when they occur within the video. Using this video analytics, you can generate appropriate content recommendations for end users and even show more contextual advertisements in lines with the content itself.

- **Speech and text-related AI services**: There are multiple AI-related aspects when it comes to text and speech analysis as well as conversions between one form to another. For the same reason, Google offers the Cloud Speech API (`https://cloud.google.com/speech/`), which can convert audio to text and can recognize over 110 languages and variants and thereby help transcribe audio content. Likewise, to convert written text-to-speech, Google offers the Cloud Text-To-Speech API (`https://cloud.google.com/text-to-speech/`) to synthesize natural-sounding speech with 30 voices, which is available in multiple languages and variants. Apart from this, Google also offers a service to detect a particular language in the text and also to convert text from one language to another using the Cloud Translation API (`https://cloud.google.com/translate/`). Another service which Google offers in this space is for the deep analysis of text by extracting information about people, places, events, and much more, which is mentioned in text documents, news articles, or blog posts. This service is a Cloud Natural Language (`https://cloud.google.com/natural-language/`), which can help understand the sentiment and intent (like positive or negative reviews) from social media content or customer conversations in call center type of text message exchanges.

- **Chatbots**: One of the most common uses of AI these days is to create conversational interfaces (or chatbots) for websites, mobile applications, messaging platforms, and IoT devices, that are capable of natural and rich interactions between users and your business. These chatbots can understand the intent and context of conversation to provide highly efficient and accurate responses. For this, Google has a service called DialogFlow Enterprise Edition (`https://cloud.google.com/dialogflow-enterprise/`), which has multiple out-of-the box templates and supports 20+ languages and integration with 14 different platforms to provide rich experience to the end users.

- **Custom Machine Learning**: In most cases, advanced users (such as data scientists) like to have more control of their algorithms, ML models, and the way the system generates results. So, for such scenarios, services like the ones discussed previously don't provide that level of deeper control and configurability, and that's why Google offers a set of services like Cloud AutoML (`https://cloud.google.com/automl/`) and Cloud Machine Learning Engine (`https://cloud.google.com/ml-engine/`), which provide greater options. As an example, if a retailer would like to classify images of various dresses as per their colors, shape, and design, then they can use Cloud AutoML to feed some sample data to train custom ML models, which can then be used to generate image recognition for actual images. Likewise, if data scientists would like to create their own custom models to perform predictive analytics, then they can use a framework like TensorFlow along with a managed service like the Cloud Machine Learning Engine, which is already integrated with many other Google services and also provides a familiar interface like Jupyter notebooks to create custom models. These services, clubbed with Cloud TPUs (TensorFlow Processing Unit, `https://cloud.google.com/tpu/`), provide up to 180 teraflops of performance, providing the computational power to train and run cutting-edge machine learning models at scale.

In order to stay up to date on the latest Google Cloud big data and machine learning-related announcements, you can subscribe to the following blog: `https://cloud.google.com/blog/big-data/`.

Kubernetes Engine

In the last few years, the developer community has embraced the use of containers (like Docker) to deploy applications in the form of images that are lightweight, stand alone, and include everything needed to run it: code, runtime, system tools, system libraries, and settings. Now, to effectively run containers at scale, you need an orchestration engine which can help in operational aspects like the autoscaling of the cluster in lines with load, auto-healing of impaired nodes, setting, and managing resources limits (such as, CPU and RAM), providing integrated monitoring and logging capabilities—which is where Kubernetes (popularly known as K8s) comes into the picture. Google is the original creator of Kubernetes and has also been using it internally for container-based production deployments for multiple years before making it open source and making it part of the Cloud Native Computing Foundation.

If you love reading comics, then this Kubernetes Engine comic is not to be missed: `https://cloud.google.com/kubernetes-engine/kubernetes-comic/`.

Kubernetes draws on the same design principles that run popular Google services and provides the same benefits—automatic management, monitoring and liveness probes for application containers, automatic scaling, rolling updates, and more.

You can quickly get started using the Google Cloud console or APIs/CLIs and deploy your first cluster, like we did in the following screenshot. You can also use the Google Cloud Shell to deploy a sample application to test out the cluster features:

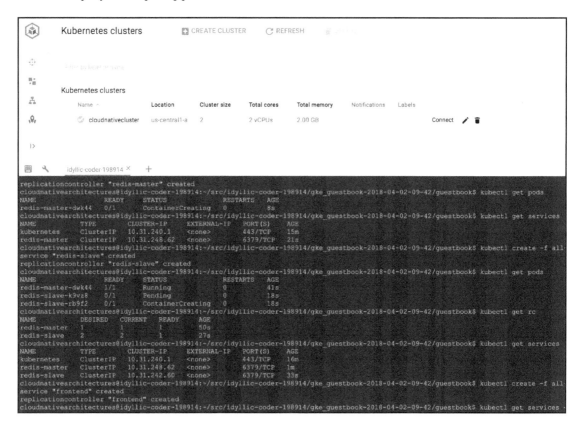

Apart from the Kubernetes Engine, Google also offers a Container Builder (`https://cloud.google.com/container-builder/`) service, using which you can bundle up your applications and other artefacts into Docker containers for deployment. As the service also supports automated triggers from source code repositories (such as GitHub, Bitbucket, and Google Cloud Source repositories), you can create fully automated CI/CD pipelines which can be initiated as soon as there's a new code check in. Another service which is related to this container ecosystem is the Container Registry (`https://cloud.google.com/container-registry/`) so that you can store your private container images and allow push, pull, and management of images from any system, VM instance, or your own hardware.

G Suite

Google has been offering online collaboration and productivity applications for independent users for quite some time. However, to make its mark in the enterprise space, Google launched G Suite (`https://gsuite.google.com/`) under its cloud business and since then has acquired multiple marquee customers:

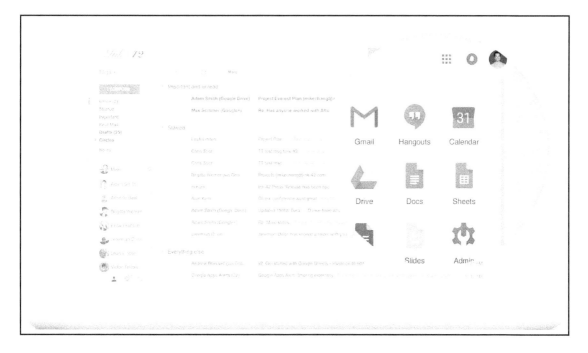

Broadly speaking, G Suite offers services in primarily four different categories, as follows:

- **Connect**: These are the set of services like Gmail, calendaring, Google+, and Hangouts, which enable better connections across the organization
- **Create**: In order to enable better collaboration, Google offers services like Docs, Sheets, Forms, Slides, Sites, and Jamboard, that can be used to create and share content between users
- **Access**: Lots of times, users want to back up and share files, videos, and other media using secure cloud storage, so for the same, Google Drive and Cloud Search come in handy
- **Control**: A final set of services are in the administration space so that enterprise controls like user management, security policies, backup and retention, and mobile devices management can be handled from a central place

 G Suite has an official blog to keep its users up to date on announcements and new features: `https://gsuiteupdates.googleblog.com/`.

Application Centric Design (CNMM Axis-2)

Now that we have explored a few interesting cloud-native services from Google Cloud, let's dive into the next topic of actually building some cloud-native application architectures and the best practices around those.

Serverless microservice

Similar to the approach we took in our previous chapters around AWS and MS Azure, we will look at creating a serverless microservice using a few Google Cloud services. In fact, before we even dive in there, it's interesting to note the way Google defines its serverless services portfolio, which can be seen in the following diagram, wherein even some early services including App Engine are included, apart from the latest ones that include Cloud Functions and the Cloud Machine Learning Engine. For more details, please refer to the whitepapers and content on the Google Cloud portal:

As for the actual application, we will again use the same sample of building a serverless weather service application, which behind the scenes will invoke the OpenWeatherMap API. Like we did in previous chapters, we will use the cloud functions capability of Google cloud, however won't be able to use Google Cloud Endpoints (managed API service) as at the time of writing this book, there's no direct integration between the two services. Also, the Google Cloud functions currently only support JavaScript and execute in Node.js runtime, so we will convert the business logic of our earlier written functions to JavaScript to demonstrate this sample use case. As a result, we will use the following reference architecture to build the sample application:

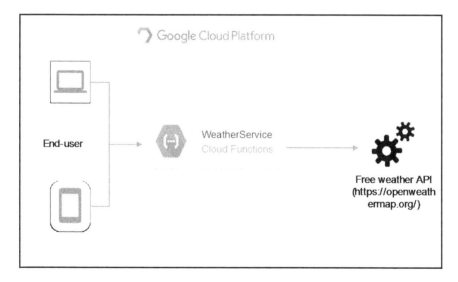

Serverless microservice – sample walkthrough

As in previous chapters, we will create a serverless microservice using Google Cloud Functions, so let's follow these to create a working example:

1. Go to Google Cloud Console and locate **Cloud Functions**, as follows:

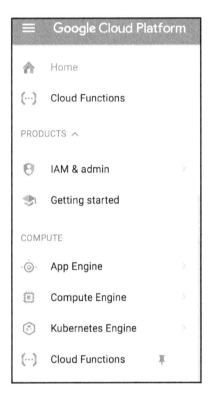

3. Use the following code in the **index.js** section to handle the main business logic of our serverless microservice. Also, please note that just below the code in the console, the value of the **Function to execute** option should be set to `weatherService`:

```
function handlePUT(req, res) {
 // Return Forbidden message for POST Request
 res.status(403).send('Forbidden!');
 }

function handleGET(req, res) {
 // Retrieve URL query parameters
 var zip = req.query.zip;
 var countrycode = req.query.countrycode;
 var apikey = req.query.apikey;

// Create complete OpenWeatherMap URL using user-provided
parameters
 var baseUrl = 'http://api.openweathermap.org/data/2.5/weather';
 var completeUrl = baseUrl + "?zip=" + zip + "," + countrycode +
"&appid=" + apikey;
 console.log("Request URL--> " + completeUrl)

// Import the sync-request module to invoke HTTP request
 var weatherServiceRequest = require('sync-request');

// Invoke OpenWeatherMap API
 var weatherServiceResponse = weatherServiceRequest('GET',
completeUrl);
 var statusCode = weatherServiceResponse.statusCode;
 console.log("RESPONSE STATUS -->" + statusCode);

// Check if response was error or success response
 if (statusCode < 300) {
 console.log("JSON BODY DATA --->>" +
weatherServiceResponse.getBody());
 // For Success response, return back appropriate status code,
content-type and body
 console.log("Setting response content type to json");
 res.setHeader('Content-Type', 'application/json');
 res.status(statusCode);
 res.send(weatherServiceResponse.getBody());
 } else {
```

```
console.log("ERROR RESPONSE -->" + statusCode);
//For Error response send back appropriate error details
res.status(statusCode);
res.send(statusCode);
}
}

/**
 * Responds to a GET request with Weather Information. Forbids a
PUT request.
 *
 * @param {Object} req Cloud Function request context.
 * @param {Object} res Cloud Function response context.
 */
exports.weatherService = (req, res) => {
switch (req.method) {
case 'GET':
handleGET(req, res);
break;
case 'PUT':
handlePUT(req, res);
break;
default:
res.status(500).send({
error: 'Something blew up!'
});
break;
}
};
```

4. Now, click on the **package.json** option and edit it to include our code-specific dependencies, as follows:

Source code
- Inline editor
  ZIP upload
  ZIP from Cloud Storage
  Cloud Source repository

index.js   package.json

```
1  {
2    "name": "sample-http",
3    "version": "0.0.1",
4    "dependencies": {
5      "sync-request": "^2.0"
6    }
7  }
8
```

Here's the code snippet to put in the **package.json** window:

```
{
  "name": "sample-http",
  "version": "0.0.1",
  "dependencies": {
  "sync-request": "^2.0"
  }
}
```

5. Click the **Create** button once you have verified that all of the settings and code are in line with the previously mentioned steps. In a few minutes, the function will be created and active in the console.

6. Now, it's time to test the function and for the same, go to your function details page and under the **Tigger** option, you will find the HTTPS endpoint for your function which can be used to invoke and test the microservice. Copy this URL which will then be used in the next step:

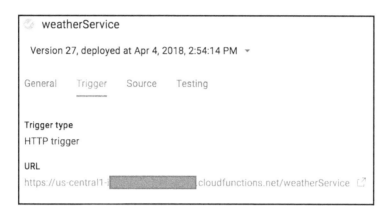

7. Now, append the following parameters to the preceding URL: `zip`, `countrycode`, and `apikey`, as follows:

```
https://us-central1-abcdef-43256.cloudfunctions.net/weatherService/
?zip=10011&countrycode=us&apikey=vjhvjvjhvjhv765675652hhjvjsdjysfyd
fjy
```

Now, use any internet browser of your choice and go to this URL and see the magic for yourself! If the function executes successfully, then you should be able to see a JSON response with weather information for the location you specified in the parameters.

8. You can also test the same using the command line by using the `curl` command as follows:

```
$ curl -X GET
'https://us-central1-idyllic-coder-198914.cloudfunctions.net/weathe
rService/?zip=10001&countrycode=us&apikey=098172635437y363535'
{"coord":{"lon":-73.99,"lat":40.73},"weather":[{"id":500,"main":"Ra
in","description":"light
rain","icon":"10d"}],"base":"stations","main":{"temp":285.07,"press
ure":998,"humidity":87,"temp_min":284.15,"temp_max":286.15},"visibi
lity":16093,"wind":{"speed":10.8,"deg":290,"gust":14.9},"clouds":{"
all":90},"dt":1522869300,"sys":{"type":1,"id":1969,"message":0.0059
,"country":"US","sunrise":1522837997,"sunset":1522884283},"id":4200
27013,"name":"New York","cod":200}
```

9. Once you have tested the function, you can also monitor it from the console, under the **General** tab of the function details. There are multiple different views available, like those based on *invocations*, *memory usage*, and *execution time*, as follows:

Invocation/sec view

10. Another important aspect of managing your Google Function is the Stackdriver **Logs** option, which can provide you with details of backend debugging from the code and function execution, as follows:

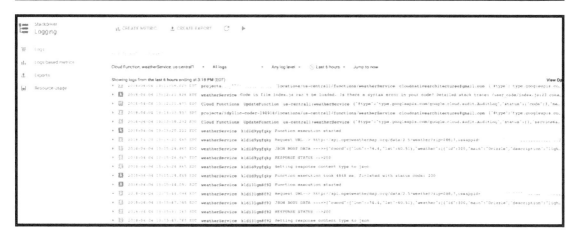

So with this, we have completed an end-to-end demo of how to design a serverless microservice using Google functions.

Automation in the Google Cloud Platform (CNMM Axis-3)

As discussed in previous chapters as well, automation is one of the key aspects when looking at optimally deploying and managing your applications in cloud. So in line with this, Google Cloud apart from offering many services which help automate processes and workflows, also has a rich set of APIs and SDKs. In fact, based on developer's individual preferences there are multiple options for SDK client libraries, including Java, Python, NodeJS, Ruby, Go, .Net and PHP, that provide flexibility and ease of automation and integration. So in the upcoming section, let's explore this further and look at various options for automation and DevOps implementations.

Infrastructure as code

Google Cloud offers a service that is very similar to AWS CloudFormation, called Google Cloud Deployment Manager, using which infrastructure components can be easily authored in a declarative fashion (YAML) to automate various provisioning and automation-related tasks. Therefore, using this, service you can create templates which can have multiple components of the application provisioned and deployed using a template.

For example, if you had a three-tier web application which is autoscaled and has load balancers in front of it, with a database for persistence, then instead of creating that manually every time you want to launch a new instance of the application, you could possibly write a YAML Cloud Deployment Manager template which can automate the entire process. To make it dynamic, you can also use template properties and environment variables in the template which can be supplied based on different individual launches. Test/Dev environments may have smaller fleet size, compared to production which has to be fully scalable.

There are a couple of other interesting features around template modules and composite types, which can help extend the functionality of Deployment Manager greatly. As part of the template modules, you can write helper files in Python or Jinja to perform specific functions, like generating unique resources names, and make your templates even more sophisticated. Using the same mechanism of leveraging Jinja or Python-based logic, you can create composite types, which is basically the ability to have one or more templates that are preconfigured to work together. As an example of a Composite type, you can create a type which is basically a specific configuration of a VPC network, which can be reused whenever you are creating a new set of application environments.

Refer to the following link for the latest supported resources with Cloud Deployment Manager: `https://cloud.google.com/deployment-manager/docs/configuration/supported-resource-types`.

Now, let's take a look at an actual sample and how that can be used to create resources in Google Cloud. To make it easy to get started, Google offers samples on GitHub and so we use a sample from there only to quickly get started and demonstrate the concepts. The following is the link to this sample, which basically creates a virtual machine in a specific Google Cloud project: `https://github.com/GoogleCloudPlatform/deploymentmanager-samples/blob/master/examples/v2/quick_start/vm.yaml`.

As also mentioned in the notes of this template, remember to update the placeholders for your project id will be `MY_PROJECT`, as well as instance family name: `FAMILY_NAME`, to properly provision sample instance using Deployment Manager.

One of the quickest ways to do this is by using Google Cloud Shell, which comes with **pre-installed gcloud (CLI)** and so requires minimal configuration. As in the following screenshot, we used the sample template to provision the resources and the command was completed successfully:

```
cloudnativearchitectures@idyllic-coder-198914:~$ gcloud deployment-manager deployments create simple-deployment --config vm.yaml
The fingerprint of the deployment is 7y7p0qjcF6g7Cp1Osq1phQ==
Waiting for create [operation-1525443310211-56b61f2a14fb8-7a136a28-eaa7aa5b]...done.
Create operation operation-1525443310211-56b61f2a14fb8-7a136a28-eaa7aa5b completed successfully.
NAME                        TYPE                  STATE      ERRORS  INTENT
quickstart-deployment-vm    compute.v1.instance   COMPLETED  []
```

Post the successful creation of your resources, you can also use the gcloud CLI to describe the created resources, as follows:

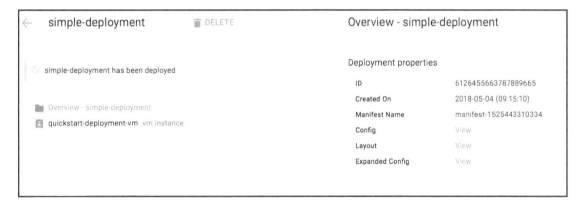

```
cloudnativearchitectures@idyllic-coder-198914:~$ gcloud deployment-manager deployments describe simple-deployment
---
fingerprint: 7y7p0qjcF6g7Cp1OsqlphQ==
id: '6126455663787889665'
insertTime: '2018-05-04T07:15:10.302-07:00'
manifest: manifest-1525443310334
name: simple-deployment
operation:
  endTime: '2018-05-04T07:15:46.580-07:00'
  name: operation-1525443310211-56b61f2a14fb8-7a136a28-eaa7aa5b
  operationType: insert
  progress: 100
  startTime: '2018-05-04T07:15:10.880-07:00'
  status: DONE
  user: cloudnativearchitectures@gmail.com
NAME                      TYPE                  STATE       INTENT
quickstart-deployment-vm  compute.v1.instance   COMPLETED
```

Apart from using the gcloud CLI, you can also use the Google Cloud Console and go to the Cloud Deployment Manager section and look at the same deployment to get more details by clicking on various sections and links, as follows:

← simple-deployment 🗑 DELETE	Overview - simple-deployment
simple-deployment has been deployed	**Deployment properties**
	ID 6126455663787889665
📁 Overview - simple-deployment	Created On 2018-05-04 (09:15:10)
🖥 quickstart-deployment-vm vm instance	Manifest Name manifest-1525443310334
	Config View
	Layout View
	Expanded Config View

CI/CD for serverless microservices

Google Cloud is still in its early stages when it comes to CI/CD-related aspects for serverless microservices. Although for source code management Google offers a service called Cloud Source Repositories (https://cloud.google.com/source-repositories/), which can also be used to manage the code for Cloud functions, beyond that, native capabilities to create a fully-fledged CI/CD environment are limited at the time of writing this book.

One of the options which helps in this process is the serverless framework, which has a plugin for Google Cloud Functions and helps create, install, package, and deploy functions related to business logic easily. More details can be found at the following link: `https://github.com/serverless/serverless-google-cloudfunctions`.

There's also an example, which can help you quickly get started: `https://serverless.com/framework/docs/providers/google/examples/`.

CI/CD for container-based applications

One of the most popular ways to deploy container-based applications on Google Cloud is by using Kubernetes. In fact, as discussed earlier, Kubernetes originated from Google's internal technologies, invented to solve problems exactly like continuous code integration and deployment. That's why if you are looking to implement CI/CD patterns in such an environment, then it's easy to do so.

It's pretty straightforward to implement release management aspects if you are using Kubernetes CLI/API as it has actions which can implement updating resources with the latest version of application code by using the latest container images. You can do this by using the rolling updates mechanism, or if during the update process there are some issues that have been discovered, then you can also abort the process or roll back to previous versions. More details on the Kubernetes CLI update operations can be found at the following link: `https://kubernetes.io/docs/reference/kubectl/cheatsheet/#updating-resources`.

 Google Cloud has an interesting comic that can help you learn the CI/CD options with Kubernetes in a fun manner: `https://cloud.google.com/kubernetes-engine/kubernetes-comic/`.

Another mechanism to implement CI/CD in the Kubernetes environment is by using Jenkins, which is an open source automation server that lets you flexibly orchestrate your build, test, and deployment pipelines. In order to do that, you need to deploy Jenkins on the Kubernetes Engine (a Google Cloud hosted version of Kubernetes) and install Kubernetes plugins for Jenkins, setting up proper configuration to orchestrate the entire deployment process. The following diagram shows the entire setup and different steps, as per the Google Cloud documentation:

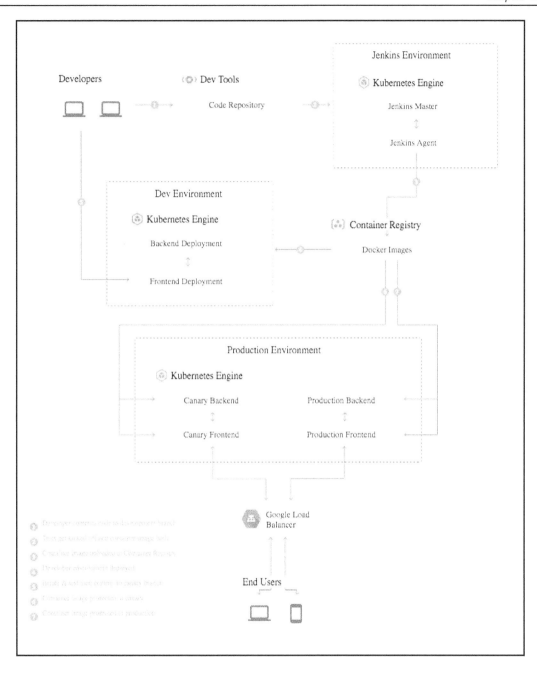

Patterns for moving off from monolithic application architectures to Google cloud native architectures

As discussed in earlier sections, originally, our focus was mainly on greenfield applications and how to leverage cloud-native capabilities like serverless, containers, microservices architectures, CI/CD patterns, and so on. However, in typical enterprise environments, most customers already have significant investment in their existing on-premise or colocation environments, so those workloads also need to be moved to the cloud to benefit holistically. To enable the same, Google Cloud offers some native services as well as partner offerings which can be leveraged across various stages of migration. Broadly speaking, Google suggests four different phases in any migration project, which includes *assessment, planning, network configuration*, and *replication*.

For most the part, during the assessment and network configuration phases, the onus is on the customer to look at the appropriate tooling, developing automation that can enable the discovery of existing workloads in on-premise environments as well as the creation of matching the network config on cloud, which can enable a seamless migration path.

For the planning phase, Google has a set of recommended partners, such as Cloudamize, CloudPhysics, and ATADATA, which can be leveraged to inspect the current on-premises environment and accordingly map them to the correct cloud services as well as right-sized instance types for best performance.

 Refer to the following link for the latest set of Google Cloud recommended migration partners: `https://cloud.google.com/migrate/`.

Similarly, for the actual VM migration phase, Google has a set of recommended partners, like CloudEndure, Velostrata, and ATADATA, which can again help replicate on-premise virtual machines directly to the cloud. Apart from these partner offerings, Google Cloud also offers an option to directly import the virtual disks using its native service capability, however that's not an optimal option for large scale migrations and partner products offer better capabilities there. You can find more details on the VM Migration aspects at the following link: `https://cloud.google.com/compute/docs/vm-migration/`.

Other than VM migrations, another very important aspect to consider in large scale migrations is around data migration. To do that, there are a few different options, as follows:

- **Cloud Storage Transfer Service**: This service helps you transfer data from other clouds (like AWS) to Google Cloud storage buckets using HTTP/HTTPS-based interfaces. You could do this directly using the Google Cloud Console, REST APIs, or even using Google Cloud Client API libraries. More details can be found at `https://cloud.google.com/storage/transfer/`.

- **Google Transfer Appliance**: Like the AWS Snowball service, Google Cloud also offers a physical appliance which you can lease from Google to transfer large amounts of data to the cloud. At present, it's available in 2 different sizes – 100 TB and 480 TB – which you can request for a few days to connect to your local storage systems, transfer data, and then ship back to Google to transfer it in one of your cloud storage buckets. Before being stored on the Transfer Appliance, all captured data is deduplicated, compressed, and encrypted with an industry standard AES 256 algorithm using a password and passphrase that you specify. With this service, you save on both cost and time, as this helps you quickly migrate the data without using your internet bandwidth. More details can be found at `https://cloud.google.com/transfer-appliance/docs/introduction`.

- **Google BigQuery Data Transfer Service**: In most cases, customers are also using many SaaS applications, like Adwords, DoubleClick Campaign Manager, DoubleClick for Publishers, and YouTube. In order to analyze the data from these services, customers can use the BigQuery Data Transfer Service to directly transfer their data to BigQuery and build a data warehouse to run analytical queries. This service ensures continuous data replication at scale, and to visualize the trends, customers can use ISV offerings like Tableau, Looker, and ZoomData, on top of the BigQuery instance. More details can be found at `https://cloud.google.com/bigquery/transfer/`.

 To understand which service is better suited for your migration projects, look at the *Choose the Right service matrix* published at `https://cloud.google.com/products/data-transfer/`.

Summary

In this chapter, we dove deep into the third significant cloud provider, Google Cloud Platform, and after understanding its origins and evolution, we focused on differentiating services like Cloud AI, Kubernetes Engine, and G Suite. Post that, we understood the concepts around serverless microservices and actually created a sample weather service application, leveraging Google Cloud functions. That led us to the next section, which focused on automation and how Google Cloud Deployment Manager can be used to create repeatable templates for treating infrastructure as code. We also looked at options for implementing CI/CD patterns in serverless environments as well as Kubernetes-based containerized deployments. Finally, we explored various options to migrate existing on-premise applications and workloads using various Google Cloud Native services as well as partner offerings. With all of the aforementioned concepts, we have completed exploring the top three public cloud providers and their capabilities to build more cloud-native architectures.

17
What's Next? Cloud Native Application Architecture Trends

In the previous chapters, we learned about multiple different aspects, starting from the core definition of the **Cloud Native Maturity Model** (**CNMM**), then peeling back different layers, and finally trying out various cloud providers hands-on. In this chapter, we are going to focus on a bunch of newer things, including looking at the future and talking about a few predictions!

Here are some of the areas we will focus on:

- Top seven predictions for the next three years – what to expect in terms of the evolution of cloud native architectures
- The future of enterprises on the cloud
- New IT roles that will possibly evolve (such as an AI Officer)

These topics will help you learn the following skills:

- Understanding the trends to future-proof your strategies and architectures
- Areas of growth and evolution in your personal career

So, let's dive right in!

Predictions for the next three years – what to expect in terms of cloud native architecture evolution

Although the cloud has already become mainstream for all types of applications and use cases, if we look at the overall market potential, it's still in its very early stages. That, coupled with the trends and advancements we are seeing, let's look at the top seven predictions that will promote the cloud native adoption in the coming three years.

Open source frameworks and platforms

Many customers are worried about lock-in aspects in the public cloud. However, this fear is totally unfounded as every piece of software and application has some vendor-specific intellectual aspects which provide value to the customer, so they shouldn't just be viewed from a lock-in perspective. As an example, for, say, word processing, many of the customers make use of Microsoft Word, so if you use that to create a document, in a way you are tied to the application, but that doesn't imply that you are locked in. However, in many of the enterprise scenarios, there are certain COTS applications which can be replaced by other open source options which both helps bring down costs and reduces dependency on a specific vendor. As a classic example of this, many of the enterprise customers who have been using Oracle databases for years have now started to go down the path to re-platform those databases to open source options like PostgreSQL or MySQL.

In the same spirit, nowadays there's a need for cloud providers to demonstrate their alignment to open source software standards, and so they have also released multiple frameworks and packages on GitHub that can be forked by anyone. A popular example of such an open source platform is Kubernetes (an open source system for managing containerized applications), which is available under the Apache-2.0 license and can be cloned or downloaded from GitHub (`https://github.com/kubernetes/kubernetes`).

Another major step in this direction to make microservice-based cloud architectures open and community led was the launch of the **Cloud Native Computing Foundation (CNCF)** (`https://www.cncf.io/`) in 2017. As this was announced, a few of the very first Platinum members were all hyper-scale cloud providers like Amazon Web Services, Microsoft Azure, and Google Cloud. Since its launch, many organizations have now become a part of this community and they continue to lead the mission of keeping the software for container-based microservices ecosystems active and open source.

 To learn more about CNCF's charter, review the following link: `https://www.cncf.io/about/charter/`.

Other than efforts around CNCF, all the public cloud providers are, in general, also making an effort to stay open and developer-friendly. The following are links to the top three cloud provider's open source microsites:

- Open source at AWS: `https://aws.github.io/`
- Open source software on Azure: `https://azure.microsoft.com/en-us/overview/open-source/`
- Open source on Google Cloud: `https://github.com/GoogleCloudPlatform`

Future trend #1

Open Source software and frameworks will continue to increase and make cloud native architectures even more developer friendly.

Increased abstraction from infrastructure services

A few years back, when the public cloud started to gain traction, the main emphasis was on the core infrastructure blocks covering Compute, Storage, Networking, Databases, and so on. However, as various cloud providers started to introduce newer services, that trend changed rapidly as the services were more higher level and abstracted the underlying infrastructure aspects greatly. As an example, we have seen services like Amazon Connect, which is a cloud-based contact center offering from AWS, and the end user doesn't have to bother about the underlying infrastructure at all and can quickly get started in a matter of minutes, focusing on their core business aspects, call routing logic, and so on.

Another aspect from an application deployment perspective we have seen is that rather than using native virtualized cloud-based instances, developers are moving towards container-based deployments or even serverless approaches using services like AWS Lambda. These techniques further abstract the user from the underlying infrastructure and let them focus on core application and business logic. In fact, this trend is not just visible in the compute layer, but even the databases (like Amazon's serverless Aurora), messaging (Amazon SQS), analytics (Amazon Athena), and so on.

As a result of the aforementioned shift, we will continue to see application deployment models change, which will be less dependent on the infrastructure specifications, as that will be automatically handled by the services itself. Another side effect of such changes will be that lines between the typical **Infrastructure-as-a-Service** (**IaaS**), **Platform-as-a-Service** (**PaaS**), and **Software-as-a-Service** (**SaaS**) aspects will continue to be blurry and everything will become cloud or cloud native, to be more accurate. We are already seeing some variations of this, even currently, where new terms like **Functions-as-a-Service** (**FaaS**) or **Anything-as-a-Service** (**XaaS**) are being used in multiple contexts.

Future trend #2

Cloud services will be more application and software oriented by changing the deployment models to be agnostic to underlying infrastructure. Also, lines between IaaS/PaaS/SaaS will become even more blurry with a greater number of cloud native services being introduced.

Systems will become smarter and AI/ML driven, starting with DevOps and moving on to NoOps

With the advent of the public cloud, we saw new types of infrastructure management patterns, which included autoscaling as well as self-healing-based techniques, making the application scaling and fault recovery process as automated as possible. During the next wave of automation, we saw DevOps become more mainstream, which was also a result of blurring lines between true developer and system operations roles due to abstracted cloud services. As a result, we saw faster and frequent deployments, easy rollback mechanisms in the case of issues, and better tools and services, which made the entire process easier and integrated. However, even with these type of advanced automation techniques, there's a need for operations and updates at certain operating system and application level aspects, which is still mostly a manual effort. Newer services like Amazon Lambda and Amazon serverless Aurora are taking that kind of heavy lifting away from the customers' hands, but still, there's a long way to go until the systems are truly smarter and can handle most of the ops-related aspects on their own. This may also mean that systems will have to be smarter, where instead of reactively responding to a situation they will proactively predict possible failures scenarios and the need for any changes, thereby reducing the need to manually correct anything or even build sophisticated automations, which may not even be needed!

To enable the aforementioned transition, technologies like Artificial Intelligence and Machine Learning will play a big role. In fact, in part, that has already started to happen, where many cloud providers' services are powered by predictive modelling techniques behind the scenes. As an example, Amazon Macie uses Machine Learning to automatically discover, classify, and protect sensitive data in AWS. Likewise, Amazon GuardDuty identifies suspected attackers through integrated threat intelligence feeds and uses Machine Learning to detect anomalies in account and workload activity. These are great examples of Machine Learning being used in the space of security, however, as we progress, the same principles and mechanisms will become more mainstream for application deployment and management models, where typical operations will change greatly.

 Refer to this interesting blog post where Amazon details the mathematical and Machine Learning-based tools it has created to handle security-related aspects in many of its services: `https://aws.amazon.com/blogs/security/protect-sensitive-data-in-the-cloud-with-automated-reasoning-zelkova/`.

Future trend #3

Cloud services and systems will be smarter, where typical requirements around infrastructure and application operations will diminish, thereby resulting in newer principles of NoOps.

Developers will natively develop new applications in the cloud, instead of first developing locally

Even though the cloud has become very popular for any type of application deployment, most of an application's development (the actual coding) happens in an offline mode where developers have IDEs on their workstations: they write the code, run the unit tests there, and once everything looks good, it is pushed to the central code repository, which again may or may not be in the cloud. However, once the entire build process runs, the actual deployment of application binaries happens in the cloud most of the time. This is primarily due to a few factors:

- In order to develop in the cloud, they need to be continuously connected to the internet, which may not always be possible.
- The IDEs and tools that the developers are comfortable with using on their workstations have never been designed for cloud-type environments.
- Some customers also fear that their codebase, which is their core IP, may not be safe to be put into the cloud.

I am sure the preceding points are just a sample of possible reasons for developing locally, but most of the preceding fears are totally unfounded. In fact, the cloud has come a long way where if developers are natively developing there, then it not only makes the process easier but also enables them to leverage many cloud services natively in their architectures, which otherwise would need to be coded on their own.

As examples of ongoing improvements in this context, Azure has Visual Studio Code to code for the cloud and likewise Amazon has AWS Cloud9, which helps code with just a browser. In the same spirit, Microsoft also acquired GitHub, which again is focusing on attracting developers and making it easy for them to develop natively in the cloud. In fact, all of this is just the beginning, and with time it will be much easier for developers to natively develop for the cloud, and the entire dev/test experience will be radically different in the future. This will further enable easy global collaboration and have applications created and managed in a decentralized manner.

Future trend #4

Cloud services will enable developers to be first-class citizens by providing multiple different options to effectively develop for the cloud in the cloud.

Voice, chatbots, and AR/VR-based interaction models will become prevalent, mainly powered by the cloud

In the last year or so, we have seen a great deal of conversations and action around Artificial Intelligence/Machine Learning, as well as Augmented Reality/Virtual Reality. Although these technologies have existed for multiple years, for effective AI/ML algorithm creation you need lots of data, and likewise for AR/VR, you need plenty of CPUs/GPUs. Now, as the cloud provides you the underlying infrastructure components at scale, you can virtually store petabytes of data and have thousands of CPUs available to you in no time for bringing your new-age applications to life. Apart from this, we have also seen tons of progress in the services and frameworks in this area, like Apache MXNet (`https://mxnet.apache.org/`), TensorFlow (`https://www.tensorflow.org/`), Caffe (`http://caffe.berkeleyvision.org/`), PyTorch (`https://pytorch.org/`), and so on. Similarly, we have seen major growth in various types of bots, ranging from simple Q&A types of bots to a full-featured bot which can complete a specific use case, like travel bookings. These bots are also becoming mainstream as part of cloud-based contact center implementations wherein, based on the call routing flow, many of the tasks can be fully handled by the bots themselves without any human dependency. These bots also function on AI/ML technologies as behind the scenes they use techniques like **Natural Language Processing** (**NLP**), voice-to-text, text-to-voice, image recognition, and **Optical Content Recognition** (**OCR**). Likewise, on the AR/VR side, we have seen the use of digital avatars being used for both end user interactions (for example, customers can digitally try dresses online), as well as industrial/enterprise use cases (like detecting problems in heavy machinery through a remote engineer). These trends are further amplified by cloud services like Amazon Sumerian, which can be used to create VR, AR, and 3D experiences that can run on popular hardware such as Oculus Go, Oculus Rift, HTC Vive Google Daydream, and Lenovo Mirage as well as Android and iOS mobile devices.

Take a look at the following Google Duplex Demo from Google IO 2018: `https://www.youtube.com/watch?v=bd1mEm2Fy08`.

Another classic example of voice-based interaction is Amazon Alexa, which is a cloud-based voice service which you can directly interact with using devices like Amazon Echo, Amazon Echo Dot, or you can even integrate in your own devices using the Alexa Voice Service (`https://developer.amazon.com/alexa-voice-service`). As a result of these integrations, and available Alexa skills, you can control your TV, temperature/lights at home, or even do banking operations (like checking a credit card's payment status or initiating a payment).

Earlier, for invoking an application, a user would typically need browser-based access or mobile app and likewise, for system level-integrations, APIs would come in handy. However, with the aforementioned new types of interaction mechanisms of chatbot, voice, or AR/VR-based interfaces, the application development patterns are also changing. In fact, not just for applications, but even for infrastructure management tasks, many organizations have started to create Alexa skills to launch an EC2 instance, get monitoring details, or even delete it. One area which is still nascent as of now is gesture-based (like hand or facial gestures without any applications) interfaces, however that too is a function of time before it becomes mainstream. As a result, in the future, applications will be more interactive, leverage multiple different interfaces, and also have a better user experience.

Future trend #5

Cloud services will enable applications to be more interactive, leveraging techniques like voice, gestures, and virtual reality/augmented reality, thereby reducing the gap between humans and machines.

Cloud native architectures will expand beyond data centers to "things"

Traditionally, applications have been designed for either server-based environments or mobile devices. However, off late, that's changing a bit, where now code and applications are also being written for "things". These *things* could be any physical device, like your light bulb, thermostat, child's toy, or an actual car, which is connected to the internet and controlled that way. As per this article from Gartner (`https://www.gartner.com/newsroom/id/3598917`), an estimated 20.4 billion such devices will be connected to the internet by 2020, thereby greatly changing the way we interact with them. In fact, with so many devices connected to the backend, the application architectures and the amount of data that's transmitted and consumed will greatly change. Again, this wouldn't be possible without the cloud as this will require scalable stream-based data processing techniques, and services like AWS IoT and Amazon Kinesis will become central to implementations. Apart from that, many devices can't also be connected to the internet all the time, as they are in remote locations which have limited internet connectivity (like sensors in oil rigs), so for those scenarios, even *edge computing* will be pretty critical. These kinds of use cases will be supported by services like AWS Greengrass, which lets you run local compute, messaging, and data caching for connected devices in a secure way. For smaller devices like micro-controllers, which again need to support such edge computing scenarios, new kernel services like Amazon FreeRTOS will be pretty critical and enable those deployments.

As the data from these edge devices will be ingested in the cloud, there will be the possibility to perform real-time, batch, or even trend analytics, which will again continue to open new avenues and evolve the architectural patterns.

Future trend #6

Cloud native applications will have an end-to-end impact, right from the edge to the backend applications to the customer facing portals, thereby changing the way applications are created and deployed.

Data will continue to be new "oil"

Data management has always been pivotal to any successful application development and deployment, and with the cloud, this trend continues to grow, as now you can harness new channels of information as well as store petabytes of data easily. In fact, many organizations are now moving to a model where they are creating centralized data lakes, where data is being fed from various different sources, which includes devices connected to the web to social media and business applications, which is then used for analytics purposes and to get deep insights and trends.

 Review these data lake architecture details on AWS and Azure:
`https://aws.amazon.com/answers/big-data/data-lake-solution/`
`https://docs.microsoft.com/en-us/azure/data-lake-store/data-lake-store-overview.`

The preceding trend has also been promoted by the fact that there are now better and faster options in order to move the data to the cloud. Until a few years back, it was only possible to transfer the data over the internet/network with options like AWS DirectConnect or by using virtual appliances like AWS Storage Gateway. However, in the last couple of years, all of the cloud providers have created physical appliances, like Amazon Snowball, which can be ordered to your data centers, connected locally to transfer data, and, once done, shipped back to cloud providers for moving data to services like Amazon S3. It's not just these smaller data transfer appliances, as now you can also request a 45-foot long ruggedized shipping container, pulled by a semi-trailer truck, that can transfer 100 PB data per AWS Snowmobile! This is just the beginning of innovation and in the future, transfer to/from the cloud will become even easier and that will further promote collection, aggregation, and analytics from vast sets of data. As data moves to the cloud, applications will follow the trend and that's the reason data will continue to be central in overall cloud adoption.

Future trend #7

Data will be central to any cloud deployment and, as data migration paths to the cloud become easier to use, cloud native architecture adoption will increase dramatically.

The future of enterprises on the cloud

Enterprises are always risk averse and so have always been slow-movers in any technology patterns. The cloud is no different in that respect, as for many years, the enterprises were watching the progress, sitting on the side-lines and waiting for others to be first-movers. It was at the same time that we saw a huge surge of many new start-ups that were all using the cloud and slowly started to disrupt the mainstream, well-established enterprises. As examples, Lyft and Uber challenged the taxi/transportation business, Airbnb disrupted the hospitality industry, and likewise Oscar Insurance radically changed the health insurance sector. These types of successes were never easier earlier, but now with the cloud, everyone has access to same set of services and infrastructure resources which they can scale up/down based on their business needs... and this changes the playing field for everyone.

As a result of the aforementioned effect, many enterprises have realized that before anyone else disrupts their business, they themselves have to do it and ride this wave of innovation with the cloud. Therefore, we have seen many enterprises not just adopt the cloud, but even go all-in in the last few years in an attempt to redefine their operational and business model. Although this list of enterprise customers is continuously increasing, we have seen customers like GE, Capital One, Adobe, Hess, Kellogg's, Novartis, Infor, Suncorp, BestBuy, Philips, Goldman Sachs, and so on have all gone public on their usage of one or the other cloud platforms.

Refer to the following links for case studies from various cloud providers:

- AWS: https://aws.amazon.com/solutions/case-studies/enterprise/
- Azure: https://azure.microsoft.com/en-us/case-studies/
- Google Cloud: https://cloud.google.com/customers/

Other than commercial entities, we have also seen government and public sector entities adopting the cloud in a big way. As a few examples, NASA, FDA, FINRA, the US Department of Homeland Security, Government of Singapore, Transport for London, Government of Ontario, Business Sweden, City of Tel Aviv, the Chilean Ministry of Health, and so on all have some or the other workloads deployed in the cloud and can be seen as public references on various cloud providers' websites.

The change for enterprises is huge, as it's not just a technology upgrade/re-platforming, but it also has many operational and business implications wherein everything is now on-demand/opex oriented versus capex, which is pretty new model for the enterprises. Other than that, in order to move fast and to truly harness the power of the cloud, they also need to have smaller teams (like DevOps, two-pizza teams) who can try out new cloud services and features rapidly and incorporate them in their application architectures. Apart from keeping this agile/innovative culture, enterprises also need to have proper governance and security controls in place so that they can demonstrate the right controls to their auditors and ensure that the laws of the land are being adhered to properly. To make these entire changes smoother, various cloud providers have come up with pretty comprehensive cloud adoption and change management frameworks, which help the enterprise customers' CIO/CTOs and various other stakeholders make the move to cloud in a frictionless and disruption-proof manner.

 Refer to the following AWS Enterprise Strategy blog for interesting nuggets of information: `https://aws.amazon.com/blogs/enterprise-strategy/`

Another change all the enterprise customers have to handle is the training of their staff on the target cloud platform. For this, all cloud providers have comprehensive programs around training and certifications, which can help the customers and employees learn about service functionality, integration techniques, and best practices. However, apart from training their own employees, enterprise customers need experts to be involved in supporting them in critical phases of the project. For the same, all cloud providers have their specialist Professional Services consultants, who can come in and advise the customer on various technical, process, and project delivery aspects. To further help with the setup of **Cloud Centers of Excellence** (**CCOE**) and delivery teams equipped with the necessary cloud knowledge, in most cases, customers also make use of various consulting partners who specialize in various areas and help make cloud projects successful.

With the previously mentioned ingredients, customers are able to bring about change in their daily work and make their cloud native journey smooth and successful. As a result of these practices, we have seen some very interesting innovations from enterprise customers, as follows:

- Capital One's Amazon Alexa skill: `https://www.capitalone.com/applications/alexa/`
- FINRA Collects, Analyzes Billions of Brokerage Transaction Records Daily Using AWS: `https://youtu.be/rHUQQzYoRtE`

- NASA JPL's presentation on, How the Cloud is Helping Answer Cosmic Questions: `https://youtu.be/8UQfrQNo2nE`
- BMW Supports Model Launch, Develops Prospects with Cloud-Based Social Marketing: `https://customers.microsoft.com/en-us/story/bmw-supports-model-launch-develops-prospects-with-clo2`
- Airbus Defense and Space improves the quality of satellite images using Cloud Machine Learning: `https://cloud.google.com/blog/big-data/2016/09/google-cloud-machine-learning-now-open-to-all-with-new-professional-services-and-education-programs`

New IT roles

One of the long-term impacts of the cloud permeating enterprises is that there are multiple new roles which have evolved. Some of these are already mainstream, whereas with evolving technology trends, some of them are starting to become more popular:

- **Chief Technology & Innovation Officer** (**CTIO**): Earlier, organizations had either a CTO or a CIO, but nowadays due to increased focus on innovation, mainly powered by the cloud, a new role of CTIO has started to appear.
- **Cloud Solutions Architect**: Earlier, we used to have Application Architects, System Architects, Integration Architects, and so on, however with the possibilities that have opened up with cloud native architectures, a new role of Cloud Solutions architect has become very popular.
- **Cloud Migration Architect**: As many of enterprises have a huge amount of technical debt which they have to remove to effectively leverage the cloud, a new migration focused on the Cloud Migrations Architect role has started to appear off late.
- **DevOps Professional/Cloud Automation Engineer**: In order to fully leverage the power of the cloud, it is important to focus on automation and orchestration functionalities, which oftentimes requires coding, scripting, and ensuring that the proper operational procedures are in place, for which DevOps Professional/Cloud Automation Engineer roles have become pivotal.
- **Cloud Security Architect**: Security controls and procedures in the cloud are very different compared to an on-premises setup. Therefore, to leverage the cloud's security controls in a proper fashion, ensuring that proper compliance and governance models are being adhered to, the Cloud Security Architect role is being adopted in many organizations.

- **Cloud Economics Professional**: This is a very unique role and still not mainstream, however some organizations have started to hire professionals who focus on cloud usage optimization more from a cost management perspective. They focus more on looking at better financial constructs (like Reserved Instances) or even help with cost segregation within the internal organization by leveraging techniques like tagging.

Along with the preceding roles, there are multiple other roles which have become mainstream because of the growth of big data, analytics, and Machine Learning powered by the cloud. In fact, as AI and ML grow in the years to come, there's already increased discussion on the possible roles which may become important in that area. One such role is a *Chief AI Officer*, who will focus on not just technology aspects of harnessing the power of AI/ML, but also look at its social implications. As an example, when AI/ML becomes smarter and is able to make decisions on its own, like driving a car, then who's responsible when that self-driving car hits a pedestrian? Is it the AI or the developer who built that AI system? It's not an easy problem to solve and that's why new roles like *Chief AI Officer* will actually focus on these types of new society-impacting situations and even work with governments and various regulatory bodies to create proper rules and frameworks to maintain the balance of the society.

So, net-net, along with the aforementioned changes, the enterprises will have to evolve and adapt to stay successful and competitive in this new innovation-led era!

Summary

This brings us to the last section of this book, and we have covered lots of ground right from the beginning. So, let's go back a bit and reflect on what we have learned through, the various chapters.

We started by defining what it actually means to be *cloud native*, as that was the core part of laying the foundation of the entire discussion in the rest of the chapters. So, as a quick refresher, the CNMM revolves around three main axes:

- Cloud Native Service
- Application Centric Designs
- Automation

So, every customer will have a varying degree of maturity of across all of these axes, but essentially, they can still be cloud native:

After this, we went into the details of the Cloud Adoption Framework and what it means from multiple different perspectives, including business, people, governance, platform, security, and operations. This eventually led us to the next important set of topics revolving around the essence of microservices, serverless, and how to build applications in the cloud using the 12-factor application framework. We then also looked at the cloud ecosystem, which is comprised of technology and consulting partners, as well as different software licensing and procurement models including marketplaces, bring-your-licenses, and so on. With all of these general concepts clearly understood, we started to take the onion-peeling approach and dived into the specifics of how you think about scalability, availability, security, cost management, and operational excellence, which are very important to understand from a cloud perspective, and how this is similar or different from the existing on-premise models.

After all of these concepts were clear, it was time to get our hands dirty by diving right into the specifics of the top three leading cloud providers, including Amazon WebServices, Microsoft Azure, and Google Cloud Platform. In each of these sections, we looked at their capabilities and differentiation based on the earlier described CNMM model. We looked at every cloud provider's key service offering, based on CNMM axis-1, followed by developing and deploying a serverless microservice based on CNMM axis-2, and finally concluded with automation/DevOps possibilities based on CNMM axis-3. This exercise gave us a deeper insight into the terms of all cloud providers and their relative comparisons as well.

Finally, in this chapter, we looked at a couple of aspects. One of the main was the top seven technology trends, which we can expect to see evolve in the next three years. This will help us look at not just current capabilities, but even plan for the future. After, we dived in to see the impact of the cloud on enterprises and how they are embracing the change. In the same section, we also learned about the new IT roles which we have seen evolve due to the cloud becoming mainstream in enterprises.

With this, we came to a conclusion, and if there's one thing you want to take away from this entire book, then that will be – *"Cloud is the new normal, and if you have to harness the full power of it, then there's no better way than being fully committed and going cloud native!"*

Other Books You May Enjoy

If you enjoyed this book, you may be interested in these other books by Packt:

Cloud Native Python
Manish Sethi

ISBN: 978-1-78712-931-3

- Get to know "the way of the cloud", including why developing good cloud software is fundamentally about mindset and discipline
- Know what microservices are and how to design them
- Create reactive applications in the cloud with third-party messaging providers
- Build massive-scale, user-friendly GUIs with React and Flux
- Secure cloud-based web applications: the do's, don'ts, and options
- Plan cloud apps that support continuous delivery and deployment

Cloud Native programming with Golang

Mina Andrawos, Martin Helmich

ISBN: 978-1-78712-598-8

- Understand modern software applications architectures
- Build secure microservices that can effectively communicate with other services
- Get to know about event-driven architectures by diving into message queues such as Kafka, Rabbitmq, and AWS SQS
- Understand key modern database technologies such as MongoDB, and Amazon's DynamoDB
- Leverage the power of containers
- Explore Amazon cloud services fundamentals
- Know how to utilize the power of the Go language to access key services in the Amazon cloud such as S3, SQS, DynamoDB and more.
- Build front-end applications using ReactJS with Go
- Implement CD for modern applications

Leave a review - let other readers know what you think

Please share your thoughts on this book with others by leaving a review on the site that you bought it from. If you purchased the book from Amazon, please leave us an honest review on this book's Amazon page. This is vital so that other potential readers can see and use your unbiased opinion to make purchasing decisions, we can understand what our customers think about our products, and our authors can see your feedback on the title that they have worked with Packt to create. It will only take a few minutes of your time, but is valuable to other potential customers, our authors, and Packt. Thank you!

Index

www.ingramcontent.com/pod-product-compliance
Lightning Source LLC
LaVergne TN
LVHW081508050326
832903LV00025B/1415